american english

american english
an introduction

◆

Zoltán Kövecses

broadview press

Canadian Cataloguing in Publication Data

Kövecses, Zoltán
        American English: an introduction

ISBN 1-55111-229-9

1. English language – United States. 2. English language – Variation – United States.
I. Title.

PE2808.K68 2000   420'.973   C00-930545-9

Broadview Press Ltd., is an independent, international publishing house, incorporated in 1985.

North America
P.O. Box 1243, Peterborough, Ontario, Canada K9J 7H5
3576 California Road, Orchard Park, NY 14127
Tel: (705) 743-8990; Fax: (705) 743-8353
E-mail: customerservice@broadviewpress.com

United Kingdom
Turpin Distribution Services Ltd.,
Blackhorse Rd, Letchworth, Hertfordshire SG6 1HN
Tel: (1462) 672555; Fax: (1462) 480947
E-mail: turpin@rsc.org

Australia
St. Clair Press, P.O. Box 287, Rozelle, NSW 2039
Tel: (02) 818-1942; Fax: (02) 418-1923

www.broadviewpress.com

Broadview Press gratefully acknowledges the financial support of the Ministry of Canadian Heritage through the Book Publishing Industry Development Program.

Type design by Hungry Eye Design.

Printed in Canada

For Lacó and Ádi, my rambunctious little boys.

Contents

Preface

This book is intended for students of American English around the world, including, of course, students who are native speakers of American English. It is an introductory book that does not require any prior knowledge of linguistics. In writing it, I made every effort to keep linguistic terminology to a minimum. This was possible because the approach to American English represented in the book is not a narrowly defined linguistic one – either in its structural or sociolinguistic form.

There have been many excellent books written on American English in the past decades. However, I feel that most of these are too specialized or narrow in focus in their treatment of the subject. My major goal with this work was twofold. One was to provide a relatively comprehensive, and yet accessible, overview of the many approaches to American English for students who first come to the study of the English language as spoken in the United States. Needless to say, any such effort to cover the wide range of approaches brings with it some inevitable superficiality – though, I hope, not a lack of important information. At the same time, it has to be kept in mind that the book represents one person's ideas and preferences about the study of American English. Nevertheless I believe that the relative superficiality in handling the diverse approaches to the subject matter is at the same time an advantage. The interested reader can get an overview of the many ways of studying American English in a single volume and can choose the one that he or she wants to pursue further.

The other goal of the book was to provide students with a new way of looking at American English. What is new about it is that it integrates into a coherent framework the impact of a variety of intellectual traditions on the development of American English. These intellectual traditions include such well-known ones as republicanism, utilitarianism, Puritanism, individualism, and rationality. I am not claiming, of course, that these traditions have not been recognized in one way or another by various authors as influencing American English in the course of its history. Instead, my claim is that no focused attempt has been made to take an inventory of the most influential intellectual traditions that have shaped the development of American English and to explain the uniqueness and specificity of American English in terms of them.

A large part of dealing with the uniqueness of American English involves a comparison of American English with British English and the comparison of the differential degrees to which the intellectual traditions that played a role in shaping them influenced British culture and American culture, respectively. In the current climate of postmodernism and multiculturalism, these ideas may sound very conservative. To talk about an American English and an American culture may sound an outgrown thing of the past. Admittedly, in this sense the present work represents a conservative enterprise, although I will show throughout the book that there is nothing incompatible between the idea of an American English and culture and the idea of America conceived as a multilingual and multicultural society. Hopefully, the reader will find by the end that what looks conservative given the current intellectual climate may not be necessarily wrong. I will try to convince the reader that there is, in general, what we can call an "American mindset" that has emerged from a particular constellation of intellectual traditions and that has produced (together with other forces) a particular variety of the English language in the United States.

The book is broken up into twenty-two chapters and can thus be conveniently used in a one-semester course on American English. To serve the student (and the teacher) better, each chapter is followed by study questions and activities. In many cases, these are designed not only to elaborate on ideas found in the chapters, but also to take those ideas further or introduce new ones. Some study questions and activities are best suited for working on at home, while others are best discussed in class (after pre-class preparation). Many of them have been tried out both in the United States and in Europe. My experience was that native speakers of American English enjoyed many of them just as much as Europeans did. The exercises in the book are doable by students anywhere in the world. I hope many of them will find pleasure in doing them.

Zoltán Kövecses
Budapest

Acknowledgments

My greatest debt goes to the people whose ideas influenced me the most in thinking about American English. They are, in alphabetical order, linguist and cultural historian Dennis Baron, cultural historian Kenneth Cmiel, sociolinguist J.L. Dillard, and literary critic David Simpson. Cmiel, Dillard, and Simpson have also read the manuscript and provided extremely valuable critical comments on it.

John Broderick gave me very useful feedback on the manuscript and suggested several important changes and new ideas. I am sure his generous help, constructive criticism, and suggestions for changes make the final product a better book than what it would have become without his help.

In addition to those mentioned above, many other people have read the whole or part of the book in manuscript form and contributed several valuable suggestions. Again in alphabetical order, they are Enikő Bollobás, Robert Dunne, George Eisen, Tibor Frank, Susan Gal, Reka Hajdu, Matthew Mancini, David Marshall, John Moore, Gary Palmer, Klaus Panther, Gunter Radden, András Sándor, Joseph Schöpp, Dieter Schulz, Walanne Steel, Linda Thornburg, Louise Vasvari, Donald Wesling, and David Williams. I am grateful to them all.

My thanks go to those students at Rutgers University, the University of Nevada at Las Vegas, Hamburg University, and Eötvös Loránd University, Budapest, who actively contributed to shaping the book in some way. Györgyi Tóth gave me invaluable assistance with turning a first, sloppy draft into a beautiful typescript.

Finally, I want to say special thanks to Donald Wesling for recommending Broadview Press to me as a potential publication outlet, to Don LePan at Broadview Press for embracing the project and helping to bring it to completion, and to Martin Boyne for the superb job he did in copy-editing the manuscript.

A phonetic alphabet for English pronunciation

(Fromkin and Rodman, 1993)

Consonants

p	pill	t	till	k	kill
b	bill	d	dill	g	gill
m	mill	n	nil	ŋ	ring
f	feel	s	seal	h	heal
v	veal	z	zeal	l	leaf
θ	thigh	č	chill	r	reef
ð	thy	j	Jill	j	you
š	shill	ʍ	which	w	witch
ž	azure				

Vowels

i	beet	ɪ	bit
e	bait	ɛ	bet
u	boot	ʊ	foot
o	boat	ɔ	bore
æ	bat		
ʌ	but	a	pot/bar
aj	bite	ə	sofa
j	boy	aw/æw	bout

chapter 1

Why study American English?

About two hundred years ago, there were many patriots in the new United States who made confident predictions about the language of their country. One of these people was Noah Webster, who made the following statement about the future of American English in 1789:

> Several circumstances render a future separation of the American tongue from the English necessary and unavoidable ... Numerous local causes, such as a new country, new associations of people, new combinations of ideas in arts and science, and some intercourse with tribes wholly unknown in Europe, will introduce new words into the American tongue. These causes will produce, in a course of time, a language in North America, as different from the future language of England, as the modern Dutch, Danish and Swedish are from the German, or from one another.... (quoted in McCrum *et al.*, 1986:241)

One hundred and thirty years later, H.L. Mencken in his monumental *The American Language* (1919) claimed that the divergence between the "two streams of English" had become so great that it was appropriate to refer to American English as a separate language, "the American language." In addition to predicting the radical separation of American English from British English, Webster, together with others (see Cmiel, 1992), made another claim about the language used in America. This was also a bold statement, and it envisioned a glorious future for American English. In 1806, Webster wrote in the preface to his dictionary:

> In fifty years from this time, the American English will be spoken by more people, than all the other dialects of the language, and in one hundred and thirty years, by more people than any other language on the globe, not excepting the Chinese. (quoted in Simpson, 1986:66)

To what degree were these confident and bold statements prophetic? Two hundred years later and in a more impassioned light, it seems reasonable to conclude that the first prediction certainly did not come true. American English today is just less different from its British counterpart than is, say, Danish from German, and it cannot be claimed that it is a separate "language" in the sense in which these two and other related languages can be said to be two separate but related languages. However, the second prediction turned out to be partially true. American English has become an enormously popular and successful world language, spoken by several hundred million people, and its influence continues to rise (see, for example, Crystal, 1975). The belief in the success of the language of the new country was shared by American politicians as well, including Thomas Jefferson, who stated:

> And should the language of England continue stationary, we shall probably enlarge our employment of it, until its new character may separate it in name, as well as in power, from the mother tongue. (quoted in Baugh and Cable, 1983:381)

What is particularly interesting about this statement is that it explicitly links the divergence of American English from the "mother tongue" to the probable future success of American English. For Jefferson, the divergence is the cause, or at least the precondition, of success.

Statements about language and its probable bright future ran parallel to statements about people. The first claim about American English was coupled with claims about the speakers of this variety of English – Americans. It was noticed very early that not only the language but also the people were diverging from their British ancestors. Some travelers, like the Frenchman Hector Crévecoeur in 1782, began to talk about a "new race of man." Moreover, similar to the predictions made about language, confident and optimistic predictions were made about the fate of Americans, the "new man." Crévecoeur also believed in the great future that lay before Americans. He wrote: "… Here [in America] individuals of all nations are melted into a new race of man, whose labours and posterity will one day cause great changes in the world" (quoted in Mitchell and Maidment, 1994:19). These changes have been commented on by several contemporary observers (see, for example, Bigsby, 1975).

The "British vs. American" issue

This book is concerned with some of the important questions that these bold predictions raise. The first such question is this: How far have the two streams of English diverged from each other by the end of the twentieth century? In other words, one of our goals is to uncover the extent of the differences that exist between British and American English. How wide and how significant is the gap today? The study of this issue has been a favorite and age-old scholarly activity among professional and amateur linguists alike (see, for example,

Marckwardt and Quirk, 1964 and Mencken, 1919). Walt Whitman and Ralph Waldo Emerson also stressed "American exceptionalism" in language in relation to poetry. The topic has also been a favorite pastime for the lay public.

Two kinds of extreme views may be distinguished, with, no doubt, several in-between or middle-of-the-road opinions. Representing one extreme, Mencken (1919), for one, emphasized the differences between British and American English and came to the conclusion that the "two streams" of English diverged so far that they can be legitimately considered two separate, though related, languages. By contrast, others, like Marckwardt and Quirk (1964), argue that the differences are there, but they do not affect mutual understanding between the two nations. The differences may be linguistically interesting, but, on the whole, they are of no major import. This latter camp emphasizes that what is dominant in the relationship between the two nations is the common, shared heritage, both in language and general culture, and whatever differences there may be, they are somehow superficial. What really matters is shared. This is a view expounded not only by some linguists, but also by other social scientists. I quote at length from one such view (Plumb, 1978:14):

> Americans are not merely English with different accents, nor are American political, legal, and social institutions entirely British, somewhat distorted by time and experience. Nevertheless, the uniqueness of America, the distinctive, quintessential nature of itself, has been overstressed in recent decades; and the common roots of much of our social and political experience and more particularly of our intellectual and cultural traditions avoided or ignored.... England and America have enjoyed, and still enjoy, ... a mutual heritage of language, institutions, and culture....

Thus both views seem to acknowledge that there are differences. Where they differ is in the amount of significance they attach to the differences. The former camp says that it is the differences that matter, while the latter camp maintains that it is the common heritage that really counts. The first view highlights the differences and downplays what is shared; the second highlights what is shared and downplays the differences.

The American "mind" and intellectual traditions

For my purposes, I do not have to participate and take sides in this on-going battle. My interest is in describing the linguistic differences as fully as possible. I wish to do this in part for its own sake. I assume that there is some inherent interest in laying out as many differences as I can find between the two varieties.

In addition, however, I want to be able to ask the more interesting question of what the differences reveal about the American "mind." This is a valid question, because it is obvious that it was the speakers, and not language of its own accord, who brought about the differences. Thus the linguistic differences can tell us about the people who have produced and use the linguistic differences.

A third concern that I have in this book is the causes that have effected the differences in mind and language. My interest here is in the factors and forces that have shaped the American mind and American English. How did what is specifically American about either language or mentality come into being? This question becomes especially interesting if we consider the fact that American English and, in many ways, American mentality (or mindset or worldview) have evolved into an enormously influential pattern that is recognized, appreciated (often also criticized), and imitated worldwide. In other words, by studying the forces that have shaped American English, we can get some idea of why American English and mentality enjoy the popularity that they do in the world at the end of the twentieth century. I do not claim to be able to offer a comprehensive and sufficiently rich and complex explanation of the totality of this phenomenon. However, I believe that the ideas that we will explore in this book will be helpful at least to begin to understand some of the major reasons for the present success of things American, including language and mentality.

What to teach: British or American?

The focus on British and American linguistic differences can also be justified by some weighty practical reasons. In the past quarter century, there have been debates about which variety of English to learn and study (not necessarily in school) and which to teach in schools for non-native speakers of English (see, for example, Strevens, 1972; Medgyes, 1982; Ryabov and Petrova, 1992). To be able to make an informed choice, we have to see clearly the ways in which American English differs from British English. But even more important, we have to see the causes of the divergences. By studying the causes, both students and educators will learn about historical events, cultural traditions, philosophical trends, and more, which in turn can make us understand why we have the differences that we do. To understand this is a first major step in the direction of leaving certain prejudices behind, prejudices that have long been surrounding British and American differences in general.

A recent example of the kinds of prejudices I have in mind is offered by Prince Charles, who launched the British Council's 2000 project. The goal of this project is to maintain the pre-eminence of the English language in the world. The *International Herald Tribune* quotes and comments on what the Prince had to say:

English "underpins human rights, good government, the resolution of conflict and the democratic process," he said. But there's a catch: "We must act now to ensure that English – and that to my way of thinking means English English – maintains its position as the world language well into the next century." American English is "very corrupting," he said. Americans tended to "invent all sorts of new nouns and verbs and make words that shouldn't be." (March 25-26, 1995)

I will show that this is not the best kind of attitude to take if we want to understand British and American differences, if we want to teach English to learners of English as a foreign language, and if we want to understand the sources of the divergences.

One might argue that the issue of which variety to teach is not really important. It can be suggested that there is emerging a new form of English, sometimes called World English or International English, that will replace national varieties (such as British and American) in the future. If this English emerges, the often mentioned differences between these two national varieties will not count. This is true, but it is also true that the newly emerging International English cannot consist of national varieties of English in equal parts; it cannot and will not contain British, American, Australian, South African, Indian, etc., Englishes to the same degree. It will have to resemble one of these more than the others. But which one? British linguist David Crystal in his *English as a Global Language* (1997) puts the question this way: "Which variety will be most influential in the development of WSSE [= World Standard Spoken English]?" (p. 138). He answers his question in the following way: "It seems likely that it will be US (rather than UK) English" (p. 138). If this prediction is correct, it gives us another reason to study American English.

Can American English reflect culture and the American "mind"?

When I say that I want to find out about the American "mind" on the basis of language, I am aware of some difficulties. Perhaps the foremost of these difficulties is that language constitutes only a partial index to the mind. Play, work, art, science, morality, customs, and others can be said to be revealing about the "mind of a nation," that is, its characteristic patterns of thought, but these things will not be considered here. The chief material of our inquiry is language, American English. In this respect, this study is an attempt at a partial characterization of the American mind, the part revealed by language. But there is even more difficulty in trying to achieve even this limited goal. The linguistic data that we will rely on come primarily from British-American comparisons. That is, it is not the totality of American English that is utilized here, but only, or mostly, those aspects of it that differ in some way from British English. However, this drawback is at the same time an advantage. By focusing on aspects of language where American English differs from British English, we can come to see what is uniquely or specifically American about American English. These uniquely American properties of English can, in turn, give us some insight into what is specific about the American mind or character.

So far I have been assuming that language reflects the mind and culture. But this is not a universally accepted and completely unproblematic assumption. Anna Wierzbicka (1986:350) poses the problem in the following way: "... how do we decide which linguistic phenomena can be legitimately interpreted as culturally significant outside language itself? Can it be done on a principled basis?" For example, English makes a distinction between arms and hands, whereas Polish does not. There is no conceivable extralinguistic explanation for this linguistic difference. But then which linguistic differences can be claimed to reflect cultural and worldview or mentality differences and which ones do not? Wierzbicka's answer is this:

> The more varied and rich our linguistic evidence is, the stronger our case. If we can explain a considerable number of differences between two languages in terms of one, or of a complex of, independently posited cultural differences, then our case will be fairly strong. (p. 351)

This is a piece of advice that I will follow in this study. Since I am interested only in the larger "design features" of American English, I will not pay attention to every single linguistic difference, but only to those that occur and manifest themselves with several others. On the basis of these differences, we can make some suggestions concerning the issue of what Americans are like. Among the properties of American English (and thus Americans) reflected by a number of linguistic phenomena, we will find a preference to be economical, rational, direct, informal, inventive, and so on.

Properties of American English: a preview

Since this is an issue to which the entire second part of the book is devoted, it serves us well to review these properties of American English early on in the book. In order to be able to isolate the characteristic features of American English in a sensible way, I have to fix at least two things. First, I have to provide a reference point, with respect to which American English can be characterized. I will choose standard British English as this reference point. Second, I have to settle on the variety of American English that is used in the comparison. As can be expected, I will choose standard American English for this purpose.

In the comparison I will often make statements of the kind "American English is more X or Y, or has more of X or Y than British English," where X and Y denote some general property of English. Obviously, statements like this presuppose that both British and American English have the feature or property in question. That is, there is only a difference in degree.

The general properties of American English listed below may not be the only ones, but they are the ones that stand out in comparison with British English:

economical
regular
direct
democratic
tolerant
informal
prudish
inflated
inventive
imaginative
success- and action-oriented

I take and use these features in a completely value-neutral way; i.e., I attach neither positive nor negative connotations to them. Below, I offer some evidence for the existence of these properties. (A much fuller treatment of each will be given in chapters twelve through twenty-one.)

The economical nature of American English is seen in several commonly observed linguistic processes, including the use of shorter words (*math – maths, cookbook – cookery book,* etc.), shorter spellings (*color – colour*), and shorter sentences (*I'll see you Monday* vs. *on Monday*). The differences can be captured in the form of what we can call principles or maxims, such as "use as little (linguistic) form as possible."

Regularity is found in the way in which American English changes certain paradigms of English that have some irregular members. Cases of this include the elimination of irregular verb forms (*burn, burned, burned,* rather than *burnt*), doing away with *shall* and keeping only *will* to indicate future, the regularization of the verb *have* (*Do you have...?*, as opposed to *Have you...?*), and many others.

Directness or straightforwardness is observed in linguistic phenomena that appear to adhere to two principles: "say what you mean and say the truth" and "say what you want to say in clear language." The first has to do with what is sometimes interpreted as American bluntness, while the second is a way of capturing the commonly observed phenomenon that American English tends to be more direct and transparent than British English. Vocabulary examples include *bedspread* for *counterpane* and *baby buggy* for *pram*. This also shows up in syntax, as indicated, for example, by the frequent elimination of the grammatical construction *so do I* in place of *I do too* (e.g., A: *I love chocolate.* B: *I do too,* instead of *So do I*), even in Standard American English.

Even more so than the others, the democratic nature of American English is a relative feature. In contrast to many other languages, English in general can be claimed to be a democratic language. Among other things, the democratic character of American English is found in the relative uniformity of American English and the availability of the prestigious standard dialect for a large number of people, a feature that contrasts sharply with British English.

Tolerance is an aspect of a democratic attitude. It is seen, for example, in the apparently low degree to which Americans observe prescriptive linguistic rules. Furthermore, tolerance exhibits itself in how Americans create new lexical forms and grammatical constructions that deviate from the canons of standard English usage (such as the ill-famed word *hopefully*), as well as in the widespread use and acceptance of these forms and constructions by Americans.

Informality can be seen as a further aspect of democracy. The notion that American English is highly informal is based, among other things, on the widespread use of first names (*Hi, my name is Kelly. I'll be your waitress/server this evening*), relationship-markers in discourse, and the free mixing of styles within a single discourse or text.

The prudishness of American English is displayed by the tendency for Americans to use highly euphemistic language to talk about aspects of life that they regard as in any way offensive, unpleasant, or sensitive. This feature of American English, at least two centuries old, may be changing now.

The high-sounding, inflated phrases of American English historically derive from the tall talk of the frontier. In today's speech it can be noticed in the language of several institutions that portray themselves as more prestigious, important, and dignified than they really are (such as *beauty salon, icecream parlor, International House of Pancakes, The World Series*, etc.). This kind of talk still enjoys the appreciation of many speakers.

Inventiveness in American English manifests itself in the high degree to which American English contributes to the English vocabulary. All the processes of word formation are put to maximum use to create new words, such as functional shift, which changes, for example, nouns to verbs (well known examples include the verbs *to interface, to impact, to access*). Additional devices of word formation are also employed.

Imaginativeness seems to pervade several aspects of the use of American English (e.g., it is one of the major reasons why American words are "imported" by other varieties of English; it is a central property of, say, business talk, the language of politics, etc.). Imaginativeness is one form of inventiveness in which linguistic processes such as metaphor and metonymy are put to use in the creation of novel phrases, words, and meanings (e.g., *lame duck, couch potato, shrink,* and many others). There are some uniquely American experiences that serve, on a large scale, as metaphorical "source domains" (such as the frontier or American sports) for the understanding of many aspects of American life.

American English can be said to be "dynamic or active," rather than "passive." This property shows itself most clearly in the American preference for goal-oriented and action words where there is a choice (e.g., *to take a shower, to take a walk* instead of *to have a shower/walk* and *hit the books* for "to study," *to grab a sandwich* for "to buy one," etc.), in the selection of action-related metaphorical source domains (such as the pervasive use of sports language in politics and business), and the general emphasis on success as a concept.

We will return to the discussion of these properties of American English in the second part of the book. For the time being, let it suffice to note that some of the features may be in conflict with each other; for example, economy or directness may be seen as contradicting the euphemizing tendency of prudishness. This creates a certain set of tensions among the features, and I take this particular set of tensions to be a further characteristic of American English.

It should also be noticed at this point that, strictly speaking, a language cannot be economical, tolerant, informal, inventive, and so on. Only the speakers of a language can. In other words, the way I characterized American English above is really a characterization of the speakers of American English. That is, we are concerned with *cultural features* that manifest themselves in language.

Explaining American English

Given these independently observable and testable cultural properties, we can ask where they come from. One of my major claims will be that they are the products of certain intellectual traditions, like Puritanism, rationalism, republicanism, and so forth, that had a greater impact on America than on Britain. I am not claiming, however, that the differences between British and American English derive solely from these intellectual traditions. The role of the unique social history of the United States and the colonies before that, like the westward expansion of the nation, is just as significant, but it has influenced other areas of linguistic differences. This aspect of the unique character of American English is especially well described in the works of J.L. Dillard (e.g., 1972, 1975, 1985, and 1992). The intellectual traditions that have influenced American English have not received much attention from scholars (but for some notable exceptions, see Simpson, 1986 and Cmiel, 1990). The present work attempts to provide an explanation of a large number of linguistic phenomena that are specific to, or characteristic of, American English in light of several major intellectual traditions. Nevertheless, no claim is made that this book is an intellectual history of American English. It is not, and what is attempted here is simply to suggest a connection between certain linguistic phenomena and certain intellectual traditions that may be held responsible for some of the large-scale linguistic peculiarities of American English. This enterprise is very much in the spirit of cultural studies (see, for example, Brogger, 1992).

Which materials are used in this book?

The linguistic facts and the ideas used in this book come from a variety of sources. The study of American English presented in this work relies heavily on published descriptions of American English and British-American comparisons. Such works abound, and I will refer to them in the course of the discussion throughout the book. The availability of a wealth of information is a fortunate situation for anyone who tries to go beyond merely identifying what is specific about American English. Most of the linguistic facts "are in"; we just have to give an account of them. I have made considerable use of these available sources. Nonetheless, as a long-time observer and student of the English language, and especially of American English, I draw also on my own observations and studies concerning American English and its differences in comparison to British English. Another large source of ideas has been the works that attempt to explain the commonly observed differences. The studies that can be helpful in this respect are much less numerous, although there are many works that deal with various aspects of American English without attempting to say what is specific about it. Perhaps the largest subcategory here includes all the works written on the sociolinguistic aspects of American English. A final source of information for the present study has been what several lay observers of the American linguistic scene have said about American English in relation to British English. These are often British people, who are in an excellent situation to notice differences. In general, the British also appear to have more interest in this than the Americans.

Structure of the book

The book is structured in the following way. I begin by presenting the major historical processes that have influenced the development of American English (chapters two and three). I then move on to discuss the main varieties of American English, including regional, social, and ethnic dialects as well as style-related varieties (chapters four to nine). After this, I describe British and American vocabulary differences and discuss some of the most important theories that attempt to give an account of the linguistic differences between the two varieties of English (chapters ten and eleven). The subsequent chapters, chapters twelve through twenty-one, provide the major part of the book. In it, I attempt to identify the specific properties of American English as these have been shaped or produced by the influence of certain intellectual traditions. Finally, a summary and a synthesis of language, character, social history, and intellectual traditions are offered in chapter twenty-two.

study questions and activities

1. Do you share Prince Charles's sentiments about American English? What attitudes can you find toward British and American English in your circles (among your friends, teachers, relatives, as well as the media)?

2. Collect additional examples for the characteristics of American English as given in the chapter. Also, collect as many counterexamples as you can. Do the claims in the chapter still stand?

3. If you are a non-native speaker of English studying American English outside an English-speaking country, check which variety of English is taught and preferred. Try to find out why that particular variety is preferred.

4. Discuss the issue of how language can express the characteristic values and thought patterns of a culture. Examine your native language first in the discussion.

chapter 2

American English: a brief history

In this chapter and the next we will be concerned with the history of American English (e.g., Algeo, 1992a). The main focus of this chapter will be on early history: the English of the first settlers and their linguistic contacts.

The historical background

It is customary to distinguish three stages in the development of American English. The first, the "colonial period," covers the period between the arrival of the first settlers in the North American continent and the end of the War of Independence; the second, the "national period," stretches from the end of the War of Independence to the end of the nineteenth century (as we will see, there is no unanimous agreement concerning the exact time frame); the third, the "international period," runs from the end of the nineteenth century to the present. These periods coincide with and are based on major historical events that played an important role in the shaping of American English.

The first period

The first English settlement was founded in Jamestown in 1607. The second permanent settlement – Plymouth Plantation – came into existence in 1620. It was founded by the Pilgrims, who made their arduous trip across the Atlantic on the *Mayflower*. These settlers were all English whose mother tongue was the English language as it was spoken around the turn of the seventeenth century. The population of the first thirteen colonies reached four million. The vast majority (according to some estimates, as much as 95%) of these people lived east of the Appalachian Mountains. It is also remarkable that most of them (again, something like 90%) came to the new continent from the British Isles. This was also the period when the importation of slaves from Africa began. As early as 1619, the first slaves were taken to Jamestown, and slavery was legalized in 1650. The process continued until the middle of the nineteenth century. (I will deal with the English spoken by the black slaves and their descendants in chapters six and seven.)

Some scholars consider this the linguistically most important period, since this was the time when the settlement of the original thirteen colonies along the Atlantic seaboard took place, and thus the first speakers of what would later become American English appeared on the North American continent. The other linguistically significant aspect of this period was that the first English-speaking settlers came into contact with a variety of other languages. First of all, the early settlers met with the native Indian population. But the Spanish were also already there. After all it was the Spanish who commissioned Cristoforo Colombo to find a westerly route to the East Indies. The Spanish had much of the South of what is the United States today in their possession. There were French settlers in the north, and the Dutch were in New Amsterdam, now New York, until 1664. The first German settlers began to arrive at the end of the seventeenth century in what is the state of Pennsylvania today. As we will see toward the end of this chapter, the extensive contact with these early non-English-speaking settlers left its mark on American English.

The Atlantic seaboard comprised three large areas – from north to south: New England, the Middle Atlantic states, and the South Atlantic states. As noted above, the first settlers reached the New England area in 1620, and established the first colony in Plymouth, Massachusetts. They then began to move up and down the coast from Massachusetts. As a result, Connecticut, Rhode Island, and New Hampshire were established in the following decades. Two thirds of the settlers around the Massachusetts Bay were from the eastern parts of Anglia. This was the region that served as the main stronghold of English Puritanism. As we will see in a later chapter, Puritanism would have a serious influence on the development of American English.

In the Middle Atlantic area, what is the state of New York today was first in the hands of the Dutch, until the British seized it and renamed the Dutch colony of New Netherlands New York in 1664. The colony of New Jersey was also founded with primarily English inhabitants, many of whom were Quakers. What is now Pennsylvania was also soon populated, primarily by Quakers, Welsh, Scottish, Irish, and German settlers. The strong influence of German settlers in this area is indicated by such town names as Germantown, which came into existence in 1683, only one year after the major city of the colony of Pennsylvania, Philadelphia, was founded. In the early decades of the 1700s, Irish settlers began to move southwest and many of them later became the first frontiersmen. Maryland was established as one of the thirteen original colonies. Delaware was also a part of the Middle Atlantic area.

The first of the South Atlantic colonies was Virginia, where Jamestown was founded. It was followed by North Carolina, South Carolina, and much later Georgia. The Carolinas received many Huguenots (French Calvinists). In general, it can be said that the population of the South Atlantic colonies was fairly mixed, both socially and geographically.

The first, the colonial, period in the development of American English closes with the ratification of the Federal Constitution in 1789, in the wake of the War of Independence.

The second period

The end of the War of Independence roughly coincides with the time when the long process of westward movement began. Tens of thousands of settlers moved west of the seaboard area toward and beyond the Mississippi River. This "march" opens the second major period in the history of American English, sometimes called the "national period." As new settlers arrived, there was an increasing demand for new, unexplored, and unoccupied territories. At first the rate of immigration was relatively slow (roughly one million people up to 1840), but after 1840 there was a dramatic increase: between 1840 and the end of the century roughly 30 million people chose the United States as their new home. Large groups of new immigrants went to the new country from Ireland and Germany. In the Irish case, a devastating potato famine (in the 1840s) drove many people away from their homes, while in the German case it was the unsuccessful 1848 revolution that was mainly responsible for people leaving their country. The exodus involved one and a half million people in both Ireland and Germany.

The main feature of the period that seems to be assumed by most scholars is that this is the time when the English spoken in the United States became and, as a result of the efforts of men like Webster, was made the national language of the new country. (We will discuss the contribution made by Webster and others to the process in several later chapters.) It is thus fitting to call this stage in the development of American English the national period. It is debatable whether it was the Civil War in 1860 or the Spanish-American War in 1898 that marked the close of the second period. What is clear, however, is that there was a significant change in the foreign policy of the United States after 1898 which brought with it an equally significant change in the international importance and recognition of American English.

The third period

This final period stretches from the late nineteenth century to the present time. The period is characterized by a new wave of immigration. The new immigrants arrived in the United States from all parts of the world, but several categories of immigrants stand out in number and importance.

The first phase of this period was marked by an influx of especially Northern European immigrants. They primarily occupied the northern states of the country. For example, the Swedish appeared in large numbers in such states as Minnesota.

Around the turn of the century, a large number of Southern and Eastern Europeans chose the United States as their new home. The immigrants from Italy came mainly from the southern part of Italy. Of the immigrants from

Eastern Europe, people from the Austro-Hungarian Empire were represented in large numbers. Between 1900 and 1905 alone, one million Austro-Hungarians moved to America. Yet another group of immigrants was made up of East and Central European Jews, three million of whom emigrated to the United States between 1880 and 1910. The most general characteristic of the immigrants from southern and eastern Europe was that they were predominantly poor, uneducated, and illiterate. Their immigration to the United States was largely facilitated by cheap travel in steamships. The low fares made it so easy that between 1865 and 1920 five million people arrived in the United States. Many of them went to the great cities of the north-east. This explains why there are, for example, quarters called *Little Italy* in several big cities such as New York.

The latest, but one of the most important, wave of immigration came from Spanish-speaking territories: Mexico, Puerto Rico, and Cuba. The immigrants from Mexico largely concentrated in the south and southwest parts of the United States, while the Puerto Ricans and Cubans concentrated in large cities in the east, such as New York and Miami. As we will see, these Hispanic immigrants developed a special variety within American English – Hispanic English, which has several distinct subvarieties. (Hispanic English will be discussed in a later chapter.)

Elizabethan English

After this brief outline of the major historical factors that, as we will see, have had a significant influence on American English, it is time to look at the English language itself as it was first used on the North American continent. Of primary importance here is the question of what the language of the first settlers was like. Since the first settlers reached the North American continent in the early decades of the seventeenth century, their language must have been similar to the English spoken in England in the late sixteenth century, the period generally referred to as "Elizabethan." I will briefly describe this language, Elizabethan English, or, more precisely, its most influential dialect. In this section I will rely on Marckwardt (1980; rev. Dillard) and McCrum, *et al.* (1986).

Pronunciation

A main feature of the speech of the early settlers may have been its considerable variation. Words like *meat, teach, sea, tea,* and *lean* were pronounced both with the sounds /i/ and /e/. Other words, such as *bird, learn, turn* had the middle sound /r/ in them and *clerk* was pronounced either /klak/ or /klərk/, the latter being the standard American pronunciation today. In addition, the sounds in words like *bite, bide,* and *rice* had the diphthong /e/ that we find in present-day *mate*. Stress patterns also varied more. In Shakespeare's time, the stress was placed either at the beginning or on the second syllable in such words as *sincere*, yielding either /'sɪnsɪr/ or /sɪn'sɪr/.

It should be noted that these are features of London speech in the seventeenth century. Speakers from other parts of England used other dialects. London speech was used by only 5% of all the speakers of English. Nevertheless, this dialect of English turned out to be the decisive one for the later development of British English, and, as a result of its variability, it also left room for American English to develop in its own way.

Pronouns

This early form of English still had the distinction between *thou* and *ye* or *you*. This had originally been a number distinction, *thou* indicating the singular second-person pronoun and *ye* or *you* the plural second-person pronoun. Later it acquired a meaning distinguishing social rank. *Thou* was used for equals, while *ye* or *you* for superiors. What is of special importance is that one religious group, the Quakers, who went to America to seek religious freedom, insisted that only one pronoun should be used, thus eliminating social distinctions in language as well. Ironically, the English language went along with this Quaker proposal, but the form that was chosen was *you*, the pronoun that was employed to address superiors. Nevertheless, the Quakers' insistence on eliminating social inequalities in language gives us an early example of how later Americans also found it important to use language in general in a democratic way.

William Bradford: History of Plimmoth Plantation

The first early settlers, the "Pilgrim Fathers," arrived in Massachusetts in 1620 from the English city of Plymouth, aboard the *Mayflower*. William Bradford was the *Mayflower*'s historian who recorded the events of the journey and the experiences of the Puritan colony. Bradford also became the first governor of the Massachusetts colony. One of the earliest documents of what can be called American English is Bradford's *History of Plimmoth Plantation*, an account of the life of the first settlers in Massachusetts Bay. Here is a sample from this text, as quoted in McCrum, *et al.* (1986):

> Being thus passed the vast ocean, and a sea of troubles ... they had now no friends to welcome them, nor inns to entertaine or refresh their weather-beaten bodys, no houses or much less townes to repaire to ... it was muttered by some that if they got not a place in time they would turn them and their goods ashore [and return] ...

But may not and ought not the children of these fathers rightly say
– Our Fathers were Englishmen which came over this great ocean,
and were ready to perish in the wilderness, but they cried unto the
Lord, and he heard their voice and looked on their adversities.

This is elegant and simple prose, in many ways reminiscent of the King James
Version of the Bible (of which, see below). The text is also characterized by, among
other things, a liberal treatment of English grammar by today's standards. For
example, in it the word *scarce* is used as an adverbial, without the ending *-ly*; it
contains sentences such as *There was but 6 or 7 sound persons,* where a plural
verb would be required today; it has what are called "dangling" participles today;
many of its sentences are long and seemingly incoherent to the modern reader.
This liberal attitude to grammar can be regarded as the root of some modern
American practices.

Our general conclusion here can be that the early form of English that the
first settlers carried with them to the new continent had a great deal of flexi-
bility which left room for the English language to develop in new directions.
This opportunity was captured by the settlers and the later immigrants.

The literary and cultural background

Elizabethan English was the language of outstanding and influential literary
figures like Shakespeare, Lyly, and Marlowe. But it was also the language of the
"Authorized Version" of the Bible, the version that became known as the "King
James Version," published in 1611. It was prepared by a team of experts, six
scholars under the leadership of John Bois.

There is one difference between the language of Shakespeare and his contem-
poraries, on the one hand, and that of the King James Version of the Bible, on the
other, that is of great importance for the study of American English. Shakespeare
made creative use of the lexicon of the English languge. Estimates vary, but the
number of different words in his works is said to easily exceed twenty thousand.
The creativity of his language perhaps needs no demonstration here. Now, in
sharp contrast to this, the Bible used only eight thousand words, all of which are
simple, everyday, and are intended for everyone. The simplicity of the Bible may
be illustrated with the following passage, taken from McCrum, *et al.* (1986):

Or ever the silver cord be loosed, or the golden bowl be broken, or the
pitcher be broken at the fountain, or the wheel broken at the cistern:
Then shall the dust return to the earth as it was: and the spirit shall
return unto God who gave it. Vanity of vanities, saith the preacher; all
is vanity. (Ecclesiastes 12)

This duality in language between simplicity and creativity will come up again and again in our account of American English. I will devote several chapters to a characterization of American English as "simple," or at least striving toward simplicity (see chapters twelve to fourteen), but I will also show how it is creative and innovative in many ways. Incidentally, this pull toward both simplicity and creativity is also characteristic of much of English literature (McArthur, 1992). According to McArthur, there are basically two linguistic traditions in English literature: one that follows the Shakespearean tradition of innovation and creativity and the other that takes the lead of the simple language of the Bible. The first is exemplified by writers such as Joyce and Dickens, the second by writers such as Hemingway.

Archaic features of American English

American English has retained many of the features of the English language spoken in England in the seventeenth and eigthteenth centuries. In this section I will briefly mention some of these important archaic features of American English. The account is based largely on Marckwardt (1980; rev. Dillard).

Pronunciation

American English sounds have qualities that were found in the English of the seventeenth and eighteenth centuries. Among these, two qualities stand out: the American use of the /r/ and /æ/ sounds. In general, it can be pointed out that /r/-preservation in words such as *bar* and *colo(u)r* and the use of /æ/ in words such as *fast* and *path* were abandoned in Southern England, that is, the speech area influenced by London, at the end of the eighteenth century. The sound corresponding to the letter *a* was mainly flat in England, even in words like *father*. This means that it was pronounced unrounded, with the lips slightly spread. There are about 150 common words in American English that have this vowel, instead of the vowel used in British English today. The /æ/ is present in American pronunciation in words in which the *a* is followed by the so-called voiceless fricatives *f, s,* and *th.* This flat *a,* pronounced /æ/, was common throughout England until the eigthteenth century.

Another well known feature of American English is the sound /r/. The /r/ sound can be pronounced in several ways. Americans pronounce it with the tongue curled back a little. This is called retroflex /r/. The retroflex /r/ had also been the normal way of saying the /r/ in England. However, British English lost it in certain positions (post-vocalically, i.e., after vowels), while American English preserved it. We will discuss this sound further in the chapter on regional dialects.

American English is also characterized by the sound /u/ in words such as *new* and *knew*, where British English has /ju/. This latter pronunciation was typical of speech in East Anglia at the time the first settlers left England and it is still recognizable in some rural parts of eastern England. However, the Americans preserved the /j/-less pronunciation, while the pronunciation with /j/ became the standard in British English.

The use of the so-called "short o" also reflects the preservation of an older pronunciation in American English. The *o* in words such as *not, hot, top,* and *lot* was flat, that is, unrounded, very close to the pronunciation of the *a* in father today. In British English it is now rounded. The flat *o* died out in England in the eighteenth century, but it has been retained in America.

In some varieties of American English the words *whale* and *wharf* are typically pronounced with the sound /ʍ/, whereas in England they have /w/. (The distinction does not, of course, apply to words such as *water*, which has /w/ in both.) This difference also goes back to Elizabethan times. The original pronunciation of these words in English in the seventeenth century, especially the English of southern England, was /ʍ/. Thus American English retained the earlier pronunciation again.

As was mentioned above, Elizabethan stress patterns were different from those of today. The words *secretary* and *necessary* had secondary stress on the last syllable in Shakespeare's time. This is general American practice today, a practice which has changed in British English, where the pronunciation of these words has only primary stress on the first syllable, yielding /ˈsɛkrɛtrɪ/ and /ˈnɛsɛsrɪ/, as opposed to American English /ˈsɛkrɛˌtɛrɪ/ and /ˈnɛsɛˌsɛrɪ/. The same applies to the stress pattern of words like *circumstance*, where American English has secondary stress on the final syllable.

We may also note that the present-day pronunciation of words such as *fertile*, *hostile*, and *missile* in American English goes back to Shakespearean times. *Fertile* was pronounced /fɜrtɪl/, *hostile* as /hastɪl/, and so forth in the seventeenth century. This is common and accepted American practice today. British English has again departed from the early practice.

There was a great deal of accent leveling in the speech of the first Americans. For example, the people from East Anglia and the West Country mixed freely in the new colonies. As a result, the children of the first generation in all probability spoke a kind of English that was the merger of accents from of variety of English dialects. The process already started on the ships and continued in the closely-knit colonies of the New World. We can consider this process of accent leveling as a major force in the shaping of American English. In particular, it must have had an impact on the relative uniformity of American English (see chapter five).

Grammar

The single best-known morphological property of American English that distinguishes it from British English concerns the verb *get*. This verb has three forms in American English: *get, got, gotten*. Present-day British English has only two: *get* and *got*, the latter both for the simple past tense and the past participle forms. The use of *gotten*, according to Marckwardt (1980; rev. Dillard), was common in England until the late seventeenth century.

In American English there are two forms with the auxiliary verb *have*: *have got* and *have gotten*. But the two constructions have different meanings. *Have got* is used to indicate something like "to possess," while *have gotten* has the meaning "to acquire, to obtain." Thus, characteristically, we find the constructions in sentences such as *I have got a good job* and *I have just gotten a good job*. In British English both of these would be expressed with the form *got*. (However, to express the sense of "acquisition" in British English some changes in the sentence would have to be made, such as the use of an adverb, as in *I have just got a good job* or the use of the reflexive, as in *I've got myself a good job*.) In British English *got* can also be used in the past perfect in sentences such as *I had got some money to spend last month*. This is not used by speakers of American English.

Another characteristic syntactic difference concerns the use of the so-called "collective nouns." These are nouns that indicate a unity or collection of individual members. Thus the focus can be on either the unity or the individual members. In British English, these nouns, such as *government, team, corporation,* and many others, are typically used with a plural verb, while Americans usually prefer a singular verb. Thus where the British would have *The government are saying ...*, Americans would have *The government is saying....* This is not a watertight rule, but it reflects a fairly typical tendency, with various kinds of exceptions. However, the main point, according to Marckwardt (1980; rev. Dillard), is that the use of the singular verb with these nouns is older, and American English maintained this usage, whereas British English departed from it in the first half of the nineteenth century.

Vocabulary

I will mention here some of the most commonly recognized cases in which American usage has kept an earlier English usage, whereas British English has abandoned or changed it.

The word *mad* is perhaps the most frequently used American word for "angry" today, as in *I am mad at him*. This goes back to Elizabethan times, when Shakespeare used it in the sense of "angry." In modern British English usage *mad* simply means "insane," although many Britishers would also recognize the American meaning of the term.

The word *platter* was used for "dish." It is not used in Britain anymore in this sense, while it is still common in the United States.

Sick originally meant "ill" in general in the seventeenth century. It is this meaning that survives in such expressions as *sickbed, sick-note, homesick,* and *lovesick* in both British and American English. The meaning of the word was not limited to "nausea" alone, which is the predominant meaning in Britain today. When used predicatively (i.e., with verbs like *to be* or *to feel*), the new British sense of the term is "ready to vomit, to feel nauseated." American English still retains the earlier, more general sense of the word, and it is used of illness in general.

One of the celebrated examples of British and American vocabulary differences is the American use of *fall* for what is *autumn* in Britain. *Fall* is the older English word of the two, and American English preserved it, although *autumn* is also found in more literary contexts.

Guess is another American English word that has captured the attention of those dealing with British-American differences. This is because, many observers find, it is overused as a verb by Americans. The specifically American meaning of the verb is "suppose" or "consider," and it occurs in sentences such as *I guess you are feeling tired after your long journey* (Oxford Advanced Learner's Dictionary, OALD). The important point about it here is that its use goes back to Chaucer in the fourteenth century, and it was used up to the seventeenth century, when it died out in standard British English (although it survives in some British dialects).

The verb *loan* originally meant "lend" in English. This use of the term is regarded as American today. Interestingly, it can be encountered in this sense in formal British English in sentences such as *Her Majesty the Queen graciously loaned the painting* (OALD).

The verb *progress* is also a remnant of an old English practice of turning nouns into verbs. The use of the word as a verb was considered an Americanism, but now it can also be found in British speech and writing. The verb *progress* was also criticized by language purists who objected to the process of coining words by making nouns into verbs.

The predominant British meaning of the noun *bug* is "small insect infesting dirty houses and beds" (OALD). However, this is a later development of the word. It originally referred to any small insect, not exclusively *bedbugs*. American English retained this older sense of the term.

The noun *druggist*, "a person who makes medicine," is an American word that was created in English in the early seventeenth century. It derives, of course, from the common English word *drug* meaning "medicine." The word *druggist* continued to be used in America, while the British later began to use the noun *chemist* for the same sense.

The word *apartment* also existed in English before it became the American word for the British English *flat*. It was used in English in 1641 in the general meaning of "a number of rooms in a house or building that belong to a single family." This is the sense that is still current in the United States. The corresponding term is *flat* in England, where the word *apartment* refers either to a "set of rooms, usually furnished and rented, especially for a holiday" or to "a private room, especially in a famous building." In this latter sense, it is commonly used in the plural *apartments*.

The noun *deck* means a set of playing cards in the United States. The term used in England is *pack*. The word *deck* is again the earlier development in the English language in this sense, and it can still be found with this meaning in some northern dialects in Britain.

The early meaning of the verb *raise* in Britain was fairly general in the seventeenth and eighteenth centuries, including the raising of children, animals, and farm products. This early unspecified meaning of the word was largely discontinued in Britain, where children are raised or brought up, horses are bred, and farm products are grown. In this case also, it is the more general earlier meaning that was preserved in American English.

The word *cabin* was employed in Britain before the first quarter of the nineteenth century in the sense of "a poor dwelling" (in addition, of course, to its nautical sense). This meaning was lost in British English, whereas in American English it continued to be in use. The continuation of the "poor dwelling" sense of the word in the United States was no doubt in part due to Harriet Beecher Stowe's famous novel *Uncle Tom's Cabin*, which greatly "popularized" it.

As a final example, we can mention the word *bloody*. Originally, the word *bloody* simply meant "covered with blood" in English. This is the meaning which was carried over to America, where the word is used in this non-taboo sense. In British English, however, it became a taboo word for the expression of anger, or other negative feelings. This is why it could create an uproar in England when it was used in G.B. Shaw's *Pygmalion* at the beginning of the century. This use of the word has not carried over to American English.

What does all this tell us about American English? For a long time it was believed that it is its archaic nature – the "colonial lag" – that provides us with the specificity of American English among the varieties of English. The widely held view has been that archaic features of the sort we have just seen define what is unique about American English. (For a critique of this misconception, see Görlach, 1991.) However, this is only partially true – and it is not even the biggest or the most important part. Archaic features represent only a fragment of "Americanisms."

In the previous chapter, we began to survey some of the features of American English that make it a unique variety. The remainder of this chapter, the whole of the next chapter, and the entire second half of the book will be devoted to spelling out in detail the rest of what is unique about American English.

The influence of languages of the colonial period

The first languages with which the English-speaking settlers came into contact in the seventeenth and eighteenth centuries include the various native Indian languages, as well as Spanish, French, Dutch, and German. In this section, I provide a brief outline of the best-known effects in the vocabulary that these languages had on American English.

American Indian languages

The first and real "owners" of the American continent were the various native American Indian tribes, speaking a large number of different Indian languages. Roughly fifty American Indian words have established themselves in the lexicon of American English. As McCrum, *et al.* (1986) say, the first English-speaking settlers called these words "wigwam" words, *wigwam* being one of the earliest borrowings into the English language in North America. McCrum, *et al.* (1986:120-121) go on to show that many of the words borrowed came from the domain of trees, plants, fruits, and animals. Indian tree names include *hickory, pecan, sequoia,* and *persimmon. Pecan* is the name of a species of nut. The settlers encountered animals and fish that were unfamiliar to them, and they readily borrowed terms from the natives: *chipmunk, moose, opossum, skunk,* and *terrapin* are some examples. Some of the loan words have to do with foods and drink; for example, *hominy* and *pemmican* are Indian terms for foods and *hooch* for drink. The political life and organization of the Indians also left its mark on American English. Such well-known American English political words as *caucus* and *mugwump* derive from Indian languages. Most of the borrowings, however, come from the domain of culture, conceived in a broad sense. Here we find well-established English words such as *totem, papoose, squaw, moccasin, tomahawk, igloo, kayak,* and *potlatch.*

In many cases, the Indian words were perceived by the settlers as too long or too difficult to pronounce. As a result, they have simplified the original Indian words, which often meant making them shorter. Thus, today American English has the word *racoon* for the animal from *aracouns,* which ultimately derives from the Indian word *raughroughouns.* The term *possum,* as in the phrase *to play possum,* comes from *opossum.* And the name of the fruit *squash* goes back to the original *askutasquash.*

McCrum, *et al.* (1986) continue their discussion of the American Indian influence on American English by examining a number of words which have changed meaning over the years. For example, *pow-wow*, which originally probably meant "he dreams," was first used in American English in the sense of a "priest, or medicine man." Then it came to mean a "ceremony with magic, together with feasting and dancing." A later development in its meaning was its extension to an "Indian council." Today its most common application is "any conference or gathering," which is a colloquial use of the word. Another term of Indian origin that has a curious history is *mugwump*. Its first meaning was "great chief." Then in 1884 it came to be used to ridicule breakaway Republicans. After that, it has been applied to any independent, especially a politician.

It is also of great interest that there are many American English idioms today that derive, in some way, from Indian languages. Some examples include *go on a scalp hunt, smoke a peace pipe, put on warpaint, fire-water, Indian file, Indian summer, play possum, bury the hatchet, go on the warpath* (McCrum, *et al.*, 1986:121). The contemporary meanings of these idiomatic expressions are based on aspects of various native Indian culture; it should be noted, however, that their use in certain contexts can be considered derogatory by many native people.

The vocabulary of Indian languages also served the settlers to give Amerindian place names to, for instance, states and rivers. In the United States twenty-six states have Indian names, including Massachusetts and the Dakotas. Some Indian river names are Merrimac and Connecticut in New England, Passaic and Raritan in New Jersey, and further south, Potomac.

French

McCrum, *et al.* (1986:124) note that the French influence came later than the native Indian influence. The settlers met the French as they moved inland. There were essentially two sources of the French influence. The early American settlers encountered the French in the north and west, along the St. Lawrence and Mississippi rivers. This contact resulted in borrowings such as *toboggan, caribous, bayou, butte, crevasse, levee, depot,* and *cache*. Some of the French words, like *caribou*, were of Indian origin. The other main contact location with the French was the south, especially New Orleans. Words such as *brioche, jambalaya, praline, chowder, picayune* ("small coin," then "anything worthless, trifling") entered American English here. As can be seen, many of these had to do with food, for which Louisiana is still famous.

One of the best-known American English words of French origin is *prairie*. This word has been "immortalized" by Western movies. The prairie was the home of the *gopher*, also a French word. Some plant names come from French as well, e.g., *pumpkin*. Many of the French borrowings have to do with toponyms, terms such as *bayou, levee, prairie, rapids*, and with building and exploration, words such as *bureau, depot, shanty, carry-all, portage, toboggan, voyageur*. This no doubt has to do with the fact that the French were among the original explorers of the continent. Interestingly, the words for the American coins *cent* and *dime* are of French origin as well.

Spanish

The early Spanish influence on American English is the most extensive of all the colonial languages. To this influence the English language owes such common words as *barbecue, chocolate*, and *tomato*, which were, incidentally, all borrowed from various Indian languages by the Spanish themselves. The settlers referred to the Spanish as *dagoes*, which is derived from the Spanish name *Diego*. The Spanish influence continues even today, and we will further discuss it in a later chapter (McCrum, *et al.*, 1986:123).

Many of the words that the settlers took over from Spanish refer to plants, such as *alfalfa, marijuana, mesquite, yucca*, and *tomato*. Others denote fish and animals, such as *barracuda, bonito, bronco, cockroach, coyote, mustang*. Plant and animal names account for almost one quarter of the total number of borrowings. Food and drink names were also frequent, yielding such familiar words in American English as *chili, enchilada, taco, tequila, tortilla, barbecue, chocolate*. As mentioned, several of these have become common English words, and several have acquired "international status." Toponyms and names connected with building also abound, such as *canyon, mesa, sierra* and *patio, plaza, pueblo* indicate. But most of the terms borrowed from Spanish reflect the main occupation of the Spanish in the American south: ranch life. As a matter of fact, the word *ranch* itself is of Spanish origin, together with numerous others such as *corral, hacienda, lasso*, and *rodeo*. Other words tell us about the ways the Spanish dressed (e.g., *chaps, poncho, sombrero*) and still others about their legal and penal system: *calaboose, desperado, hoosegow, vigilantes*.

Finally, there is a mixed bag of words that are difficult to place in any one of the large categories above. These include such well known and common words as *filibuster, hombre, loco, stevedore, tornado, vamoose*, and *stampede*.

Dutch

Until 1664, what was then called the town of New Amsterdam was in the hands of the Dutch, before the British seized it and renamed it New York. The early Dutch history of the city is reflected in the names for parts of New York, such as Brooklyn, Harlem, and Bronx.

As McCrum, *et al.* (1986:124-125) tell us, overall the number of Dutch words is not great in contemporary American English. However, many of the Dutch borrowings are well known and even have a certain amount of reputation in lay and expert linguistic circles alike. *Waffle, coleslaw, cookie, pot cheese, dumb, landscape, caboose, sleigh, boss, snoop, spook, poppycock* (literally meaning "soft dung") all derive from Dutch, and so do *Santa Claus* and *Yankee*. This last one has given much headache to people who tried to figure out its origin. Those who believe in its Dutch origin say that it comes from *Jan Kees*, meaning "John Cheese." The American English word *boss* also originates in Dutch, where it meant "master," which is closely related to its contemporary American application as "employer or chief." James Fenimore Cooper noted in his *The American Democrat* that *boss* is a word that white servants used in place of the term *master* (or *massa*, employed by Black servants) as, for them, a more appealing alternative. *Boss* entered American English through another route as well. In Black English the word means "fine, excellent" in slang phrases such as a *boss chick (girl)*. Interestingly, this use also has to do with Dutch. Its probable source is Suriname creole, which is based in part on Dutch.

Some Dutch toponyms have also found their way into American English, as exemplified by the word *bush* meaning "back country." Two American English words from the domain of farming that derive from Dutch are *hay barrack* and *saw buck*, words that indicate very early contact with the Dutch.

German

There is one important difference between the early German settlers and the other settlers mentioned above. While the Spanish, Dutch, and French were rival colonists to the British settlers, the Germans were the first non-colonizing immigrants, who were rather fleeing from religious persecution at home. The German settlers began to arrive on the new continent in 1683, their main destination being Pennsylvania. These early settlers came from Bavaria, and belonged to Amish and Mennonite sects, which were well known for the austere lives they led. The German settlers maintained many of their language habits, which gave rise to what is called *Pennsylvania Dutch*. This was of course a misnomer based on the German word for German, which is *Deutsch* (McCrum, *et al.*, 1986:125).

Several "German cities" in the United States accommodate the seven million Germans. They include Cincinnati, Milwaukee, and St. Louis. Many German words have been taken over by American English, several of them being in daily use, such as *check* (from *Zeiche*), *cookbook, delicatessen, ecology, fresh* (from *frech*), *kindergarten, rifle* (*groove*) (McCrum, *et al.*, 1986:264-265). Most of the German words that have been borrowed have to do with food and drink.

These are words such as *delicatessen, hamburger, frankfurter, noodle, pretzel, sauerkraut, cookbook,* and *lager.* The word *hot dog* is an American coinage that came about as a result of a change in American attitude toward the Germans in the wake of the First World War. The brief rash of anti-German feeling at this time made many change their names, and the wave of "Americanizing" German words produced *hot dog* in place of *frankfurter.* The Germans were respected for the quality of their education, and American English borrowed several German words from this domain, such as *festschrift, semester,* and *seminar.* I will mention some more American borrowings from German in the discussion of American slang (see chapter nine).

Pidgin Englishes

In addition to these influences, the early settlers came across various kinds of pidgin English (see Dillard, 1985, 1992). The influence of pidgin English, like the mixture of Dutch-English and Indian-English, must have been substantial in the early formative period of American English. A nice illustration of this situation is an event reported by William Bradford, in which he tells us that, "about 16th of March [1621], a certain Indian came boldly among them and spoke to them in broken English, which they could well understand but marvelled at it.... At length they understood by discours with him, that he was not of these parts, but belonged to the eastern parts where some English ships came to fish, with whom he was acquainted and ... amongst whom he had got his language" (Quoted in McCrum, *et al.*, 1986:120). The pidgin English spoken by this Indian was spread among the Indian tribes by trading ships on the east coast.

The influence of later immigrants

As McCrum, *et al.* (1986:263) observe, the word *immigrant* itself is an American term that was coined in 1789 to refine the word *emigrant.* With the exodus of people in the nineteenth and twentieth centuries, the United States became, in a real sense, a country of the "huddled masses." In the previous section, we have surveyed the linguistic influence of the early settlers. It is important to see, however, that the settlement of North America is not limited to this early period. Instead, it is a long process that has continued to the present time. Moreover, the immigrants from the different countries came to the United States not all at once but at different times. As we have seen, the German case is a good example of this.

In the present section, I will briefly mention some later immigrant groups and the influence they have had on American English. Most of the data in the remainder of this chapter come from McCrum, *et al.* (1986:263-265).

Italian

As I noted in the first section, there was an influx of Italians, especially from southern Italy, around the turn of the century. The linguistic influence of Italians is not remarkable. The words that they contributed to American English are largely names of food and vegetables, including *pizza, pasta, spaghetti, lasagna* (and other pastas), *espresso, parmesan, vermicelli, broccoli,* and *zucchini.*

Yiddish

The Jewish immigrants also made their linguistic contribution to American English. Such well-known words as *chutzpa, kibitzer, gonef, lox,* and *bagel* have entered American English from Yiddish. Many idiomatic expressions also derive from Yiddish. Perhaps the best known of these is *Enjoy!,* an American counterpart (but not equivalent) of *Good appetite.* In addition, expressions like *Give a look, He knows from nothing, If you'll excuse the expression, I'm telling you, I need it like a hole in the head,* and *I should worry* all derive from Yiddish. I will say more about the Yiddish influence in the chapters on regional dialects and slang.

Hispanic influence

We have seen the early Spanish linguistic influence in the previous section, where it was noted that the Spanish were a rival group of colonists to the British. However, later Spanish-speaking immigrants were very different from these early settlers. The second largest non-British ethnic group in the United States is the Hispanic. This comprises the Mexicans, Puerto Ricans, and Cubans, among others, who have come to the United States in the course of the nineteenth and twentieth centuries. The nature of the linguistic contact between American English and the Spanish of these groups will be described in the chapter on ethnic dialects (see chapter seven).

Other groups

In addition to the ethnic groups mentioned so far, there have been many others. Groups of immigrants came to the United States not only from Europe, West Africa (the black slaves), and Central America (Mexico, Cuba, Puerto Rico), but from all over the world. Almost all of the ethnic groups and their languages have contributed something or other to what is American English today. This is especially clear in the case of such large Asian ethnic groups as the Chinese and the Japanese.

study questions and activities

1. Try to find as many words as you can in American English that do not originate in English. Check where they come from and roughly when they entered American English. Use a good dictionary of American English (at least of the collegiate size). What do these words tell you about the history of American English and the U.S. in general?

2. Check in a recent British dictionary all the words in the chapter that were given as examples of the alleged archaic character of American English. What does the dictionary reveal about the words concerning their meaning and current British or American status? You can also check this with native speakers of British English.

3. Take a good grammar of English that lists the most common collective nouns. Collect examples of their use in British and American newspapers. What regularities do you find? Different collective nouns may reveal different patterns of use. What does the variation depend on in particular cases?

4. What immigrant languages are most conspicuous in recent American fiction and movies? To determine this, arrange with members of your class to read as many recent American novels or short stories and/or to see as many American movies as you can. Make note of all the words and expressions that represent immigrant languages in the U.S. today. Discuss in class what you have found.

chapter 3

A new nation

A merican English has been shaped by more than early language contacts. A
new continent, new activities, new institutions, and new technologies had
to be named. This task of naming, much of which took place in the nineteenth
century, will be our topic in this chapter.

The task of naming

Of the many tasks that awaited the settlers and immigrants on the new continent, perhaps the most basic and immediate one was the naming of all the new
things that confronted them when they arrived. This task continued during
their westward march across the continent. As a result of a new climate and
different fauna, flora, and resources, new activities emerged that helped the
people survive, live comfortably, or get rich. Since the very first days of their
arrival, and even before that, they had come into contact with other peoples
speaking languages other than English. As we saw in the previous chapter, the
settlers and immigrants very often freely borrowed from these languages in the
course of their various activities. Old technologies they brought with them
from England were continued and new ones introduced, but both countries
often created their new terminologies. They also had to set up institutions that
in many cases differed from the institutions they had left behind and thus
required new names. In other words, the making of a new nation was not only
a physical, mental, or an emotional task, but very clearly and importantly also
a linguistic one. As Thomas Jefferson put it, "new circumstances ... call for new
words, new phrases, and the transfer of old words to new objects" (McCrum,
et al., 1986:121-122).

Two of the "namers": Lewis and Clark

In 1804, two army officers, Meriwether Lewis and William Clark, were commissioned by Jefferson to explore the West, the huge area west of the Appalachian
mountains. The journals of the expedition give us a sense of what it was like to
first encounter a new and unexplored continent, what the task of naming the
"new circumstances" involved, and how the early settlers may have gone about
the task. Although the language of the journals is, strictly speaking, Virginian

English, the kind of English spoken by Lewis and Clark, the journals of the expedition provide us with a valuable source of information concerning the state of American English in general at the time (see Simpson, 1986).

One characteristic of the journals is their liberal spellings. Lewis and Clark use *clift* for *cliff, whin* for *when, bofore* for *before, furin* for *foreign*, these spellings probably reflecting the fashionable pronunciation of these words. There is also a mixture of traditional or conservative English spelling and the new American spelling in the journals. Lewis and Clark sometimes preserve the Johnsonian *-our* for Webster's *-or*. On the other hand, they tend to use the Websterian *-er* for the Johnsonian *-re* spellings.

The vocabulary of the journals is also noteworthy. Lewis and Clark established several new Americanisms, including words like *creek, bottom, bluff, slay* (their spelling of *sleigh*). At the same time, as Simpson (1986) notes, they tended to be conservative in naming. Although they used new words, they mostly gave old names to new things. Nevertheless, it is appropriate to characterize Lewis and Clark's naming activity as an "orgy of naming" (Simpson, 1986). They named timely events or coincidences peculiar to the expedition, such as *Elk rappids, birth Creek* (on the occasion of Clark's birthday), *rattle snake clifts*, and *Panther Creek*. Some of the names they employed were platitudinous, such as *Travellers rest*. Most of these names did not survive. They also gave new names to significant features of landscape, in which case they used more aggrandized and aggressive naming, like *Smith's River*, after the then Secretary of the Navy, and *Jefferson's River*, after the president. *Jefferson's River* had two tributaries, which they called *Wisdom* and *Philanthropy*. This aggrandizing feature in naming prefigures a more general tendency in American English to elevate the status of things with the help of applying dignified language (see chapter eighteen). However, the main point is that not only did Lewis and Clark produce an "orgy of naming," but, as also remarked by Simpson (1986), they did not appear to show any sense that the places might have already been named by the native Indians. In this respect, Lewis and Clark can be said to possess a great deal of political power and can be regarded as typical colonizers, who ignore the rights and possessions of natives.

The naming of things

Plants

The plants that the settlers first encountered and had no word for needed naming. For example, the British English word *corn*, which meant and still primarily means "wheat" in England, came to be used for "maize." In American English *corn* denotes the same thing that *maize* does in Great Britain. But the use of English words was just one possibility. Another was the borrowing of terms from those languages that the new inhabitants came into contact with. As we have seen, these were often the indigenous Indian languages. The tall, red pine trees in northern California were called *sequoya*, borrowing the term from the native Indians. Some other new, American English words include *endive, hickory, live oak, sweet potato, eggplant,* and *squash.*

Animals

Obviously, many of the animals the white men encountered for the first time were new to him. The settlers recognized some similarity between the bird they called *robin* in England and a bird they found on the new continent. This gave rise to the use of the old word to denote the similar but also different bird with the word *robin*. In America a robin is a red-breasted thrush. Here again, the old linguistic resources were made use of in a slightly different meaning. The word *turkey* indicates a distinctive American bird. The American *buffalo* is closely related to the European *bison*. Many of the animals were known to the settlers, but for some reason or other the old names to denote them were replaced by new ones. Further examples of American English names for animals that have European equivalents are *ladybug, bug* (for insect), *German shepherd,* and *rooster.* (The reasons for the change from *cock* to *rooster* will be discussed in a later chapter.) Additional American English animal names like *bullfrog, groundhog,* and *garter snake* give us a sense of the creativity and imaginativeness with which Americans went about the task of naming the animals that they encountered on the new continent.

Geography and landscape

Obviously, the geography and landscape also needed new names. Proper names were used for individual rivers, lakes, and mountains. As already noted, many of the names for rivers came from Indian languages. But new common names were also needed for other aspects of the landscape. Thus in American English we find *bluff* as a noun (meaning "high, steep, broad-faced cliff or rock"), *notch, gap, divide* as a noun (meaning "watershed"), *clearing* (meaning "an area of land cleared of trees"), and others. These new words all represent cases where old words in the English language acquired new meanings in American English.

The frontier and the West

But the center of the "orgy of naming" was the frontier that was bustling with new activities, new ways of life, and new ideas. The orgy was going on in much of the nineteenth century, and, as we will see in this chapter and in chapter eighteen, it has left an indelible mark on American English and American mentality. The actors on the frontier are the *cowboys, backwoodsmen, beaver trappers, squatters* ("persons who settle on unoccupied land"), and many others. These are new "occupations" and also new words. The new activities include gambling, drinking, driving cattle, fur trading, mining, logging, and so forth. We will take a quick look at these new activities in light of their most direct contributions to American English. A detailed treatment of the influence of these domains on American English can be found in Dillard (1985, 1992).

Gambling

I will talk about the effects of gambling on American English in somewhat more detail in the chapter on slang. I simply note here that most of the gambling was taking place on the Mississippi River, and that it resulted in many American expressions that are widely used to the present day. A *fair deal* today is fair treatment, and the poker word *deal* was picked up by President Roosevelt in his *New Deal*. When you give up and surrender, you *throw in your hand*, when you imitate someone, you *follow suit*, and the situation in which *the chips are down* may demand your best efforts. These are some of the American English expressions that originated in gambling in the West.

Drinking

Drinking was a major part of the new way of life in the West. Some new words, like *firewater*, tell us about language contacts and how the drinking habits of the *white man* "spilled over" to the native Indian tribes. The chief location of consuming alcohol was the *saloon*, where the *bartender* could give you *bourbon* or make a *cocktail* for you. In the later Prohibition era, the big word was *bootlegging*, which was smuggling *whiskey* (not *whisky*) in flat bottles in the leg of one's boots. The *bar-rooms* and *groggeries* were smokey, and if you wanted to get drunk, you *went on a bender* and *took your liquor straight*.

The cowboy

The mythical figure of the American West was the cowboy. The activities and work tools of the cowboy have produced a large number of new words in American English, of which only a fragment can be reviewed here.

A less known fact about *cowboys* or *cowpunchers* or *vaqueros* is that about one third of them were Blacks or Mexicans. The peak of the cowboy as a profession was after the middle of the nineteenth century. This was the time when the number of cows increased almost uncontrollably in Texas and there was also a great demand for their meat in the new big cities in the north. The challenge that confronted the owners of cattle was how to get the cattle from the south to the north. They soon found that this was lucrative business. They could get 40 dollars for a cow in the north that was worth three or four dollars in the south. Some people who were successful in selling the cows at the northern markets made huge amounts of money.

The way to do it was to drive the cattle through the plains from Texas to some northern towns. This was the job of the cowboy, and it was a tough and demanding job for very little pay. The cowboys drove the cattle of the *cattle barons* along established paths, called *trails*. There were three historically famous trails from Texas, especially from San Antonio, to some northern destinations: the Western Trail, the Chisholm Trail, and the Shawnee Trail. By the 1860s, the railroad reached the state of Kansas, where the cows could be put on train in such *cow towns* as Abilene, Wichita, Dodge City, or Kansas City to take them to northern cities like Chicago.

One thing that made the drive along these trails dangerous was the fact that the trails ran through Indian territory in Oklahoma. The cowboys carried guns to protect themselves not only from the Indians but also from *rustlers* or cattle thieves. The guns that became famous were the *Colt caliber .44* or *.45* and the *Winchester repeating rifle*.

The cowboys drove cattle herds of several thousand cows. There was one cowboy to every 200 or 300 cows. The cowboys had to be fed, and each herd was accompanied by a "rolling kitchen," the *chuck wagon* with all the basic foods, like *sourdough*, coffee and beans, pots and other kitchen utensils.

The cowboy's main job was to drive the cattle to their destination. To be able to do this, he had to be an excellent rider of his sometimes half-tamed horse, the *mustang* or the *bronc(o)*. One of the most feared events that could occur during the drive was the *stampede*, the wild run of the entire herd. The *lasso* or *rope* was the cowboy's most important tool. It helped him catch stray cattle, pull the wagons stuck in mud, and many other things. The clothes of the cowboy were adapted to the job he had to do. He wore a broad-brimmed hat, often a *Stetson*, to keep the sun out of his eyes; the leather *chaps* protected his legs from thorns and from chafing during the long rides; the *bandana* or *neckerchief* was his filter against the dust.

By the end of the nineteenth century, an extensive railroad system had been built throughout the United States. This development and the large-scale appearance of farmers who put up barbed-wire fences around their land obviated the need for cattle drives in the traditional way, and brought an end to the cowboy as a profession.

Fur traders

Already in the seventeenth and eighteenth centuries, many *backwoodsmen* and *mountain men* were roaming the uninhabited wilderness. Some of them were criminals, but most of them were people who liked the complete freedom of their life in the wilderness. At the beginning of the nineteenth century, by a lucky turn of events for them, fur hats, especially *beaver hats*, became fashionable in Europe, and this gave them a new source of livelihood. They trapped and skinned the beavers, and then sold the beaver skins to fur traders. They were called *beaver trappers*, or *free trappers*, as they preferred to call themselves. They had extensive contacts with a variety of ethnic groups, and many of them spoke several languages, like French, Spanish, and Indian languages, or pidgins. To them, American English owes such idiomatic expressions as *eager beaver* and *to work like a beaver*.

Miners

In early 1848, gold was discovered in California. The following year attracted tens of thousands of people from the United States and all over the world to try their luck. All the fervor that this event created was called *gold fever*, and the rush to California was called the *gold rush*. The people who participated in the gold rush were the *forty niners*. In 1848 San Francisco had about 850 inhabitants, which swelled to forty thousand in 1849.

McCrum, *et al.* (1986:252-253) list the numerous words and phrases which entered American English as a result of the Gold Rush. The luckiest *gold diggers* found a *bonanza*, a rich vein of gold (the word *bonanza* coming from Spanish meaning "fair weather"). *Stakes were claimed*, that is, it was important for the miners to establish exclusive rights to land. The place where the prospectors mined for gold was called *diggings* or *digs*. The word *prospector* came from *prospect*, a promising place for gold. The verb *to prospect* was also used in the sense of searching for such a place. If you made a *big strike*, you found a lot of gold. But many miners were *panning* for gold in mountain streams, and if you had some gold left on the bottom of your pan, you *panned out*, that is, you were successful.

The gold on the surface was soon exhausted, and gold mining became profitable for large companies only. The individual gold diggers disappeared by the 1860s.

The railroad

In 1862, Congress commissioned two large companies to build the railroad between Nebraska and the Pacific Ocean. The company called *Central Pacific* was building the tracks from west to east, while *Union Pacific* was going from east to west. In 1869, the tracks met at Promontory Point, five miles east of the town of Ogden in what later became the state of Utah. This event marked, in many ways, the beginning of the end of the frontier and the West. The westward "march" came to an end, and, with it, many of the activities that formed such an integral part of frontier life.

The terminology of the American railroad borrowed from the terminology of the sea journey. This explains many of the nautical terms that we can find in the vocabulary of the railroad, words such as *berth, purser, steward, fare, cabin, freight*. Incidentally, the same applies to certain aspects of conquering the prairie, as indicated by the use of words like *prairie schooner*, the large covered wagon used by the settlers (Dillard, 1985).

The word *railroad* was also an American invention, together with such common Americanisms as *to sidetrack, to backtrack, cowcatcher*, and *streamlining*. The railroad produced many American idioms as well, including *on the gravy train* ("to live well without having to work hard") and *whistle stop tour* ("a trip with brief stops by a politician in a campaign"). It is to the railroad that American English owes the expressions *to be in the clear, to make the grade, to have the right of way, to reach the end of the line, to go off the rails*, many of which can be used both literally and metaphorically (McCrum, *et al.*, 1986:256).

As Dillard (1985) explains, the railroad in America was the dividing line between old and new communication, and even perhaps between an old and a new way of life. Travel and communication was made incredibly faster and shorter by new technologies. And the new technologies also had an impact on American English.

Language and technological developments

There were several technological developments in the United States toward the end of the nineteenth and the beginning of the twentieth centuries. These developments all contributed to American English.

Particularly in the area of transportation, with the arrival of the car, and with it road traffic and forms of public transportation, a range of words referring to parts of cars, types of car, and aspects of car travel entered the language, among them *windshield, station wagon, stop lights*, and *freeway*. Further technological developments gave rise to what Dillard (1985) calls "special varieties" of American English, for example, radio, television, film, telephone, and computers. The vocabulary associated with these developments is so common that it needs no further elaboration here; indeed, the language of computers adds more words to American English on a regular basis. For further examples, see Gozzi (1990).

Setting up new institutions

The kinds of institutions that we will survey in this section include new geographical, political, financial-commercial, and educational institutions. The setting up of these institutions was accompanied by large-scale naming and renaming.

Geographical institutions

When people are in a position, as the settlers were, to give names to geographical institutions like states, cities, and towns, they have a variety of options available to them. One of the chief researchers of American place-names, George R. Stewart (1970), suggests that Americans have made use of the following major methods of naming places: they used descriptive names, commemorative names, transfer names, possessive names, incident names, coined names, commendatory names, and shift names. Let us look at some of these briefly and examine the main features of American place-naming practices.

Transfer names

These are already existing place-names transferred to a new location. The new location is obviously the United States and the country from which many of the American place-names derive is England. Most of these occur in what once was the original thirteen colonies, but some can be found in other states as well. Examples of British transfer names are *Dover* in Delaware and *Boston* in Massachusetts. American transfer names often have the modifier *New*, as in *New England* and *New London*. There are twelve *New Londons*, eight *New Bostons*, and four *New Baltimores* in the United States. But Germany is also well "represented." The twelve *Berlins*, seven *Germantowns*, four *Bismarcks*, and five *Fredericks* illustrate American place-names based on transfer. Many exotic American place-names are derived from transfers of place names, as *Athens* in Georgia and *Euclid* in Ohio indicate. The giving of classical place-names to American cities and towns was once fashionable. Many of them occur in the state of New York (e.g., *Ithaca*).

Personal commemoratives

Personal commemorative place-names are commonly given in honor of a famous person. In a way, transfer names can also be regarded as commemoratives – place-names honoring locations, rather than persons. An example of a personal commemorative place-name is *Washington*, D.C. Many of the founding fathers and American presidents have been honored by giving their names to a place. *Madison, Jefferson, Monroe,* and *Franklin* are all place-names commemorating these famous Americans.

Commemorative place-names are evenly spread throughout the United States. However, they have an interesting feature. We can find British place and person commemoratives only before the Declaration of Independence, while after this only American heroes, politicians, and towns are thus commemorated. There seem to be no British person commemoratives west of the Appalachian Mountains. This makes sense if we consider the date of the Declaration of Independence and the beginning of westward movement.

Incident names

Incident names may be thought of as yet another kind of commemorative place-names. These can indicate a place where a memorable incident occurred, as in the name of *Battle Creek*, Michigan, or where animals were killed or seen, as in *Cascabel*, Arizona, or where any, once remarkable, event took place such as someone exclaiming, as in the case of *Eureka* in Northern California.

Descriptive names

Descriptive names record a sense impression, the long-enduring qualities (e.g., the geographic features) of a geographical location. One example of this place-naming practice is *Hot Springs*, South Dakota. But impermanent associations are also possible within this category, such as *Hollywood*, Florida or *International Falls*, Minnesota. Some place-names may also be relative descriptives, that is, names that describe a relationship, as in *Westerly*, Rhode Island. Descriptive names are evenly spread in the United States, and they were commonly used. This is an extremely general place-naming practice. Consequently, it was employed by both the settlers and the native Indians, who frequently named places after a natural feature. Well-known examples include *Long Island* in New York, and *Long Beach* and *Big Sur* in California. The famous mountain range, the *Rocky Mountains* (or *Rockies*), is also a product of this place-naming process.

Commendatory names

Commendatory place-names focus on a pleasant or attractive feature of a place. They often offer space, extensive view, good climate, good farming conditions, and so forth. Examples include *Richfield* in Utah and *Lakeview* in Oregon. Names like *Enterprise* and *Commerce* appear in several states, reflecting the hopes and desires of their inhabitants. Commendatory names are common throughout the United States. It makes sense to believe that they were an important factor to attract people to a lesser-known region.

Shift names

These are place-names that are based on two entities being in each other's proximity or vicinity, such that one has a name, the other does not. The place that does not have a name takes over the name of the entity that does. *Salt Lake City* in Utah is a good illustration of this kind of place-naming, where the city was built next to the lake that had the name.

Coined names

These are place-names that are consciously constructed or manufactured, for example, out of fragments of other words or names. The town of *Texarkana* in Texas blends the names of three states: Texas, Arkansas, and Louisiana.

Amerindian place-names

Amerindian place-names abound in the United States. It is mistakenly believed by many people that Amerindian names were simply learned and then adopted by the early European settlers. This simplifying assumption is false in two ways. One is that Amerindian place-names are often displaced, that is, are not applied where they were originally used (Algeo, 1992b). Second, most of the place-names of Amerindian origin appear in later periods of the settlement, more specifically, after the middle of the nineteenth century. This was a time when the native Indians and their culture were looked at in a romantic light (Simpson, 1986).

Twenty-six states have Amerindian names. These state names come from a variety of different Amerindian languages, for example, *Idaho* from Apache, *Minnesota* from Siouan, and *Ohio* from Iroquoian. Several of these state names entered American English in an indirect way, for example, through French or Spanish. *Illinois* is an example of a French-mediated state name, while *Arizona* may illustrate the name of a state that came into English from a native Indian language through the mediation of Spanish. In addition to state names, many place-names designating towns, cities, and counties also derive from Amerindian names. One well known example is *Chicago*, from originally an Algonquian word meaning "onion field." This place-name was also mediated by French.

Spanish place-names

As can be predicted, place-names of Spanish origin are especially prevalent in states like California, Texas, New Mexico, Lousiana, and Florida. Among others, *California, Nevada*, and *Florida* are Spanish state names. Southern California, in particular, has a large number of counties, cities, towns, villages, universities, and streets with Spanish names. *San Diego, La Jolla University,* and *Via Posada* will serve as examples.

French place-names

State names deriving from French include *Louisiana* and *Maine.* The Great Lakes have French names, and there are many settlements with French names in Louisiana and along the Mississippi and Missouri rivers.

Religious place-names

Many American place-names are religious. This is especially true for many of the early Spanish place-names. For example, many of the Spanish missions that had religious names later became towns or cities. This accounts for such place-names in California as *San Diego, Santa Ana, Los Angeles, San Louis Obispo, Santa Cruz,* and *San Francisco.*

The Puritans also used this practice of naming, though to a lesser degree than the Spanish. *Salem,* Massachusetts, is one example. This was later transferred to Oregon as well.

Political institutions

The political institutions that Americans set up in the wake of the American Revolution were similar to but at the same time different from the corresponding institutions in England. These differences, for many Americans at the time, justified and, indeed, demanded new names. The best case in point is the presidency. After a prolonged debate, Americans decided to call their chief executive the *President,* rather than the *Prime Minister.* Many additional changes in the vocabulary of politics and government were also made. In the United States, the government is usually referred to as the *administration.* The *Congress* consists of the *House of Representatives* and the *Senate.* The ministry dealing with foreign affairs is the *State Department,* and the official in charge of it is the *Secretary of State.* These are only some of the examples of the renaming process in the political sphere.

The domain of banking and commerce

The vocabulary of banking and commerce also changed considerably. In the United States one can have a *checking account* and/or a *savings account* in a bank. Some people have *stocks,* and everybody pays *tax.* The people dealing with land are called *realtors.*

Getting down to a more mundane level of life, as we saw in the previous chapter, Americans adopted the word *check* from German, and they continued to use the word *druggist*, while the British began to call it *chemist*. Americans stand *in line*, and they can purchase things through an *installment plan*. In *stores*, they are helped by *sales clerks*.

People and their homes

Perhaps it is not immediately obvious that even the names of people and the vocabulary of the home have undergone changes on the hands of Americans. But they did, and in this section we highlight some examples of this process.

People and their names

It may appear only natural that people who settled down in the United States preserved their names. This is indeed what happened in most cases – though not in all. Even the names of people underwent modification, or change, as a result of the large-scale renaming. Many immigrants have changed their last names. Stories have long circulated about how ill-educated immigration officials changed people's names when they first arrived (McCrum, *et al.*, 1986). This happened especially in the case of long, difficult-to-pronounce, and "un-English-like" names. One group of "sufferers" were Central or Eastern European Jews, who had, for the immigration officials at least, strange, unpronounceable names. In many cases, the Jewish names were "anglicized," such that, for example, Ouspenska became Spensky. For many other Jews and other immigrants, however, the name-change was not necessarily an undesirable consequence but a welcome happening, an event in which the new name started a new life for the bearer of the name.

There is a tendency among many Americans to choose religious first names for their children. Our studies have shown that this tendency is much stronger among Americans than among the British. When asked why parents give names like *John*, *Patrick*, or *Gregory* to their children, the response often was that the child was born on that particular saint's day. Another source of religious first names given to American children is the Old Testament. First names such as *Aaron*, *Benjamin*, and *Joseph* are taken from the Old Testament. The frequent use of religious first names has no doubt to do with the strong religious heritage of many Americans.

Food

A major American way of preparing meat is the *barbecue* (a word we already had occasion to mention in the previous chapter), grilling the meat over pieces of burning coal. *Hotdog* and *hamburger* or *burger* and *French fries* are also American terms for food that have become familiar to people the world over.

Houses and households

In America, the flat that you own is a *condominium*, or a *condo* for short, and the flat that you rent is an *apartment*. A building with many apartments in it is an *apartment house*. The floor of a house that is level with the ground is called the *first floor*. Houses have *faucets* for water and *sockets* or *outlets* for electricity. The (usually) grassy area in front of and in back of a house is a *yard*, a *frontyard* and a *backyard*, respectively. (Of course, Americans can also have gardens *in* their yards. After all, having a garden is one of the things one does with a yard.)

study questions and activities

1. If you watch a western movie or read a novel about the American west, write down the words that you suspect to have originated in the "Wild West." Check in a good and sufficiently large American dictionary whether your guesses were correct or not.

2. Find a book in your school or local library about technological inventions. Find as many inventions as you can that were made by Americans. Check in a dictionary if the inventions resulted in a linguistic Americanism.

3. Read some issues of one or several American newspapers. Try to find all the words and expressions that portray American political institutions and practices. Describe the system emerging through language. (Save the words and your summary for later use.)

4. Take a detailed map of the United States that gives the names of all the place names. Choose a state and examine naming practices there. Compare what you find for one of the 13 original states with the naming practices in one or two later states.

chapter 4

Linguistic geography in the United States

L inguistic geography is a way of studying variation in language. The serious linguistic study of variation in, and of the specificity of, American English began
when the American Dialect Society was established in 1889. One goal of the
society was to eventually produce a dictionary of regional words. As we will see,
however, this took a long time. In the present chapter, I will describe the most
important features of the methodology, its accomplishments, as well as the weaknesses of linguistic geography in the United States. In the next chapter, I will present in some detail the main regional dialects of American English. Later chapters
will take up the issue of social, ethnic, and stylistic variation in the United States.

Some history

Most observers of American English – especially in the seventeenth and eighteenth centuries – were struck by the apparent homogeneity of English in
North America. These American observers or foreign travelers (British or other)
often expressed the view that there appeared to exist only three distinguishable
varieties of American English. One was the English that was used in New
England. Clearly distinct from this seemed to them to be the English spoken
in the South. The third variety was the most widespread in that it was used in
the geographically largest region of the country and by the largest number of
people. The region was assumed to extend from the Appalachian Mountains to
and later beyond the Mississippi River and was the size of a continent. This is
the variety that came to be known as General American (GA). It gave observers
the impression that American English was an extremely homogeneous dialect
of English with only two noticeably different subvarieties: New England and
Southern American English.

There was of course a very good reason for this general impression. The
impression arose from comparisons with the situation in Britain. The reason
was that relative to the size of the country Britain displayed a much more
diverse range of dialects than the United States.

The belief that American English consists of General American and the
Eastern (Northern) and Southern dialect varieties was called into question by a
group of American scholars in the 1930s. Most important among them was the
Austrian-born scholar Hans Kurath, who spent a large part of his long life and
academic career studying this issue. In 1930 Kurath was named the director of

an ambitious project called *The Linguistic Atlas of the United States and Canada*. He patterned the project on a similar European undertaking that had been completed some years before the American project started: *Atlas linguistique de la France*, which ran between 1902 and 1910. Given the results of their work, Kurath and his co-workers challenged the belief that American English had the varieties Eastern, Southern, and General American. Instead, they suggested that American English is best viewed as having the following major dialect areas: Northern, Midland, and Southern. That is, they did away with the elusive notion of "General American" and replaced it with the dialect area that they called Midland. In order to provide a better understanding of this project and its results, we have to be clear about the relationship between the notions of language, dialect, and idiolect.

Language, dialect, and idiolect

What does it mean that American English has three major regional dialects? What is a dialect and what is the relationship of the term to language and idiolect? These terms and the relationships among them are notoriously difficult to define in a precise manner. It is customary to distinguish the notion of dialect from that of language in terms of two criteria: (1) mutual intelligibility and (2) systematic differences. When the English of a group of speakers shows systematic differences but these speakers can nevertheless understand each other, we have different dialects of English. When speech communities show systematic differences without the speakers of the different groups understanding each other, we have different languages. Unfortunately, these definitions are not as simple and clearcut as we would like them to be. For example, Norwegians and Swedes show many systematic differences in their speech but they can understand each other. Given our criteria of lack of mutual intelligibility and systematic differences, we would have to call Norwegian and Swedish two different dialects of the same language, but this is not what we do. We consider Norwegian and Swedish two languages because the two groups of speakers live in different countries. Although there are difficulties of this kind, I will talk about dialects when the speakers of a group can mutually understand each other despite systematic differences in their speech. In this sense, then, British and American English are different dialects of the same language.

In addition, individual speakers each have their characteristic ways of speaking – ways that are unique to each individual. We call these different ways of speaking idiolects. An idiolect is the speech patterns of an individual at a particular age. It is necessary to add the qualification "at a particular age" because we obviously speak differently as we go through various age periods. The many idiolects used among a group of speakers make up a particular dialect.

In sum, we can suggest that language is made up of dialects, and dialects are made up of idiolects.

Linguistic geography

As we saw above, linguistic geography is the scientific study of dialectal diversity in a language. Linguists have used many terms to talk about the study of dialectal diversity. These include dialectology, word geography, area geography, dialect geography, and linguistic geography. We will use this last designation because it is this that is most commonly employed to discuss dialectal diversity in the United States. As we noted above, the name of the project that had as its goal the mapping of dialect variation in the United States was *The Linguistic Atlas of the United States and Canada*. Below I attempt to characterize this project briefly.

It is useful to begin with a summary statement of what linguistic geography is about. We find the following short introduction to the notion in Carroll Reed's book *Dialects of American English* (1977:6):

> Within the last hundred years a new science, known as dialectology, or linguistic geography, had made its appearance in the field of cultural history. Its methods are briefly as follows: A concise questionnaire is constructed for the purpose of testing speakers of a language as to the way their particular dialect makes use of that language. The speakers are chosen on the basis of their economic, social, religious, or educational background, and are sought in both rural and urban areas. When enough speakers have been sampled in the required areas, their responses can be recorded graphically on a map, so that any variation in usage can be observed quite readily. Geographical deviations, involving groups of different features, then permit us to draw "isoglosses" on the map. These vaguely resemble isobars on a weather map, but they serve to mark somewhat sharper differences than the arbitrary point of transition symbolized in the weather map.

For example, if we examine the occurrence of the word *mudworm* in this manner, we find that its use is limited to the New England area. Other parts of the country will use *earthworm,* or some other variant.

Let us now see in some more detail how linguistic geography was put to work in attempting to find dialect diversity in American English. (In presenting the methodology of linguistic geography below, I will rely on Finegan and Besnier, 1989, and Malmstrom and Ashley, 1958.)

The methodology of linguistic geography

The selection of communities

As one of the necessary initial steps in doing linguistic geography, certain communities had to be selected in a region. These were typically ones that had played an important part in the history of the region. (This implies that the researchers who planned to study dialectal diversity had to study the history of a region first.) This way the communities selected provided (at least ideally) a cross section of the region's historical, cultural, economic, and geographic composition.

The construction of survey questionnaires

In addition, a survey questionnaire was constructed that contained various items of usage in a region. Linguistic items that appeared on the questionnaire were chosen for three reasons: (1) because they referred to common things which were expected to be known to most of the people of the region; (2) because they were easy to introduce into a friendly conversation that took place in the course of going through the items of the questionnaire; and (3) because they were known to have regional or social variants.

Certain topics were especially well suited for inclusion and linguistic representation in the questionnaire. Many linguistic items that were included had to do with the weather, home, food, clothing, farm, animals, crops, vehicles, utensils, and others. These were topics that were familiar to the people who were asked, they were easily and naturally talked about, and they produced several regional variants. Altogether, roughly one thousand items were included in the questionnaire.

The questionnaire aimed at eliciting information on various aspects of linguistic usage. Thus, in addition to information concerning words (lexis), some items were designed to reveal differences in pronunciation (phonology) and structural patterns (morphology and syntax) among regions. Below are some examples that demonstrate the kinds of questions used in the questionnaires. The sample also contains the fieldnotes of the fieldworker, which in turn consist of potential variants of an item and the response of the informant or respondent. The sample questions and the fieldnotes are taken from Wolfram and Schilling-Estes (1998a:127).

Pronunciation
What are the two parts of an egg? One is the white; the other is ___.
Variants: *yok, yelk, yulk, yilk, yoke*
Response: *yulk; "heard": yelk*

Grammar

I wanted to hang something out in the barn, so I just took a nail and ___.

Variants: *drive, druv, driv, drove, droove*

Response: *drove a nail*

Vocabulary

Where did you keep your hogs and pigs? Did you have a shelter or was it open?

Variants: *hog pen, pig pen, hog lot, hog crawl, cattle crawl*

Response: *hog pen, pig pen;* "old-fashioned or obsolete": *crawl, hog crawl, cattle crawl*

Informants

Together with the communities, certain individual speakers belonging to a community had to be selected. Three categories of informants, or respondents (or subjects, as we would call these persons today), were recognized: (1) old-fashioned, rustic speakers of eighth-grade education; (2) younger, more modern speakers of high-school education: and (3) "cultured" speakers of college education.

Interviews

Each of the selected informants had an interview with a field worker. Field workers (who were not necessarily linguists) were people who went through several weeks of intensive training preparing them for how to conduct the interviews and how to register the information obtained in a systematic way. The interviews concentrated on the items in the questionnaire. The interviews themselves were conducted in the homes of the respondents. Given the large number of linguistic items on which information was sought, the interviews lasted 6 to 20 hours. This meant that in some cases the field worker visited the same person on several occasions.

Later on, a new method of obtaining information was introduced; this was called "postal check list." It involved sending out a questionnaire to respondents, asking them to fill out and return the questionnaire. An obvious advantage of this method was that a much larger number of people was reached and no field workers were needed. Problems with it included the fact that information concerning pronunciation could not be obtained this way and that there was no opportunity to ask the respondents for clarification or other relevant comments.

Analysis: isoglosses and maps

A key term in the analysis of the information obtained from the questionnaires is "isogloss." When an item is used in a definite region, the field worker can draw a line on the map of the region, the line showing the outer limits of the distribution of a particular usage. The boundary line that indicates the distribution of an item is called an isogloss. This way it is possible for the researcher to draw a map for the item in question. Finegan and Besnier (1989:395-396) explain the rest of the procedure in the following way. As the next step, the researchers stack these maps one on top of the other. To understand how this procedure works, imagine that the maps are drawn on transparencies. If we stack them, it will show which isoglosses from the different maps coincide. The ones that coincide show dialect boundaries.

The isoglosses often coincide and they define a dialect region. In the *Linguistic Atlas* project, researchers found that, for example, the linguistic items *I want off* ("I want to get off"), *sook!* (a call to cows), and *snake feeder* ("dragonfly") "bundled" together; that is, the isoglosses for these items coincided on the maps. These and other items with a similar distribution pattern were seen as making up the Midland dialect area.

A Word Geography of the Eastern United States

The first real improvement on the impressionistic classification of dialects in North America mentioned at the beginning of the chapter came with the pioneering work of Hans Kurath. Kurath began to study the dialects of American English in the eastern United States in the 1920s. Together with his colleagues, he did an extensive study of dialects that was primarily based on lexical evidence. A distillation of dialect maps changed the dominant view of what dialects there were in American English. The new classification based on real evidence yielded the following dialect areas: Northern, Midland, and Southern. The Northern region extended from New England along the Canadian border to the northern coast of the Pacific. The Midland area started out around Philadelphia in a narrow band and fanned out beyond the Appalachian Mountains covering the entire Midwest and West, all the way to the Pacific. The Southern speech area started in Virginia and included the Carolinas, Kentucky, Tennessee and the Gulf states. Kurath's research was published in 1949 under the title *A Word Geography of the Eastern United States*. This study focused on the speech areas of the Atlantic Coast down to South Carolina. On the basis of lexical evidence, eighteen smaller speech areas were isolated under the more general regional dialect areas (Northern, Midland, Southern).

Kurath has this to say about what they found concerning vocabulary:

> Regional and local expressions are most common in the vocabulary of
> the intimate everyday life of the home and the farm – not only among
> the simple folk and the middle class but also among the cultured ...
> Food, clothing, shelter, health, the day's work, play, mating, social
> gatherings, the land, the farm buildings, implements, the farm stocks
> and crops, the weather, the fauna and flora – these are the intimate
> concern of the common folk in the countryside, and for these things
> expressions are handed down in the family and the neighborhood
> that schooling and reading, and a familiarity with regional or national
> usage do not blot out. (1949:9-10)

To illustrate this, let us take the concept of mating. Atlas research found that,
in addition to the standard word *bastard,* several others were in use for "a child
born out of wedlock." They include *woods colt, come-by-chance,* and *old-field
colt* in the Eastern United States. *Woods colt* is characteristic of Virginia and
North Carolina. *Come-by-chance* is a term used in most of Pennsylvania and
parts of New York State. *Old-field colt* can be found in coastal Virginia.

Sectional atlas studies

In addition to the large-scale study of regional variation in American English,
smaller projects were also carried out. These were confined to less extensive
geographical areas and were called "sectional atlas studies." Some of these were
published and they include studies of the Great Lakes region, Chicago,
California, and other regions. Reed (1977) provides useful information concerning sectional studies carried out before the 1970s.

The further west the atlas studies moved, the more difficulties they
encountered. Researchers were confronted with a more complex situation than
they were in the east. In the east, it was relatively easy to find long-established
communities with more or less homogeneous populations. By contrast, the
western states were settled more recently and most communities represent a
greater mixture of people coming from a variety of different regions.

Main findings

The main findings of the *Linguistic Atlas* project are both linguistic and cultural
in nature. The main linguistic result, as was shown above, was a new classification of regional dialects in American English. The new classification was based
on real evidence unlike the previous impressionistic judgments about dialectal

diversity. Thus, the project was also important from a methodological point of view.

However, the *Linguistic Atlas* project was not an exclusively linguistic one. As Reed's summary statement above concerning linguistic geography suggests, the "atlas projects" were also studies in cultural history. By detecting divergent patterns in the distribution of linguistic items it became possible to detect settlement patterns, or patterns of migration, in the United States. Indeed, this was considered one of the chief results of linguistic geography. In several publications, Kurath himself also concluded that "speech boundaries reflect settlement boundaries" (see, for example, Kurath 1972:253). A leading contemporary researcher gives us a concise summary in this connection (Kretzschmar, 1998). This is how he summarizes Kurath's and others' position in regard to the importance of settlement history to variation in American English:

> Each region corresponds to a major settlement pathway: The Northern region matches migration westward to territories claimed by northern colonies (e.g., the Western Reserve) and to other places via the Great Lakes; the Midland region begins in the great colonial city of Philadelphia, both westward towards Pittsburgh via the National Road and southwest through the Shenandoah Valley; the Southern region includes the old Virginia and South Carolina plantation areas, centered around Richmond and Charleston, and their westward expansion into suitable plantation country in the Deep South. (p. 25)

Dictionary of American Regional English

Another major undertaking attempting to map American regional dialects is the *DARE* project (short for *Dictionary of American Regional English*). The main figure in this project is Frederick Cassidy, who is also the editor-in-chief of the dictionary that is based on the project.

The *DARE* project focuses on regional lexical variation in American English. Despite its narrower focus, in some other ways it is an even more ambitious project than the *Linguistic Atlas* project was. *DARE* used a questionnaire that consists of nearly 2000 questions on linguistic usage and its surveys were conducted in roughly 1000 different communities across the country. Work on the *DARE* project started in the 1960s and lasted throughout the 70s. The evaluation of the data is carried out by the assistance of computer technology. So far, three volumes of this monumental enterprise have been published: one in 1985, one in 1991, and the most recent in 1996. See Cassidy (1985), Cassidy and Hall (1991, 1996).

General assessment of linguistic geography

The methodology of linguistic geography has changed considerably since its early days. Researchers within the linguistic geography paradigm noticed, for example, that Kurath may have been biased in the selection of isoglosses, on the basis of which he isolated the main dialect areas of American English. Kretzschmar (1998), for one, notes that "Kurath's knowledge of settlement history aided his selection of isoglosses for presentation" (p. 25). In view of this potential weakness, more objective techniques were developed. This primarily means the use of highly sophisticated computer technology in the reanalysis of Kurath's data, as well as collecting and analyzing new data. American linguist Edgar Schneider's new volume *Focus on the USA* provides a comprehensive survey of these new ways of doing linguistic geography (Schneider, 1998).

Murray (1998), in his overview of theory groups in American sociolinguistics, offers an assessment of American dialectology, or linguistic geography. He observes that linguistic geography had only a very small influence on American linguistics in general, and sociolinguistics in particular, as this new field of linguistics emerged after World War Two in the United States. Murray mentions several reasons for this situation. One is that after World War Two American linguistics took a decidedly theoretical turn. Mainstream linguistics became theory-oriented and began to study "autonomous" aspects of language, and, consequently, regional, social, and cultural aspects of language faded into the background. Work concentrated on syntax, not on social or communicative dimensions of language use. Another, and maybe even more important, reason was that the methodology (and, eventually, the results of linguistic geography) was not really suitable to the study of the language and society of a modern urban America. Concerning the issue of methodology, Murray quotes Pickford (1956):

> by using techniques developed for some of the most stable peasantries of Europe, American linguistic geographers have come to confusion in the country and chaos in the city. They have tried to muddle through the manifest linguistic heterogeneity by limiting observation to a restricted segment of the total linguistic material[, ...] deliberately confin[ing] most of their research to life-time residents of culturally-subordinate communities. (pp. 179-180)

Their methodology did not enable American dialectologists to study class differences, urban problems, recent migrations within the country, or the influence of mass media on language habits. For example, by confining their research to "life-time residents of culturally-subordinate communities," dialectologists could not promise to solve certain urban problems. It became increasingly obvious in the 1960s and 1970s that a new kind of linguistics was needed to study language diversity and variation in a complex postwar society. We will take up the discussion of these changes in the American linguistic scene in chapters six to eight.

study questions and activities

1. Test your knowledge of American regionalisms. Here's a quiz for you from the *DARE* homepage. Try to match up the words in the two columns:

1. arigato	__ a ball of bread dough fried in deep fat
2. goose nest	__ to be infatuated or in love
3. iron man	__ a celebration for a newly married couple
4. crimmy	__ cold, chilly
5. election pink	__ disgusted with, sated by
6. mean	__ a dollar
7. kiss-me-quick	__ to eat noisily, chew loudly
8. nebby	__ to flirt or court
9. leppy	__ a jazz dance step
10. mouse	__ a lump or swelling caused by a blow
11. comb one's head	__ a moonshiner
12. fish tail	__ an orphan calf, lamb, or colt
13. jewlark	__ a rhododendron
14. blockader	__ a sinkhole
15. infare	__ snoopy, inquisitive
16. get one's nose open	__ a sudden dip or rise in the road
17. keekling	__ thank you
18. chank	__ a type of pastry
19. feest	__ to whip, beat, scold severely
20. holy poke	__ very, exceedingly

    You can check your answers in the first three volumes of *DARE*.

2. Choose a novel by an American author and try to find the linguistic regionalisms in the book. (Use an American dictionary that provides information on regional usage.)

3. Compare a work by Faulkner, Twain, Salinger, Steinbeck, and Dreiser in terms of American regionalisms. How many regionalisms do they use? To

what extent do these works "rely" on the regional usages they exhibit? For what artistic purpose do the authors presumably use them?

4. Have you noticed any regionalisms in a recent American movie that you saw? (With especially some of the older movies, you can make good use of Frederick Cassidy's dictionary mentioned in the chapter.)

chapter 5

Regional dialects of American English

In the previous chapter we saw the methodology with which scholars have attempted to isolate varieties of American English. In this chapter we will look at some of the linguistic features of the most important varieties of American English, as established by linguistic geography. The linguistic variation under consideration here is based on how people living in various geographic regions of the United States speak differently. The dialects that have emerged in this way are called "regional dialects." (An excellent survey of American regional dialects that also challenges some of the early results of linguistic geography can be found in Carver, 1987. Recent introductions to variation in American English, with teaching implications, are Glowka and Lance, 1993, and Wolfram and Schilling-Estes, 1998a; 1998b.)

The study of American regional varieties

As was shown in chapter four, a major linguistic result of Kurath and his colleagues' work was a new classification of American regional dialects into a Northern, Midland, and Southern dialect area. Ever since Kurath and his colleagues' pioneering work, however, other linguists have been trying to refine and improve on these findings. As a matter of fact, the *DARE* project that was briefly discussed in the previous chapter also offered results that point to a subtler picture. Evidence suggests (see Carver, 1987) that it might be more appropriate to think of American English regional dialects as comprising a Northern and a Southern region, both divided into upper and lower (with further subdivisions in each). But other classifications of the major dialect areas also exist. For example, Baugh and Cable (1983) report the existence of the following areas: Eastern New England, New York, Inland Northern, North Midland, South Midland, and Southern. These are the areas that Baugh and Cable identify with labels that reflect a regional classification. They also add General American and Black English as further dialects. General American here corresponds to what is called Network Standard today. Both Network Standard and Black English are best viewed as social dialects and will be discussed in the next chapter. As can be seen, the major differences between the classification suggested by Kurath and the one reported by Baugh and Cable involve the following. Kurath's Northern is further differentiated into Eastern New England, New York, and

Inland Northern, while Kurath's Midland dialect is divided into North Midland and South Midland by Baugh and Cable. A still different and more recent classification is proposed by Bailey (1992). His scheme of speech areas includes the North, Coastal South, Midland, and West.

The issue of what the major dialect areas of American English are is a hotly debated topic, and I cannot do justice to this complex issue in an introductory text (but see Carver, 1987, Schneider, 1998, and Wolfram and Schilling-Estes, 1998a for useful overviews). Neither is it possible to take inventory of all subdialects and "isolated" regional dialects of American English. For example, because of a lack of space in this kind of text I will not be able to discuss what Walt Wolfram and Natalie Schilling-Estes call "post-insular island communities" on the eastern seaboard. However, the interested reader is recommended to consult their publications on this fascinating area of the study of American English (see, for example, Wolfram and Schilling-Estes, 1998b).

For simplicity's sake, I will make use of Richard Bailey's scheme in presenting the main dialects of American English; that is, I will briefly characterize the Northern, Southern, Midland, and Western dialect regions, with some of their subdialects. In the sections to follow I will note some of the typical phonological, grammatical, and lexical features of these dialects. The presentation below is primarily paraphrased from Bailey (1992), whose examples will be used throughout, although occasional examples from other authors will also be mentioned.

The Northern dialect

The northern region stretches from New England and New York to Oregon and Washington, along the northern border of the United States. The major northern cities include Boston, New York, Buffalo, Cleveland, Detroit, Chicago, and Minneapolis. Boston and New York differ in some ways from the others, but nevertheless remain basically linguistically northern speech areas.

Pronunciation

In terms of pronunciation, the northern region seems to be characterized by what is called rhoticity, that is, the use of the sound /r/ in words like *bird* and *car*. Exceptions to this are New England (especially eastern New England) and New York, which, although geographically belonging to the North, do not pronounce the /r/ in a post-vocalic position (i.e., after a vowel) and at the end of words.

Another feature of Northern pronunciation is that the vowels in words like *cot* and *caught* are not pronounced in the same way, unlike other dialect areas, where there is a general tendency to "merge" the two distinct vowels into one, the vowel found in *cot*. Regarding vowels, Wolfram and Schilling-Estes also note that in the North the pronunciation of *root* has a short vowel, as in *foot*. This sound is opposed to the long vowel of *boot* (1998a:108).

Finally, in the Northern dialect words like *matter* and *madder* are pronounced with the same medial consonant, which is called the "flap," represented as /D/. (The sound is called the "flap" because the tongue flaps against the alveolar ridge. This happens in both cases.)

Grammar

In Northern grammar, we find sentences such as *That's all the farther I could go*, which means *That's as far as I could go*. The construction "*all the* + adjective" seems to be a regional feature. Bailey limits the use of this construction to the comparative degree, as in the example. Finegan and Besnier (1989:398-99) discuss a similar construction ("*all* + adjective"), but they do not mention that it is found in the comparative degree only or that it requires the definite article *the*. The example they provide is *My hands are all greasy* (meaning "My hands are covered with grease"). They note in connection with the feature that it occurs in the New England region of the Northern dialect.

Wolfram and Schilling-Estes (1998a:108) observe that the dialect has the expression *sick to/at the stomach* as opposed to *sick in/on the stomach* found in other parts of the U.S. Also, the verb *dive* has its past tense in *dove* in the North. Characteristic of the region is the use of auxiliaries such as *had ought / hadn't ought* instead of the more common and standard *ought / ought not*.

Vocabulary

Northern vocabulary contains items that together define the region. This means that although the words given below may occur in other regional dialects, together they occur only in the Northern region. This applies to the other dialect regions as well. Such words include *bitch* ("complain"), *bloodsucker* ("leech"), *cabbage salad* ("cole slaw"), *comforter* ("heavy quilt"), *cowboy* ("reckless driver"), *nightcrawler* ("large earthworm"), and *sub(marine)* ("a kind of sandwich").

We may note several additional regional markers for the Northern dialect of American English. One is that less cultivated Northerners have a tendency to use the word *youse* for the plural of *you*. The region is also marked by some Northern European influence: especially Finnish influence in Michigan and Swedish influence in Minnesota. Buffalo and Detroit are characterized by some Polish-English influence. Russian-English influence can also be found in the region. One example of this is the word *babushka*, meaning a "large kerchief covering the head and the shoulders."

New York City

New York speech is a distinct subdialect within the larger Northern dialect. Its characteristic features are easily recognizable and are well known among most speakers of American English. The features briefly discussed below jointly define this subdialect.

Unlike the general Northern dialect area, New York is mostly /r/-less (but see Tierney, 1995); that is, the /r/ is not pronounced in words like *car* and *park*. (I will discuss some of the social complexities in connection with this feature in the next chapter.) New Yorkers use what linguists call the linking /r/. As noted, New Yorkers do not generally pronounce the /r/ in words like *gopher*. However, before a word beginning with a vowel many of them would pronounce it in such sentences as *The gopher is lost*, where the /r/ in *gopher* is followed by the vowel /ɪ/ in *is*. This linking /r/ is a more general property of the East New England region. In addition to the linking /r/, New York also has what is termed intrusive /r/. In the word *sofa* there is no /r/ at all. However, when a word such as *sofa* is followed by a vowel, an /r/ may "intrude" in the speech of many New Yorkers. This yields utterances like *The sofa/r/ is lost*. It is notable that intrusive /r/ is a distinctive feature of many British English dialects too.

New York speech is also characterized by some special vowel sounds. There is a long, tense, relatively high vowel, /æ/, in words like *cab* that lends a unique quality to the speech of many New Yorkers. Another characteristic vowel commonly used is the long, tense, and very round vowel /ɔ/ in words like *caught*. In general, New York pronunciation is perceived as nasal. (New York City pronunciation will be further discussed in the next chapter.)

The idiomatic phrases used by New Yorkers may also differ from those used by speakers of other American dialects. One example is *to stand on line*. This is the New York version of the idiom which is more typically *to stand in line* in other parts of the United States.

New York speech is influenced by several of its immigrant and ethnic populations. Perhaps the group that has exerted the greatest influence is the large Jewish community. Their Jewish English is one of the hallmarks of New York speech in general. The impact has been primarily on the vocabulary and words like *chutzpa*, *schlemiel*, *schmooze*, and *gonef* are associated with New York's Jewish population in the minds of most Americans. What made it possible for these and other words to enter the general vocabulary of American English was the fact that New York is the media and entertainment "capital" of the United States and that several New York-based writers, like J.D. Salinger, made use of these words in their works.

Boston speech

Similarly to New York City, Boston speech is also /r/-less. Sentences like *Park the car* are pronounced without the /r/. We also find the intrusive /r/ in Boston speech. For many, the use of the intrusive /r/ in the Boston area was epitomized by J.F. Kennedy's speech – especially in such well known examples as *The idea/r/ is ...* and *Cuba/r/ is a problem.* Another noticeable feature of Boston pronunciation is the special quality of the vowel /a/ in sentences like *Park the car.* It is a long, flat vowel, which is produced with the lips spread, rather than with the mouth open as in *father.* More generally, in the same way as New York speech is perceived as nasal, Boston speech is said to have a "twang."

The Coastal South

This dialectal region includes Virginia, the Carolinas, and the Gulf states, extending to the western end of Texas.

Pronunciation

A major feature of pronunciation in the Coastal South is that it is not rhotic, that is, it is /r/-less. Words like *car, bar,* etc. are pronounced /ka/ and /ba/. Also, because of a tendency to diphthongize single vowel sounds (monophthongs) in words like *torn* and *born,* the pronunciation of these words will be similar to that of *tone* and *bone* in some other dialects. The overall result in Coastal South pronunciation will be /ton/ and /bon/.

Sounds that are diphthongs in other dialects are monophthongs in the Coastal South. Words like *hide* will be pronounced as /had/, as opposed to /hajd/, say, in the North.

A typical feature of coastal South pronunciation (but also that of the North Midland region) is the merger of /ɛ/ and /ɪ/ before a nasal consonant. Words like *pen* and *pin, cents* and *since,* etc. are /pɛn/ and /sɪns/, respectively.

Taken together, these distinctive pronunciation features make up what is known as "Southern drawl," which is regarded as a characteristic trait of the Southern accent.

Grammar

Concerning grammar, I will mention three features. The first is the invariant *be.* This means that the same form of *be* is used in all persons and the singular and the plural. For example, the sentence *I am pretty busy* often becomes *I be pretty busy* in this dialect. (More about this feature can be found in chapter seven.)

A second feature is the frequent use of double modals. Thus, southerners might use sentences like *She might can do it* or *Could you may go*.

Finally, in the south there seems to be a greater tolerance for the form *ain't* than in other dialects. This happens in cases like *I'm a fool, ain't I?*, but not in cases like *They ain't here*.

Words and phrases

In the South, *thank you* often becomes *(ap)preciate it*. This feature seems to be spreading to other regions as well. What is called a *brook* or a *stream* is a *branch* in Coastal South and a *farm worker* is often referred to as a *hand*. One's relatives are one's *kinfolk*. As in this last example, it is a general property of the South that much of its vocabulary is regarded as archaic elsewhere. Many cultivated Southerners use *you-all* for the plural *you*. The region also abounds in words that come from a variety of ethnic groups living in the area. Thus, words like *hominy, cooter* ("turtle"), *gumbo, bayou, jambalaya, vaquero* ("cowboy"), and so on are typical here.

Subdialects

There are several interesting subdialects within this general region. One of the most remarkable of these is the English spoken in the Virginia "tidewater" area. The English of Tangier Island has maintained many archaic features of the West Country dialect in late seventeenth-century England. Some subdialects are popularized by movie series about life in the region. For example, the refined speech of Texans in Dallas has become both nationally and internationally known and identifiable through the *Dallas* series. Cajun English is yet another subdialect spoken in Louisiana that has many French and Creole traces.

The Midland dialect

The Midland region begins on the East Coast in Philadelphia, and moving inland it fans out and extends westward (into Ohio, Indiana, and Illinois) and southwest (through Kentucky, Tennessee into the interior parts of the Southern coastal states and Missouri and Arkansas). Some dialectologists consider the language spoken in Ohio, Indiana, etc. as belonging to the Northern dialect, while the language spoken in Kentucky, Tennessee, etc., forms a part of the Southern dialect region. This region is obviously more difficult to study than the long-established communities in the Eastern United States. Timothy Frazer, one of the main researchers of this region, provides an overview of the many complexities in the linguistic study of the Midwest (see Frazer, 1998). One of these is the difficulty of precisely delimiting the area itself.

Carver (1987) goes even further and argues against taking the Midland dialect region to be one of the three major dialect regions in the U.S., suggesting that this idea is mostly a remnant of Kurath's early division of American dialects into Northern, Southern, and Midland. Carver maintains that evidence does not support this widely held view, and that the view ultimately emerged "because there has been no unified collection of data covering the country as a whole" (Carver, 1987:182). It should be noted that Carver does not claim that the "Midland" does not exist as a dialect; rather, his suggestion is that it does not have an equal status with the Northern and Southern dialects in its relative importance. In Carver's words, "given its relatively small number of isoglosses, and its great overlap with the Upper South, it simply does not have the primary status in the dialect hierarchy that Kurath assigned to it" (1987:183).

Despite this possibility, I will follow the traditional classification and consider, together with many others, the Midwest as a dialect region on a par with the North and the South. Here again, I rely heavily on Bailey's (1992) characterization of this dialect.

Pronunciation

Midland pronunciation is also rhotic, as is the case in general in the United States. It is interesting to note that Philadelphia is the only rhotic city along the Atlantic Coast, where, it will be remembered, New England (especially Eastern New England) and the Coastal South are /r/-less as well.

Another point of interest in connection with pronunciation is that the /ɔ/-/a/ merger begins in Pennsylvania. Thus in this region people pronounce word pairs like *cot – caught* and *tot – taught* in the same way, using the /a/ of *cot* and *tot* for the /ɔ/ of *caught* and *taught*.

Grammar

In the area of grammar, Midland speakers often use *a*-prefixation; that is, they add *a* to the verb with an *-ing* ending. For example, one comes across sentences like *She went a-visiting yesterday* and *They were a-coming across the bridge* more frequently than in other dialects.

There also exists a special construction with *anymore*. We find examples like *We use a gas stove anymore*, in which *anymore* means something like "nowadays." Another example for the same construction is provided by Finegan and Besnier: *Anymore, they build shopping malls everywhere* ("Nowadays, they build shopping malls everywhere") (1989:399).

As a result of German influence, the Midland also uses *all* in a special construction. Here *all* has the meaning of "run out." Thus the sentence *The pot roast is all* means that it is gone or that there is nothing left. Possibly related to this construction is the example given by Finegan and Besnier (1989:398), where *all* means "the only." This meaning of *all* can be found in such sentences as *This is all the coat I've got* ("This is the only coat I have").

Vocabulary

Regarding vocabulary, the Midland also has certain words that are more common here than in other parts of the country. Here people use *blind* ("window shade"), *fishing worm* ("earthworm"), *mango* ("sweet or bell pepper"), *woolly worm* ("caterpillar"), and, based on Carver (1989:264), more examples can be added: *snake feeder* ("dragonfly"), *sook!* (a call to cows), *fat meat* ("bacon"), *rick (of hay)* ("hay stack"), and *white mule* ("illegally made whiskey"). In the Midland region, formerly limited usages became general (*bucket – pail*). The expression *want + particle* is common here: *I want off now* ("I want to get off now"). Foreign influence is negligible in the region, probably as a result of poor soil and poverty, especially in the southern part of the Midland.

Subdialects

Perhaps the best known subdialect in the Midland region is the kind of American English recognized by Americans and foreigners alike in country-western music. This English comes from the lower Midland area, or, as some dialectologists would put it, from the Upper South. More specifically, the American English commonly used in country-western music and that has gained national and international prominence originates from the Appalachian and Ozark regions. This variety of American English was further popularized by movies and many people who imitate it (e.g., truck drivers).

Pennsylvania Dutch has had some impact on American English. As was noted in chapter two, the term is a misnomer for German (*Deutsch*). Pennsylvania Dutch is the language of the Amish and Mennonites in eastern and central Pennsylvania who settled down in the United States in the seventeenth and eighteenth centuries.

The West as a dialect region

The West is by far the geographically largest region comprising the territory west of the Mississippi, extending to the Pacific Ocean. The settlement of this enormous area was completed after the California gold rush in the 1850s. A demographic characteristic of the West is that the settlers came from all the other major areas, the North, Midland, and the South, thus producing a great deal of intermingling, both demographically and linguistically.

Pronunciation

In this region, which covers most of the Pacific coast, we find rhoticity. The /r/ is universally pronounced post-vocalically and at the end of words.

The merger of /a/ and /ɔ/ is complete and word pairs like *tot – taught, cot – caught,* and *don – dawn* are pronounced alike, with the vowel /a/.

A newly emerging feature of pronunciation along the Pacific, and especially in California, is the shift from the monophthong /ɛ/ to the diphthong /e/. Thus we hear words like *measure* and *edge* pronounced with the diphthong of *bait* and *age.*

People not living in California perceive the pronunciation of *really* as that of *rilly,* with short /ɪ/.

Grammar

There are many subcultures in California and some of them developed their own syntax. One of these is the drug culture. A characteristic feature of their dialect is a simplified syntax, for example, in sentences like *I been tripping for three weeks.* The teenagers living in San Fernando Valley also developed their characteristic patterns of speech. The word *like* is one of their favorites in a construction such as the following: *Like, no biggie.*

Vocabulary

Some of the vocabulary of the West is distinctive. Words like *bear claw* ("a large sweet pastry in the shape of a bear's paw"), *chesterfield* ("a sofa"; a word shared with Canadian English), and *sourdough bread* ("bread started with a piece of fermented dough") are more or less unique to this region. Many words that are commonly used in everyday life reflect the influence of foreign languages in the region. Of these the most influential is Spanish in its Mexican variety. Some of the Spanish words in almost daily use include *adios, adobe, bronco, embarcadero, hombre, Santa Ana, frijoles, tortilla,* and many others. Even Hawaiian (a Polynesian language) has its influence felt in such words as *aloha* ("a friendly greeting") and *lei* ("garland").

Subdialects

As we have seen above, several subcultures in this region – especially in California – have contributed to what can be termed the Western dialect. I will discuss some further subcultures and their linguistic input to American English in general when in a later chapter we focus on American slang. California has also produced a language that is not strictly speaking a subdialect, but rather a certain style of speaking that can be called "laidback" style. It is characterized by an informal and casual way of speaking, reflecting a similar lifestyle. (The issue of style will be discussed in chapter eight.)

In general, it may be noted that the West, and especially California with all its subcultures, began to contribute to the linguistic repertory of the nation as a whole. Thus, a process that in the past went from east to west seems to have been reversed. Today the Western dialect affects the language habits of many speakers of American English in the non-Western regions.

Some general regional markers

So far in this chapter, I have dealt with linguistic features of American English which, taken individually, may or may not uniquely characterize a given regional dialect. (However, taken together, they do identify a regional dialect.) In this section, I will look at two individual linguistic features that identify a region uniquely. That is, when the feature is used, we can be reasonably certain about the region the speaker comes from.

The two features are the different synonyms for two concepts: "carbonated soft drinks," on the one hand, and "automobile highways," on the other. If we look at the various synonyms for these two concepts, we find an interesting pattern of distribution for the synonyms (Marckwardt, 1980; rev. Dillard). In the case of carbonated soft drinks, we find that speakers of American English refer to them with a variety of terms, including *coke, cold drink, pop, soda,* and others. Now it turns out that these terms, or synonyms, tend to be associated with different regions in the United States. The words *coke* and *dope* are used in the South (*dope*, of course, has other meanings elsewhere); *cold drink* in the lower Mississippi Valley; *pop* in interior North and West; *soda* or *soda-pop* in Los Angeles; and *tonic* in Boston.

The words referring to "limited-access automobile highways" once showed a considerable amount of semantic specialization. Today, however, the words given below are roughly synonymous. What is interesting about them is that they reveal regional differences in their use. Thus, *parkway* is the term used in Eastern New York, New Jersey, Connecticut, and Rhode Island. The word *turnpike* is preferred in New Jersey, Pennsylvania, Massachusetts, Maine, New Hampshire, Ohio, Indiana, and Florida. In New York, people often refer to the same kind of highway as *thruway*. In Michigan, one drives on an *expressway*. Finally, people in California are blessed, and sometimes cursed, with their extensive system of *freeways*. (For more regional words, see Cassidy, 1985, Cassidy and Hall, 1991, 1996, and Carver, 1989.)

Reasons for uniformity and variation in American English

We have seen above that American English is characterized by both uniformity and variation or heterogeneity. On the one hand, American English is remarkably uniform, in that roughly two thirds of its population speak the same dialect, this being a situation very different from what we find in England. On the other hand, there is also some degree of variation, in that there are clearly identifiable regional dialects within American English. It is interesting and instructive to see why both the uniformity and the variation have come about. Let us begin with the question of uniformity.

Although it seems impossible to point to a single and clear factor that explains everything in this regard, we can suggest some ideas concerning the issue of relative uniformity. First, we can mention the mingling of settlers. The people who came from linguistically different regions in Britain intermingled a great deal and especially in the course of the westward movement. This must have been an enormous stabilizing factor in the development of American dialects. Moreover, as Dillard (1992) suggests, the mixing of dialects must have begun as early as the arrival of the first settlers, who spent several months together in their boats. Today's mobility may also contribute to the levelling of dialects, and although some researchers doubt the significance of media in this process, we may be certain at least that the media does not help diversification.

Second, there have been several strong forces in the United States that are likely to have fostered uniformity, rather than diversity. One of these is the influence of Noah Webster. Webster's attempts to standardize American English with his extremely popular spelling book and his American dictionaries must have been at least partially responsible. Another early grammarian, Murray, must also be given credit for the uniformity which he helped produce with his successful grammar. American public education may be a further source. I will talk about this second category of reasons for relative uniformity in the next chapter.

Third, a social-psychological reason that is often mentioned as an additional factor is the alleged conformity of Americans. People point to the American tendency to wear the same kind of clothes (such as blue jeans and T-shirts), drive similar cars in a given period (e.g., small Japanese cars), and live in houses that look alike (e.g., in the song by Pete Seeger: "Little boxes look the same"). In other words, the ready acceptance of emblems of group allegiance or identification on the part of many Americans is offered as an explanation of their linguistic uniformity as well.

Now we can ask what brought about the variation. As I pointed out earlier, this must have been at least in part the result of the settlers coming from linguistically different parts of England. Furthermore, the attitude of the settlers to the language of the mother country differed significantly. Those settlers who stayed on the Atlantic seaboard maintained much closer contact with England than those who moved inland. For example, many people in New England and the South sent their children to school in England. It was also easier for these people to have access to books from England and to maintain family contacts. As we have seen in this chapter, the dialects of American English that evolved on the Atlantic seaboard at an early stage of settlement show more similarity to British English today than do the dialects that came into being later. This can be exemplified by the distribution of the sound /r/ in the general practice of Americans today. The first settlers arrived from the southern regions of England: from the southeast the pilgrims went to the Massachusetts Bay area and from the south and London they went to tidewater Virginia. These early settlers had no /r/ in their accents, which began to disappear in the southern part of England in the sixteenth century. It is these settlers who populated much of the Atlantic seaboard. Philadelphia was an exception. The Philadelphia region was settled by the English from the south of England and the Germans, but also by people from Northern Britain (they were Scottish and Irish). The Scottish and Irish were /r/-pronouncing, and they were the settlers who moved inland west or south-west and who became the pioneers par excellence. This accounts for the /r/-pronouncing character of General American and the /r/-lessness of the Atlantic seaboard.

study questions and activities

1. If you have Frederick Cassidy's dictionary in your library, check the pronunciation of the word *greasy* in it. Based on what you find, which theory of American regional dialects do you think it supports?

2. If you are a movie fan, find out where an American movie you have not seen takes place. Study the characteristics of this region's dialect more closely and go to see the movie. How does the language of the movie compare with what you have learned about the dialect?

3. If you live in the U.S., observe the characteristics of the speech heard around you. Try to make an inventory of the most common characteristics in pronunciation, grammar, and vocabulary.

4. If you live outside the U.S. and are a non-native speaker of English with an American around you, try to study the characteristics of this person's speech. Make a hypothesis concerning the part of the U.S. in which you think the person was raised. Ask the person if your hypothesis is correct.

chapter 6

Social dialects of American English

In the previous two chapters we saw that American English varies according to which general geographical area a speaker comes from. It was pointed out that recent research has identified four such general geographical areas: the North, Midland, Coastal South, and the West. However, physical space is not the only factor that produces variation in language. An equally important factor (and some would claim, an even more important one) is the social context in which a language is spoken. Thus, in addition to geographical variation, there is also social variation. American English, similarly to other languages, varies according to social context.

Social vs. regional variation

The scientific study of this aspect of American English began with the pioneering work of the best known American sociolinguist, William Labov. Labov (1966, 1972) used especially two techniques in his research in the 1960s. In one, he went to different department stores in New York City: Saks Fifth Avenue, Macy's, and Klein's. These department stores were respectively regarded by New Yorkers as being upper (middle) class, middle class, and working class. Labov asked sales assistants certain questions (such as *Where can I find the lamps?*) and based on their responses he isolated certain, what he called, linguistic variables. For example, he found interesting differences in the use of the sound /r/ in the three department stores. Sales assistants used more /r/s in expressions like *fourth floor* in the upper-middle-class Saks than in middle-class Macy's. In the working-class Klein's, the sound was almost completely missing in positions exemplified by the expression *fourth floor*. This finding becomes interesting in the light of what was said in the previous chapter about the distribution of the sound /r/ in American English. There it was pointed out that the post-vocalic (including word final) /r/ is one of the characteristic features of standard American, as opposed to British, English. Pronouncing the /r/ is the norm in the Northern, Midland, and Western dialect regions, that is, in the greatest part of the country. Most television and radio announcers also prefer the use of /r/ in this position. Pronouncing the /r/ has more prestige in the United States than not pronouncing it. On the other hand, however, it was also pointed out that in general New York is not an /r/-pronouncing region. What the research by Labov shows is that high social status correlates with the use of certain linguistic forms. There was more /r/ used in Saks than in Macy's than in Klein's. Furthermore, there is also a correlation between socioeconomic class and prestigious linguistic forms. The sales assistants in Saks and Macy's preferred the prestigious /r/-pronouncing variant of the form, while the sales assistants in the working-class Klein's stayed with the nationally less prestigious local /r/-less variant.

But how was Labov sure that his findings were the result of socioeconomic status, and not of something else, such as being black rather than white, or being a sales clerk rather than a stock boy, or being a woman rather than a man? If it turns out that he spoke with more blacks than whites, with more sales clerks than stock boys, or with more women than men, the particular pattern in the pronunciation of /r/ could have been produced by any of these other factors (i.e., ethnicity, occupation, and gender). In order to check that his findings really derived from socioeconomic status, Labov took a second look at his data. He chose the largest homogeneous group in his sample of speakers (that is, the group that does not exhibit any ethnic, occupational, or gender differentiation) and he checked this group's use of the /r/ sound. This group was female white sales clerks. The speakers in the sample of female white sales clerks differed from each other in one respect only: socioeconomic status (in that they worked for Saks, Macy's, and Klein's, respectively). As it turned out, the numbers obtained for this homogeneous group indicated that those working for Saks pronounced more /r/s than those for Macy's, and those for Macy's more than those working for Klein. Thus Labov managed to show that the differences in the pronunciation of post-vocalic /r/ were indeed the result of socioeconomic status, and not of other potential factors.

As we just saw, Labov examined the pronunciation of post-vocalic /r/ within a homogeneous group (female white sales clerks) across three socioeconomically different department stores. But he was also interested in the issue of how narrow a social ranking can get and still show linguistic differences. In other words, he wanted to find out what would happen if he limited the sample of speakers to a single department store (i.e., if he narrowed the range of social ranking to one, not three). For this purpose, he selected Macy's (because he had the largest number of respondents from this department store). This time Labov checked the data he obtained from the three occupational groups at Macy's: the floor-walkers, the sales clerks, and the stock boys. He found that the floorwalkers produced the most /r/s, the sales clerks less, and the stock boys the least. This way he showed that the pronunciation of /r/ is socially stratified in New York City, in that higher-ranking social groups produce more /r/s than lower-ranking ones.

The other technique Labov used in his research consisted of interviewing a couple of hundred New Yorkers from Manhattan's Lower East Side. He examined a representative sample of the residents of the Lower East Side, including blacks and whites, men and women, Jews and Italians, and parents and children. He obtained extensive sociological information about each of the interview subjects – information concerning their education, income, and occupation. On the basis of this information, he was in a position to assign each subject to a particular socioeconomic group or category. This situation made the study very different from the one that was reported above. Another difference lies in the fact that he tape-recorded the interviews; the interviews with each respondent lasted for several hours. The tape-recorded conversations made it possible for Labov to analyze in detail and depth the characteristic patterns in the speech of these New Yorkers. In these studies, Labov looked again at the use of the sound /r/ and several other linguistic features, such as the voiceless fricative /θ/ in words like *think,* having the variant pronunciation /t/; the voiced fricative /ð/ in words like *this* or *that,* having the variant /d/; the pronunciation of the *-ing* suffix, as in *running* with the pronunciation variants /ɪŋ/ and /ɪn/, and the pronunciation of the vowel in words like *bad, care,* and *sag,* where the vowel alternates between /æ/ and /ɪə/. Again, Labov found that in each of these cases the socioeconomic status of the respondent correlates with linguistic variables. Thus, upper-middle-class respondents produced most /r/s. Moreover, they also produced more /θ/, /ð/, /ŋ/, and /æ/ than the lower middle-class and the working class. In general, then, Labov convincingly showed that pronunciation differences reflect subtle differences in socioeconomic status. The important part of Labov's study discussed here is not that language reflects socioeconomic differences (that was known before him), but that it can do so in extremely subtle ways.

Using these techniques, Labov was able to describe some of the linguistic features of New York City and to correlate them systematically with differential socioeconomic status. Thus, he described a part of American English (spoken in New York City). However, the patterns that he found for the distribution of the linguistic variables are not limited to New York City, but are much more general. For example, his findings were later extended from pronunciation to syntactic data. Moreover, similar patterns of distribution were found in other dialects of English. Peter Trudgill, the British sociolinguist, studied some of the same linguistic variables as Labov in the English city of Norwich and found a strikingly similar pattern of distribution for socioeconomic class. For example, the higher the social class the more /ɪŋ/ pronunciation (as opposed to /ɪn/) it will produce.

Incidentally, more than thirty years after Labov's work, a linguistically-minded New York journalist, John Tierney, repeated Labov's experiment (Tierney, 1995). He went to the same department stores that Labov went to and asked some questions that elicited the /r/ sound or the absence of it. Tierney's experiment was, of course, only an informal one, but nevertheless he asked sixty sales clerks at Saks, Macy's and Bradlees (the last is close to where Klein's used to be). The results he obtained confirmed Labov's findings. The sales clerks at Saks used more /r/s than at Macy's and at Macy's more than at Bradlees (he asked 60 clerks altogether, compared to Labov's 264). Interestingly, the percentages were higher than what Labov found: 50% of the clerks produced an /r/ at Saks, 40% at Macy's, and 15% at Bradlees. This shows that the tendency to pronounce the /r/ in post-vocalic position could be growing in New York City. It also shows that one of the characteristic features of New York City speech is still very much alive today, suggesting that this vernacular is not likely to go away soon.

But in demonstrating the close and subtle correlation between language use and socioeconomic status, Labov also did more. He showed that variation in the use of language may not be primarily a matter of geography, that is, a question of physical space. What matters just as (or more) importantly is to which social group one belongs. In other words, he found a way of handling the issue that had baffled linguistic geographers, namely, the issue of how to account for linguistic variation in dense and complex urban communities. He began to offer solutions to problems where linguistic geographers only saw, to use Pickford's word, "chaos."

Factors in social variation

All linguists would agree that variation resulting from which social class one belongs to is a matter of social dialects. Many sociolinguistic studies indicate that differentiation in American English is the result of the differentiation of American society into middle class and working class, with further finer distinctions in both. Thus socioeconomic class is viewed as a factor that can produce social dialects. But it is not the only one. Sex (or more appropriately, gender) is another factor. As has been shown by several authors, American women have characteristics of speech not found in the speech of American men. It is also commonly observed that different generations of speakers of American English speak differently. The English of children is different from that of middle-aged speakers and old people, and the way teenagers speak is often incomprehensible to everybody else. A celebrated example is Salinger's *The Catcher in the Rye*. Race and/or ethnic group is also responsible for the creation of social dialects in American English. What is generally referred to as Black American English is different from Hispanic American English, and both are different from the English spoken by many whites. Education also leads to social variation in American English. College- and university-educated people tend to speak differently from people without college education. Finally, there is also a noticeable difference in the English of Americans who live in big cities and those who live in rural areas. (On social variation in American English, see Wolfram, 1974; Glowka and Lance, 1993; Wolfram and Schilling-Estes, 1998a.)

Gender

That American men and women speak differently has been shown by several authors (e.g., Lakoff, 1975; Gilligan, 1982; Tannen, 1990). Often it is the choice of words that distinguishes the speech of women from that of men. Hendrickson mentions a study in which it is suggested that women use words like *trousers, china,* and *houseguests* in situations where men say *pants, dishes,* and *visitors* (1986:14). Robin Lakoff (1975) claims that what she calls "women's speech" is characterized by six features. In addition to differences in lexical choice, women use question intonation in statements (*When will dinner be ready? Oh, about eight o'clock?*); hedges and question tags (*He's a nice guy, isn't he?* and *It's kind of hot in here.*); emphatic modifiers and intonational emphasis (*so, such, very: It's so beautiful!*); hypercorrect grammar and pronunciation (more formal syntax, prestigious accent); and superpolite forms (*Would you please open the window if you don't mind?*). Lakoff's main point is that all of these features show how women have less social power in American society than men do. Her description of speech by women was based on her own intuitions.

However, Wolfson (1989) cites evidence that most of these findings are false, or debatable, or require further research. The findings that seem to be supported by independent empirical evidence include the use of tag-questions and hypercorrect grammar and pronunciation. Wolfson mentions studies which show that women indeed use more tag-questions than men. However, she also points out that tag-questions have a variety of different functions and that women use them not necessarily because they have less power but because they put tag-questions to more uses than men. In regard to hypercorrect grammar and pronunciation, Wolfson points out that Lakoff's findings receive some support from research by Labov (1966), who found that women do significantly more hypercorrection than men. This was especially typical of lower-middle-class women.

American men and women also seem to differ with respect to their "conversational styles." Tannen's (1990) work indicates that men and women employ different strategies in everyday conversations, strategies that may lead to misunderstanding between them.

Age

Whether a speaker is young or old can also make a difference. In other words, age also produces social dialects. The most obvious way in which young and old speakers of American English can differ is the choice of words. Older generations tend to use words like *spigot* for what is more commonly called a *faucet* in the United States and a *tap* in England. They would also use *icebox* and *tape recorder* for what younger generations would call *refrigerator* (or *fridge*) and *stereo*, respectively. In addition, young speakers tend to use more slang than older ones, who have a tendency to express themselves in more traditional ways. The general issue of slang in America will be taken up in a separate chapter.

Race and ethnic group

Race and ethnic group appear to be major sources of social variation in language in the United States. All the major races and ethnic groups in the United States are clearly distinguishable by the dialect of American English they use. I will discuss social dialects based on race and ethnic groups in a separate chapter, where I describe some of the major features of Black and Hispanic English.

Education

Education is perhaps the main factor that produces the distinct varieties that we know as Standard vs. Nonstandard (or Vernacular) American English. The social dialects of standard and nonstandard American English will be the topic of the next section of this chapter.

Region

In this chapter, by "region" I mean not geographical region, but the social region of urban and rural areas and the contrast between the dialect used in urban as opposed to rural areas. The English of American city-dwellers in general can be differentiated from that of people living in the country mostly by the fact that the English of city-dwellers bears closer resemblance to the national standard than the English of people in the rural parts.

In conclusion, socioeconomic class, gender, age, race and ethnic group, education, and region (city vs. rural area) are the main factors that bring about social variation in language in general, and specifically for our purposes in American English.

Standard and nonstandard American English

Standard American English (SAE)

When we ask what Standard American English is, the social factors listed above prove useful. Standard American English is not a variety of English that is inherently "standard," or better, or more beautiful, or more logical than other forms of English. What makes it standard is that some speakers of American English have the social power to impose the variety of English they happen to use on speakers of other varieties. They are in a position to make their English the prestigious form of English. They can do so thanks to their social power. Since this social power is desired by other people, the English spoken by people with power is also desirable for others. In this sense, the possession of the prestigious variety is the possession of social power.

But who are the people who possess this social power and the prestigious form of American English that goes with it? It seems reasonable to suggest that these people are those on the top of the socioeconomic hierarchy (the middle class, especially upper-middle class); they are predominantly males; they are mostly whites; they are middle-aged (probably upper middle-aged); they are college- or university-educated (especially with a higher degree from a prestigious private or state university); and come from major industrial areas (as opposed to rural). This is of course not to say that all speakers of Standard American English possess all of these characteristics; for example, many Afro-Americans in the United States speak the standard variety of American English. However, these are the predominant characteristics of those who possess social power and who therefore "control" SAE.

Perhaps the typical embodiment of Standard American English is what has been referred to, especially in the past, as General American. This term has two uses. One refers to the allegedly uniform kind of American English spoken outside the New England and Southern areas, that is, the vast majority of the United States. This is the sense in which Krapp (1924) introduced the term, and it is still employed in this sense especially by laymen in discussions of American English. In light of what we saw in the previous two chapters, we must conclude that the term General American is not really a valid descriptive concept: in place of a uniform General American we have found three large dialect areas (Northern, Midland, and West). Nevertheless, we can find some useful application for the term in another sense. The other use of the term refers to a certain norm or "standard" of pronunciation that derives primarily from the Midland and Western regions and that is thus characteristic of the majority of Americans. The notion of General American is closely related to that of Network Standard.

What is recognized as Network Standard today has in all probability evolved from General American. As was mentioned in the previous chapter, the Midland and the West cover a huge geographical region in which a great deal of intermingling took place. The West was settled by people from a variety of different regions, speaking in a variety of different accents. This was also the region where many people came who spoke no English at all. The schoolteachers must have played an especially important role here in teaching children to speak "proper" English. As Hendrickson (1986) explains: "Here pronunciation very likely followed the rule of schoolteachers in 'sounding out' words by syllables. The current dialect that most of the TV networks use as a standard was probably born in the one-room schoolhouse" (p. 22). Since Network Standard probably developed from General American in the first sense (i.e., the American English of the Midland and West), Network Standard is rhotic, the flat /æ/ sound is used in words like *half* and *path*, and a flat, not rounded, *o* /ɑ/ is pronounced in words like *hot* and *top*. It has some other notable features as well, but these are the ones that most clearly distinguish it from other major American English varieties, as well as from British English.

In this latter application of the term as a norm or standard to be followed, General American can be conceived as a geographically neutral dialect. The question is whether it is also neutral in relation to social dialects. It does not seem to be so. If the factors listed above are indeed the ones that produce social dialects, then General American as Network Standard is anything but socially neutral. It is defined by the people who have the most social power in American society. Network Standard can be heard on the main radio and television stations in the United States. This variety of American English has become widespread since the 1960s, beginning with the appearance of television on a large scale in the U.S. The main figures transmitting this variety of English are the nationally known TV newscasters of the major television networks. Most middle-class, white, educated Americans regard the English used by these figures as their standard. This has become, for them, the most prestigious variety of American English. This relatively recent development has changed the sociolinguistic situation in the United States. Previously, each region had its own regional standard that had prestige for the people living in the region. These regional centers are now in the process of disappearing, giving way to Network Standard, which has acquired prestige nationwide.

But Standard American English does not consist solely of an accent. It involves other systems of language as well, especially syntax. To see what the syntactic characteristics of standard American English are, it is best to look at features that are considered *non*standard.

Nonstandard (or Vernacular) American English

Nonstandard (or vernacular) English in the United States is primarily a matter of education, or more precisely, a lack of it. Lack of higher education often makes it difficult for people to acquire the standard. Correspondingly, as we have seen above, Standard American English is associated with people who have college education. But nonstandard American English is also correlated to factors such as socioeconomic class, race and ethnic group, and region.

What are the properties of nonstandard (vernacular) American English? Here only a brief selection of the most representative features can be given (Gramley and Pätzold, 1992:377).

Perhaps the best known feature of nonstandard American English is the phenomenon that is called "multiple negation." This is exemplified in sentences like *I didn't say nothing* and *They don't need none*. In these sentences, negation is expressed by more than one linguistic item: *not* and *nothing* in the first and *not* and *none* in the second. Negative items like these are not limited to two in many cases.

The contraction *ain't* is also a typical nonstandard form. It can mean "be + not" or "have + not." Thus the sentence *He ain't no buddy of mine* means "He isn't a friend of mine," the sentence *I ain't got no money* means "I don't have any money," and the sentence *I ain't done it yet* means "I haven't done it yet." (Notice also the frequent use of multiple negation in sentences with *ain't*.)

Subject and verb often do not agree in nonstandard English. Thus *don't* can occur with a third person singular subject, as in *He don't love her*. On the other hand, plural subjects are often not followed by the plural of *be*, as in *They was pretty hungry*. Another way of putting this is to say that irregular verb forms are regularized, that is, exceptions in verbal paradigms like *does* are eliminated.

The pronoun *them* can be used in a demonstrative function. What this means is that *them* can replace the standard demonstrative pronoun *those*. Thus, we hear sentences like *Give me them things* for the standard *Give me those things*. Similarly, the use of the standard demonstrative pronoun *this* can be reinforced by the deictic place adverb *here*. This results in sentences like *This here man wants something*.

We can find in nonstandard American English the application of double modals, like *might could*. This results in sentences like *They might could help us out*.

Often the subject relative pronoun is missing in defining relative clauses, as in *The fellow wrote that letter is here*. The standard version of the sentence would be *The fellow who/that wrote that letter is here*. That is, in the nonstandard sentence the relative pronouns *who* or *that* that can be used to refer to the subject of the main clause (and thus would be the subject of the defining relative clause) can be left out.

The simple past tense can be expressed by verb forms that are considered past participle forms in the standard. Thus *done* and *seen*, for example, can be used to indicate simple past tense: *He done it* and *John seen 'em*. Regularized verb forms are used for the same purpose, as in *She knowed it* (instead of *knew*). We also have past tenses such as *come* (for *came*) and *drownded* (for *drowned*).

Standard irregular past tense forms are also used for the past participle. Thus, *took, went, tore, fell, wrote,* which are irregular past forms in standard English, can function as past participles, yielding sentences such as *He had went home*.

One frequently heard misconception about nonstandard American English, especially on the part of users of the standard, is that nonstandard American

English is somehow less "logical" and "systematic" than the standard. The example that is often brought up in this argument is multiple negation. The claim is that the use of multiple negation reflects a less logical way of thinking, since two negatives in a sentence cancel each other out and result in a positive statement. What this argument misses is that language and languages do not function according to the canons of classical logic. Shakespeare commonly used multiple negation, and perhaps nobody would want to say that there was something wrong with his "logical capabilities." Moreover, there are many languages in the world where multiple negation is the norm and the standard. It seems then that there is no correlation between the use of multiple linguistic negation and inferior reasoning abilities. Again, the proper conclusion seems to be that the standard can be defined in a variety of ways, the definition depending on what the preferred language habits of people are who happen to be in a position to define it.

Nonstandard American English is also often claimed to be less systematic than the standard. To see whether this claim is a valid one, let us look at two cases. The first case is the system of possessive pronouns. In standard English these are *my, your, his, her, its, our, your,* and *their.* The so-called "absolute forms" of these pronouns are *mine, yours, his, hers, its, ours, yours,* and *theirs.* We can notice three very different processes in the formation of the absolute form. As Marckwardt (1980:151-152; rev. Dillard) notes, the absolute form *mine* is derived from *my* + *-n* and the forms *yours, hers, ours, theirs* from the adjectival use of the possessive pronouns *your, her, our, their* plus *-s.* The absolute forms *his* and *its* cannot be distinguished from their adjectival possessive forms. In other words, we get a paradigm that is not very systematic or regular. Contrast, however, the corresponding nonstandard forms for these pronouns. We have *mine, yourn, hisn, hern, ourn, yourn,* and *theirn.* That is, in all cases the absolute form comes from the systematic application of the rule: "add *-n* to the adjectival form of the possessive pronoun." This is a process that can be said to be more regular and systematic than the standard. As another illustration of the same point, we can observe the same in the case of the reflexive pronouns. The standard has *myself, yourself, himself, herself, itself, ourselves, yourselves, themselves.* Here, *myself, yourself, ourselves,* and *yourselves* are combinations of the possessive pronoun and *self* or *selves. Himself* and *themselves* derive from the objective case of the personal pronouns *he* and *they,* whereas *herself* and *itself* could come from either the possessive pronouns or the objective case of the personal pronouns. The nonstandard forms are again more regular. They are *myself, yourself, hisself, herself, ourself, yourself,* and *theirself.* These forms all derive from the adjectival possessive pronouns plus the form *self.* An added advantage of the nonstandard system is that it eliminates the redundancy of marking the plural twice: the singular form *self* is used throughout and plurality is indicated by the form of the possessive pronouns *our* and *their.* As Marckwardt

(1980; rev. Dillard) notes, the only ambiguity in this system is in the second person; *yourself*, where *your* has lost the singular-plural distinction anyway.

Attempts at standardizing American English

The standardizing influence of the Network Standard mentioned in a previous section has not come about as a result of the conscious effort of some TV newscasters. It is not the intention of radio and television stations in the U.S. to change anybody's English. It is the social desirability of their English that makes people want to acquire it. However, there have been very conscious attempts in the United States to change the language habits of people who do not conform to the norm or standard as envisioned by the powerful "language experts" of the white middle class. Of these attempts and processes, I will mention only three.

If the main transmitters of General American or Network Standard are the TV newscasters and radio announcers, then the main enforcers of the proper use of standard American English are the school teachers. English teachers have long been engaged in the teaching of what they regard as "proper" English. In general, public education has been seen as one of the main standardizing influences in the United States. The ideologists behind the efforts by school teachers are the language educators, who provide them with the rationale for their struggle. The main argument of the language educators has been for a long time that the English language in America is constantly deteriorating and that the process will lead to its death. Some of the major contemporary figures who hold this view include Edwin Newman and William Safire.

A different but related attempt to standardize American English is more politically oriented. In 1983 an organization called "US English" was established under the leadership of the linguist Senator Hayakawa to make English the official language in the United States. The U.S. Constitution does not state that English is the official language of the country. This causes fear among members of the group. They are concerned that languages other than English (e.g., Spanish) might overtake the role of English as the virtual official language in some areas. The pressure group has been relatively successful. As a result of their efforts, English was made the official language in several states.

The major single figure in the standardizing process was the famous American lexicographer Noah Webster. Webster realized that American English could not be standardized in the manner of some European countries, like France, where the final arbiter of usage is the Academy. Attempts to establish an academy to legislate over linguistic issues had failed invariably in the United States (for example, one attributed to John Adams). Webster's efforts at standardization were much more pragmatic and he was partly successful. Whatever the degree of the standardization of American English today is, it is to a considerable extent the result of his work. He published between 1783 and 1785 *A Grammatical Institute of the English Language*, which consisted of a spelling book, a grammar, and a reader. His success in standardization is most remarkable in the area of spelling and pronunciation. (We will come back to his specific proposals in a later chapter.) His influence on speakers of American English is shown by the fact that the spelling book sold 80 million copies, which is second only to the Bible. His other major work was his *American Dictionary of the English Language*, published in 1828. In the area of vocabulary, he was less successful in his efforts. This was the time when the vocabulary of American English was expanding rapidly, especially along the westward moving frontier (Claiborne, 1983). It was impossible to standardize vocabulary in this period of incredible growth. Indeed, this period and process have often been compared with the parallel situation in Elizabethan times in England.

Webster saw three major reasons for the need to standardize American English. First, he held the view that Britain is too far from the United States to serve as a model. Thus he saw the standardization of American English as a practical issue. Second, there was a political motive. Being a patriot, Webster wanted not only political but also cultural independence from England, and cultural independence for him naturally implied linguistic independence. A new and different kind of English was for him the ultimate proof of cultural independence. Third, Webster clearly saw that the new nation, in order to become a unified nation, needed a national language. He sought to bring together the diverse people of the new nation with the help of a new – an American – English. Webster offered standard American English as a common language to the immigrants speaking a wide variety of different languages.

It is also often mentioned that there are certain psychological reasons that have facilitated the relative success of the standardizing process in the United States (e.g., Baugh and Cable, 1983; Marckwardt, 1980 [rev. Dillard]). One of them is the American respect for experts. Another, as we saw in the previous chapter, is the often mentioned conformity of many Americans, which is also seen in domains outside language use, for example, in the way many Americans dress.

Attitudes toward dialects of American English

It is obvious from what has been said in this chapter that standard American English is a prestigious dialect for many Americans. It is also obvious, maybe even more so, that nonstandard American English has no prestige for most Americans. As was pointed out, this is because the standard dialect is associated with (social, political, cultural) power, while the nonstandard one (or ones) is associated with a lack of power.

But at least three further important questions arise concerning the attitudes to dialects in general: (1) How do Americans perceive their own regional dialects and those of others? (2) How is American English (especially the standard variety) perceived by foreigners, and, among them, especially the British? (3) How do speakers of American English perceive British English?

American attitudes to regional dialects

The question of attitude to dialects is a huge and complex one. It is also a socially important one because our attitude to dialects and the people speaking those dialects may determine the way we act toward these speakers. Linguists are just beginning to investigate attitudes to American dialects in a scientific manner. This new and fascinating research has acquired the name "perceptual dialectology" (see Preston, 1998). In this section, I offer only some informal observations concerning the issue. (Readers seriously interested in this topic should consult Dennis Preston's works.)

Many Americans think of their own dialects as bad. For example, people from the Ozark mountains regard their speech as "hillbilly" or "poor" and Labov found that most New Yorkers do not like their own accent. This attitude, and some of the complexities that go with it, can be seen in a comment on Tangier Island speech. One former inhabitant who studied the speech of the islanders writes:

> Tangiermen are painfully aware that the way they talk is different – even bad, as they say – from the speech of the surrounding areas and seem to be ashamed of their speech in front of strangers. In speaking with them, they consciously distort a feature or two, those that they feel are the most conspicuous to others, toward that of the standard, an act for which they teasingly accuse each other, either at the time or later, of "putting on airs" or "talking proper." (McCrum, et al., 1986:108)

But dialects deviating from the standard are also seen in a negative light from the outside, that is, on the part of speakers outside a given dialect area. New York speech is regarded by many as "unrefined" or "rough." The Southern dialect is stereotyped as "slow," and the drawl characteristic of the region is also looked down on by many people and is often ridiculed. In contrast, there are Americans who seem to have a great deal of appreciation for the way New Englanders speak. Interestingly, the Northern dialect draws very little comment, and the (North) Midland and Western dialects appear to be perceived as having the fewest stereotypes. This might have to do with the fact that it is these dialects in the United States that come closest to the Network Standard, the dialect (accent) that seems to have the most prestige.

British attitudes to American English

The British attitude to American English exhibits two contradictory features. One is that the British say, either explicitly or implicitly, that their English is superior to that of Americans (Finegan, 1980). This attitude is amply documented in the long history of the language debate between the British and Americans (see, for example, Finegan, 1980; Baron, 1982; Simpson, 1986). There is, however, a tendency in the relationship between British and American English that undercuts this view. In the twentieth century, American English has had a much greater influence on British English than vice versa. This is especially clear in the domain of vocabulary, as we will see in chapter ten. The outcome is an extremely complex sociolinguistic and cultural situation.

American attitudes to British English

The American attitude to American English is characterized by what Baron (1982) calls "linguistic insecurity," "the feeling that many Americans have that their language is somehow not quite up to snuff, that it is out of control, riddled with errors, or simply unskillful or gauche" (p. 227). Baron suggests that this linguistic insecurity has two sources: the notion of more or less prestigious dialects, on the one hand, and the exaggerated idea of correctness in language, on the other. Baron explains in the following way: "Two major forces in our culture cooperate to produce linguistic insecurity: the ranking of social and geographical dialects as superior and inferior, and an educational system based on a doctrine of correctness and purity in language that invariably conflicts with the observable facts of English usage" (p. 228). It might be additionally suggested that this American linguistic insecurity comes, historically, from a third source: a feeling of cultural inferiority (or insecurity), of which a special case is the belief that somehow American English is less good or proper than British English. Indeed, one can hear frequent comments made by Americans that indicate that they regard British English as a superior form of English.

Dialects and social problems

Many of the topics that have been discussed in this and the previous chapters are of course not only linguistic in nature. The topics of "standard" and "non-standard" (or vernacular) American Englishes and their relationship to each other, as well as that of the attitude to various dialects of American English and to British English often appear as social issues. Handling them in one way or another may have, and often does have, serious social consequences in contemporary American society. Such issues include whether speakers of vernacular

English should be taught to read standard English first at schools, whether tests for vernacular speakers should be given in standard or nonstandard English, whether the use of nonstandard dialectal forms in school should be regarded as a failure or a problem, whether lower scores on standardized tests by vernacular speakers also point to some kind of cognitive deficiency on the part of these speakers, whether students should or should not be taught a second dialect in school and, if yes, how it should be done, and many others. As is obvious from this list, all of the issues raise important social questions and consequences for American society. American linguists Walt Wolfram and Donna Christian provide an extensive survey of these and several other dialect-related issues in their highly readable *Dialects and Education* (Wolfram and Christian, 1989). We will return to one of these questions (the so-called "Ebonics" debate) in the next chapter.

study questions and activities

1. Read a recent book about the differences between men's and women's speech in the U.S. (e.g., Tannen's *You Just Don't Understand*). Summarize and discuss the differences.

2. Read a recent American novel or short story that features the American English of poor, uneducated whites. How does their English differ from the American English that is taught in schools?

3. Study the pronunciation of the leading newscasters on some major American TV channels or radio stations. Compare this with that of some of the "guests" in talk shows and so on on the same channels and stations. What do you find?

4. Try to find data on how young children in the U.S. talk and are talked to. How would you characterize the main features of their speech? Do these features resemble child language in your country?

5. What is your opinion of the *English Only* movement in the U.S.? Read up on this issue in available sources (one of these is the Internet). Discuss in class what arguments are offered in favor of it and against it.

6. Do you think that an Academy is needed to "regulate" the English language?

chapter 7

Ethnic dialects of American English

In this chapter, we will survey the most important ethnic dialects of American English. Particular attention will be paid to Chicano English and Black English, since these are the dialects spoken by the most people.

Hispanic American English

Hispanic Americans form the second largest ethnic minority in the United States (next to African Americans). Many of them are Cuban Americans who live primarily in concentrated communities in New York City and Union City in New Jersey and in the cities of Florida. A second large Hispanic American group is Puerto Ricans, American citizens who have been able to travel freely between their island and the United States for a long time. Characteristic of their English is the influence of two nonstandard forms of American English: Puerto Rican English and Black English. However, the largest group of Americans from a Hispanic background moved to the United States from Mexico. This has happened, and is still happening, mostly for economic reasons. The English of this group of people is called Chicano English. Chicanos live especially in the American Southwest – an area including Texas, New Mexico, Arizona, and California. Chicano English is the most uniform of the varieties of Hispanic English. For many people, it is the expression of ethnic solidarity.

Chicano English

The features that set off Chicano English from Standard American English are largely phonological, but syntactic and lexical differences can also be found. A close investigation of this ethnic dialect was done by Joyce Penfield and Jacob L. Ornstein-Galicia (1985). In this section I will present the major distinguishing characteristics of Chicano English on the basis of two summaries of the detailed study by Penfield and Ornstein-Galicia: Victoria Fromkin and Robert Rodman's *An Introduction to Language* and Stephan Gramley and Kurt Michael Pätzold's *A Survey of Modern English*. The latter work contains several additional references that may be useful for those who wish to pursue the topic further. Two points should be kept in mind for the discussion to follow. One is that Chicano English shares many features with other Hispanic dialects of English. The second is that many speakers of Chicano English are bilingual (that is, they can speak both Chicano English and Standard American English).

Phonological properties

1. In Chicano English, there is a tendency to devoice and harden final voiced consonants, like /z/. As a result of this process, the word *please* is pronounced like *police*, *easy* /izɪ/ becomes /isɪ/, and *guys* /gajz/ becomes /gajs/. /d/ is devoiced and becomes /t/, as when the word *hid* is pronounced /hɪt/.

2. The sound /v/, a labio-dental fricative, is realized as a bilabial stop [b] or a bilabial fricative [B].

3. The American English consonants /θ/ and /ð/ are pronounced differently in Chicano English. /θ/ is realized as /t/ and /ð/ as /d/. This occurs when /θ/ and /ð/ are word-initial. For example, *thing* /θɪŋ/ is pronounced /tɪŋ/ and *they* as /de/.

4. A commonly noted feature of Chicano English is what is called "word-final consonant simplification." This simplification of final consonant clusters occurs in a number of situations. A single consonant sound may be left out from the end of a word, as in *start*. Thus, *star* and *start* are pronounced in the same way: /star/. An entire suffix may be deleted, as is the case with the past tense morpheme /d/. A word like *towed* is pronounced /to/, as opposed to /tod/. The third person suffix /s/ may also be left out in cases like *loves*, which becomes /lav/.

5. Speakers of Chicano English produce alternation of /č/ and /š/. That is, words, like *check*, that have the initial sound /č/ are pronounced with /š/, resulting in /šɛk/, and words, like *show*, that have the initial sound /š/ are pronounced with /č/, resulting in /čo/. The Chicano pronunciation of *chicken* /čɪken/ is often /šɪken/. Since Spanish has no /š/, the use of the sound in words like *chicken* is the result of hypercorrection on the part of speakers of Chicano English.

6. Standard American English has eleven stressed vowel phonemes: /i/, /ɪ/, /e/, /ɛ/, /æ/, /u/, /ʊ/, /o/, /ɔ/, /a/, /ʌ/. Spanish has only five: /i/, /e/, /u/, /o/, /a/. Consequently, speakers of Chicano English use the five Spanish vowels for the eleven English vowels. This results in the merger of some vowel sounds. For example, Chicano speakers produce a merger of /ɪ/ and

/i/, yielding /i/. For example, the words *ship* and *sheep*, containing /ɪ/ and /i/, respectively, are pronounced with the vowel of *sheep*, that is, /i/.

7. Stress patterns often differ from those of Standard American English (SAE). This occurs especially in compounds and long words. For example, the word *'miniskirt*, which has the main stress word-initially in SAE, becomes *mini'skirt* in Chicano English, with the stress on the second part of the compound, and the word *an'ticipate* is pronounced *antici'pate* with final stress in Chicano English.

Another aspect of pronunciation differences is that Chicano English uses rising pitch in declarative sentences, whereas in SAE falling intonation is used.

Syntactic differences

1. In Chicano English a negative sentence may include a negative morpheme before the verb even if another negative appears, resulting in a "double negative." For example:

   I don't have any money.   I don have no money.
   I don't want anything.   I no want nothin.

2. The use of the comparative construction may also differ. The word *more* is often employed in the sense of "more often" in Chicano English.

   I use English more often.   More I use English.
   They use Spanish more often.   They use more Spanish.

Morphology

There are also some morphological differences. For example, Standard American English mass nouns are frequently used as count nouns in Chicano English. Thus, a Chicano speaker may talk about *vacations* (instead of *vacation*) and about *an applause* (instead of *applause*). In both cases mass nouns are turned into count nouns.

Lexical differences

Some lexical differences involve the meanings of words. For example, the verb *borrow* may replace *lend* in Chicano English. Thus the sentence *Lend me a pencil* in SAE becomes *Borrow me a pencil*. To take another example, the word *until* has a negative meaning in Chicano English. In a conversation, like **Q:** *Is X here?* **A:** *Until 3*, until 3 means "not until 3."

Chicano English borrows many words from Spanish. For example, the Spanish word *quinceañera* is used for a special party for a 15-year-old girl. Other words from Spanish include *comadre* ("godmother") and *compadre* ("godfather").

We can ask why Chicano English is characterized by these particular distinguishing features. It was noted in the section on phonology that the Spanish sound system (e.g., the smaller number of vowels in Spanish) has a role in shaping this dialect. This is an obvious reason for the Chicano phenomena mentioned above, but there may be more to the issue, as Jon Amastae (1992:210) notes: "Differences from other varieties are due to at least four factors operating over several generations: interference from Spanish, learning errors that have become established, contact with other dialects of English, and independent developments."

The Black English vernacular

Where does American Black English come from?

There are many varieties of Black English, including the Krio of Sierra Leone, Caribbean creole, the Gullah dialect on the coast of South Carolina, American Black English, and others (see Dillard, 1972; McCrum, *et al.*, 1986). The question we have to begin with is: Where does American Black English come from? Black English in the North American continent (called Black English Vernacular, or BEV for short) has a long and complex history. An early theory of the development of BEV was that BEV came from the regional dialects of the British slave-owners (variously identified as Irish, East Anglian, and West Country). According to this view, African slaves learned English from their colonial masters as a second language. Black children learned a variety of regional British English from their parents, and Black American English (BAE) is the final product of this process.

Today most linguists do not take this explanation seriously. Although there is no agreement among linguists on every issue of the development of BEV (concerning these controversies, see Bailey and Cukor-Avila, 1991), we can sketch a brief history that is more or less accepted. As was mentioned in the first chapter, the first slaves from Africa appeared in the colonies shortly after the first settlers. The city that had become the center of the "slave trade" was Charleston, South Carolina. Many slaves first arrived here and then they were transported inland to the plantations. However, some of the slaves stayed in the Charleston area, on what is called the Sea Islands. The creole language of the large black population in the region is called Gullah, spoken by about a quarter of a million people. It is a language that is probably most similar of all varieties of Black American English to the original creole English that was used in the New World and the West African Pidgin English of the earliest slaves. These slaves, who spoke different African languages (like Wolof), invented a form of English, West African Pidgin English, which incorporated many features from West African languages. Gullah could survive because it was relatively self-contained and isolated from the rest of the world. Its major feature is that it has preserved a large number of Africanisms. The basic finding concerning the history of BAE seems to be that BAE (and BEV) is the end product of a long process that began with West African Pidgin English, continued with Carribean creole, and reached the North American continent in the form of Gullah.

A large part of the development of BAE took place on the plantations of the South. For over 200 years "plantation talk" was the main form of Black English in North America. In the North, the Blacks adjusted their English much more to the English of the Whites. We will see that in the South a reverse process occurred. The life of Blacks on the plantations gave American English many of its words and phrases. One of these is *to sell down the river*. The idiom derives from the practice of slave-owners in, say, South Carolina to sell black slaves to the lower Mississippi regions, where conditions were usually the worst. Thus the sale of a black slave *down the river* was often regarded as a punishment. The present meaning of the idiom, "to take advantage of someone," reflects this. After the freeing of the slaves by Lincoln, many Blacks moved north to the big industrial cities. This event also gave rise to a phrase, this one being limited to Black use: *to sell out to the Yankees*. The meaning of the expression is simply "to move to a northern industrial area" (Clarence, 1994).

With this development a new phase began in the history of Black American English. Words from BAE entered the lexicon of white Americans. Most of these words had to do with aspects of Black culture and had their roots in the plantations. At the end of the nineteenth and the beginning of the twentieth century, white America got to know jazz and the blues, and in dance the cake-walk, the jitterbug, and later the break. The big cities of the north were thriving with black culture, especially in music and other forms of entertainment. In addition, a new black ghetto culture appeared in the big industrial cities, which gave rise to an almost new language. Much of this language became a part of American slang, and was imitated by several other subcultures, such as the hippies.

The black civil rights movement intensified after the second world war. In fact, the phrase *civil rights* came into use during this period (in the sense of the rights guaranteed by various Amendments to the U.S. Constitution). This was also the time when the word *Negro* came to be replaced by the word *Black* with reference to Afro-Americans. The new concept of "Blackness" and the new use of the word *Black* in the sixties spawned several new concepts and the phrases that denote them: *Black power, Black studies, Black history,* and, last but not least, *Black English*. Other words that entered general American English in the period had to do with what the civil rights activists were fighting for. One such thing was busing, the transportation of school children to schools outside their neighborhood in order to desegregate the schools. The word *busing* is well known to all Americans.

But what are the major characteristics of Black American English? I offer a brief survey of these below.

Characteristics of Black English vernacular

The survey is based on descriptions by Baugh (1992), Gramley and Pätzold (1992), and Fromkin and Rodman (1993). There seems to be general agreement among these and other authors concerning what the main characteristics of Black American English are. The examples presented below derive largely from these authors, who in turn often take them from earlier work by Labov, Baugh, and several others.

Phonological properties

1. A characteristic of BEV is /r/ deletion. /r/ deletion is common except before a vowel. Thus word pairs like *guard – god, nor – gnaw, sore – saw, poor – pa, fort – fought, court – caught* are pronounced identically. This feature makes BEV non-rhotic and thus similar to Southern, New England, and British English pronunciation.

2. The /l/ is also deleted in BEV under certain phonological circumstances. This occurs at the end of words and before labials. Examples include *toll – toe* and *all – awe* for the end of words and *help-hep* for labials like /p/.

3. The phonetic process "consonant cluster simplification," mentioned already above in connection with Chicano English, is yet another feature of BEV. This occurs especially at the end of words and if one of the consonants is /t/, /d/, /s/, or /z/. Thus in BEV we get pronunciations like /mɛn/ for *mend*, /pæs/ for *past*, /dɛs/ for *desk*, and /tɛs/ for *test*. Past tense endings are also absent in such clusters, as in *passed* /pæs/, *talked* /taŋk/, and *looked* /lʊk/. The process is not fully productive, though. While *paste* is /pes/, *chased* is not /čes/ but /čest/. Consonant cluster simplification is not a unique property of BEV; it occurs in many other dialects of (American) English, including Standard (American) English. However, the feature is most frequent in Black English.

4. Syllabic /n/ replaces /ŋ/ in *ing*-forms. Thus we get /sɪngɪn/ for *singing* and /wəkɪn/ for *working*. This is one of the best known features of BEV pronunciation, but again it is not unique to it. It can be found, for example, in several varieties of Southern and Midland dialects.

5. The SAE consonants /ð/ and /θ/ in word-initial position become /d/ and /t/ in BEV. Thus *that day* is /dæt de/ and *I think* is /a tɪn/ in BEV. In other positions the /θ/ is pronounced /f/ and the /ð/ is pronounced /v/, as in the words *Ruth* /ruf/ and *brother* /brʌvə/, respectively. The word *south*, which is /sawθ/ in SAE, is /sawf/ in BEV.

6. BEV pronunciation does not distinguish between SAE /ɛ/ and /ɪ/ before a nasal. The resulting sound in BEV is closer to /ɪ/, as in *pen* and *pin*, where the BEV pronunciation would be something like /pɪn/. This lack of distinction between /ɪ/ and /ɛ/ before nasals is also characteristic of many regional dialects, such as the Midland and Southern dialects.

7. There is also a lack of distinction between the sounds /aj/ and /aw/, in that the diphthongs become the monophthong /a/, as in the words *why* and *wow*, where the resulting pronunciation is /wa/. As another example, consider the pronunciation of *I think* in item five above.

8. A similar process of monophthongization occurs in the case of the diphthong /ɔj/, which becomes /ɔ/, as in *boil* and *boy*, which are pronounced alike as /bɔ/.

Syntactic properties

1. A widely known syntactic property of BEV is the use of double negatives. Thus, in BEV we find sentences such as *He ain't got no clothes on* or *She don't know nothing*. However, as we have seen in this and previous chapters, this is not an exclusive property of BEV, but can be found in several non-standard dialects of English.

2. Existential *it* can replace existential *there*. The SAE sentence *There is no food in the house* would be *It ain't no food in the house* in BEV.

3. Characteristic of BEV is the omission of the plural, possessive, and singular present 's. Thus speakers of BEV produce sentences like the following:

   He got ten cent. (instead of the plural *cents*)

That's my brother book. (instead of *brother's*)

She like new clothes. (instead of *likes*)

This process is also operative in the case of the past -*ed* suffix, yielding such past tense forms as /wak/, instead of the SAE /wakt/ for *walked*.

4. Another commonly recognized feature of BEV is the deletion of *be* from sentences. For example:

SAE:	BEV:
He is nice/He's nice.	He nice.
They are mine/They're mine.	They mine.
I am going to do it/I'm gonna do it.	I gonna do it.

5. Equally well known is the feature called "habitual *be*." The use of *be* in the habitual sense can often be "translated" with such words as *always, generally*, or *sometimes* that denote habitual occurrences of events. However, when there is no *be* in the sentence, it can indicate that the sentence applies to a situation *now*. The following examples from Fromkin and Rodman (1993:290) make this clear:

(a) John be happy.	"John is always happy."
(b) John happy.	"John is happy now."
(a) He be late.	"He is habitually late."
(b) He late.	"He is late this time."
(a) Do you be tired?	"Are you generally tired?"
(b) You tired?	"Are you tired now?"

The sentences marked (a) exemplify the habitual use of *be*, whereas those marked (b) indicate situations that obtain at the time of speaking only.

6. A meaning similar to habitual *be* can be expressed with the aspectual usage of the word *steady*. This can be done before progressive verbs or with heavy stress in sentence-final position. For example:

We be steady rapping. (progressive verb follows)
We be rapping 'steady. (sentence-final position)

The meaning of both sentences is "We are always talking."

7. When *be* is present in the sentence, it is often not conjugated. This is called the "invariant *be.*" This *be* remains the same in the singular and plural and in all persons. This is the basis of the joke in a cartoon in which a character says: *I be, You be, He be, We be, Y'all be, They be. I love conjugating verbs in jive!* The word *jive* is here used as a synonym of BEV.

8. In BEV the auxiliary *do* can replace *be* in a negative statement, such as *It don't all be her fault,* corresponding to *It isn't always her fault* in SAE.

9. *Been* is often stressed when it is used to refer to long-standing events with long pasts in such sentences as *I 'been seen dat movie* and *She 'been had that hat.* The SAE sentences are *I have seen that movie* and *She has had that hat for a long time.*

10. Intention can be expressed with the particle *a,* as in the example *I'm a shoot you,* meaning "I am going to shoot you."

Vocabulary

1. The vocabulary of BAE was, and still is, a major source of American slang, as we will see in chapter nine. But in addition to being a source for slang, it also contributed words that form a part of the vocabulary of standard American English. These words include *jazz, blues, ragtime, boogie woogie, jive, rhythm and blues,* to mention just a few. (Holloway and Vass, 1997, is an interesting recent collection of words of African origin in American English.)

2. Many BEV words have their sources in West African languages. Words with West African roots include *goober* ("peanut"), *yam* ("sweet potato"), *tote* ("to carry"), *buckra* ("white man"). (In discussing the African origins of many Black English and contemporary American English words and phrases Holloway and Vass, 1997, attempt to provide the precise African languages from which the words and phrases come.)

3. BEV has many pejorative terms for whites, just as American English has many pejorative words for African Americans. BEV words for whites inlude *honkie, ofay,* and *whitey.* According to Clarence (1994), the first two have African origins.

Similarity of BAE to White Southern American English

It is commonly observed that BEV is similar in sound to the English of white southerners. This raises the question of how this similarity came about. Whose English influenced whose? Did the Blacks acquire the accent of the Whites, or did the Whites acquire the accent of the Blacks? For a long time it was assumed that it was the slaves who had learned the English of the white Southerners. This prejudice is amply documented by McCrum, *et al.* (1986) throughout the nineteenth and the first half of the twentieth century. More recently, however, a much less prejudiced view has been expressed on the part of several linguists studying BAE concerning the relationship between the two dialects. In the new view, BAE is seen as having influenced southern white talk, rather than the other way around. There are a number of reasons for this influence. First, the black and white children typically grew up together up to the age of six. We know from the study of language acquisition that these are crucially important years in learning a language. Since the white children were greatly outnumbered by black children in these linguistically most formative years, the influence of the black children's linguistic habits was stronger than those of the whites. Second, most white babies and children were nursed and raised by black women. This must have have produced a very significant influence on the language of white children. Third, it was also observed early that it was especially Southern white women whose speech was changed by black linguistic forms. This is because it was the white women who mixed most with the black slaves on the plantations. The white women in turn spent more time raising their own children than the men. This may also have reinforced the speech habits that the white children were exposed to in the company of black children.

Black speaking styles

The Black community has a rich system of verbal rituals. These are speech events that are governed by rules. Many of these are linguistically creative performances. Originally, rapping was voluble and eloquent talk. Jiving is deceiving the whites through verbal trickery. It is a form of deceitful, insincere talk. One of the best known verbal games is *playing the dozens*. The dozens is ritually insulting another's mother. It is also called the dirty dozens, sounding, or signifying. In this verbal game, two black boys ritually insult each other's mother, and the loser is the player who first gives in to anger. The object of the game is to test emotional strength. If, as a result of the insults thrown at you, you explode in anger, you have failed the test. The winner is the participant who can stay calm in the face of the most offensive insults. Here's a short example taken from Kochman (1981):

Pretty Black: "What'chu laughing 'bout Nap with your funky mouth smelling like dog shit."

Nap: "Your mama motherfucker."

Pretty Black: "Your funky mama too."

Nap (strongly): "It takes twelve barrels of water to make a steamboat run; it takes an elephant's dick to make your Grandmammy come; she been elephant fucked, camel fucked and hit side the head with your Grandpappy's nuts." (p. 55)

Many of these verbal rituals go back to African origins. (Note, however, that verbal rituals are characteristic of oral-based societies in general.) The popularity of the rituals reflects the traditional fondness of Afro-Americans for good verbal (as opposed to written) performance. People with better than average skills in verbal performance are highly respected. The language of the games and rituals is highly creative and imaginative. The creative and imaginative character of Black speech may have been a major source for the inventiveness and imaginativeness of American English in general (see, for example, Dillard, 1985 and 1992).

The debates surrounding Black English

In the 1970s, Black American English became a major issue in a debate that is still going on in the United States. Black activists wanted to have Black American English recognized in schools with black children. Their argument was based on some newly available linguistic findings coming from such eminent linguists as William Labov, William Stewart, and J. L. Dillard. These and other experts argued that Black English is just as systematic and "logical" as Standard American English. Several Black activists took up this argument and demanded not only a recognition of civil rights but also language rights. If Black English is just as good as SAE, then, they claimed, it should be taken into account in planning the school curricula. In a landmark court decision in 1979 the demand was first met in the Ann Arbor school district.

A different but related debate flared up in the United States in the late 1990s. It became known to many Americans as the "Ebonics" debate. (The term Ebonics derives from a combination of *ebony* and *phonics*.) The controversy started when the Oakland (Calif.) school board passed a resolution to treat Black English (Ebonics) as a second language, a language that is different from standard English. The idea behind this was that if Ebonics is regarded as a language, federal funds that are available for bilingual programs could also be requested by schools where there are students whose first or home language is Black English. The goal was to teach students in their primary language (Ebonics) and to help such students master standard English by means of teaching them in their home language. This was considered necessary because students whose home language was Black English performed below every other group in their studies, including English. There was a general outcry against the resolution. The main counterargument was that Black English (or Ebonics) is not a language different from English but a dialect or variety of it. This view is justified. As we saw, despite the many systematic differences much of the vocabulary, grammar, and phonology of Black English is shared by other varieties of English, including Standard American English. As a result of the backlash, its proponents qualified the original resolution.

Nevertheless, some of the methodological aspects of how to help students with Black English as their home language master standard American English seem useful. In certain schools of the Oakland school district some teachers experimented with using Ebonics in the teaching of standard English. They used a kind of "contrastive analysis," in which students were asked to compare linguistic features of texts in Ebonics with their standard English counterparts. For example, in the course of reading a story they asked students if a certain form or construction was in Black English or standard English. (One example of this was the syntactic construction *I be Flossie Finley*, a construction mentioned above.) The teachers reported definite improvement in the oral skills of the students who were taught English in this manner. (Wolfram and Christian, 1989, provide a very accessible account of the role, place and "problematics" of Black English in language and non-language education in general.)

The debate whether Ebonics or Standard American English should be used in schools with students whose home language is the Black English vernacular is likely to continue to rage. A narrowly sociolinguistc examination is not really helpful, no matter how objective or well-meaning it aims to be. Interestingly enough, large segments of the Afro-American community reject the idea of the use of the Black English vernacular in the schools. This situation suggests that without first understanding clearly the symbolic significance and function of Ebonics to the Afro-American community, as well as understanding the symbolic significance and function of Standard American English to the same community, it will be difficult to come to general agreement concerning this issue.

study questions and activities

1. Read a novel by a well known African American author that is about the life of African Americans in the U.S. Make note of the linguistic phenomena that reflect Black English. Summarize what you find.

2. Do the same with a Chicano author.

3. Do the same with an author you choose who represents a third ethnic group in the U.S.

4. Discuss the issue of the possible symbolic significance of Black English for African Americans. Are there any such ethnic dialects in your own country? What possible symbolic significance does their language have for them?

5. Read up on the Ebonics issue (one of your sources can be the Internet again – using Ebonics as the word you want to do a search on). What do you think about the issue? Discuss your views in class.

chapter 8

Style in American English

So far we have looked at varieties of American English that are defined by such factors as geographic location, socioeconomic status, age, gender, ethnic group, and others. These factors characterize the users of American English, in that all speakers are brought up in a particular geographic location, are members of a socioeconomic class, go through a number of age periods in the course of their lives, and are born to a race or particular ethnic group. In other words, these factors that define regional, social, ethnic, and other varieties are more or less inevitable from the perspective of speakers. The linguistic term that was used for varieties of this kind was "dialect." But there is another kind of variation in American English (and of course in other languages as well). This kind of variation depends not so much on inevitable factors such as the above, but on various factors that make up communicative situations, that is, the situations in which we speak, write, or communicate in other ways with others. The most important factors that are elements of communicative situations include the setting, the subject matter, the medium, and the audience. All of these can define certain situational styles in American English. It should be noticed that these styles depend primarily on aspects of use, not on inevitable characteristics of the user. This kind of use-related variation can be called "situational style." Each speaker of a language has a number of such situational styles at his or her disposal. For example, speakers of American English use a different style when they talk to their friends and when they talk to their teachers or doctors. The situational styles that a speaker has available for use in various communicative situations is called his or her "linguistic repertory." In any given communicative situation speakers, of course, use a situationally appropriate style as part of a regional or social dialect.

Similarly to dialects, situational styles are characterized by a variety of linguistic features. It is convenient to classify these as phonological, lexical, and syntactic.

We begin our discussion of situationally-defined styles in American English with setting and then go on to subject matter, medium, audience, and some related issues in the study of style.

Setting

Several situational syles can be defined by the setting of the communicative situation, i.e., social context. Users of American English adjust the way they speak or write according to the social context. They speak and write differently at home, in the office, at a ballgame, while giving a lecture to a large audience at a university, or at a state ceremony. Some of these call for an "elevated" or "refined" style, while others for a more "down-to-earth" or "simple" style.

What counts as elevated and refined or down-to-earth and simple is of course a matter of conventions, and the conventions might change from culture to culture, region to region, or from one historical period to another. For example, the dominant refined style of the nineteenth century in the United States was a highly literary style that would sound pompous or inflated to contemporary ears. To provide a sense of some of the characteristics of this style, below is an excerpt from a speech delivered in 1863 at the commemoration of a cemetery for Civil War soldiers in Gettysburg. The speaker was a professional orator from New England, Edward Everett. We can assume that he was invited to give the speech on this important occasion because he was thought to possess the qualities and skills needed to be a good orator at the time.

> Lord Bacon, in "the true marshalling of the sovereign degrees of honor," assigns the first place to "the Condirotores Imperiorum, founders of States and Commonwealths"; and truly, to build up from the discordant elements of our nature, the passions, the interests and the opinions of the individual man, the rivalries of family, clan and tribe, the influences of climate and geographical position, the accidents of peace and war accumulated for ages – to build up from those oftentimes warring elements a well-compacted, prosperous and powerful State, if it were to be accomplished by one effort or in one generation would require a more than mortal skill. (from Bryson, 1994:79-80)

As Bryson notes, the speech was highly acclaimed in the press afterwards, and again, we may assume that it was well received because it displayed the linguistic features and accomplished the goals that were associated with a public speech on such a ceremonial occasion as the consecration of a state cemetery during the Civil War. We can observe several linguistic features of this sentence. What is immediately obvious is that the sentence is extremely long. Indeed, one wonders how the 15,000 people present were able to understand it at all. The speech lasted for roughly two hours and consisted of about 1,500 sentences, most of which were equally long. Structurally speaking, the sentence is exceedingly complex; it contains several subordinate clauses and parenthetical remarks, and the relationship among these is anything but clear. In addition, it makes references to a number of historical events, but it does not clarify why those events are relevant to the occasion at hand. It also uses a highly flowery vocabulary that sounds pompous by today's standards. All in all, we can be sure that these linguistic features contributed to the success of the speech. An important state ceremony called for length (in speech and sentence size), complexity (in structure), grandeur (in reference), and floweriness (in vocabulary), rather then shortness, simplicity, mundaneness, and directness.

Sometimes it is possible to capture the moment of a historical shift in the paradigm that people adopt in handling the different stylistic needs of social situations. Up until the middle of the nineteenth century there was practically no alternative to the elevated, literarary style to be used on an important public occasion. However, in 1863 all that changed in American English. This is because there was another speaker at the commemoration in Gettysburg. His name was Abraham Lincoln and he gave the following speech:

> Four score and seven years ago our fathers brought forth on this continent a new nation, conceived in liberty and dedicated to the proposition that all men are created equal.
>
> Now we are engaged in a great civil war, testing whether that nation or any nation so conceived and so dedicated can long endure. We are met on a great battlefield of that war. We come to dedicate a portion of that field as a final resting place for those who here gave their lives that that nation might live. It is altogether fitting and proper that we should do this.
>
> But, in a larger sense, we cannot dedicate – we cannot consecrate – we cannot hallow – this ground. The brave men, living and dead, who struggled here have consecrated it far above our poor power to add or detract. The world will little note nor long remember what we say here, but it can never forget what they did here. It is for us, the living, rather, to be dedicated here to the unfinished work which they who fought here have thus far so nobly advanced.
>
> It is rather for us to be here dedicated to the great task remaining before us – that from these honored dead we take increased devotion to that cause for which they gave the last full measure of devotion; that we here highly resolve that these dead shall not have died in vain; that this nation, under God, shall have a new birth of freedom; that the government of the people, by the people, for the people shall not perish from the earth.

This speech indicated a turning point in the development of situational styles in America because it challenged everything about what a speech should be like on a serious and highly significant public occasion (Wills, 1992, provides a detailed analysis). It was short, it was simple, it was, in a sense, mundane and down-to-earth, and it was to the point throughout. Indeed, we can say that it was the exact antithesis of the speech by Edward Everett before him. Lincoln's speech had anything but a warm reception in the press. The *Chicago Times* called Lincoln's sentences "silly, flat and dishwatery." And Lincoln himself thought it was a failure. Nevertheless, this speech, which came to be known as the *Gettysburg Address,* later became one of the greatest American speeches. Now we know why. It was successful because it was short, simple, down-to-earth, and to the point. Lincoln's genius was not that he spoke this way. After all, he came from the frontier where this way of speaking was the norm. His genius was that he had the courage to speak this way on this particular occasion – a state ceremony. In short, Lincoln elevated a regional dialect characterized by brevity, simplicity, down-to-earthness, and directness to the status of "elevated style." As we will see in later chapters, these features have been preserved to the present day and have become the hallmarks of American English.

Subject matter

Many subject matters require their own style. The styles related to subject matter, or topic, are most typically – though not exclusively – defined by a specialized vocabulary. Speakers of American English are surrounded by many such styles, including legal language, the language used by doctors, the languages of sports, the language of computers, to mention just a few. Several of these "languages" have acquired special names. Thus, we can, for instance, talk about legalese and computerese. (Several ideas and examples in the remainder of the chapter will be taken from Zwicky, 1980.)

These subject matter-related languages, or styles (though the everyday meaning of "style" seems less appropriate here), are sometimes also called technical languages or professional jargons, which have certain interesting characteristics. Perhaps the most obvious of these is that jargons are very clear and precise for those on the inside. To achieve clear and precise reference, subtle distinctions are made – distinctions that are not made in ordinary language. For example, professional decorators often use terms for various shades of red, such as *garnet*, *magenta*, *vermillion*. Further well-known examples include the rich and detailed terminologies used by horse and dog breeders or collectors of all kinds.

The terminologies used by specialists are such that while the terms are sensible and obvious for insiders, they are often irritatingly incomprehensible for outsiders. This happens even if, in addition to the specialist term, there is an ordinary word for a thing. For example, a doctor may say that we have *dermatitis* even though we simply have a *rash*. While the meaning of the term is obvious for doctors, it is not transparent for most patients.

This raises the question why it is necessary at all for professionals to use elusive terminologies. One reason is that, sometimes, jargon is used to impress people. Thus doctors might use *rhinoplasty* for what we would call a *nose job* or *rhinitis* for a *runny nose* or *dermatitis* for a *rash*. The same applies to the language used by lawyers. Possibly, if these professionals employed ordinary language, we wouldn't be sure they know more about their job than we do.

Medium

When we use language, we either speak or write. The American linguist Douglas Biber hypothesized that several linguistic features tend to co-occur in various genres, some of which come from speech and some from writing (Biber, 1988). He designed a large-scale study in the course of which he analyzed a huge corpus with the help of computer. He found that certain linguistic features do indeed cluster together along various dimensions. For example, he found that the following features co-occur in his corpus, characterizing different kinds of genres or texts (taken from Finegan and Besnier, 1989):

Set A:
first and second person pronouns (*I, me, we, us, you*)
that-deletion from subordinate clauses (*She said he lied.*)
private verbs (*think, consider, assume*)
demonstrative pronouns (*this, that, these*)
emphatics (*really, for sure*)
hedges (*kind of, more or less, maybe*)
sentence relatives (*Then he lied, which bothered her a lot.*)
sentence-final prepositions (*the teacher I told you about*)

As Finegan and Besnier point out, these features occur together because they characterize a particular kind of speech situation, one in which the two communicating parties share a context. There is a specific speaker and addressee typically in a face-to-face situation, they normally express their personal views and emotions concerning the topics they discuss, and they are familiar with the situation (though they are not necessarily face-to-face with each other) in which the communication takes place. The situation is also informal as suggested by the presence of the last feature: the use of sentence-final prepositions.

Set B:
frequent nouns and prepositions
longer words
lexical variety
attributive adjectives (*the tall buildings*)

These features characterize a situation in which the exchange of information is most important. As can be seen from the lack of the use of personal and demonstrative pronouns, hedges, emphatics, and private verbs, this is a speech situation in which the speaker and the addressee are not "involved," that is, they do not interact. In this type of situation, the chief emphasis is on sharing information without the two parties interacting.

As Biber suggests, the two sets of features represent the end poles of a single dimension of stylistic variation; namely, the "interactional (or involved) vs. informational" dimension. Different kinds of texts and discourses can be placed along the dimension. Some of them will be "more interactional or involved," while others "more informational." Thus, for example, telephone conversations, face-to-face conversations, personal letters, spontaneous speeches, and interviews are (to a decreasing degree) closer to the interactional end of the dimension, and official documents, academic prose, science fiction, and prepared speeches are (again to a decreasing degree) closer to the informational end.

Most importantly for our purposes here, we find that most of the kinds of text and discourse that are closer to the interactional end are spoken ones and most of those closer to the informational end are written ones. Biber's study provides us with an excellent way of distinguishing the major linguistic features of speech and writing. His study also shows that although a genre is written its features may be more characteristic of interactional style (a case in point is personal letters); and although a genre is spoken, its features may be more characteristic of informational style (e.g., prepared speeches). Nevertheless, it is clear that the linguistic features associated with interactional style predominantly characterize spoken genres, and the features associated with informational style predominantly characterize written genres.

I will make further use of Biber's work in the second part of the book, where I will discuss the unique features of American English.

Audience

The final significant factor that we may consider here in the definition of styles is the audience. This means that the social relationship between speaker and listener can influence the way we speak. We vary our speech style according to who our communication partner is. It is customary to distinguish several styles that are defined by the speaker's relationship to his or her audience. These include informal (or casual), formal, and neutral styles of speech. This three-way classification is sometimes enlarged to include more styles. For example, in an influential study, the American linguist Martin Joos (1967:11) proposed a five-way classification: intimate, casual, consultative, formal, and frozen. It is important to note, as Joos points out, that these are all "usage-scales of native central English" (p. 11). That is, they all characterize the linguistic repertory of "mainstream" native speakers of English. While recognizing the value of the five-way classification proposed by Joos, for simplicity's sake, in the following I will be describing some of the major features of the commonly employed three-way system: informal (casual), neutral (consultative, somewhat careful), and formal (highly careful).

Vocabulary

Our characterization of the three styles begins with the discussion of vocabulary. A major feature of informal style is the extensive use of slang. Slang words almost routinely come up in conversations between friends, close peers, and the like. Wherever there is an intimate relationship between the speaker and hearer, the use of slang is justified and sometimes even required for the sake of demonstrating and maintaining "solidarity" between the parties. (We will discuss American slang in the next chapter in detail.)

Words from different styles may apply to a single referent (or thing). This is commonly the case. Take, for example, cars. In American English we can refer to this class of referents with a variety of terms, such as *wheels, car,* and *automobile. Wheels* is a slang term, *car* is neutral style, and *automobile* is slightly formal. In this case, we have a stylistically neutral term among the words that refer to the same thing. However, in other cases there is no such neutral way of referring to something. This happens especially commonly with body wastes, bodily functions, and sexuality as referents. For example, in American English there is the slang expression *to take a leak* (among many others), the vulgar term *to piss,* the formal and euphemistic word *to void,* the formal verb *to urinate,* and the extremely formal word *to micturate.* It seems, then, that American English does not have a stylistically neutral term for passing water (which is of course another formal and euphemistic expression).

It is another tendency in English that short forms of a word are generally informal (at least at the beginning of their use), while the full form is neutral or formal. A few decades ago *TV* and *fridge* were regarded as informal, while their full forms *television* and *refrigerator* as neutral or formal. Today, however, *TV* and *fridge* seem to be neutral terms.

The formality scale applies not only to what are called "open system" items, such as nouns and verbs, but also to "closed system" items, such as conjunctions and sentence adverbs. Some conjunctions and sentence adverbs are formal, some neutral, and some informal in American English. Examples of formal ones include *ergo, therefore, perhaps, nonetheless,* and *thus*; neutral ones include *and, but, or,* and *anyway*; and informal ones include *anyways* and *at any rate. Maybe* is neutral for some speakers of American English and informal for others.

Pronunciation

The various audience-related styles are also revealed, or associated, by phonological features, that is, features of pronunciation. One of the most systematic studies in this regard was done by Labov (1966, 1972) in the course of his work on the linguistic stratification of English in New York City. Let us now take another look at this.

In his studies, Labov compared data that he obtained in the following four ways: from casual speech, from the reading of a paragraph, from the reading of lists of unrelated words, and from the reading of paired words (such as *God – guard*). These ways of collecting data represent different degrees of formality, ranging from very informal (casual) to very formal (very careful). The production of casual speech requires hardly any attention on the part of the speaker, the reading of a paragraph requires some, the reading of a list of words more, and the reading of paired words requires a considerable amount of attention on the part of the reader. Given these different contexts for the production of speech, the subjects of Labov's research used /r/ more often in the more formal situations (contexts) and less often in the less formal situations (like casual speech). This finding was consistent for all speakers, regardless of socioeconomic class. In other words, both upper-middle and working-class speakers used less /r/ in less formal situations and more /r/ in more formal situations. This was of course a relative finding: whereas in the case of upper-middle-class speakers the increase from very informal casual speech to the very formal reading of paired words was 20% to 60%, in the case of working class subjects it was 10% to 30%. The important point is that both increased their production of /r/ as a result of the increase in the formality of context.

Written texts can also be more or less formal. A personal letter to a good friend is usually informal, while a letter of application is mostly highly formal. One characteristic of informal written style is the frequent use of contractions. Contractions often indicate varying degrees of informality. Thus, in very informal style we can often observe contractions such as *he'd'a* (he would have) and in casual style contractions such as *he'd've* (he would have). Some contractions may show up in neutral or careful style as well (such as *he'd* for "he would" or "he had"). Interestingly, children often write "*of*" for "have" because these words sound the same in casual speech.

Syntax

Finally, let us turn to the characterization of different styles in the area of syntax, that is, the arrangement of words in a sentence. I will only give illustrative differences here, rather than provide a description of all the syntactic properties of informal, neutral (or consultative), and formal styles. I will discuss only casual and formal style in this section, since these are the two stylistically-marked cases.

Casual style

We can begin with informal or casual style. One syntactic property of this style is what linguists call "ellipsis." This means that certain words are deleted from the complete sentence. For example, the pronouns *I* and *you* often disappear from the beginning of sentences (that is, in subject position). Another case is where *have* and *be* drop out in their uses as auxiliaries. For instance, the sentence *What are you doing?* frequently becomes *Whatcha doin'?*

Another syntactic property of casual style is "topicalization," a syntactic process in which the object of a sentence is moved to the front of the sentence. Thus, in casual style we often find sentences such as *That I'd like to see!*, which derives from the stylistically more or less neutral sentence *I'd like to see that!*

As a final illustration of the syntactic features of casual style, in this style the clauses of a sentence are more often linked by co-ordinating conjunctions such as *and* than in more formal styles. This is especially noticeable when children relate an event.

Formal style

One syntactic feature of more formal styles in American English is the use of the subjunctive. Here are two examples to illustrate this syntactic construction: *He demands that you leave at once* (for *He demands that you should leave at once*) and *I hereby request that this be done* (for *I hereby request that this should be done*). The frequent use of the subjunctive is especially characteristic of American journalistic writing, while sentences with *should* are more typical of British English.

In more formal styles, we find a preponderance of subordinate clauses, as opposed to structures of co-ordination that we saw above for casual style. Subordinate clauses represent a higher degree of syntactic (and cognitive) complexity. It thus makes sense that subordination is used mainly in formal styles that allow the speaker and hearer more time to produce and understand the more complex structures.

The subject of a sentence can be a "clausal subject." This simply means that the subject of the sentence is a clause. Clausal subjects are especially common in formal styles. We can illustrate this with a sentence such as *For a man of his age to divorce is a sure mark of immaturity.*

Characteristic of formal styles is the syntactic pattern where there is a negative adverb in sentence-initial position. An example is: *Never have I seen such a sight.* In a neutral style this would be *I've never seen such a sight.*

A well-known feature of formal style is the use of structures that signal higher levels of politeness in making requests. Thus, the construction *Would you mind closing the door (please)?* is more polite and formal than the imperative *Close the door, please.*

Mixing styles

Although there are prescriptive rules that prohibit the mixing of different styles in English, style-mixing is a fact of life, not only in the United States but in most other cultures. Style-mixing can be deliberate or unintentional.

Deliberate style-mixing occurs where speakers try to achieve certain communicative goals by relying on several disparate styles in the same speech situation. One such goal can be persuasion. If, for example, politicians want to get the nomination of their constituencies in a rural or working-class area, they often resort to "folksy" words, sentence structures, and the like in their speeches. Another example is provided by some parents or teachers who try to imitate the linguistic habits of their children and students. As we know, this is a dangerous strategy because it is very difficult to use appropriately, say, the slang words of teenagers.

Americans, just like people in other cultures, also mix styles in an unintentional way. As a matter of fact, however, Americans are often made fun of for doing this by other speakers of English, especially the British. The assumption here is that Americans are somehow less refined than others in keeping their styles distinct and homogeneous. This observation is also extended beyond linguistic habits, and often applies to, for example, the ways American dress. We will return to the issue of style-mixing in chapter sixteen.

study questions and activities

1. If you are an internet "buff," describe the main features of the language used on the internet. In what ways is it different from general American English? Which of the words have entered general American usage and what new senses have they acquired?

2. Read (a few passages of) the Declaration of Independence or the Constitution. How can you characterize them in terms of their style?

3. Go to see an American movie that features two close friends in it. Try to describe the language they use in terms of pronunciation, vocabulary, and grammar.

4. Find examples of different kinds of letters: some letters to the editor in American newspapers or magazines, some official letters that you or somebody else received from an American institution (such as a bank, telephone company, etc.), and some personal letters you received from an American friend. Compare the characteristics of each of the three kinds of letters in light of what you learned in the chapter.

5. How would you rank the following words in order of their formality-informality? (They may not mean precisely the same thing.) *Drunk, plastered, high, inebriated, boozed, bombed, tight, juiced.* In addition, what subtle differences of meaning can you discover between them?

chapter 9

American slang

Slang occupies the extreme informal end of the informal-formal (or casual-careful) scale that we saw in the previous chapter. The "style of slang" makes itself manifest mostly in a distinctive vocabulary. It is this distinctive vocabulary to which we now turn in our characterization of American dialects and styles.

American slang is a major hallmark of American English. To understand what makes American slang unique and a major part of the American experience, we have to look at how it emerged, what its sources are, and which subject matters it deals with. American slang, similar to American English in general, varies both regionally and socially, but it also has a large shared part. An example of descriptions of regional slang is *The City in Slang* by Irving Lewis Allen (1993), who provides a fascinating account of New York City slang, and an example of descriptions of social variation in American slang is Connie Eble's widely acclaimed book *Slang and Sociability* (1996) and her other works (such as Eble, 1998). Despite the existence of such variation in American slang, in this chapter we will primarily deal with features of what can be called "general American slang."

History of the study of English slang

The first slang dictionary of the English language was published in London in 1785. The author was Francis Grose, a soldier and champion drinker. He gave his dictionary the title *The Classical Dictionary of the Vulgar Tongue*. These facts show several interesting things about the study of slang. Slang was primarily regarded as a matter of what is vulgar in language, a view that quite a few people share even today. In addition, the first slang dictionaries were often done by amateur linguists, who had real life experience with the use of slang, as Grose's example as "soldier and champion drinker" indicates. Finally, the interest in slang in English goes back at least two hundred years, which is a long time in the history of slang dictionaries, but a short time considering the existence of the English language.

The first comprehensive slang dictionary of English, which contained much more than vulgarities, was produced by John S. Farmer and William E. Henley. Their dictionary was called *Slang and Its Analogues Past and Present*. It appeared in seven volumes with close to a thousand pages between 1890 and 1904.

The first definitive slang dictionary of the English language appeared in 1937. Its author was Eric Partridge and he gave his dictionary the title *A Dictionary of Slang and Unconventional English*. As the title indicates, Partridge had a very broad conception of slang, including any unconventional language. This dictionary was updated several times and its eighth edition was recently published.

The authors mentioned so far are all British and their works concentrate mainly on British English. The first major American slang dictionary that was widely recognized as such was published in 1960. *The Dictionary of American Slang* was edited by Harold Wentworth and Stuart Berg Flexner. Revised editions came out in 1967 and 1975. Since then several new American slang dictionaries have been made and most of them draw heavily on the work of Flexner and Wentworth (for example, Robert Chapman's *New Dictionary of American Slang*). A thesaurus of American slang that represents an incredible amount of work and contains over one hundred thousand slang words and expressions is Berrey and Van den Bark's *The American Thesaurus of Slang* first published in 1942. The most recent, the most comprehensive, and the "new definitive" dictionary of American slang is J.E. Lighter's *Historical Dictionary of American Slang*, which spans three hundred years of slang in America. It consists of three volumes, of which two have been published so far (1994, 1997).

The emergence of American slang

American slang began with the emergence of American English. Between 1619 and 1772, American slang was mostly limited to anatomical terms used by the 20,000 felons who were transported to the colonies from England. Slang began on a large scale only after the Civil War. Before then, the small agricultural population was scattered over a huge area, there was no serious urbanization, there was no youth culture, and communications were slow. In addition, the subcultures that are most conducive to the emergence and development of slang only appeared in the twentieth century. From the beginning of the twentieth century, however, slang became an "established" part of the American linguistic scene and it gained more and more attention in the United States. This is clearly shown by the number of pages devoted to the topic of American slang in successive editions of H.L. Mencken's monumental *The American Language*.

With the communications explosion at the beginning of the century, a typically American slang has become regarded as one of the hallmarks of American English. What were the conditions that led to the emergence of American slang? The answer to this question is given by Lighter (1994) in the following way. First of all, a written language was required, together with a "public consciousness of a normative standard written language" that places such labels on language use as "reputable" and "disreputable." Also needed was the formation of certain subcultures with distinctive vocabularies that could be regarded as less respectable than the language of the mainstream culture. In addition, there must have been interaction between the mainstream culture and these subcultures, and this interaction must have made prominent the "unconventional" or "nonstandard" vocabularies of the subcultures. A further requirement was a situation in which speakers of the mainstream culture resisted the new vocabularies of the subcultures by branding them as bad and unacceptable English, thus excluding them from generally acceptable usage. Finally, there must have been enough "respectable" speakers who found good use for the branded vocabularies despite the admonitions of the – what we might call – saviors of the standard. In other words, for slang to exist, American society must have reached a stage in its development where it became a "literate, complex, heterogeneous culture[s] recognizing a standard usage whose primacy is upheld by a strong pedagogical tradition" (Lighter, 1994:XVIII). As we saw in a previous chapter (chapter six), the insistence on a standard and a resulting pedagogical tradition became a prominent aspect of American English by the middle of the nineteenth century.

The ideas by Lighter mentioned above give us a working definition of slang: Slang is a variety of language which is used by its speakers to differentiate themselves from or to go against existing norms of the standard variety and the corresponding dominant mainstream culture.

Sources of American slang

In this section, we will consider the major sources of American slang, the sources that contributed most significantly to what was or has been recognized as slang in American English. Needless to say, we can only mention some of these and give a few representative examples here. It is useful to draw a distinction between general slang and specialized slang. General slang is used or at least understood by most native speakers of a language, whereas specialized slang is restricted to particular groups or subcultures. General slang in part arises from the creative use of language by speakers of the standard and it also draws on specialized slang for its words and expressions. The specialized language is often called cant or jargon. Cant or jargon produces some words and idioms that are taken up by most speakers of the language who in turn use these with the purpose of showing differences with, or explicitly denying values and norms of, the mainstream.

Criminal underworld

A major source of American slang was, and still is, the criminal underworld that speaks a kind of cant or argot. An especially productive period when criminal slang entered general slang was the early part of the twentieth century. The place was the major American cities, particularly Chicago with its gangs and the mafia. Perhaps the best known word that is related to the Mafia is *godfather* ("the leader of the Mafia"), further popularized, also outside the United States, by the three movies with the same title in the 1970s. Several American slang words that are still used or recognized today originate from that general period. (However, the examples that are given do not all necessarily come from this period or place.) For example, the criminal who obtains money in a confidence game is called a *grifter*. The policeman who patrols the street is a *flatfoot*. The professional who receives stolen goods is a *fence*. This word, like many others, is no longer considered slang. In addition, it has a British origin and serves as an example of how American slang took over several words from already existing British slang words. Additional slang words originating from the criminal world that have gained currency in American slang include

> gun moll, gunsel, torpedo, to case a joint, big shot, hoodlum, racketeer, rough house ("physical violence"), hot seat ("electric chair"), to do the dirty work, hatchet man, protection racket, loan shark

Some of these have acquired more general meanings. A *hot seat* is not simply an "electric chair"; it has come to be used for any difficult situation. Similarly, a *hatchet man* is not restricted any more to the original meaning "hired killer," but can also be applied to certain people in a political context, where *hatchet men* do the dirty work for a politician.

Armed forces

The armed forces also contributed a large number of words to American slang. The two World Wars were especially productive times. In World War I, a U.S. marine was called a *leatherneck*, after the leather part in the uniform's collar. American sailors or soldiers called their British counterparts *limey*. The name comes from the lime juice given to British sailors to prevent scurvy. The term was later extended to Englishmen in general. *Frog* was a word used by Americans to describe French soldiers and later Frenchmen, and it is still used derogatorily or in a humorous context in the extended sense. The word for food or mealtime was *chow*, and it is common in this sense even today. Other American slang words and phrases that go back to World War I include *bump off* ("to kill"), *ammo* ("ammunition"), *foxhole, dogtag, brass hat*.

World War II was even more productive. For example, it gave Americans one of the best known acronyms in American English: *snafu*. It is customary to "decode" it in two ways, one rude, the other polite. According to the rude but the originally intended version, it is "situation normal, all fucked up," while the version used in more polite circles is "situation normal, all fouled up." Here's a selection of some more WW II slang:

> G.I., brass, chew out, boondocks, goof up, sweat it out, blitz, foul up, shack up, hit the sack, skivvies, buy it, sad sack, pissed off

Many of these are in common use today.

In addition to these more direct products of World War II, some other words, though not necessarily "hard core" slang, were made famous by novelists writing about the war. Perhaps the best known example of these is Joseph Heller's *Catch-22*, from the novel with the same title in 1961, describing a paradox from which there is no way out for the victim.

More recent wars that involved Americans had less influence on American slang. The Korean War produced some slang words like *whirlybird* and *chopper*, both for helicopter. Vietnam's influence was also relatively small. It gave American slang some additional words for killing, like *zap* and *waste*, for the Vietnamese (*Nam*), any Asian (*gook*), the Vietcong (*Charlie*), a Vietnamese village hut (*hootch*), and American infantry soldiers (*grunt*).

The frontier

The frontier also played a significant role in the formation of American slang as we know it today. The words and phrases used by gamblers, cowboys, gold diggers, fur traders, and other participants in frontier life to talk about their activities became an integral part of American slang. (See the earlier discussion in chapter three, and McCrum, *et al.*, 1986:252-255.)

Gambling

We can begin our brief survey with gambling. Some of the gambling terms that have gained general currency in American slang include

> you bet (emphatic affirmation, "yes"), put up or shut up, to pass the buck ("shift responsibility"), square deal, fair deal, rough deal, big deal, bluff, the cards weren't stacked against you, to have an ace up one's sleeve, to up the ante, to hit the jackpot, to load the dice, to throw in one's hand, to play a wild card, the chips are down

The craze for gambling swept through the frontier and the favorite card game was poker – especially an American version of it called *stud poker*. It was played in the *saloons* and on the steamboats of the Mississippi. Today the same gambling spirit may be observed in the *casinos* of Las Vegas and the reappearance of riverboat casinos and casinos on Indian reservations.

Gold diggers

The craze for gambling was matched only by the craze for gold. When gold was discovered in California (the *Golden State*) at the middle of the nineteenth century, it attracted tens of thousands of people (for more detail, see chapter three). The search for gold produced some well known American slang expressions, including *pan out, strike it rich, big strike, lucky strike*.

Cowboys

The cowboy, this quintessential American figure, is also responsible for a number of American slang phrases. His activities often demanded that he communicated with people who were not speakers of English. A go-between language was required and it was often some kind of pidgin. The use of pidgin resulted in such expressions as *long time no see* and *no can do*. A characteristic article of the cowboy's outfit or clothing was the bandana – a scarf to prevent the cowboy from inhaling dust. The bandana was usually worn around the neck and when the cowboy got angry he perceived a rise in body heat in the neck area. This produced the idiom *to be hot under the collar* ("to be very angry"). The dusty plains of the Southwest and the common experience of death led to the humorous slang expression *to bite the dust* ("to die"). According to McCrum, *et al.* (1986), the idiomatic phrase *the real McCoy* derives from the name of an early *cattle baron* in the 1860s named Joseph McCoy. The phrase means what *kosher*, the slang word from Yiddish, means: "genuine, real, authentic; hence worthy."

Black English

Immigrant and ethnic populations contributed a great deal to American slang. The most productive sources have been Black English and Yiddish. We can first look at some examples from the former. Black English slang words that are well known outside the Afro-American community include *soul brother* and *soul sister*, which were originally used by black men and women to address other black men and women. After the sixties, however, the expressions, especially *soul brother*, were almost entirely taken over by whites. More generally, the word *soul* is used to describe any characteristic of black people, including their food, music, language, handshake, etc., as in *soul food, soul music, soul language, soul shake*. It is a word suggesting a deep cultural identity among African Americans. Many terms originating in Black English slang have been taken over by members of the mainstream culture and are no longer recognized by speakers of American slang as coming from Black English. One such word is the verb *badmouth*, which means "to criticize" or "to disparage." Another is *dig* as it is used in sentences like *He don't dig you*, meaning "to understand"; *Dig, man!*, meaning "to pay attention, look, see"; and *Hey, I really dig that jacket!*, meaning "to like or love." Supposedly, the word used in these senses comes from the language of black jazz musicians in the first quarter of the century. One of the commonest American slang terms for an attractive woman also finds its origin in black slang. The word *fox*, as in *Dig that fox!*, is generally known, although it is considered somewhat dated today. More and more white speakers of slang employ the black slang verb *dis* in examples like *Don't dis me!* The meaning is "to insult someone, to be disrespectful to someone." While this word is still primarily associated with Black English, the word *nitty gritty* is not. Although it derives from black scatological slang, it has become part and parcel of general American slang in the sense of "the raw facts, the basics." The same applies to one of the best known American slang words for "enthusiastic approval or liking," *cool*. Today the word *cool* can be heard from the mouths of distinguished white university professors. As a result, the most authentic users of slang do not find it powerful enough any more. The following additional American slang words all derive from Black slang (McCrum, *et al.*, 1986:224):

> cakewalk, funky, jive, juke joint, main man, ofay, salty, wig out, bad, hummer (noun), beat, beat up, cat, chick, groovy, have a ball, hip, hype, in the groove, jam, joint is jumping, latch on, mellow, out of the world, pad, riff, sharp, solid, square, stache, too much, yeah man

> From jazz: jazz (formerly obscene meaning "to have sex"), jive, hepcat, OK (oll korrect), dig, cat

Many other examples can be found in a recent collection, *The African Heritage of American English*, by Holloway and Vass (1997).

Yiddish

Another major source for American slang is Yiddish. One observer of the American slang scene remarked that if we want to have an idea of the number and kinds of Yiddish words that entered American slang, all we have to do is turn to the words beginning with the letters *sch* in any good American dictionary. Even a brief glance at *Webster's New World Dictionary* gives us *schlemiel, schmaltz, schmo, schmooze, schmuck, schnook, schnorrer,* and *schnozzle*. A *schlemiel* is an ineffectual person or one who is easily victimized. *Schmaltz* refers to oversentimental music or language and it comes from the word denoting the melted fat of chiefly goose or other fowl. A *schmo* or a *schmuck* is a foolish or contemptible person, and it is a near synonym of the common American slang word *jerk*. The verb *schmooze* means "to chat or gossip" and the resulting activity can also be referred to by the same word used as a noun. A gullible person is often called a *schnook*, among the many other American English slang words for this type of people. A *schnoz* or a *schnozzle* is a nose, and someone who lives by begging is a *schnorrer*. Many of these Yiddish slang words have also entered the slang of cultures that had close contact with Jewish ethnic groups in Europe. One such case is Hungarian culture. Additional words or phrases of Yiddish origin that have become slang include:

> gonef, chutzpah, kibitzer, yenta, shlep, momzer, mensch, nebbish, kosher, get lost, I'm telling you, I need it like a hole in the head, actor-schmactor ("comedian")

German

Of the foreign languages, German contributed significantly to American slang. This is especially characteristic of earlier slang. These American slang words are common even today. Here are some examples:

> bummer, hoodlum, nix, fresh, phooey, scram!, spiel, yesman, and how!, no way

Subcultures

In recent years, several new subcultures have emerged in the United States whose language have had a considerable impact on general American slang, as McCrum, *et al.* (1986:348-349) tell us.

Surftalk

One such group that developed a distinctive vocabulary is the surfers, especially on the beaches of Southern California. They go out *to catch a surf* and then they relax with a *Heinie* or a *Lowie*, referring to a can of Heineken or Löwenbräu beer, respectively. The words that they use may be specific to the activities they perform as surfers, such as the special surfing maneuver called *getting air*. It is not the expressions such as this that have influenced more general slang. As McCrum, *et al.* (1986) note, the real power of their slang or jargon may be the result of the usages that they popularize through the desirability of their lifestyle. They use expressions that they obviously did not invent, yet by serving as some kind of role model for many young people these usages are imitated. This is what happened in the case of words like *awesome*. This term, meaning "excellent, fantastic," has become extremely popular with teenagers in California and throughout the nation. A similar impact on more general slang usage can be observed in their use of *for sure* for "the expression of approval."

Valleytalk

The surfers' slang or surf talk has met and combined forces with what has become known as "Valleytalk," a white teenager slang spoken primarily in middle-class suburbs north of Los Angeles, stretching into the San Fernando valley. This is slang first used mainly by teenager girls in the area and then adopted by larger and larger segments of the young student population of Southern California and almost throughout the entire United States. Together with the surfers, they have popularized the use of *awesome* for things that you like very much. They are also "responsible" for the present popularity of enthusiastic expressions of intensity, such as *totally* and *to the max*, meaning "completely." In their lingo *to barf* means "to vomit" and the things that can make you do so are *grody*. In contrast, good things are *vicious*, as when you say *My Mom can lay some vicious vittle*, that is, she can provide excellent food. The example also suggests that these speakers of slang are sensitive to the slang of other subcultures, in this case to Black slang, shown by the word *vicious*, which, together with *bad*, means "very good, excellent."

Surftalk and Valleytalk are the languages of very young speakers of American English. As we have seen, they influenced each other and, due to the appeal of the lifestyle of their speakers, they have influenced the speech habits of young speakers in general. As is commonly the case, the process does not stop here with the young speakers, but this language, at least some aspects of it, becomes a part of general American slang. Indeed, student slang in the United States, and also many other countries, is a major source and supplier of general slang. One could say that, in some reverse genealogy, the language of the children becomes the language of the parents, that is, the slang of teenagers becomes the slang of adult speakers of slang. When the process reaches this stage, young slang speakers "find the time ripe" to begin to invent new slang.

The slang of homosexuals

A process similar to what happened to Surftalk and Valleytalk is happening to other jargons. We can take as a recent case in point the slang used by homosexuals. Homosexuals, as every relatively closed subculture, have their own special language. A homosexual who conceals his homosexuality is called a *closet queen*. A *drag queen* is a male transvestite. A heterosexual female who likes the company of male homosexuals is referred to as a *fag hag*. There are many other examples like these that denote many of the subtle semantic distinctions that people make within the gay community. But what is of more interest here is that some of the slang primarily or originally used by homosexuals is beginning to enter general American slang. Originally, the expression *to come out of the closet* meant "to reveal one's homosexuality openly." Now this expression is common with respect to almost any situation in which an assumed or socially stigmatized undesirable property of a person is finally revealed. So when a politician finally reveals his or her true political stance, he or she can be said *to have come out of the closet*. Similarly, the word *drag* was originally used among homosexuals for the clothes worn by homosexuals. Today men may be said to go to the office in their *business drag* (McCrum, *et al.,* 1986). Clearly, much of the slang of the group is no longer restricted to homosexuals.

More recent jargons

Sports

Sport is a major source of slang in many cultures. For reasons that we will discuss later (see chapter twenty-one), this is especially so in the United States. The terminology of baseball and American football gave rise to many American slang expressions. Some examples from these two sports are *bush league, first base, score, touchdown*. But other sports, like boxing, ice hockey, horse racing, and so on, have also contributed.

Drug users

This is a large source domain for general American slang. Many of the slang words adopted for general use have to do with losing control or having very pleasant experiences. Thus, we have general slang expressions like *freak out, flip out, be stoned, out of this world, out of one's mind, be tripping*.

Beat and hippie movements

The *beats* and *hippies* of the 1950s and 1960s created their own language and reality. This process was in part original and in part borrowed from other subcultures, especially from Black culture. One example of this latter development may be the frequent use of the word *man*. The hippies were called by mainstream America the *flower children* or *people*, and they were said to be the *flower power*.

Other more recent source domains of American slang include the computer, television, show business and the film industry, ghetto language, and, interestingly, the language of bureaucracy, management, executives, talk shows, and yuppies.

The subject matters of American slang

According to Wentworth and Flexner (1960, 1975), the subject matter or conceptual domain that has most attracted the creation of new slang is that of drunkenness. Indeed, the following list is just a small selection of words that have or once had to do with being drunk in American English:

canned, knocked out, loaded, lushed up, shit-faced, soaked, tanked up, zonked out, bombed, pissed, sloshed, ripped, plastered, stoned, blitzed, fried, hammered, polluted, slammed, smashed, toasted, wasted, be high, have a buzz

Interestingly, drunkenness in these examples is seen as some kind of destruction. This is a theme that is shared with being under the influence of drugs.

The conceptual domain of drunkenness involves more than just the words for being drunk. Some of the other items also involved include the people who do the drinking and the alcoholic beverages used. So there are long lists of words for these aspects of the domain as well. We could come up with items like *wino*, *booze-hound*, *lush*, and *alky* for the former, and *booze* (perhaps the best known American slang word for "alcoholic drinks"), *hard stuff*, *suds* ("beer"), for the latter.

The meanings of the items on our list for "drunk" indicate varying degrees of drunkenness, ranging from mild to extreme degrees. In the mild category we have, for example, *have a buzz*. Some representative examples from the extreme end of the scale include *stoned* and *smashed*. It is noteworthy that these latter items often come from the usage of drug culture to describe the effects of various kinds of drugs on people. Thus it can be said that the experience with drugs is a major metaphorical source domain for drunkenness; that is, words for various degrees of being under the influence of drugs are used to talk about drunkenness.

However, others would disagree with Wentworth and Flexner's assessment that it is the conceptual domain of drunkenness that has produced the most synonyms and near-synonyms. We could agree with Lighter (1994) who suggests that the subject matter most productively elaborated in American slang is sex. This seems to be supported by collections of slang in a thesaurus format. For example, Chapman (1989), Berrey and Van der Bark (1947), and András and Kövecses (1989) all appear to show that slang items related to sexuality are the most numerous. Some of the conceptual components of this domain include the men and women who are the objects of sexual desire, the sexual desire itself, the sexual organs of the people having sex, the sexual act itself with its infinite varieties, and many others. This is a complex conceptual domain with many component parts. Here is a short list of words for the sexual act itself:

ball, get laid, check the oil, get one's rocks off, fuck the pants off, give somebody the time, shaft, shtup, pull, get one's banana peeled

For the male sexual organ:

banana, bone, dick, dong, dipstick, pecker, schlong, schmuck, tally-whacker, wienie

These are words that have been around for a long time. Now let us see some additional ones of more recent standing:

the Chief, Kojak, buddy, heat-seeking moisture missile, garden hose, leaning tower of please-her, love wand, cave dweller

These words, among many others, were produced in a linguistic experiment in which twelve college students (both males and females) were asked to list words for the "male member" in a 30-minute period (Cameron, 1992). Altogether nearly 150 words were listed. This result gives us an idea of the remarkable creativity of speakers of American slang.

The lists above give us some sense of the variety of words and expressions concerning sexuality in American slang. These may be very productive, but may not be specific to American slang. Some of the domains that are likely to be more specific to American culture include:

money (wealthy, rich)
success (win, achieve, failure)
car
people, men, women and their properties (stupid, insane, weak, fat, thin, strong, clever, ...)
ethnic groups
food and eating (eating, hunger, food, satisfaction ...)
movement (walk, drive, leave, arrive, run, escape, ...)
talk (talk, gossip, nonsense, lie, ...)
body parts, processes, products (genitalia, buttocks, piss, spit, ...)
intense emotions (anger, fear, love, happiness, ...)

criminal world (gun, police, kill, steal, rob, victim, prison, ...)
aggression/fighting (hit, beat, fight, ...)
drugs (selling drugs, marijuana, LSD, cocaine, heroine,
    opium, crack, ...)
homosexuality
attitudes to people and things (negative-positive)
communicative acts (agreement-disagreement, dismissal,
    expression of emotion [anger, dislike, surprise, pleasure])

Some of these domains of slang, like those of money, success, cars, ethnic groups, may be culture-specific. Or, at least, we can say that the degree to which they are elaborated in American slang is culture-specific. This leads us to the issue of what is characteristically (though not uniquely) American about American slang.

Distinctive properties of American slang

American slang has certain features that distinguish it from the slang of other English-speaking cultures or the slang of other languages. I will discuss here its productivity, action-orientedness, male-centeredness, and cultural-embeddedness.

Productivity

One characteristic of American slang is the incredible productivity of its speakers. This can be observed in the extent to which they make use of the existing ways of creating new words and expressions and in the extent to which they resort to new ones.

Compounding

American slang creates new words by putting two existing words together. Some examples include:

airhead, homeboy, barn-stormer, bench warmer, big timer, bone-shaker, bootlegger, bronco buster, bullshitter, cradle-snatcher, egg beater, eye-opener, go-getter, gold-digger, lush-roller, party-pooper, switch-hitter, tear-jerker

Some of the words that are utilized for this purpose recur frequently:

-gate: Watergate, Whitewatergate
-artist: bullshit artist, make-out artist, rip-off artist

-bug:	money bug, car bug, movie bug
-jockey:	bench jockey ("mechanic," or "substitute"), juice jockey ("electrician"), disc jockey, desk jockey, highball jockey ("bartender")
-head:	juicehead, acidhead, airhead
-job:	blow job, mental job, put-up job, sex job, snow job
-joint:	beer joint, grease joint, gyp joint, rip-off joint
-monkey:	grease monkey, powder monkey, road monkey

Some of them are what are called prefix-words:

real-:	real cool, real crazy, the real George, the real McCoy, real sharp
mega-:	megabucks, megawork, megabeers

Some others are various particles:

out:	blimp out ("overeat"), schiz out ("to break down emotionally")
off:	blow off ("ignore")
on:	hit on ("to make sexual overtures to")

Derivation

Many slang words are derived from existing English words by adding common English endings, or suffixes, to them. American slang produces a vast variety of slang words in this way.

-er: barn-stormer, bench warmer, big timer, blooper, boner, bone-shaker, bootlegger, bronco buster, bullshitter, bummer, buster, clinker, cradle-snatcher, downer, egg beater, eye-opener, fiver, go-getter, gold-digger, homer, howler, joker, kisser, lifer, lush-roller, party-pooper, porker, scorcher, smacker, sticker, stinker, sucker, switch-hitter, tear-jerker

-ie, -ey, -y, -sie, -sy: baddie, goodie, birdie, cutie, sharpie, sweetie, buddy, Chevvie, Caddy, doggie, freebie, hickey, leftie, kneesies, lousy, meany, mommy, tough cookie, steady, rookie, shortie, quickie

-age: bookage, fundage, sleepage (collective nouns): e.g., *I am about to ask my folks for some major fundage.*

-o: blotto, bozo, combo, dildo, desperado, doggo, Fatso, gismo, kiddo, lesbo, weirdo, wacko, wino

-*ster*: dragster, gangster, hipster, mobster, shyster
-*ville*: dullsville, hicksville, endsville, sleepsville

There are some word endings that are borrowed from other languages and appear to be unique to, or at least most characteristic of, American slang. These include:

-*eroo* (Spanish): buckeroo, buddyroo, flopperoo, sockeroo, stinkeroo
-*fest* (German): bullfest, gabfest, slugfest
-*nik* (Russian): sputnik, beatnik
-*eteria* (Spanish of the Southwest): cafeteria, lunchateria

Certain sounds

There are certain sounds that are used to create some characteristically American slang. Here are two of these:

z: zazzy from jazzy; scuz from scum; zap from slap and whap
oo: cigaroot, bazooms (from bosoms), smasheroo

Functional shift

What is called "functional shift," or the transfer of a word from one word class to another, is a major source of much American slang. Functional shift is used to transform many nouns to verbs:

Noun to verb: chin, ditch, eye, ink, jaw, stomach

But transfer from verb to noun is also common:

Verb to noun: break, combine, hit, kick, kill, sell, show, smoke

Acronyms

American slang is noted for its fondness of letter words, or acronyms. This might be a characteristic that also applies to American English in general. Some slang examples include:

G.I., A.W.O.L., snafu, I.O.U., C(-note), G, B.S., s.o.b., ac-dc, D.J., K.O., O.D., o.j., P.D.Q., P.O.W., B.L.T., T. and A., O.T.L. (out to lunch), V.J. (video jockey)

Imaginativeness

American slang is not only inventive, it is also imaginative. It not only creates new words but the words it creates are frequently imaginative. This means that many of the new words are based on such figurative processes of language as metaphor, metonymy, irony, idiom, and hyperbole.

Metaphor

We can get an idea of the pervasiveness of metaphor in American slang if we look at more expressions that refer to the sexual act. The expressions given below come from the slang of college students, collected by American linguist Pamela Munro (1990):

> to do the deadly deed, to lay pipe, to beat someone with an ugly stick, to get some trim, to do the nasty, to play hide the salami, to jump someone's bones, to ride the hobby horse, to give a hot beef injection, to throw the dagger, to do the bone dance, to do the wild thing, to bump fuzz

These expressions indicate not only the extent to which American slang is metaphorical, but also that the metaphors used form *idioms*, that is, phrases whose meanings, according to the traditional definition, are not predictable from the meanings of the component parts. Another property of American slang that they reveal is the humorous nature of many slang expressions. It seems as if speakers of slang revel in *humor* in talking about sexual intercourse and, as we have seen above, about many other domains. It is noteworthy that the basis of both idioms and humor is often metaphor, as indicated by the expressions.

Moreover, metaphor also commonly underlies *hyperbole*. Hyperbole appears to be a major process in the production of much American slang. The users of American slang, chiefly men, describe their experiences in terms of extreme language (Flexner, 1960). A woman is either a *knockout* or a *dog*, a book is either *great* or *crap*, people either have *guts* or they are *chickens*. As we have seen above, you are not simply drunk or even very drunk but *blitzed, fried, polluted, paralyzed*, and *wasted*. In using hyperbole, speakers often create realities that are grander or more impressive than the actual reality. This property of hyperbole links it with a frequently commented-on characteristic of American English: tall talk, which goes back to the frontier in the nineteenth century. Tall talk has to do with the self-advertisement or self-aggrandizement of the speaker. We will return to the discussion of this aspect of American English in a later chapter (see chapter eighteen).

Metonymy

Metonymy is another important feature of American slang, though perhaps less pervasive than metaphor. In metonymy, typically a part or property of a concept stands for the whole concept. For example, we can see metonymy at work in such words as *brew* and *chill* for beer. In both cases, a property of beer (how it is made and how it is served) is used to stand for the drink. Just as hyperbole and idioms are commonly based on metaphor, so is *irony* often based on metonymy. A well known example of this process in American slang includes words like *bad, mean, wicked, vicious, killer,* and others. Used in the appropriate context, all of these words may mean "excellent" or "very good," the opposite of the original meaning of the words. "To be excellent or very good" and "to be bad" are complementary opposites. In this kind of metonymy, one member of a pair of complementary opposites ("bad") stands for the other member ("good") of the pair.

These figures of speech, like metaphor, idiom, metonymy, and others, add novelty and spice to linguistic expression. This makes speakers of slang creative users of American English. The linguistic creativity of slang is vitally important to counterbalance the tendency of the standard language to become conservative and stale. Many novel slang expressions disappear from the language, but quite a few of them become a part of the standard. It is the creative aspect of American slang that seems to have captured the great American poet Walt Whitman's imagination. Whitman said: "Such is slang, or indirection, an attempt of common humanity to escape from bald literalism, and express itself illimitably" (*Slang in America*).

American slang as male language

That slang is the language of men is common knowledge. However, this accepted piece of wisdom must be qualified in at least two ways when we consider slang in the American situation. First of all, much (though not all) American slang is not simply the slang of men, it is the slang of a special type of man: the macho man. The man who is, or tries to be, macho wants to impress others and a part of trying to achieve this is to use slang that has "shock value." Often, taboo words are used for this purpose. In the *Historical Dictionary of American Slang* (Lighter, 1994), as one reviewer tells us, the word *fuck* occurs over 1,100 times. The reviewer comments: "... the dark jewel in America's lexical underbelly stands revealed in all its scapegrace vigor and variety" (Parshall, 1994:61). It seems then that a speaker of American slang can "shock" people in quite a broad range of meanings with the use of just one short word and its idiomatic extensions. Another related aspect of macho talk is the emphasis on short, often monosyllabic words.

Many slang words are like this and there seems to be a preference for them in the language use of many macho men. They include not only taboo words, but also words like *bread, dough, booze, split,* etc. These words derive their force from their brevity. They are means of being, attempting to be, or attempting to be perceived to be, "direct" and "straightforward." Monosyllables or other short words are felt to be more direct and sincere than longer words. With their help, one can really *call a spade a spade*. These words are also felt to have the power to call attention to social pretense, the archetypal enemy of slang. They show the attitude, the real opinion of the speaker of slang to anything that is *fake* or *phoney*. (For a literary illustration of this point, see the novel *The Catcher in the Rye* by Salinger.) The other qualification I must add to the initial statement of this paragraph is that there is an increasing number of women in the U.S. today who use slang. One large category of women who use slang is college students. In one study, mentioned already above, it was shown that the women in a college who participated in an experiment could list 50 different terms for the "male member" in 30 minutes. Most of the words were slang terms and the women produced almost the same items that the men did in the experiment. This is quite an impressive result that shows that at least college women are familiar with a good deal of slang vocabulary that was thought to be in the possession of men only. The other category of women using primarily male or macho slang consists of those women who attempt to be like men, and who, perhaps mistakenly, believe that it is their linguistic assimilation to men that will bring them equal social treatment.

Action or violence-orientation

There are many slang phrases in American English that seem to be more characteristic of American slang than of other national varieties of English slang. Consider the following idioms:

> bite the dust, break luck, break the news, break up, catch a surf, cut class, cut someone, let's cut, draw pay, pull a boner, make a score, grab some sleep, grab a sandwich, feed our face, hit someone up for money, hit it off with someone, hit on someone, hit the books, hit the booze, hit the deck, hit the hay/sack, hit someone with something, hit a dead-end, hit the road, hit the ceiling, hit the panic button, kick (a topic) around, kick down (the gearshift), kick in (money), kick someone upstairs, kill a beer, kill time, pull a boner, pull an all-nighter, pull an en foldo, pull a job, pull something off, push a hack/cab, push fifty, pusher (of illegal goods), push off, push the panic button, push up daisies, rip off (something), shoot (a movie),

shoot someone a line, shoot one's cookies, shoot off one's mouth, shoot the bull, shoot up, split, split the scene, split up

What we have in these and many other similar cases is that the speaker makes himself the active doer of an event even if he is not one (Flexner, 1960). It appears that idiomatic expressions such as these are more typical of American slang (and American English in general) than of other national varieties. The claim is not that they do *not* occur in other varieties. Notice that in each case there is a transitive verb that suggests a conscious, deliberate agent and typically an inanimate thing that is acted on. We draw, pull, hit, make, etc. something and kill somebody. However, in many of the idioms above people are not the agents of an action but the "patients" or "sufferers," or experiencers of an event that happens to them, or they are the patients, sufferers or experiencers of actions performed by somebody else. And even if they are the wilful agents, the action that they perform is not as aggressive or violent as is suggested by the verbs used. For example, in *pull a boner*, which means to make a mistake, we are anything but wilfull agents and yet the verb *pull* is used that suggests this agency. In *draw pay* the agent is somebody else, the person or institution that gives us the money. We are not doing an action, but an action is done to us. In *hit the road*, which means "to leave," we are the agents of leaving, but the action that we perform is not as "forceful" or "violent" as suggested by the verb *hit*. These examples show that Americans, in the course of their informal use of language, have a tendency to project an image of force, activity, and dynamism where, strictly speaking, it does not exist, or it is not called for. This tendency appears to fit the image of Americans (either of themselves or by others) as active, dynamic agents that have control over their world. (We will take up this issue in some later chapters as well.)

Lack of certain kinds of slang

In addition to what we have seen so far, what sets American slang apart from other national varieties of slang are some properties that it lacks. Major characteristics of British and Australian slang are "rhyming slang" and "back slang." American slang does not seem to possess either of these, or possesses them to a much smaller degree. Rhyming slang is a major property of Cockney speech, spoken in the East End of London, and of Australian slang. Rhyming slang starts out with expressions like *plates of meat* for "feet," *twist and twirl* for "girl," and *daisy roots* for "boots" that contain a word that rhymes with the word that is substituted. In the examples these are *feet, girl,* and *boots.* In rhyming slang the conjunction (like *and*) or the preposition (like *of*) and the rhyming word of the phrase (*meat, twirl,* etc.) are commonly left out, yielding one word that does not rhyme with the word that is substituted. Thus, the word for feet becomes *plates*, the word for girl becomes *twist*, the word for boots become *daisy*, and so forth. Although this kind of slang appears to be almost entirely absent from American slang, rhyme does occur in the formation of new words. The process is called "reduplication," and it produced such American English slang words as *buddy-buddy*, *okey-dokey*, and *hanky-panky*. Slightly different from reduplication is the process that yielded phrases like *wheeler dealer* ("a scheming person in business and social life; a clever manipulator") and *legal beagle* ("lawyer"). Another property of British slang is the word-formation process called back slang, where words are simply spelled in reverse. This yields words like *yob* ("boy, youth") and *ecilop* ("police"). In more recent British slang the word *yob* acquired the more specialized sense of "lout, or hooligan." This process did not gain any popularity among speakers of American slang.

Cultural knowledge

Perhaps the most obvious way in which American slang distingushes itself from other national varieties is the cultural context from which much American slang derives. Many American slang words and phrases are impossible to understand without familiarity with the appropriate cultural context that motivates them. Take, for example, the American slang word *Henry* or *Henrietta* that was used at the beginning of the century. To understand the word, speakers needed to know that a particular make of American car was manufactured by a person who was called Henry Ford. The name of the manufacturer came to stand for the product. Or, as an another example, consider the verb *bogart*, as used in the song lyrics *Don't bogart that joint my friend / Pass it over to me*. The understanding of the word requires sophisticated cultural knowledge. The hearer needs to know that there was a famous American movie star called Humphrey Bogart and that in his movies he habitually got things by intimidation, or he took more than his share of things. It is this latter meaning that applies to the example, namely, that one should not smoke more than one's share of a marijuana cigarette. These and similar examples (many of which we have seen above in this chapter) show that American slang (or any other national slang for that matter) is intimately linked to the cultural context in which it is born. It is this cultural knowledge that can greatly facilitate the successful learning of American slang for non-native speakers of American English.

American attitude to American slang

How common is slang among Americans? According to Lighter (1994), slang makes up at least ten per cent of the words the average American knows. Slang is the language American use, either in the form of vulgarity, or profanities, or humor, In very informal situations. Americans seem to like slang, if the number and kinds of slang dictionaries available in the United States are an indication. Slang dictionaries of all kinds abound, and there seems to be a great demand for them by Americans. In addition to the "standard" slang dictionaries, one finds such works as *The International Dictionary of Obscenities, Dangerous English, Forbidden English*, and many others.

At the same time, the American attitude to slang is ambivalent. According to some, slang is the "grunts of the human hog." Some others have a more positive view of it, and say that it is the "poetry of the proletariat." On the whole, teachers and parents discourage it. One frequently comes across the parental admonition "Don't use slang!" However, it may turn out that the same parents or teachers who are so discouraging about slang enjoy slang in their hearts of heart. Many middle-class Americans enjoy movies like *Grumpy Old Men*, which is about two old men and their life in a northern city. This is a movie about deep and fundamental human emotions and values, like friendship, love, loyalty, faithfulness, and so on. Yet at the same time, one of the things that many middle-class Americans most enjoy about it is the part in which one of the two grumpy old men's father gives a list of slang expressions for sexual activity. The expressions are sometimes hilariously funny. Here is a selection of them, given by the character called Chuck in several takes in a trailer, not in the main film:

"Looks like he's going to enter the holy of holies, coitus uninterruptis."
"Looks like Chuck's gonna put the hot dog in the bun."
"Looks like Chuck's takin' the skin-boat to Tuna Town."
"Looks like Chuck's takin' a ride in the wild balogna pony."

The point is that it is difficult to enjoy expressions like these and admonish your children and students not to use such expressions. But it is exactly this ambivalent attitude to slang that seems to be characteristic of many Americans.

Impact of American slang on other varieties of English

American slang has become the "slang of the English language." This is no doubt due to the political, economic, and cultural power of the United States in relation to other English-speaking countries. The British, Australians, and Canadians are taking over hundreds of American slang words every year. If we look at, for example, some British slang dictionaries (like Thorne, 1990; Ayto and Simpson, 1993), we realize that a considerable number of the entries, or the submeanings of entries, come from American slang. The reverse situation is much less frequent; American slang dictionaries contain hardly any slang words that are of British origin. This is a general tendency concerning the impact of American English on other "Englishes," a topic to which we will return in the next chapter.

In light of this situation, it is not surprising that there is a great demand for American slang among foreign students of English. American slang is slowly becoming a part of the English-language curriculum. A useful book on American slang is *Street Talk*, which is designed for intermediate or advanced students of English. Today's English books, movies, magazines, and newspapers can hardly be understood without at least some familiarity with American slang.

study questions and activities

1. Which features of American slang are reflected in the following American slang expressions? (Note that the expressions all have to do with death.) *to kick the bucket, to assume room temperature, to become a future source of oil, to fertilize mushrooms, to check out, to be metabolically challenged, to go to fertilize the lawn.*

2. Find additional examples of American slang that have become well established with speakers of British English as well.

3. Look at American slang in the domains of being drunk and having a drug experience. What similarities and differences can you find?

4. Read a British and an American play and/or go and see a British and an American movie in which people often express their anger. (Ask around which plays or movies would be best for the purpose.) Make note of the ways in which anger is expressed through language in English. What percentage of the linguistic expressions is slang? Why is the expression of anger a "good" and productive domain in slang? Can you find any differences between British and American English?

5. What other "speech acts" are expecially conducive to slang? Why do you think these lend themselves to a "slangy" way of talking?

chapter 10

Vocabulary differences between British and American English

That British English and American English represent two different varieties of the English language is a commonplace. It is also commonly assumed that most of the differences can be found in the vocabulary. Before we give an account of the nature and extent of these vocabulary differences, it is appropriate to provide a brief general characterization of that part of the vocabulary of English that is uniquely American – at least regarding its origin.

Words of American origin

According to *Webster's New World Dictionary* (1991), there are about 11,000 English words that are of American origin. So far, no detailed linguistic-statistical analysis of these words has been given (but see Gozzi, 1990). My students and I have only recently begun an informal study of this part of the English vocabulary. The observations to follow are based on this cursory and informal study.

Of the 11,000 English words of American origin (including of course American borrowings from other languages), the majority of the words (roughly two-thirds) are new American coinages, that is, the products of certain word-formation processes. Let us call these "new coinages." All the other words (about one-third) are the new uses of already existing English words, that is, words that have acquired a new meaning in American English. Let us call this case the "new use of old words."

As regards the grammatical class or category of all the new words, the largest class by far is that of nouns. The next most frequent category is that of new verbs (very crudely estimated, about one-fourth or one-fifth of the nouns). This is followed by new adjectives and various kinds of idioms. There are very few new adverbs, prepositions, and interjections. These results make intuitive sense.

In the case of new coinages, the most productive word-formation process is compounding, that is, putting two existing words together to form a new word (for more detail, see chapter nineteen). Another productive process that gives rise to many new American words is adding "prefixes" (like *de-* or *anti-*) or "suffixes" (like *-ee* or *-er*) to words. A third very productive process to form new words seems to be shifting, that is, the changing of the grammatical category of a word (see also chapter nineteen). Of all the possible grammatical shifts, the one that yields the largest number of new American words is the "noun to verb" shift. Other word-formation processes are also at work, but they seem to be less productive. (On this issue, see chapter nineteen.)

In line with what we saw in chapter two, many new American words are borrowings; that is, they are words borrowed by Americans from a variety of languages with which they came into contact. These include languages like Spanish, French, native Indian languages, and others. We will come back to this topic in a later section in this chapter.

Finally, if we look at the stock of words which are uniquely American, we may observe that there are certain subject matters that are especially productive. Some of the subject matters that stand out in this respect include nature (plants, animals), science and technology, politics and government, and food and drinks (see also Gozzi, 1990). The productivity of these and other domains makes sense in light of what we saw in chapter three concerning the naming and renaming of a new continent and nation. I will say more about the linguistic details of these domains in a later section.

Vocabulary differences: some questions

Before we move on to a more detailed study of these subject matters in relation to British English, it is important to clarify some issues first. These include such questions as the causes of British and American vocabulary differences and the extent and stylistic level of the differences.

The causes of vocabulary differences

One question that naturally arises is this: What are the main causes of the vocabulary differences between British and American English? The causes are in part social-cultural, in part technological, and in part linguistic. Let's begin with the social-cultural ones.

Social-cultural causes

There have been certain social and cultural developments since the early days of the emergence of what had become the United States. For example, the educational systems in the two countries developed somewhat differently, leading to differences in such words as *form* and *grade*, and many others. *Co-ed* was originally an American word (a noun denoting a female student at a coeducational school) that came to be used also in Britain, where it is used as an adjective only meaning "coeducational." Different sports had also emerged, developing their own terminologies. Whereas people in Britain are well known for playing cricket, people in the United States are equally well known for their love of baseball. Social-geographical causes also contributed. For example, the word *panhandle* in American English is a uniquely American development and it emerged as a result of a uniquely American experience. As the map of Texas shows, the western part of that state has the shape of a panhandle. This resemblance led to the use of the word *panhandle* as a description of this part of Texas (and other states like Florida).

Technological causes

Technology has also produced different vocabularies in British and American English. For example, the car industry developed in a parallel but distinct way in both countries, and, as a result, what was called *windscreen* in England was referred to by the word *windshield* in the United States.

The *Oxford Companion to the English Language* provides some interesting generalizations about the main tendencies concerning British-American differences in the domain of technology. It suggests that in the areas of technology that developed before the settlement of America, the differences in vocabulary are small. The example given is sailing, an activity that existed well before the settlement. Another claim is that in those areas of technology that developed in the nineteenth century, the differences are much greater. These areas include rail and automotive transport. We will see several examples of differences for these two areas in this chapter. Finally, it is suggested that in technological developments in the twentieth century, differences are again few. For example, the language of the computer industry is basically the same.

As can be seen from the examples above and many others, the new American words are either uniquely American (*panhandle*) thanks to uniquely American experiences, or they are new words that developed parallel to their British counterparts (*grade – form*).

Linguistic causes

The task of naming new social-cultural and technological objects and experiences had to be undertaken by specific linguistic processes. Many of the linguistic processes that participated in naming have already been mentioned, so we will confine ourselves to just a brief overview and survey.

One linguistic process that was used to meet the demands of naming the new was borrowing. We have seen a large number of examples for this phenomenon in American English in earlier chapters, when we discussed the influence of early contact languages such as American Indian languages (*moccasin, skunk, wigwam*, etc.), Dutch (*boss, coleslaw*), Spanish (*bronco, rodeo, ranch*), and French (*prairie, chowder*). The influence of later immigrant languages has also been mentioned, including African languages (*goober, jazz, banjo*), German, Yiddish (*schmalz, schlep, schlock*), Italian, and many others. On the other hand, British English has been influenced by other languages. When talking about different sources for vocabulary items in British and American English, the most obvious source that needs to be mentioned in the case of British English is Hindi (a language spoken in India). Many words in British English have an origin in Hindi.

Independent linguistic change may also be responsible for differing vocabulary items in British and American English. One variety may preserve an archaism that the other has lost. We have seen several examples for this process in chapter two, including *I guess, mad, sick*, and many others.

New words may be made up of old resources in one variety. For example, American English has new words like *lengthy, Americanism, Briticism*, and others, which are American words made up of the old resources of the English language. For example, *lengthy* is a combination of the word *length* and the ending (suffix) *-y*, and the word *Americanism* consists of the adjective *American* and the ending *-ism*. These words and endings had all been in the English language for a long time before American English put them to new use. We will examine the details of this process in American English in a later chapter.

Two additional linguistic processes must be mentioned: the extension of meaning and the narrowing of meaning. An example for meaning extension is the American use of the word *school*. The meaning of the word is generalized in American English. While in British English *school* is applied mainly to pre-university education (except in some institutional names, such as the *London School of Economics*), Americans employ the word without any such restriction. The narrowing of meaning can be demonstrated by the word *corn*. *Corn* in England primarily means "grain," which is thus a part of the meaning of such plants as wheat, maize, oat, etc. The meaning of *corn* in America was narrowed to what the British call *maize*.

The extent of vocabulary differences

A further question that can be raised in connection with vocabulary differences is the extent of these differences. How many differences are there? Or, perhaps more precisely, how many different terms are there in British and American English that can potentially cause confusion? *Webster's New World Dictionary* marks 11,000 items as Americanisms. Bryson (1990:177) estimates this number at 4,000 words in common speech. Even this latter estimate is a very large number if we consider that *in common speech* people are not likely to use many more words than this at all. Bryson mentions such everyday words as *lift* (British) and *elevator* (American), *dustbin* (BE) and *garbage can* (AE), and *biscuit* (BE) and *cookie* (AE) as examples.

At which stylistic level are differences most common?

Finally, it can be asked at which level of use the differences are most common. Alternatively, taking an American vantage point, we can ask: Which stylistic levels are most productive of a distinctively American vocabulary? There seems to be some agreement among scholars concerning this question. For example, Strevens (1972) suggests that it is primarily in popular speech, at the level of informal language, that American English vocabulary is significantly different from British. Strevens' examples include American slang and colloquial expressions such as *blow one's top* ("get angry"), *bump off* ("kill"), *case a joint, give the once-over, hijack, hustle, moonlight*, and *take it on the lam*. These are all originally American English expressions. Since the first time of their American use in these meanings, some of them have ended up in British English and some of them have also lost their originally slangish character (e.g., *hijack*). Other scholars express a similar view to that of Strevens. In making the same point, Baugh and Cable (1983) provide a different set of examples, including items like *bawl out, bonehead, boob, bootlegger, dumbbell, go-getter, grafter, hootch, peach of a, pep, punk*, and *razz*. Looking at the linguistic situation from a non-linguistic viewpoint, Max Lerner, in his *America as a Civilization* (1987), claims that what is distinctively American about American English can be largely found in popular speech. Thus there seems to be some consensus that what is distinctively American in the vocabulary can be largely found in the realm of popular, informal speech.

The main subject areas of British and American English lexical differences

Which subject areas provide most of the lexical differences between British and American English? We can get some idea of this, if we keep in mind some of the areas where American English developed its own distinct vocabulary. We have surveyed these areas (like geography, technology, education) in chapter three. These are the likely sources of British-American differences. However, it is difficult to answer this question with any precision because the scholars (especially the linguists) who deal with the issue at all do not base their views on anything like a reliable statistical survey. They simply make certain judgments concerning what appears to them to be subject areas with a number of differences. On the other hand, those scholars who have come up with alphabetically-arranged dictionaries of lexical differences between British and American English (like Moss, 1973; Schur, 1980) do not make an attempt to specify the vocabulary domains in which the items listed fall. For these reasons, all we can do is survey the works of the authors who have attempted to say something about the issue, and come up with some generalizations based on their impressionistic judgments.

With this question in mind, I examined six particular works: Baugh and Cable, 1983; Benson, Benson, and Ilson, 1986; Claiborne, 1983; Gramley and Pätzold, 1992; Strevens, 1972; and Trudgill and Hannah, 1982. Of the works surveyed, most of them agree that the subject areas that produce a significant number of lexical differences are those of food and cooking, government and politics, and the railroad and the automobile – that is, transportation in general. These were mentioned by four or five of the authors. Education and clothing were mentioned by three, and geography and landscape, animals, and plants by two. Some items mentioned only once include household, military ranks, law, and farming. Although these works did not set as a their goal the statistical survey of the main areas of differences, they provide us with some idea of the approximate kind and number of domains involved.

Below I give a list of these and some additional domains with some representative examples of lexical differences. The domains are presented in no rank order. First the British, then the American equivalent is given.

DOMAIN	BRITISH	AMERICAN
Building and household	groundfloor	first floor
	lift	elevator
	point	socket
	tap	faucet
	flat (rented)	apartment
	cupboard	closet
	eiderdown	quilt/comforter
	flat (owned)	condominium
	cot	crib
	dustbin	trashcan
	garden	yard
	nappy	diaper
	drawing pin	thumbtack
	torch	flashlight (powered by batteries)

DOMAIN	BRITISH	AMERICAN
Food	tin	can
	sweets	candy
	chips	French fries
	crisps	chips
	porridge	oatmeal
	jam	jelly
	milk	cream
	to take away	to take out/to go
	biscuit	cookie
	candy floss	cotton candy
	cornflour	cornstarch
Clothes	dinner jacket	tuxedo
	trousers	pants/slacks
	underpants	(under) shorts,
	vest	undershirt
	waistcoat	vest
	tights	pantyhose
School and education	lecturer	instructor
	senior lecturer	assistant professor
	reader	associate professor
	professor	(full) professor,
	main subject	major
	subsidiary subject	minor
	hall of residence	dormitory/residence hall
	mark	grade
	postgraduate	graduate
	secondary school	high school
	university	college/university
	maths	math
Entertainment	cloakroom	checkroom/coatroom
	booking office	ticket office
	film/movie	movie
	cinema	movie theater
	interval	intermission

DOMAIN	BRITISH	AMERICAN
Shopping	bill	check
	chemist	druggist
	queue	line
	hire purchase	installment plan
	shop assistant	sales clerk
	hoarding	billboard
	jumble sale	rummage/yard/ garage sale
Business and finance	current account	checking account
	deposit account	savings account
	shares	stocks
	note	bill
	estate agent	realtor/real estate agent
Road, traffic, and transportation	car park	parking lot
	diversion	detour
	pavement	sidewalk
	motorway	freeway
	roundabout	traffic circle
	taxi/cab	cab/taxi
	traffic lights	stop lights
	high street	main street
	underground	subway
	coach	bus
	tram	streetcar
	sledge	sled
Accommodation and travel	luggage	baggage
	page boy	bell hop
	left luggage office	baggage room
	receptionist	desk clerk
	to book	to make reservations
	timetable	schedule
	toilet(s)	restroom
	return ticket	round trip ticket
	single ticket	one way ticket

DOMAIN	BRITISH	AMERICAN
Car number plate	license plate	
	boot	trunk
	dynamo	generator
	petrol	gas
	caravan	trailer
	lorry	truck
	motorcar	automobile
	windscreen	windshield
	estate car	station wagon
	bonnet	hood
	wing	fender
	mudflap	splash guard
	dip switch	dimmer
	indicator	turn signal/blinker
	silencer	muffler
	aerial	antenna
Telephone and post office	post code	zip code
	engaged	busy
	ring up	call up
	reverse charges	call collect
	postman	mailman/mailcarrier/ postal carrier
	parcel	package
	ex directory	unlisted
Newspaper	leader	editorial
	newsagent	newsdealer
	paperboy	paperboy/newsboy
Train	railway	railroad
	goods train	freight train
	points	switches
	carriage	car
	engine-driver	engineer

DOMAIN	BRITISH	AMERICAN
Plants	maize	corn
	chickory	endive
	corn	grain
	stone	pit
Animals	ladybird	ladybug
	insect	bug
	Alsatian	German shepherd
	cock	rooster

One way of systematizing these categories would be to say that many of the differences center around the theme "people and their immediate environment," including the subcategories household, clothing, food, shopping, and buildings. Slightly removed from this central theme, we have the theme "human interaction and communication." This involves such subcategories as travel and accomodation, personal communication (telephone and post), and transportation (car, train, road). Next, we could set up the theme "social institutions" with such subcategories as school and education, business and banking, and media and entertainment. Finally, the subcategories of plants and animals could be viewed as parts of the theme "natural environment." We could imagine these themes as concentric circles with people and their immediate environment in the center.

It should be remembered that the list of lexical items above is just a representative sample of a much larger number of items that differ in British and American English. What is striking about this list is that they are not in any way slangish, or even colloquial expressions. They represent perfectly standard British and American usage that people commonly use for their everyday purposes in talking about these domains. This finding goes against the view that the major or dominant stylistic level where differences can be found is the level of very informal language use. This may only be true in terms of sheer numbers, that is, if we look at how many terms differ and at which level. But if we also consider the frequency of occurrence in standard, stylistically neutral exchanges, it may turn out to be the case that the lexical differences are equally significant at a more neutral stylistic level of communication.

The interaction between British and American English vocabulary

So far, the impression may have been created that British English has developed one set of terms in these domains and American English simply developed a different set in the same domains. This would be a simplistic picture. There has been, and there still is, a great deal of interaction between the two varieties regarding their vocabularies. In this section, we will look at the nature of this interaction.

American English words in British English

First, let us take a look at some words that were originally American, but later entered British English. Bryson (1990:171-172) offers the following list:

> commuter, bedrock, snag, striptease, cold spell, gimmick, babysitter, lengthy, sag, saggy, teenager, telephone, typewriter, radio, to cut no ice, to butt in, to sidetrack, hangover, to make good ("be successful"), fudge, publicity, joyride, bucket shop, blizzard, stunt, law-abiding, department store, to notify, to advocate, currency (for money), to park, to rattle ("unnerve, unsettle"), hindsight, beeline, raincoat, scrawny, to take a backseat, cloudburst, graveyard, know-how, to register (in a hotel), to shut down, to fill the bill, to hold down ("keep"), to hold up ("rob"), to bank on, to stay put, to be stung ("cheated"), grapevine, fan, gimmick, phoney

The Oxford Companion to the English Language adds to this list the following items:

> airline, boondoggle, checklist, disco, expense account, flowchart, geewhiz, halfbreed, inner city, junk food, kangaroo court, laser, mass meeting, nifty, ouch, pants, quasar, radio, soap opera, teddy bear, UFO, vigilante, wholehearted, xerox, yuppie, zipper

Interestingly, the two lists share one word only: *radio*.

Most speakers of English, native or foreign, could not tell the origin of the words above. These American words have become a part and parcel of the general word stock of English. Some of the words and expressions that we take to be typically British also derive from American English. The expression that describes an allegedly British attitude is *a stiff upper lip*. Curiously, the expression comes from American English. To take another example, the British counterpart of the American *traffic circle* is *roundabout*. Bryson (1990:171) tells us that the British term was invented by Americans, and that before the 1920s the British English term was *gyratory circus*.

Some American words appear to compete with British ones. Examples include, according to Svejcer (1978), the following: *shop – store, luggage – baggage, dinner jacket – tuxedo, dressing gown – bathrobe*. His suggestion is that the originally American words (given second) are beginning to gain ground in Britain as well. Some other American words that have been picked up by the British are claimed to be in the process of replacing their British counterparts. For example, Bryson (1990:175) suggests that this is the case for such pairs as *truck* for *lorry*, *airplane* for *aeroplane*, and *billion* (1,000,000,000 for 1,000,000,000,000). The important point about these examples is that they reflect the tendency of how American English words enter British English. Some of the individual examples may be debated, but the tendency is clearly there.

The case of idioms offers a particularly interesting situation. There seem to be many idioms where the difference between British and American English can be found in only one word. Examples include *sweep under the carpet* (BE)/*rug* (AE), *blow one's own trumpet* (BE)/*horn* (AE), *the lie* (BE)/*lay* (AE) *of the land,* and *put in one's penniworth* (BE)/*two cents' worth* (AE). In other cases, however, both the British and Americans use idioms that are specific to their variety of English. On the British side, we find such idioms as *drop a brick, in queer street, hard cheese,* and *a turn-up for the book,* meaning "blunder," "in debt," "bad luck," and "a surprise," respectively. Specific American idioms include *a bum steer* ("bad advice"), *out of left field* ("unexpectedly"), *feel like two cents* ("feel ashamed"), and *right off the bat* ("without delay"). In some other cases, British and American idioms may consist of the same words but have opposite meanings. The metaphorical idiom *to be a bomb* exists in both varieties, but it means "to be a success" in British English and "to be a complete failure" in American English. Obviously, cases like this may cause all kinds of (sometimes humorous, sometimes embarrassing) misunderstandings.

British English words in American English

However, the reverse process has also been going on for a long time. American English has also taken over words from British English. We can find the following words that were originally British in current American usage: *smog, weekend, gadget, miniskirt, radar, brain drain, gay* (in the sense of "homosexual"). This list is Bryson's (1990). To it, we can add another list by Strevens (1972:63-64), who also mentions *smog,* and in addition *awfully, jolly, ripping, cheerio, righto, copper, cop, headmaster, opposite number, penny, shop, to miss the bus* (not the train), *to wangle,* and *what price...?* Again, opinions may differ in judging the extent to which these British words and expressions have become a part of American English. It is the general phenonenon that is important, namely, that vocabulary items also go in the British to American direction.

However, as the surveys show, there is a much greater number of American words and expressions in British English than vice versa. The much stronger flow of borrowing seems to go from American to British. Moreover, in general speakers of British English appear to know more Americanisms than speakers of American English know British words and expressions. As, for example, Alwood's study reported in Svejcer (1978) shows, British students are more familiar with Americanisms than American students with Briticisms.

Which words from American English are taken over by the British?

A particularly interesting and important question that the discussion above raises is this: Which American words end up in British English? That is, which are the American words that are most readily accepted by speakers of British English? In answering this question, Svejcer (1978) sets up four categories. First, those American words and phrases are taken over that "designate objects and phenomena which did not have established appellations in British English" (Svejcer, 1978:158). Svejcer's examples include *commuter, blurb, job-hop, know-how, babysitter*. In other words, these are cases where the British had no name for something and needed one. The simplest thing for them to do was take over the American word. Second, Svejcer suggests that some of the Americanisms are "cultural borrowings," a term that he takes from Bloomfield. The *jukebox, milk-shake, sundae, chewing gum, Western*, and the *bikini* are American cultural "inventions" that the British also came to like, or at least came to live with. Third, there is a category of words that reflect "American realia which are widely known in Britain." Examples include such things as *ranch, congressman, Secretary of State*, and *rodeo*. These words indicate aspects of American reality with which many people the world over are familiar. Svejcer's fourth and last category includes "words and set phrases which have a distinct expressive-stylistic coloring" and are used for stylistically neutral ones. Svejcer provides the following examples (citing the American word first): *to steamroller – suppress, gimmick – trick, graft – corruption, boost – publicize, foolproof – simple, up-and-coming – promising, bunk – nonsense*, and *brainwashing – indoctrination* (Svejcer, 1978:158-59). According to Svejcer, the American words have gone over to British English, because of their "distinct expressive-stylistic coloring." (We will take up this last issue in chapter twenty, where we will discuss the imaginativeness of American English.)

The same cause is noticed by Gramley and Pätzold (1992:359) when, discussing why one variety of English borrows from another, they write:

> In this causal approach, the vivid and expressive nature of a number
> of words and phrases is held to have helped them expand, for example,
> many of the informal or slang items from AmE such as *fiend* (as in
> *dope fiend* or *fitness fiend*), *joint* ('cheap or dirty place of meeting for
> drinking, eating etc.') and *sucker* ('gullible person').

Apparently, Baugh and Cable (1983:388-89) also believe that the expressive nature of some American words is a good "selling point." This is what they say in connection with the issue:

> Generally speaking, it may be said that when an American word expresses an idea in a way that appeals to the English as fitting or effective, the word is ultimately adopted in England. Mr. Ernest Weekley, in his *Adjectives – and Other Words*, says: "It is difficult now to imagine how we got on so long without the word *stunt*, how we expressed the characteristics so conveniently summed up in *dope-fiend* or *highbrow*, or any other possible way of describing that mixture of the cheap pathetic and the ludicrous which is now universally labelled *sob-stuff.*"

However, it is not the case that all "expressive" and "vivid" American expressions end up in British English. Many have not been assimilated. The main barrier, according to Svejcer (1978:159) is "a lack of clarity as to their inner form for Englishmen." This is why expressions deriving from, for instance, characteristically American sports, not well known to the British, are less likely to be assimilated by the British. For example, expressions from baseball, despite their often expressive and picturesque character, have not been borrowed. Here are some such American baseball phrases: *to pinch-hit* ("substitute"), *off one's base* ("wrong"), *with two strikes against one* ("in an unfavorable position"). A similar example from American football is *huddle* ("secret consultation"). Obviously, the same explanation applies to why Americans do not assimilate some British phrases despite their expressivity or "color" (e.g., the British cricket expression *sticky wicket*, meaning "a difficult situation").

However, the clarity of other American expressions has helped them get into British English. We can find in British use such American phrases as *to strike oil* ("get rich") from oil drilling, *lunatic fringe* ("extremist minority"), *hit the headlines* ("become famous") from journalism, and *hold down a job* ("to keep a job") from the cowboy's activity. Even though the activities from which some of these expressions derive might not be very familiar to British speakers, the phrases have transparent meanings, and this may have been responsible for the British borrowing them. We will discuss the issue of clarity and transparency in American English in the chapter on directness (see chapter fourteen).

study questions and activities

1. Have some native speakers of British and American English describe any of the areas (such as household, school, car, etc.) mentioned in the chapter. Do you find additional differences in the terms they use?

2. Take some newspaper reports about the same topic (e.g., an event demanding world-wide interest) in British and American newspapers and magazines. What systematic differences can you find?

3. Try to find an article, a short-story or novel in a language other than English (such as French, Chinese, Japanese, Italian, Arabic, German, etc.) that was translated by both a British and an American translator. Do research on the differences in translation.

4. On the internet, invite British and American native speakers to respond to some question or issue you pose to them. Do their responses reveal any differences?

chapter 11

General accounts of British-American linguistic differences

In the previous chapters we have seen how various aspects of British and American linguistic differences are accounted for. The focus was on particular linguistic phenomena and particular explanations for those phenomena. In this chapter, our focus will shift to general accounts that have been offered in the study of British and American linguistic differences. These accounts range from the scholarly or scientific to lay views as used by nonlinguists, or combinations of the two. The treatment of the approaches will be necessarily brief, because we have already dealt with most of them in previous chapters. Only the "form-referent typology" and the "intellectual traditions" approaches will receive slightly more detailed treatment. This is because the former has not been discussed so far and it is clearly a very important approach, and the latter because it forms the basis of the chapters that follow.

The "linguistic geography" approach

We have dealt with this approach in some detail in a previous chapter. The main idea of the approach is that the origins of American English are somehow contained in the various regional dialects of British English (see, for example, Kurath, 1949). The proponents of this view stress the continuity of American English arising from British English. According to one critique of linguistic geography, it is assumed that "speakers of British regional dialects brought a great amount of dialect diversity to the Americas, enough to form the basis of all subsequent dialect diversity in the latter" (Dillard, 1985:55) and that "British 'regional' varieties redistributed themselves regionally within the United States" (Dillard, 1975:161-162). We have seen examples of this process in previous chapters in the accounts of pronunciation, vocabulary, and grammar differences. For example, the distribution of the /r/ sound in the United States and how it acquired prestige was explained with reference to where and when the settlers and the later immigrants from the British Isles came in their new country. In other words, in this approach the specificity and diversity of American English are seen primarily as the product of British immigration patterns.

A collection of British archaisms

Closely related to the view favored by the advocates of linguistic geography is the notion that whatever is specific about American English comes simply from earlier stages of British English. It is suggested that after the early settlement of North America by the English-speaking settlers, the language of these early settlers preserved many of the properties that were characteristic of seventeenth-century British English (see chapter two). The claim is that, after this, British English began to develop in a different direction and left some of these features behind, and later developed new ones. Here again, in chapter two we have seen a number of examples in pronunciation, vocabulary, and grammar. More examples can be found in Marckwardt (1980; rev. Dillard, ch. 4). The pervasiveness of this view can be seen in the popular conception that American English is often thought to be a direct continuation of Elizabethan English, the English used by such authors as Shakespeare.

Social history

The approach to British-American differences we will consider next could be called the "socio-historical view." This view arose largely as a critique of the previously mentioned accounts. It is especially embodied in the works of J.L. Dillard. Dillard maintains that scholars like Kurath attach undue importance to immigration patterns in the development of American English. While he does not deny that immigration patterns might have played some role in the production of a specifically American variety of English, he suggests that a number of significant factors have been ignored as a result of the preconceptions that are involved in dialect or linguistic geography.

Perhaps foremost of these factors in Dillard's research are the various pidgin and creole languages with which the settlers and the later immigrants came into contact. He also suggests that a kind of "pidginization" process started as soon as the earliest settlers, the Puritans, left England and sailed to Holland. It is important to point out that by American English Dillard means American Englishes rather than American English, and talks about several different varieties of American English, including Black English. In this regard, he claims, for example, that it is not possible to explain the origins of Black American English on the basis of British regional dialects, as scholars within the tradition of linguistic geography attempted to do.

Several scholars have shown that what is known as American English today owes a great deal to many of the contact languages that the settlers had come across on the new continent. For example, we saw in chapter two, referring to Marckwardt (rev. Dillard, 1980), that a variety of native Indian languages, Dutch,

Spanish, French, and, somewhat later, German, and many other languages have left their marks on the vocabulary of American English.

Another major source of British and American English differences can be found in an extremely significant event in American history: the westward movement, and the frontier life that accompanied it (Dillard, 1985; Hendrickson, 1986). In the chapter focusing on the creation of a new nation, we saw how such frontier activities as the cattle trade, trapping, mining, gambling, and drinking, all contributed to a distinct American English vocabulary. Also, in the course of their westward movement the settlers came into contact with languages and cultures not mentioned in the previous paragraph (see Dillard, 1992).

Dillard (1985) also takes note of the many special varieties that can be found in American English. He discusses such varieties as those associated with the radio, television, movie, stage, telephone, computer, and religion, among others, and explains how these varieties all form a part of the general process that makes American English different from British English (for more detail, see chapter three).

Parallel lists

The approaches mentioned so far represent attempts to *explain* how American English came to be different from British English. However, not all approaches attempt to do this. What is called the "parallel list" method by some scholars (like Algeo, 1989) consists simply of listing the existing differences between American and British English. They often contain British and American word correspondences, or assumed equivalences, as in the following:

BE: – AE:
postman – mailman
lift – elevator
tram – streetcar
pavement – sidewalk
luggage – baggage
autumn – fall
strip cartoon – comic strip, etc.

These parallel lists are often used for teaching the two main varieties of English for foreign learners (e.g., Janicki, 1977). They can also take the form of language guides for travellers. The British collect items that are considered to be Americanisms and Americans items that are Briticisms (e.g., Moore, 1991). Thus the lists often serve the purpose of facilitating travel. Parallel lists can also be found for more specific purposes, such as facilitating the reading of British mystery novels for Americans. Most parallel lists are concerned with vocabulary differences, but other lists of differences may also be included. Schur (1980), for example, provides not only a dictionary that handles words and expressions, but also offers several appendices dealing with spelling, pronunciation, grammatical structures, etc.

"Form-referent" typologies

A number of scholars have noted that the parallel list method is defective for the simple reason that straightforward equivalences between items on the lists are the exception rather than the rule (e.g., Algeo, 1989; Benson, Benson, and Ilson, 1986). These scholars suggest that there are complex relationships – and not simple equivalences – between any two items. The particular relationships that these authors identify and specify vary slightly, but the general ideas and principles on which they base their statements of the kinds of relationships are more or less the same. They assume that words (forms) refer to things in the world (referents). Furthermore, they assume that different forms can be used to refer to the same thing and that a single form can refer to more than one referent. The former case is called synonymy (several words, one referent) and the latter, polysemy (one word, several referents). They also recognize that forms and referents can be general and limited. If a word is general, it is a part of Common English; if it is limited, it belongs to either British or to American English. If a referent (thing, event) is general, it exists both in Great Britain and the United States; if it is limited, it exists either in Great Britain or in the United States. Given these distinctions, a number of relationships can be isolated between corresponding British and American items (forms and referents). The following survey is based especially on Algeo's work (1986, 1989). In presenting his system, I will deviate from his scheme in some minor details, beginning with cases where there is a single form and a single referent.

Three gaps

Given that we are talking about two cultures and two corresponding varieties of English and that form (word) and referent (thing) are distinguished, we get several possibilities for gaps in the vocabulary of either British or American English.

Cultural gap

One possibility is that there is a limited form and a limited referent. *Airing cupboard* is a phrase in British English that does not exist in American English because the referent of the phrase also does not exist in the U.S. This situation can be called a "cultural gap."

Lexical gap

It is also possible that there is a limited form but a general referent. The word *fortnight* is a well known word in British English, but it is not used in American English. However, this limited form denotes a general referent, that is, "two weeks." It may be suggested that there is a "lexical gap" in American English to express this particular concept. The same applies to the American English word *block* that is not used in British English in the sense of "a block of houses," a referent that is obviously shared in the two countries.

Referential gap

The name *Big Ben* can be viewed as a term shared, but whose referent is limited to Britain. This might be called a "referential gap."

Synonymy

Next we turn to cases of synonymy. As has been noted, in synonymy we have several forms and one referent. Again, different possibilities may be distinguished.

Interdialectal synonymy

Let us take as the first example the telephone numbers that the telephone companies are not allowed to give out. This referent is shared in Britain and the U.S., but is referred to as *ex-directory* in Britain and *unlisted* in the United States. In other words, we have a case of a shared, general referent and two limited forms. *Underground* and *subway*, *articulated lorry* and *trailer truck*, *aubergine* and *eggplant* are further examples. This phenomenon is called "interdialectal synonymy."

A version of this is provided by the three terms *Brit*, *Britisher*, and *Briton*. The first of these is limited to Great Britain, the second to the United States, and the third is shared. That is, we have two equivalent terms and a common one.

One-sided dialectal synonymy

A different possibility within synonymy arises when one term is general and the other is limited to one of the dialects. The case in point is *autumn* and *fall*. *Autumn* is used both in Great Britain and the United States, although its

American use is constrained by stylistic factors. It is viewed as a somewhat literary or formal term. Examples like this can be called "one-sided dialectal synonymy." Other instances for overlapping terms include *advert* and *ad*, *subway* and *underpass*, *agony aunt* and *sob sister*, *all-in* and *all-inclusive*, *dump truck* and *dumper truck*, *expensive* and *dear*.

Polysemy

A further group of cases involves polysemy, that is, one form having several referents, or meanings. Several cases can be distinguished.

Interdialectal polysemy

This case can be exemplified with the word *robin*. As noted in previous chapters, the settlers often made use of old words for things that were new to them, but at the same time sufficiently similar to something they were familiar with in Britain. Thus a general English word like *robin* acquired a new meaning. Hence it became polysemous between British and American English; a general form has two different and limited meanings.

One version of this situation is when a term has in addition a common (general) meaning as well. An example of this is the word *chancellor*. This word denotes "the chief minister of a European country" (Germany), a meaning that is common to both British and American English. However, in Britain it has the additional sense of "the honorary head of a university," while in the United States the additional sense is "the chief executive officer of a state university system."

Interdialectal diversity

A case that resembles both *robin* and *chancellor* is provided by the verb *to table something*. It resembles *robin*, in that it has two limited referents, and it is like *chancellor*, in that it has a general referent as well (the thing table). The two limited referents of *table* are "to bring up for discussion at a meeting" (British) and "to remove from discussion at a meeting" (American). What makes this case especially interesting is that the two limited meanings of the verb *to table* are opposites, an uncommon situation for polysemous words.

One-sided dialectal polysemy

The word *chapel* represents yet another case within the broader category of polysemy. The general meaning of the term is "a small place of worship or a place of worship in larger building (church)," while in British English it also has the meaning "nonconformist church." Thus, there is one form with (at least) two meanings, one general and the other limited (in this case to British English).

More inclusive terms

A final case of polysemy-based relationships between British and American English is the situation in which the referent of a general form is more inclusive in one variety than in the other. A good example of this is the word *staff*. In British usage the referent of the word is something like "employees in general," be it a hospital, a hotel, or a university. In the United States, however, *staff* is most commonly and naturally used for non-academic employees, such as secretaries, clerks, and maintenance personnel. Thus the meaning of the term is wider, more inclusive in British English. It may be noted that the equivalent of the British English word *staff* in the sense of "teachers at a university" is *faculty* in American English.

Interlocking terms

Interlocking terms involve multiple forms and multiple referents (as opposed to the first category, where there was a single form and a single referent). Both terms are used in the other variety, but there are also unique situations in which the terms are employed in the two varieties. A case in point are the words *luggage* and *baggage*. *Luggage* is used in both Britain and America when people talk about empty, new suitcases and small cases (e.g., *buy luggage, luggage rack*). At an airport, suitcases are generally (though not exclusively) called *baggage* (e.g., *baggage claim area, excess baggage fee*) in both Britain and America. However, in some other situations people in Britain would prefer to use *luggage* (e.g., *luggage van, left-luggage office*), whereas Americans tend to use *baggage* (*baggage car, baggage room*). The distribution of such word pairs as *post* and *mail* represents an equally complex case of interdialectal variation.

Homonymy

I mention homonymy-based interdialectal variation only for the sake of presenting the complete system of this approach, rather than for its significance. Interdialectal variation that is based on homonymy (as opposed to synonymy and polysemy) involves one form with two (or more) meanings, such that (unlike polysemy) the meanings are not related. An example is the British word *Taffy* and the American term *taffy*, both pronounced /tæfɪ/. *Taffy* means "an Irishman" in British English, while *taffy* is a kind of candy in the U.S. (The British word for the same candy is *toffee*.)

Functionally analogous referents

This case involves multiple forms and multiple referents, where the referents have roughly the same function. The words *Parliament* (BE) and *Congress* (AE) exemplify this situation. The two institutions referred to by the two words are different in several ways, yet they obviously have very much the same governmental function. We thus have two different words, referring to different referents, but the referents are analogous in their function. It is this functional analogy that is the distinguishing characteristic of this category of cases. Other examples include *muesli* (BE) and *granola* (AE), *British Library* and *Library of Congress*, and *the West End* and *Broadway*. The number of examples in this category is fairly large, but they seem to represent varying degrees of functional analogy.

As Benson, *et al.* (1986) claim, the "form-referent typology" approach is not applicable only to vocabulary. It can also be extended to the study of inter-dialectal variation in pronunciation and grammar. However, most of the work so far along these lines has been done in the description of vocabulary differences.

A weakness of the "form-referent typology" approach is that it is not an explanation but a description of existing differences. It is a sophisticated description, but it does not offer an account of the causes of the divergences. The "social history" approach attempts an explanation of the causes, but does not always take into account all the linguistic differences that exist between the national varieties. On the other hand, the "form-referent typology" approach pays attention to all the details without trying to account for how they have come about.

"Intellectual traditions" approach

The approaches to British-American differences surveyed so far in this chapter all have their merits, and each has its use in the study of the two national varieties of English. However, I suggest that there is even more to the story of the divergences between British and American English. It may be that there is a further set of factors that are responsible for many of the linguistic differences. I propose that these factors have to do with certain intellectual traditions and certain national characteristics of the British and the Americans, respectively. This idea is, of course, not new. It goes back to at least Mencken (1919, 1963), and it surfaces occasionally in other authors as well (e.g., Marckwardt; rev. Dillard, 1980). Not surprisingly, it can also be found in the works of authors who approach the question of what is specifically "American" about America and Americans. One example, mentioned in the previous chapter, is Max Lerner, who claims that American English reflects the national characteristics of vigor and creativity in Americans. This is a common observation – also made by Mencken and by Marckwardt and Dillard. Others link national traits in thought and behavior to intellectual traditions. For example, Bellah, *et al.* (1985) relate the notion of American inventiveness and creativity to the American intellectual tradition that they call "expressive individualism," embodied, for example, in the work of Walt Whitman.

It will be argued in the chapters to follow that the specific American traits that appear to manifest themselves most clearly in the language of Americans include linguistic economy, rationality, propriety, directness, democracy, informality, inventiveness, imaginativeness, and some others. These traits are intended in a value-neutral way. In ordinary language use, some have positive, some have negative connotations. I wish to use the terms referring to the traits or properties without these connotations when analyzing the linguistic data in subsequent chapters.

To say that these are characteristically American traits is not to say that other nations do not have them. They clearly do, and obviously, the British have them as well. As Ernst Leisi puts it, American English is even "more English" than British English (Leisi, 1985:229). The same applies to the two peoples. These are relative concepts with which I will try to characterize what might be called the "American character" or the "American worldview." Their relativity means that Americans, as far as this can be ascertained on the basis of language, exhibit more of these properties in comparison to the British. The basis of the comparison will be British English and what we can say about the "British mind" on the basis of British usage. Independent evidence will also be surveyed and taken into account when I try to characterize what is British and what is American, including works by sociologists, psychologists, philosophers, anthropologists, writers, and observant lay persons, who have noticed characteristic differences between the British and Americans.

The systematic study of the American national character in the last half century, often compared with the British, goes back to Margaret Mead and continues to the present day in the works of such American authors as Bellah, *et al.* (1985) and such British authors as Wilkinson (1988). This is a respectable tradition, but, in it, very little attempt is made to systematically link linguistic differences with psychological, intellectual, and behavioral ones. The linguistic tradition of dealing with British-American differences features equally respectable names, but, conversely, the linguists pay very little attention to how linguistic facts correlate systematically with the psychological, intellectual, and behavioral properties. A major goal of this book is to attempt to relate the findings of linguists with those of social scientists in a systematic fashion. This requires us to look at the large body of data that linguists have gathered concerning British and American English differences, and to attempt to correlate these findings with evidence of differences in character traits from nonlinguistic sources. It will be shown that this can be done and that the linguistic differences can be seen as arising from systematic differences in "national character."

It might of course be asked where this national character comes from. I will adopt a simplified view of the relationships between American English as a dialect of English, the American national character, and American intellectual traditions. Obviously, these aspects of a nation are related to each other in complex ways. However, I propose that it is the national character that is chiefly responsible for many properties of American English, and that the national character is, to a large degree, a product of a variety of intellectual traditions and social-historical processes operative in the two countries. Thus, American English has acquired its unique properties that distinguish it from British English as a result of an again unique American character, which in turn derives from a number of intellectual traditions and social-historical processes. It could also be argued that it is the national character that somehow brings about intellectual traditions and even, *à la* Benjamin Lee Whorf (1956), that it is language that shapes thought. I think that these possibilities are all, to some degree, operative in the interaction of language, character, intellectual traditions, and social history. Nevertheless, for the sake of clarity, I adopt the more conservative view of the interaction, and the major claim that I make in this regard is that it is the national character, intellectual traditions, and social history that jointly shape a language – in our case, American English. The remaining chapters will provide abundant evidence to support this claim. They will also show that we can go a long way in accounting for British-American linguistic differences if we investigate the influence of the American national character and American intellectual traditions on American English.

study questions and activities

1. Given what you have learned in the chapter and in the previous chapters, write an essay in which you summarize the main goals and results, as well as the main strengths and weaknesses, of the approaches that deal with the relationship between British and American English. Add some ideas concerning how you would improve on the approaches.

chapter 12

Economy in American English

As the popular saying goes, Britain and America are "two nations divided by a common language." The question that we need to ask is this: How exactly are the two languages different? In discussions of British and American English differences, the most commonly heard observation, on the part of experts and lay people, natives and foreigners alike, is that American English tends to be somehow "simpler" than its British counterpart. I use "simplicity" as a general cover term that includes a variety of related linguistic phenomena. Simplicity may manifest itself in many linguistic ways and for several different reasons. It can be seen in spelling, word forms, syntax, discourse, and more. The driving force behind simplification may also be manifold, but three general intellectual traditions appear to be chiefly responsible: puritanism, the rationality of the Age of Enlightenment, and republicanism. In this chapter we will deal mostly with the process of simplification in spelling and, to some extent, in word forms, as largely driven by some Puritan values, especially thriftiness.

The historical context

A remarkable feature of the tendency for simplification in American English is that, at least in its historical beginnings, it was a conscious and planned process. The historical context was provided by the War of Independence. A key figure in the "cultural and linguistic War of Independence" was, as we saw in a previous chapter, Noah Webster. Webster wanted to have a new and uniform English in the new country, a vision that was most fully shared with him by H.L. Mencken more than a hundred years later. However, the attempt to change American English in a deliberate manner was not merely a goal set by linguists. Although never at the level of official politics, several influential politicians participated in the debates concerning *how* to change the English language in an effort to adjust it to the new circumstances. Most prominent among these was Thomas Jefferson. For example, Jefferson made the following comments in 1779 (quoted by Simpson, 1986:32):

> Will it not be better ... while we are reforming the principles to reform also the language of treaties, which history alone and not grammar will

justify? The articles may be rendered shorter and more conspicuous, by simplifying their stile and structure.

There are several points about this passage that are relevant to our discussion. First, Jefferson wants to reform politics simultaneously with the language of politics. That is, he finds it desirable if political and linguistic reform go hand in hand. Second, the particular linguistic domains that would be affected by the change are style and structure. Third, the way he wants linguistic reform to go is in the direction of greater simplicity. Simplicity, for Jefferson in this passage, means shortness of form and transparency or "conspicuousness" of meaning. Fourth, the reasons for the desired change to shortness of form and transparency of meaning that Jefferson mentions are twofold: the ideal of economizing with resources (in this case, with linguistic forms) and the ideal of the widespread social availability of commodities (in this case, that of meanings). As will be shown below, the first ideal may be linked to the Puritan value of thriftiness and the second to republicanism, that is, democratic ideas about social sharing and the role of any privileged class in interpreting language for other less privileged classes. Indeed, this is also Simpson's interpretation of the passage by Jefferson. Simpson introduces the passage with these words (1986:32): "Jefferson, in 1779, comments on the potential for a simultaneous reform of politics and language by simplifying the language of politics and making it available to a wider audience." His comments following the passage above are even clearer and show that language reform in the new country has its roots in certain republican or democratic ideals. Simpson writes: "We may infer that along with such a simplification would go a demystification of the role of the patrician as executive and interpreter, ..." (1986:32). (The issue of the transparency of meaning will be taken up in the chapter on directness. See chapter fourteen.) Although Jefferson's statements have to do with reforming the language of politics, we will see that the kinds of changes that he recommended in the passage above for political language can be seen as overall changes in American English in general.

Spelling reform

Perhaps the most obvious domain in which Americans tried to simplify English is that of spelling. Spelling reforms started at about the end of the eighteenth century. Attempts at changing the complicated spelling system of English were not only numerous but involved some "big names," including Benjamin Franklin, Noah Webster, and Mark Twain. Twain, for example, worked on what he called "a simplified alphabet." We will discuss some of the details of Webster's ideas later in this section.

In 1876 the Spelling Reform Board was founded. The Board drew up a list of about 300 words where it recommended simplifications in the spelling. These included changes in the spelling of such words as *axe* (to *ax*), *judgement* (to *judgment*), *catalogue* (to *catalog*), *programme* (to *program*). In these cases the recommendations of the Board were accepted, and today the second versions of the spellings above are all regarded as possible American alternatives. However, many of the Board's other suggestions were not successful. Later the Board went overboard, so to speak, with its recommendations. Perhaps fueled by their initial success, it suggested simplified spellings that did not meet with the approval of the public. For example, they wanted to have *tuf* for *tough*, *def* for *deaf*, *troble* for *trouble*, *yu* for *you*, and many others. There was a great deal of resistance to these changes, and simplified spelling slowly went out of fashion.

Almost a century before the days of the Spelling Reform Board, Webster published his *American Spelling Book* (later called *Elementary Spelling Book*) in 1788. In this book he suggested a number of changes in English spelling, but many of these were not accepted. These included *bred* for *bread*, *soop* for *soup*, *wimmin* for *women*, *fether* for *feather*, *tuf* for *tough*, *groop* for *group*, *medicin* for *medicine*. Some of his other suggestions were more favorably received. Some of the best known cases of changes that Webster successfully suggested include the shift from *-ll* to *-l* (as in *woolen*), from *-re* to *-er* (as in *theater*), from *-our* to *-or* (as in *color*), and *-ce* to *-se* (as in *defense*). Some of his suggestions concerning individual words were also adopted. An example is the American spelling (and pronunciation) of *aluminum*, in place of the British *aluminium*. In those cases where British English had alternative spellings, Webster always recommended the simpler form for American usage. For example, British English had at the time both *music* and *musick*, and it also had *risk* and *risque*. Since then, both varieties of English have opted for the simpler versions of these cases.

Economy

One manifestation of simplicity in language is economy – economy of linguistic expression. This can take a variety of forms and can occur at various levels of linguistic structure.

Spelling

As a first set of examples, let us look again at some of the suggestions for simplifying spelling in American English. As we saw above, American spelling, in the majority of cases, is consistently shorter than British spelling. Consider again the examples, where the changes are indicated from British to American:

-mme to *-m*: *program(me)* and *kilogram(me)*.
-our to *-or*: *colo(u)r, neighbo(u)r, hono(u)r, valo(u)r, flavo(u)r,*
and *behavio(u)r*.
-gg to *-g*: *wag(g)on* and *fag(g)ot* (*Faggot* means "homosexual" in AE
and "unpleasant person" in BE).
-ll to *-l*: *counsel(l)or* and *wool(l)en*.
-logue to *-log*: *catalog(ue), dialog(ue), monolog(ue)*.
judgement to *judgment*.
moustache to *mustache*.
aluminium to *aluminum*.

These spellings did not all arise as a result of Webster's efforts, but, as we saw
above, some of them did. What is more important is that in *all* of these examples of American spelling we have the process of simplification at work
through reducing or shortening the written form of words. We can ask why
the changes in spelling occurred in this particular way. Why not some other
way? We can get a fairly clear answer to the question from Webster himself.
Webster translates linguistic economy into real economy, as the following passage
indicates (taken from Simpson, 1986:53):

> Such a reform would diminish the number of letters about one six-
> teenth or eighteenth. This would save a page in eighteen; and a saving
> of an eighteenth in the expense of the books, is an advantage that should
> not be overlooked. (Webster, 1789:397)

Given that changes had to be made in the English of the Americans, the
changes, according to Webster, had to go in the direction of linguistic economy, because it is also "commonsense" real economy. This idea was especially
prevalent among the Puritans of New England, the home of Webster. We can
rely on Simpson's interpretation again, who apparently assumes that
Webster's reasoning derives from the Puritan value of thriftiness. Simpson
says, "Before dismissing this as a hyperbolic example of Yankee thrift, we
should remind ourselves once again that Webster thought and wrote within a
society for which the circulation of information and opinion through print
was held to be of the greatest importance" (Simpson, 1986:53). Strictly speaking, Webster was not of course a Puritan, but he seems to have inherited several
strong Puritan views, possibly including the one to economize with resources
in general and with linguistic resources in particular. What makes the quotation above especially interesting is that Webster manages to combine real
economy with a linguistic one in his argument for the simplification of
American spelling.

Others strove for spelling reforms for slightly different reasons. For example, Robert Ross, who produced another American spelling book in 1785, justifies his efforts in the following way:

> *Dilworth's* Spelling Book recommending Subjection to a foreign Power has a Tendency to promote Disaffection to the present Government, and must therefore be very improper for the Instruction of the *Freeborn* Youth of *America*, since we have become an Independent Nation.... And if our own Productions and Manufactures are as good as those of other Nations, why should we import from Great-Britain? (Quoted in Baron, 1982:68)

Dilworth was the British author of a spelling book widely used in American schools at the time. As Baron tells us, Ross recommended his own book because it was cheaper than European imports. More important is his nationalistic argument that the youth of a free nation should not learn how to spell from a book coming from the former oppressor.

The principle underlying Webster's proposals seems to be: "use as little (linguistic) form as possible." In addition to this principle, a second distinct way in which American English appears to make use of simplification through economy is what can be stated as "use forms you already have." It is a tendency in English in general to change the *-ae* and *-oe* letter-combinations into *-e*. Nevertheless, British English seems to have retained both the *-ae* and *-oe* spellings, in addition to the *-e* spelling in words like *mediaeval, foetus, paediatrician, oesophagus, manoeuvre, anaemia, amoeba*, etc. American English, however, seems to prefer the simplified *-e* spelling in these cases. Thus, in American English the usual spellings of these words are *medieval, fetus, pediatrician, esophagus, maneuver, anemia*, and *ameba*. Since the *-ae* and *-oe* spelling does not exist in the regular writing system of English, the principle on which the American choice is based seems to be: "use only letter-combinations that you already have in the regular orthographic (writing) system." This principle accounts for the American preference, but it is not a watertight rule. One clear exception is the existence of both the *-ae* and *-e* spellings in *aesthetics* and *esthetics* in American English. The difference between British *connexion* and American *connection* may exemplify the same principle.

Simpson's words may be helpful again at this point to understand the process of simplification through economy:

> When Johnson spells *errour*, because of some reputed analogy with the French, from which the English word might have been secondarily derived, but speaks and pronounces it as *error*, he is not just

unnecessarily ingenious but also socially divisive, as Webster points out in the preface to his *Compendious Dictionary*. (Simpson, 1986:53)

The key words for us in this passage are "he is not just unnecessarily ingenious." In other words, if there is no compelling reason to do so, we should not indulge in the luxury of using more linguistic form than is needed; we have to be economical with linguistic resources as well. It should also be noted that the phrase "socially divisive" refers to another reason for linguistic economy. It is a democratic one. To ignore the principles of linguistic economy may divide society into those who understand and those who do not.

Words

Economy as a simplification process may also appear at the level of words (or, more technically, morphology) in American English. This happens when a word in British English is similar to one in American English. In these cases, American words have a tendency to be shorter than British ones.

Several words, especially nouns, that end in *-s* in British English are used without the *-s* in American English. Examples include *maths – math*, *innings – inning*, and *overheads – overhead* (the last example meaning "expenses to keep a business running"). But the same distinction can also apply to adverbs. *Towards* and *backwards* are British usage, while *toward* and *backward* are used in the U.S.

Furthermore, some words that end in *-ing* in British English do not have the *-ing* form in their American English counterparts. Words that exhibit this property include *sailing boat – sail boat*, *sparking plug – spark plug*, and *parting – part* (of the hair).

There are also cases where the *-er* suffix is present in the British English but not in the American English word. An example is *dumper truck* as opposed to *dump truck*. It has to be noted that *dump truck* is not an exclusively American English term; it belongs to common English. However, *dumper truck* is limited to British English.

The *-al* suffix behaves in the same way as the cases mentioned so far. For example, British English has *musical box*, whereas we find *music box* in American English.

Finally, the suffix *-ery* is used in British English in words like *cookery book*, which is simply *cook-book* in American English.

What these cases and the examples suggest is that American English has a tendency to use the shorter forms. If a word ends in a suffix in British English, American English simply omits the suffix. This can be regarded as another form of the simplification process in American English that is based on the economy of linguistic expression – here, the use of a shorter form.

Interestingly, we can think of the other principle "use (linguistic) forms you already have" that we saw in connection with spelling as having its analog in the vocabulary as well. The fact that American English has retained many archaic words that British English has lost may be a lexical manifestation of the same principle. Given those well established words, Americans have kept and continued to use them. Conversely, the same principle may explain why Webster found it important to discourage the use of French words in the new republic (quoted in Simpson, 1986:72):

> All our ladies, even those of the most scanty fortune, must dress like a dutchess in London; every shop-keeper must be as great a rake as an English lord; while the *belles* and the *beaux*, with tastes too refined for a vulgar language, must in all their discourse, mingle a spice of *sans souci* and *je ne scai quoi*. (Webster, 1785, p.47)

If the principle is "use forms you already have," then there is no need to use French words. Webster's argument here is based on two notions. One is the traditional Puritan distrust of ornament and affectation, while the other is again economic, possibly Puritan thrift. (However, we should not imagine a direct link between Puritan origins and linguistic economy; literary writings from the 1600s and early 1700s do not demonstrate this kind of linguistic economy.) Economy (possibly Puritan) seemed to be a part of the spirit of the time. Simpson notes that the journal *American Museum* recommended the adoption of a national dress in place of foreign clothes to avoid the potential economic damage to the country (Simpson, 1986:264). Of course, the argument against the use of French and Latinate words could also be supported by certain democratic principles. However, this is not the option chosen in the passage above (which does not mean that democratic ideas are not used for linguistic economy in other cases).

Syntax

Webster links the principle "use as little form as possible" with Puritan thriftiness. We do not know if thriftiness is also the driving force for the general tendency to shorten words in American English. However, the tendency is not incompatible with it. As we have seen above, linguistic economy may also be driven by the republican ideal. We will see that rationality can also lead to the shortening of linguistic forms (see chapter thirteen). In other words, simplification through economy may result from several distinct factors or forces, and these forces may also act simultaneously. This is probably the case in the next set of examples that come from the domain of syntax.

Consider the sentences below, where the first sentence of each pair is more typically British, while the second is more typically American:

(a) The exams started on Monday.
(b) The exams started Monday.

(a) We'll stay at home today.
(b) We'll stay home today.

(a) You can do it in any way you like.
(b) You can do it any way you like.

(a) He'll come to see us soon.
(b) He'll come see us soon.

(a) Where do you want to get off?
(b) Where do you want off?

The second sentence of each pair is shorter than the first. The sentences that are regarded as more typically American lack a particle or function word (in the last pair also a verb) that the more typically British sentences all have. It could be suggested that this is because the principle of "use as little (linguistic) form as possible" is more effective in American English. Furthermore, it may also be that the principle itself is more prevalent in America than in Britain because of the more explicit presence in America of some Puritan values. However, this is not likely to be the only, or even the major, cause of the differences above. In the next chapter, I will point out that rationality, another driving force, may also play some role in how American English came to be different from British English.

In the previous paragraph, we saw how the principle of "use as little form as possible," which was fairly explicitly stated for the systematic differences in spelling, has its counterpart in syntax. The other principle, "use (linguistic) forms you already have," may also be present in syntax. If there is an auxiliary in an English sentence, the repetition of the verb phrase of which the auxiliary is a part is indicated by repeating the auxiliary. For example, a response to the question *Have you cleaned your desk?* is *Yes, I have*, where the auxiliary *have* stands for the entire verb phrase *have cleaned my desk*. This is common to both British and American English. However, British English also has the possibility of responding with *Yes, I have done*. This grammatical construction is called *do*-substitution. *Do*-substitution in these cases is only available for speakers of British English. The reason might be that speakers of American English observe the principle "do not introduce a new auxiliary to the sentence; use the one you already have." This in turn can be regarded as a special case of the principle "use forms you already have." As we have seen, this can refer to the lack of an item in the spelling system or to the lack of an item (such as the auxiliary *do*) in a sentence.

Literary discourse and economy

Linguistic economy can also be at work in literature. This can take a variety of forms. Perhaps the best known American writer of fiction to make use of linguistic economy in his works was Ernest Hemingway. One of Hemingway's goals was to avoid the "tricks" of high literature. To this end he employed certain simplifications in his prose of the 1920s (Cowley, 1973). One of Hemingway's "favorite" stylistic devices was to "strip" sentences to their bare essentials. In his writing, he made a deliberate effort to avoid adjectives and adverbs, while keeping nouns and verbs. For Hemingway, the adjective and adverb did not belong to the essential parts of a sentence; they were something unnecessary that could be left out. In this respect, he can be viewed as following the ideas of the Saxonist movement in the United States, a purist approach to English that wished to replace foreign, especially French, words with Anglo-Saxon words and that also treated nouns and verbs as the most important parts of speech. This aspect of Hemingway's stylistic "revolution" influenced several American writers and is the key to understanding and appreciating much of his later work. Here is a passage to illustrate this style from the short story "Indian Camp," in the short story collection *In Our Time* (1925):

> He pulled back the blanket from the Indian's head. His hand came away wet. He mounted on the edge of the lower bunk with the lamp in one hand and looked in. The Indian lay with his face toward the wall. His throat had been cut ear to ear. The blood had flowed down into a pool where his body sagged the bunk. His head rested on his left arm. The open razor lay, edge up, in the blankets.

The extreme case of linguistic economy is silence. This extreme possibility as a stylistic device is utilized frequently in novels by Fenimore Cooper. The kind of silence Cooper is fascinated by is that of the Native American. The character that embodies the silent American in Cooper's novels is Natty Bumppo. Indeed, Cooper identifies silence as an essential aspect of the American character. In *Miles Wallingford*, he writes (quoted in Simpson, 1986:197): "It is lucky for us that the American character inclines to silence and thoughtfulness, in grave emergencies; we are noisy, garrulous, and sputtering, only in our politics"

(p. 281). Maybe Cooper is right. Some time ago the British novelist Graham Greene wrote a novel with the title *The Quiet American*. Could he have written a novel entitled *The Quiet Englishman*?

Linguistic economy (i.e., less linguistic form) in literature does not, of course, mean less meaning. Shorter sentences do not carry less meaning – silence is not meaningless. On the contrary, linguistic economy in literature is one way of adding layers of meaning to a literary work. Simpson (1986) argues that Natty Bumppo's silence is rich in meaning. In Hemingway's case, we find that the deliberately short and simple sentences were intended to be the tip of the iceberg. The reader is supposed to figure out the rest, and by far the most, of the meaning in Hemingway's stories.

But as noted earlier in the chapter, we should not suppose a direct influence from Puritan origins on the style of American literature in general. Despite the obviously economical tendencies in ordinary language and some of American literature, there was still fascination with ornamental style in the British mode.

Obviously, the linguistic phenomenon discussed in this chapter is just one small part of British-American differences. But the important point to remember is that given a certain deeply ingrained intellectual tradition, it manifests itself in language, no matter how small the scale of the linguistic phenomenon is.

study questions and activities

1. Try to find more examples for linguistic economy for some, or all, of the cases that were discussed in the chapter. Try to find counterexamples as well. Do the generalizations offered in the chapter still stand? Or do we have to abandon them completely and replace them with other generalizations? (Save your counterexamples for later use because you may be able to account for them with the help of some other characteristic of American English we'll deal with in later chapters.)

2. If economizing with resources in general is indeed an important American trait, there must be several proverbs that reflect this value. (Proverbs typically convey values and truths held important in a culture.) Look up the concept of *waste* (as verb, noun, adjective, and their synonyms) in Wolfgang Mieder's *Dictionary of American Proverbs* to see how many American proverbs have to do with this Puritan value. See also what other culturally important notions these proverbs bring into focus. Compare the results with what you find in your own culture concerning waste.

In thinking about the American proverbs, try to check whether they are old or recent. Can you see a shift in present-day American society away from the norms as given in the proverbs?

3. Look at the first few passages of Hemingway's *The Old Man and the Sea,* Twain's *The Adventures of Huckleberry Finn,* and Cooper's *The Last of the Mohicans.* How do they compare in terms of linguistic economy?

4. Can you find the same economizing tendencies in such major American documents as *The Constitution* or the *Declaration of Independence?* If not, why not? What possible reasons can you think of?

chapter 13

Rationality in American English

In the previous chapter a possible connection was pointed out between the Puritan value of thriftiness and what was called "linguistic economy." However, it was suggested that thriftiness might not be the only motivation for linguistic economy. It was mentioned that the democratic ideal might also play some role in American English, developing linguistic forms that are shorter than the corresponding forms in British English. The present chapter will focus on a third motivating force, rationality (or rationalism), a key component of the philosophy of the Enlightenment. When applied to American English, rationality can be seen as manifesting itself in at least the following three ways: (1) linguistic economy; (2) regularity; and (3) iconicity. We dealt with linguistic economy in the previous chapter, but we return to it here as well, because linguistic economy may also be brought about by the ideas that in part constitute rationality. Indeed, several of the linguistic phenomena discussed in the previous chapter can be viewed as probably arising from rationality as well, not just Puritanism. We will discuss these after a brief survey of some important ideas of rationality as a philosophical view, with particular attention to its American linguistic context.

What is rationality?

Rationality is a philosophical view which is the product of the Age of Enlightenment. Its most important notion is human reason. It is reason, and not our senses, that lead to the understanding of the world, and it is reason that is supposed to govern human affairs in general. There is a universal reason found in all human beings, and it is this universal reason that should be the basis of our judgments about all issues, including language.

A major advocate of the ideas of rationality concerning issues of language in the United States was Noah Webster, who lived and worked in the last part of the eighteenth and first half of the nineteenth century. Webster was in part a son of the Enlightenment. Simpson (1986:54) tells us that "there is much in Webster's early writings that identifies him as a true son of the Enlightenment, a believer in the prospect of rational universals and in the gradual supplanting of error and superstition by truth and good feelings." For Webster, rationality is closely linked with economy, as we saw in the previous chapter. Moreover, this rationality-based economy in language is necessary for a higher political purpose. Again with Simpson: "Within this manner of thinking cheaper books would have meant a wider readership and an enhancing of the opportunity for a unified nation" (p. 54). In other words, the overall political purpose for Webster is a unified American nation, and this goal can be best achieved if cheaper books are available to everyone.

The common man who is supposed to read these books is endowed with certain rational dispositions. One of these is that there is a natural dislike in the common man for anything that is unnecessary or superfluous. A natural inclination of the common man is for the avoidance of redundancy. For Webster and others, redundancy makes no sense; it is nonrational. This applies to language as well. A language that is rational is based on one-to-one correspondences between sound and letter and between meaning and form. These ideas about language are, of course, not limited to Webster and the American situation. We also find them in much of contemporary British writing. One example of this is given by Baron (1982), who reports that the British linguist Gilchrich argues, in the name of one-to-one correspondences between form and meaning, that in a rational language there should not be synonymy. My claim here is that in America the principles of rationality in relation to language were extremely influential, and were more so than in England.

According to the principles of rationality, a language must be regular, and it must be based on analogy. This is another aspect of universal human dispositions. Analogy and regularity are the natural dispositions of the human mind. The common man has this "natural instinct" (Simpson, 1986). For Webster, the language used by the common man reflects this natural instinct for analogy or regularity, or in Webster's words: "The tendency of unlettered men is to *uniformity* – to *analogy*" (quoted in Simpson, 1986:75).

One linguistic significance of this is that issues of usage are, for Webster, to be determined by analogy, and not by authority. It is this "logic of the common man" that should be evoked to judge what is acceptable and unacceptable usage. Linguistic authority should not play a role in the decision. Again, this rationality-based logic is useful for political purposes, namely, for the creation of a unified American English and, with it, a unified American nation. This relationship among language, the logic or the reason of the common man, and political goals is given by Webster in his *Dissertations* in the following way:

> This language is the inheritance which the Americans have received from their British parents. To cultivate and adorn it, is a task reserved for men who shall understand the connection between language and logic, and form an adequate idea of the influence which a uniformity of speech may have on national attachments. *(Dissertations*, p. 18; quoted in Baron, 1982:45)

Webster's ideas about analogy and uniformity determining linguistic usage were picked up by several later grammarians in the 1820s (Cmiel, 1990). These new grammarians rejected refined speech and custom in general as the authority in linguistic issues. The new basis for judging and determining linguistic usage that they offered was, following Webster, analogy or uniformity, that is, rationality. In their view, "reason must replace custom as the standard of good English" (Cmiel, 1990:76). They found rationality in the usage of the common man, who naturally possessed a disposition for analogy and regularity in his linguistic usage. The new grammarians had the vision of a rational American English, an English that was free from arbitrary custom, no matter how refined, and which was governed by reason and logical principles. According to Cmiel (1990), the historical context provided by the America of the 1820s did not favor these ideas and the ideal of a rational grammar. Populism was on the rise and popular orators did not want a grammar governed by universal logical principles; they wanted freedom to express themselves in a variety of voices and by means of a variety of linguistic resources, including "bad" grammar, slang, folksy ways of speaking, vulgarity, but also refined forms of language. So we can ask what became of the insistence on reason as the final arbiter of linguistic usage in America. Our answer will be that despite its failure in the 1820s, it became a major force in the shaping of American English. To see this, we have to look at some of the details of how American English differs from British English today, and see whether the differences are informed by the "logical principles" of rationality that Webster and the other grammarians thought so highly of in their vision of a new, American English.

Linguistic economy: the elimination of redundancy

In this section, I re-analyze some of the examples that were discussed in the previous chapter. These examples can be thought of as being cases of redundancy. Redundancy, as defined here, is a situation in which (1) a spelling is not "faithful" to the corresponding pronunciation, in that it contains more letters than is necessary, and (2) a meaning is expressed by more than one linguistic form. The claim will be that linguistic economy in the examples re-analyzed here may have also been produced by a rationalistic conception of language, possibly in combination with some Puritan ideals. In the next section, we will look at some additional examples of linguistic economy. However, I will suggest that those cases are different from linguistic economy as a kind of redundancy, the form of linguistic economy taken up in this section. The distinction is neatly captured by James Ewing in 1798 in relation to spelling reforms, proposing the following principles as the bases for his suggested spelling reforms:

1st No character should be set down, in any word, which is not
pronounced.

2d Every distinct simple sound should have a distinct character to
mark it, for which it should uniformly stand.

3d The same character should never be set down as the representative
of two different sounds. (Baron, 1982:78)

The first principle has to do with what we will call linguistic economy as
redundancy; in spelling no letters are required that are not pronounced. The
second and third principles together characterize what I will call linguistic
economy as "one value, one form." In the domain of spelling this means that
one letter must stand only for one sound value.

Sound and spelling

As noted in the previous chapter, one suggestion by Webster and other
spelling reformers was the shift from British English *-mme* to *-m* in such
words as *program(me)* and *kilogram(me)*. The underlying principle behind the
change seems to be that the *-me* part is superfluous in these cases because the
"faithful" orthographic representation of the pronunciation of these words
does not require the *-me* part. The *-m* does all the job that is needed since the
pronunciation is /progræm/ and /kilogræm/. Similarly, the *u* part of the British
English spelling of *-our* at the end of words such as *colour, neighbour, honour,*
valour, flavour, and *behaviour,* seems to be superfluous. It does not reflect a
sound in writing, since the pronunciation of *-our* has /ə/ in it, and does not
have anything resembling /u/. Thus, here again, the principle seems to be
"avoid superfluous elements in form," where "superfluous" is defined relative
to the sound shape of the word in question. Where British English usually has
-gg-, American English usually has *-g-* in words like *waggon.* Also, words that
normally have *-ll-* in British English are spelled with *-l-* in American English.
Examples include *counsel(l)or* and *wool(l)en.* It can thus be claimed that the shift
from *-ll* to *-l* in American English is a consequence of the underlying principle
that elements that are superfluous in the above sense are to be best avoided in
the written form. The same principle seems to apply to the shift in spelling from
British English *-logue* to American English *-log.* The *-ue* part of *-logue* does not
reflect anything from the pronunciation of words like *catalogue, dialogue, mono-*
logue, and others. Indeed, Webster explicitly suggests that the spelling reform can
be made in three steps, one being the "omission of superfluous or silent letters"
(Baron; 1982:63).

The same argument can be readily extended to the domain of semantics.
This is the domain of British and American differences to which we now turn.

Meaning and its expression

The next set of examples, examples that we already saw in the previous chapter, has to do with the economical expression of meaning, including the expression of time, place, manner, purpose, and direction. The principle that appears to be involved is "avoid redundancy in the expression of meaning."

Time

The relationship between an event and the time when the event takes place is commonly expressed by a preposition in English, especially by such prepositions as *on* and *by*. In the sentence *The exams started on Monday*, the relationship between the starting of exams and the time of this event is expressed by *on*. However, it can be suggested that the statement of the relationship by *on* is redundant; it is obvious that the expression *Monday* marks the time-frame in which the event (the starting of exams) took place, and so it does not have to be explicitly stated. Indeed, this seems to be the choice of many Americans. It is mostly speakers of American English, but not of British English, who can also say *The exams started Monday*. The point here is not that this is an extremely productive process (it may be limited to some time prepositions such as *on*), but that when it occurs it occurs in American English and not in British English.

Other examples that are commonly observed include sentences like the following:

He works by day and studies at night.
He works days and studies nights.

On Saturdays we go to town.
Saturdays we go to town.

The second example in both pairs above is a typically American English sentence that is unlikely to occur in British English.

Place

The same general phenomenon may be observed in the case of place prepositions such as *at*. Consider the sentences

We'll stay at home today.
We'll stay home today.

At in these examples may be considered redundant in the same sense in which *on* was redundant in its temporal usage above. Again, the second sentence is viewed as American.

Manner

What we said about time and place can be extended to manner, as these examples show:

> You can do it in any way you like.
> You can do it any way you like.

It seems that the second sentence, without the preposition *in* indicating manner, is more common in American English.

Purpose

The previous cases have to do with how a linguistic expression (a preposition) that marks an obvious relationship between two things (e.g., an event and the time of the event) may be omitted. There is a similar situation in cases like *He'll come see us soon*. This is a sentence found primarily in American English. What makes it interesting as an example of simplification through rationality is that it derives from the sentence *He'll come to see us soon*, which is found chiefly in British English. We have two actions in this sentence: coming and seeing, and a relationship between them, namely, that the purpose of the coming is the seeing. Now one common way to express purpose in English is by means of the particle *to*, as in *to see*. With the motion verbs *come* and *go*, we commonly associate a goal, or purpose; we come and go to a place for a reason, which is the purpose of the motion. Given this assumed relationship between motion and purpose, we do not have to make the relationship explicit; the *to* part of the infinitive may be left out. Again, this is the choice that American English makes. In other words, if it can be assumed that motion to a place has a purpose associated with it, then in (especially informal) American English we do not have to state the obvious; the purpose-marker may be omitted. Actually, the situation is slightly more complicated. This is because there is also an intermediate sentence between the two we have seen so far: *He'll come and see us*. This seems to exist both in British and American English. However, this sentence (the *come and see* type of construction) probably came into existence in American English first and came to be used by speakers of British English. In any event, what is remarkable about it is that it also does not mark the purpose-relationship between motion and action.

Whether or not it was American English that started the construction, the point is that the process was carried further in American English, where the nature of the relationship between motion and action does not need to be marked at all.

The same kind of explanation seems to hold for other cases that involve a motion verb and a purpose, e.g.,

Go (and) fix the car.
Can I come (and) have coffee with you?

We may even be able to extend this account to cases involving not only motion verbs. One such verb may be *help*. The difference in the use of this verb between British and American English is well known. Consider the examples

I'll help to mow the lawn.
I'll help mow the lawn.

The first sentence is typically British, while the second American. In the American version, the preposition indicating purpose may be omitted. However, the version of the construction with *and* is not available in either variety.

Direction

As a final example for this kind of simplification process, let us take the American English construction *want + particle*. When somebody says *Where do you want off?*, what is meant is where we want to get off or where we want to be dropped off. That is, there is an action that is understood to link the want and the direction; this is typically a motion. The motion between the want and the direction does not have to be made explicit; it is understood. When we say *The cat wants out*, we mean that the cat wants to go out. This construction is not used in British English. (But interestingly enough, it is used in Scottish English, where the American usage derives from.) We surmise that what made this admittedly trivial and limited construction more acceptable to speakers of American, rather then British, English is the American preference for not marking a relationship between two semantic units if the relationship is obvious since it can be assumed. It is important to see that I am not suggesting that this happens every time it could happen, but that when it happens it happens more commonly in American English.

We can add further similar cases to the ones discussed above. These include questions and the so-called "present perfect tense."

Questions

There is a type of informal question in American English that does not make use of auxiliary inversion. An example is *You want to leave now?*, said with rising intonation. What is missing here, compared with the normal way of asking a question, is that there is no auxiliary (*do*) and there is no inversion of the auxiliary with the subject (*do you...*). The principle that seems to be involved is something like "use only one form (intonation) to indicate questions," which is a special case of the more general principle "avoid redundancy."

The kind of question called "uninverted response question" presents a similar situation. In this case, although there is an auxiliary, there is no inversion. In the short dialog, *A: John went home, B: He did?*, of the three things usually needed for questions (auxiliary, auxiliary and subject inversion, and rising intonation) only two are present: auxiliary and question intonation. Again, this kind of question is more typical of American than of British English.

Finally, there is a type of question in which the auxiliary repeats the auxiliary used by the first speaker in a dialog; for example, *A: I'll do it, B: You will?* In this case it is also the intonation that signals the question; there is no inversion. (Incidentally, this type of question indicates mild surprise or interest.) It seems then that in all these cases American English reduces redundancy in the expression of questions to a considerable degree.

The "present perfect tense"

Students and teachers of English commonly make the observation that the use of the "present perfect tense" is somehow simpler in American than in British English. The key component of the use of the present perfect tense in English is the idea that an action or state has to do with the present, as in the following examples:

> They have already left.
> Has the baby eaten yet?

This idea of "up to the present" is clearly involved in the use of such adverbs as *already*, *yet*, and *still*. With these adverbs, American English may omit the use of the present perfect (*have* + *V-en*). Instead, it can have sentences such as

> They already left.
> Did the baby eat yet?

Thus, American English may choose between the use of *have* + *adverb* + *V-en* or *simple past* + *adverb* (e.g., *already*, *yet*, *still*). This second choice can be seen as another case in which redundancy is avoided. Since the adverbs express the idea that the present perfect tense does (i.e., that an action or state has to do with the present), it is not necessary to use both forms. The principle appears to be "don't use both forms if one is sufficient for the purpose." It should be noted, however, that this is considered informal usage in American English that is increasingly spreading to British English as well (Crystal, 1991).

Linguistic economy: one value, one form

Another form of linguistic economy is a case where it is thought that one linguistic value (a particular sound or meaning) must correspond to only one linguistic form. As we will see, this is related to, but also slightly different from, the idea of economy in language that manifests itself in the avoidance of redundancy or superfluity. The linguistic value can be either a sound value or a meaning. We begin with the discussion of "sound-to-spelling" correspondence.

Conventionality in sound-to-spelling correspondence

Linguistic economy sometimes consists in the selection of a more conventional item. What this means here is the following. In "sound-to-written form" correspondences or relationships, there are usually several distinct written forms (letters) that correspond to any given sound in English. (An amusing example of this is G.B. Shaw's alternative spelling for the word *fish*, which could, according to Shaw, be also spelled *ghoti* by making use of English "sound-letter" correspondences.) However, one of these tends to be one that is most closely associated with a sound, and thus can be said to be the most conventional written form, or representation of the sound in question. When this is the case, American English typically adopts the most conventional written form. Thus, ideally, there will be only one letter corresponding to each sound. Discussing Webster's thoughts about the issue, Simpson expresses the idea in the following way: "Changes in speech will occur, and writing can follow and transcribe them in a regular and rational way, with the same letters representing the same sounds throughout" (Simpson, 1986:61). Apparently, Webster also believed that each letter is inherently linked to a single sound (Simpson, 1986:58):

> The unavoidable consequence then of fixing the orthography of a living language, is to destroy the use of the alphabet. This effect has, in a degree, already taken place in our language; and letters, the most useful invention that ever blessed mankind, have lost and continue to lose a part of their value, by no longer being the representatives of the sounds originally annexed to them. (1806, p. vi)

In our terminology, this means that there was an assumption that each sound is conventionally associated with a given letter. Let us now take some cases where differences between British and American English can be explained along these lines.

The change from c to s

Consider first such pairs of words as *defence – defense, offence – offense*, and *pretence – pretense*, words that are spelled with a *c* in British and *s* in American English. *C* and *s* are alternative written representations of the sound /s/ in English. The letter *s* can be seen as a more conventional written symbol for the sound /s/ than the letter *c*. As the examples show, American English typically chooses this more conventional symbol to represent the sound /s/. A counterexample is provided by the word pair *practise – practice*, where the words are verbs. In this particular case, it is British English that uses the more conventional symbol for /s/. However, the general tendency for American English is to have *s*, rather than *c* in these cases.

The change from -ise to -ize

Furthermore, the spelling of the suffix *-ise/-yse* (as in *characterise, analyse, paralyse*) is regarded as the British variant of the same suffix with *z*, which is considered the standard American usage. Both *-ise* and *-ize* (and also *-isation* and *-ization*) are pronounced with a /z/. The letter *z* is a more conventional orthographic representation of the sound /z/ than the letter *s*. American English again favors the variant that is simpler in that it is more conventional.

First names

A further set of examples is provided by the different spellings of such first names as *Marc* (BE) and *Mark* (AE) and *Geoff* (BE) and *Jeff* (AE). It is reasonable to suggest that *-k* is a more conventional written representation of /k/ than *-c* is and *-e* is more so for /ɛ/ than *-eo*.

Phonetic spelling

Finally, we can take what is called "phonetic spelling." In the case of phonetic spelling, the principle could be stated in the following way: "to represent sound shape in writing, use only letters or letter combinations that are the most conventional written representations of sounds." Take the following examples for phonetic spelling from Gramley and Pätzold (1992):

plough, draught, through, though, light, high, night

Both British and American English use these spellings, but American English also has alternative written representations for these words (especially in informal contexts). Some of the spellings below (like *lite, hi, nite*) are often disapproved of, but some (like *plow* and *thru*) have become quite respectable and are accepted sometimes in standard usage:

plow, draft, thru, tho, lite, hi, nite

-ow can be said to be a more conventional written representation of the sound /aw/ than *-ough*; *-f* more of /f/ than *-gh*; *-u* more of /u/ than *-ough*; *-o* more of /o/ than *-ough*; and *-i* more of /aj/ than *-igh*.

In the cases discussed in this section, a more conventional form is selected over a less conventional form. Thus, in these cases linguistic economy consists in the preference for the most conventional form (letter). In this sense, typically, American English can be said to be simpler than British English, in that it favors a letter that is thought to be most conventionally associated with a given sound.

Syntax and morphology

Cases of "one value-one form" can be found in syntax and morphology as well. This occurs when a single meaning is expressed by a single linguistic form. A special case of this is what could be called "symmetry of forms."

The so ... as construction

This construction exists both in British and American English. Trudgill and Hannah (1982) give the following example:

It's not so far as I thought it was.

In addition to the *so ... as* construction, American English has its own version, where we can also find the sentence:

It's not as far as I thought it was.

In other words, the American alternative is *as ... as*, which shows a preference for a symmetry of forms. It should be noted that the construction as such appears in limited contexts: either in negative or conditional sentences. Here are some additional examples to show this from Trudgill and Hannah (1982):

> So long as you're happy, we'll stay.
> As long as you're happy, we'll stay.
>
> That one isn't so nice as the other.
> That one isn't as nice as the other.

It must be pointed out that some speakers of British English do not accept these expressions as more characteristic of either British or American English. Since we do not have any statistical information concerning the present-day distribution of the construction in the two varieties, we simply assume that Trudgill and Hannah's description was correct at some time but the situation may be changing now. However, this does not really affect the argument presented here.

Conditionals

In English there are several forms to express present hypothetical conditionality: the conjunction *if* and the auxiliary *would* (in British English, also *should*) in the dependent clause and the "past tense" in the main clause. An example of this type of conditional is the sentence *I would do it if I had time*. That is, *would* is used to express the notion that the conditional is a hypothetical and present one (as opposed to the past hypothetical conditional). But many Americans can also say sentences like *I would do it if I would have time*, which is considered less educated usage (but we can hear it said even by university professors). The point is that this latter sentence seems to conform to the principle of "use only *would* to express present hypothetical conditionality." Let us take another example.

> If it rained, everything would be okay. (both BE and AE)
> If it would rain, everything would be okay. (AE)

In educated or standard usage, the first sentence has *if*, the "past tense," and *would* to express conditionality. However, Americans also use and accept conditionality as being expressed by *if* and *would*, where *would* replaces the "past tense." This is one form of simplification based on the principle of "one meaning, one form."

The principle also extends to past hypothetical conditionals in American English. Consider the following pairs of examples:

> If I had seen one, I would have bought it for you. (both BE and AE)
> If I would have seen one, I would have bought it for you. (AE)

I wish I had done it. (both BE and AE)
I wish I would have done it. (AE)

As the examples suggest, in standard usage the past hypothetical conditional makes use of *would* + *have* + *verb-en* in the main clause and the "past perfect" (*had* + *verb-en*) in the dependent clause. American English has, in addition, the option of replacing the past perfect with the *would* + *have* + *verb-en* construction in the dependent clause. Here again, American English uses one form (*would have* + *verb-en*) to express a given meaning (past hypothetical conditionality). The choice of the form is also revealing about American English; it chooses the form that expresses the meaning more directly and transparently (which is *would*, rather than the past tense or the past perfect tense).

Regularity

A second major way, in addition to the two forms of economy we have looked at above, in which greater simplicity is achieved in American English is what can be called "regularity." Regularity manifests itself in American English in several ways.

In the first section we already observed the relationship between the common man and rationality. For Webster and many others, the common man or the yeoman is a "rational and rational*izing* being [who] will tend to provide order where it does not exist" (Simpson, 1986:75). This rational faculty is also attributed to the unlearned:

> The tendency of unlettered men is to *uniformity* – to *analogy*; and so strong is this disposition, that the common people have actually converted some of our irregular verbs into regular ones.... This popular tendency is not to be contemned [sic] and disregarded, as some of the learned affect to do, for it is governed by the natural, primary principles of all languages. (Webster, 1807a, pp. 119-20, quoted by Simpson, 1986:75)

As can be seen, a major part of this rationality is the natural inclination of the common man for "uniformity or analogy." We will call this inclination toward uniformity "regularity" in what follows in this chapter.

First we will take some cases of regularity in American English from morphology, then we will discuss some examples from syntax.

Regular and irregular verbs

As Webster noted in 1807, speakers of American English have a tendency to convert irregular verbs into regular ones. This is frequently observed by those interested in British-American linguistic differences even today. The phenomenon is called the "regularization of verb forms" (Gramley and Pätzold, 1992). Let us take some nonregularized examples first from present-day English:

burn	burned	burnt
dream	dreamed	dreamt
dwell	dwelt	dwelled
kneel	knelt	kneeled
lean	leaned	leant
learn	learnt	learned
spell	spelt	spelled
spill	spilt	spilled
spoil	spoilt	spoiled
smell	smelt	smelled
leap	leapt	leaped

These are the verb forms for the infinitive, the past tense, and the past participle in British English. As can be seen from the examples, in all these cases British English has two forms for the past tense and past participle (e.g., *burned* and *burnt*, *spelt* and *spelled*); that is, both forms can function as both the past tense or the past participle of the verbs. (The form preferred in British English is given first in the table.) In contrast, American English has only one form for both the past tense and the participle; it is the regular form (verb *+ed*, such as *burned, dreamed, kneeled, learned*) for both. Thus in predicative function American English has *burned* and *spelled* for both the past tense and the past participle. That is, a verbal contrast is expressed through only one form, rather than two as is the case in British English. One exception to this generalization is the verb *get*, which is more regular in British than in American English. As mentioned in chapter two, the British use *got* for both the past tense and the past participle, while Americans use *got* and *gotten*. However, the clear tendency is for American English to regularize these verb forms, while British English keeps the irregular forms.

Central and noncentral verbs

English verbs can be classified as central (regular) ones and noncentral (semi-regular) ones. Central verbs are lexical verbs like *walk, read, look at, think,* etc., while noncentral verbs include auxiliaries like *dare, need, used to,* etc. In American English there is a strong regularization process going on to make the noncentral verbs similar to the central ones. One of the things that makes a noncentral verb noncentral is that it can be negated directly, that is, without the use of *do*. For example:

I dare not think that it will happen.

This occurs mostly in British English. American English, and as an alternative also British English, would mostly have:

I don't dare (to) think that it will happen.

Similarly, both British and American English have

I don't need to tell you how much I like it,

but mostly British English has

I needn't tell you how much I like it.

Or to take another auxiliary, *used to*, we find sentences like the following:

He used not to go there. (chiefly BE)
He didn't use(d) to go there. (both BE and AE).

The underlying principle that American English appears to observe to a greater extent than British English is "Treat noncentral verbs as central ones." Of course, the end result of the process is likely to be the disappearance of the distinction between central and noncentral verbs. But this is not the point. The point is that American English is leading the way in the direction of greater simplicity in English, and this simplicity arises from the process of regularization.

Have

In British English, the verb *have* meaning "possession" can be treated as both a central and a noncentral verb. It can stand alone in declarative sentences (*I have a car*), but it can be used as an auxiliary as well in questions, for example (*Have you a car?*). In American English, however, it came to be used as a central verb. This is the result of the process of regularization.

In English, in sentences without an auxiliary, the normal, regular way to form questions and negate sentences is to use the auxiliary *do*, as in *Did you hear about it?* and *She does not go to parties*. This happens when there is no other auxiliary in the sentence. The principle appears to be "Use a regular construction in as many cases as possible." American English adopted this principle more than British English in that it extended it to the verb *have*. Questions and negation with *do* in conjunction with *have* are more common in American than in British English, although there is an increasing tendency to adopt this practice in British English as well, as the examples below suggest:

Do you have a car? (both BE and AE)
I don't have a car. (both BE and AE)

Have you a car? (only BE)
I haven't a car. (only BE)

Auxiliaries

The shall – will paradigm

One of the best-known cases of regularization is provided by the use of the auxiliaries *shall* and *will*. In American English, *shall* is hardly ever used to talk about future events (except in literary style). Whereas British English still retains *shall* in first person statements about the future, American English uses *will* for all persons, singular and plural.

I shall come back tomorrow. (chiefly BE)
I will come back tomorrow. (chiefly AE, increasingly used in BE)

What we find in this case is that a single form (will) is used throughout the paradigm in American English. The regularization process here takes the form of homogenization.

Should – would

Similarly, *should* is replaced by *would* in conditional sentences of the following kind:

I should do it if I could. (esp. older speakers of BE)
I would do it if I could. (AE and younger speakers of BE)

Here again, the first person *should* is dropped from the paradigm and *would* takes its place in American English. The principle seems to be that if there is a paradigm with an irregular member (i.e., a form limited to first person), American English eliminates this member in favor of a more regular one (i.e., a form that is less limited).

Shall – should

This is not to say that *shall* has no function in American English at all. It does; it is used in suggestions and offers to do something:

Shall we go?
Shall I get you a drink?

However, when permission for action is requested, *should* replaces it:

Shall I drink this now? (BE)
Should I drink this now? (AE)

In other words, *should* in American English is taking over a function that is performed by *shall* in British English. This kind of phenomenon is not limited to auxiliaries like *shall* and *should*.

Ought to and should

Ought to is also giving way to *should* in American English, where *should* is more common than *ought to*.

You ought to do it. (obligation)
You should do it.
They ought to be there by now. (tentative conclusion)
They should be there by now.

Used to and would

We find the same process in *used to* and *would*. These auxiliaries are used to express habitual or continuous activity in the past.

He used to go there every weekend. (BE and AE)
He would go there every weekend. (mostly AE)

In American English *would* in this sense occurs in longer stretches of discourse, especially in narrative contexts.

Must and have to

The English modal *must* has the meaning of "obligation" and "logical necessity." (Linguists also use the term "epistemic necessity" for what I call "logical necessity" here.) For example:

> You must leave at once. (obligation)
> He is not here. He must have left. (logical necessity)

Must is used infrequently in the "obligation" meaning in American English. However, it occurs commonly in the "logical necessity" sense. In this sense, speakers of American English can negate *must*:

> He must not be in. His car is gone.

Must in the "obligation" sense is replaced by have to in American English:

> You have to leave at once. (obligation; AE)

Need and have to

In the same way as *must*, *need* as a modal auxiliary is hardly ever used in American English in the sense of "obligation" and its function is also taken over by *have to*. *Need*, in British English, is used to indicate an "absence of obligation":

> You needn't do it. (absence of obligation; chiefly BE)
> You don't have to do it. (chiefly AE)

In American English, this is expressed by *(not) have to*.

In sum, we can observe an American tendency to use fewer modal auxiliaries than are used by the British. Instead of five modals (*shall, used to, ought to, must, need*), American English makes extensive use of just *should, would*, and *have to*. (There are, of course, other modals, like *can* and *may*, that are used both in British and American English.) Furthermore, these are auxiliaries that are used to perform very general and common functions in the modal system of English, while the auxiliaries that they replace (e.g., *shall, used to, need*) and that are more common in British than in American English perform much more specific tasks. In this again, we can see another instance of a more complete simplification process in American English.

Syntax

American English also seems to be more regular concerning many of its syntactic patterns. We will consider four such patterns: verbs with a direct and indirect object, adjectival constructions, the use of articles, and inversion.

Ditransitive verbs

Ditransitive verbs are verbs that take both a direct and an indirect object. Examples of this class of verbs are *give, send, show*, and many others. These verbs appear in two basic syntactic constructions. In one, the verb is followed by the direct object followed in turn by the indirect object. The indirect object is commonly expressed by the preposition *to* (less commonly by *for*). An example is:

Will you give it to me? (both BE and AE)

The other construction has the indirect object first, followed by the direct object:

Will you give me it? (both BE and AE)

Now there is a third construction that is only available to speakers of British English:

Will you give it me? (BE)

Here, the direct object is immediately followed by the indirect object, without the preposition *to*. The construction is irregular and thus not used in American English.

Noun phrases with modifiers

There are certain noun phrases that characterize British but not American English. These include river names and various noun phrases expressing temporal relationships. Noun phrases in English have the general, productive, hence regular, structure *(article +) adjective (modifier) + noun*. Take river names first. In American English we have such river names as *(the) Mississippi River, (the) Missouri River*, and *(the) Hudson River*, where the name functions as an adjective that specifies the generic common noun *river*. In British English, however, we have names like *(the) River Thames, (the) River Humber*, and *(the) River Avon*, where it is the noun *river* that appears in the position of the modifier (adjective). This only occurs in American English in the case of names that derive from French, like *Lake Superior* and *Lake Erie*. Thus American English can be said to be more regular in this respect.

Noun phrases expressing time relationships are another case in point. We find some differences between British and American English in this area as well. Here are some examples:

BE:	AE and BE:
on Sunday next	next Sunday
during January last	during last January
Monday last	last Monday

The examples under BE are exclusively British English, while the examples under AE and BE are shared. The adjectives *next* and *last* modify the nouns *Sunday, January,* and *Monday*, respectively. In this function, according to the basic rules of English syntax, they should come before the nouns. This happens in the case of some shared usage but not in the exclusively British usage. In this respect, British English is again less regular.

A similar account may apply to what is known as the "appositive construction," such as the following:

> Margaret Thatcher, the British Prime Minister, arrived in Washington today.
> British Prime Minister Margaret Thatcher arrived in Washington today.

The first sentence represents shared usage, while the second is typically recognized as American.

Articles

The productive structure for noun phrases in English is *article (+ adjective) + noun* and for prepositional phrases *preposition + article + noun*. Again, British English seems to deviate from these structures more often than American English, as indicated by the examples with the article *a*:

> He was seized with cramp. (BE)
> He got a cramp. (AE)

> He has earache. (BE)
> He has an earache. (AE)

to go to (a) university (BE)
to go to a university (AE)

She often gets stomachache. (BE)
She often gets a stomachache. (AE)

half an hour (shared)
a half hour (AE)

The same can be said of the article *the*:

to go to hospital (BE)
to go to the hospital (AE)

This difference applies to cases where the construction does *not* indicate a specific, concrete instance of being taken to the hospital. However, it may be noted that when it is used in the sense of "to be hospitalized," the construction makes use of *the* in British English as well.

Other examples include:

Leave your key at reception. (BE)
Leave your key at the desk. (AE)

at the end of term (BE)
at the end of the term/semester (AE)

in future (BE)
in the future (AE)

I saw him next day. (BE)
I saw him the next day. (AE)

However, proper names, like the names of countries, do not regularly require the definite article *the* in English. We find that American English observes this rule more fully than British English. Consider the following examples:

the Argentine (BE)
Argentina (shared)

the Gambia (BE)
Gambia (AE)

the Lebanon (BE)
Lebanon (shared)

the Sudan (BE)
Sudan (shared)

As the examples suggest, the definite article *the* occurs only in British English.

Inversion

As we saw above in the case of some types of question, American English has a tendency to avoid the inversion of subject and auxiliary. This phenomenon seems to be a part of a more general pattern in which inversion is avoided in other constructions as well, or at least is not used very commonly. For a further example, consider first the conditional construction again. The constructions in the second column below are alternatives to the ones in the first:

If I had been there, ...	Had I been there, ...
If you need help, ...	Should you need help, ...
If this continues, ...	Were this to continue, ...

What is shared by the examples in the second column is that they all employ inversion – inversion of subject and auxiliary, plus the omission of *if.* This inverted conditional construction is less common in American than in British writing, and when it is used in American English it is viewed as extremely formal.

Incidentally, a similar account may also apply to such cases as *during January last*, *Friday last*, and *Tuesday next*, discussed above. The versions that are shared by both varieties of English are *during last January*, *last Friday*, and *next Tuesday*. These latter phrases seem to be more regular because they avoid the inversion of the basic *modifier + noun* structure in English.

A further construction

In British English we can find such temporal phrases as *a week this Tuesday*. The equivalent and shared construction to this in American English is *a week from this Tuesday*. The difference is that the British phrase omits the preposition *from* from a prepositional phrase *(from this Tuesday)*. Thus British English uses a derived version of a larger noun phrase that contains a prepositional phrase. Noun phrases with the structure *article + head noun + preposition + determiner + noun* are much more regular in the syntax of English than noun phrases with the structure *article + head noun + determiner + noun*.

In sum, given all these differences, it can be suggested that American English uses more regularized syntax than British English.

Iconicity

There is a set of cases in which simplicity appears as similarity. In the examples discussed below, the similarity is between sound shape and written representation. We can call these cases "iconicity." The principle that seems to be at work is this: "make written form similar to sound shape." We will consider two cases for this principle. (For a general discussion of iconicity used in a similar sense and spirit, see Haiman, 1985.)

The change from -re to -er

When we pronounce words like *theatre* (BE) – *theater* (AE) and *centre* (BE) –*center* (AE), the sequence of the final sounds is this: /tə(r)/. Notice that in the British spelling the sequence of the actual sounds, /ə+r/, is reversed, yielding *-re* in writing. Given the British spelling, the sequence of sounds should be /t+r+ə/ and not /t+ə/, which is actually the case. The American English spelling of these and similar words, however, closely follows the sequence in which the sounds are actually pronounced. The spelling and the pronunciation coincide: *-ter* corresponds to the sound sequence /t+ə+r/. In this sense, the spelling and the pronunciation may be said to be similar or iconic.

The marking of stress

Another case in which iconicity is at work can be found again in the relationship between pronunciation and spelling. In American English spelling seems to follow pronunciation more closely than in British English. Consider some examples from Gramley and Pätzold (1992:346) again:

A:	B:
re'bel > re'belling	'revel > 'reveling
re'pel > re'pelling	'travel > 'traveler
com'pel > com'pelling	'trammel > 'trammeled
con'trol > con'trolling	'yodel > 'yodeled
pa'trol > pa'troller	'marvel > 'marveling

British and American English share the spellings in group A, but group B reflects American English spellings (British spelling would have *-ll* for group B as well). As Gramley and Pätzold point out, in group A the stress is on the second syllable of the root morpheme, whereas in group B it is on the first syllable. Furthermore, the words are all spelled with a single letter vowel (either *o* or *e*). In American English, the general rule for these cases seems to be that polysyllabic words with stress on the final syllable and with *e* or *o* that end in *l* double the *l*, if the suffix that follows begins with a vowel (as in *-ing*, *-ed*, *-er*). That is, American English seems to indicate the stress pattern of these words via their spelling. Stress on the final syllable is shown by *-ll*. In contrast, British English has the double *l (-ll)* for group B as well, and as a result does not show the differences in stress patterns between groups A and B. Thus, American English can be said to display more iconicity between its pronunciation and spelling.

It can be argued, however, that British English is simpler than American English because it uses a more regular spelling pattern: it has *-ll* for both groups. This is correct, but this kind of simplicity is gained at the loss of another kind of simplicity. British English has overall regularity in spelling at the expense of iconicity between pronunciation and spelling.

Despite the rejection of rationality as the basis of American English grammar in the early part of the nineteenth century, we can find many "rational or logical" principles at work in American English that were advocated by the new grammarians in America and that inform many of the present-day differences between British and American English. The principles of the elimination of redundancy, the preference for one-to-one correspondences, the large-scale use of regularity or analogy, and what can be called iconicity all suggest that, although the idea of rationality was not favorably received in the 1820s, it was not discarded from the linguistic consciousness of Americans. Instead, the ideas surrounding linguistic rationality or rationalism can be viewed as a major force in the shaping of American English.

study questions and activities

1. There is a general belief about American English around the world that it is easier to learn than British English. Do you share this belief? Do you think that what was said in the chapter has anything to do with the belief?

2. One of my students in Budapest, Zsuzsanna Bokor, did an interesting study to compare British with American English in terms of the dimensions of economy and rationality as discussed in this and the previous chapters. She gave a questionnaire to five native speakers of British English and five native speakers of American English. The questionnaire looked like this:

Questionnaire

Instructions:

1) Cross out any letters that you think are superfluous.
2) Cross out any words that you think are redundant.
3) Eliminate any punctuation you consider unnecessary.
4) Change any word to its shorter "equivalent" if you know it and would use it in the context.
5) Do not rewrite the sentences and bear in mind that changes can be made only by keeping the original meaning and grammaticality. Important: Make only those changes that you yourself would use in speech or writing regardless of what you think common or correct usage is in your culture.

1) The colours of the United States flag are red, blue, and white.
2) We are going to run out of petrol soon.
3) Go and prepare some dinner.
4) The first convoy of the United Nations' peacekeeping forces has arrived in Bosnia today.
5) I ran into her in the city centre, in front of a jewellery shop. She said, "How are you doing today?"
6) "Good-bye," he said after the movie.
7) Tonight we went into this drive-through restaurant for coffee and doughnuts.
8) He looked at me really strangely when I said I have always dreamt of becoming a singer.
9) Come and help me to repair the car.
10) The Mediaeval history exam will start on Monday so I am staying at home to study.
11) Do me a favour, will you?
12) The first time he travelled to Los Angeles was in the 1960's.

According to Zsuzsi, 38 changes (i.e., shortenings like letter subtractions or contractions) can be made altogether in these sentences. Check if you can find all, or most, of them. Zsuzsi did the experiment with five British and five Americans. It turned out that the Americans made far more shortenings (of different kinds) than the British. Do the experiment with as many native speakers as you can and see if you get the same result. Calculate the percentages for both groups.

3. In this chapter and the previous one, no mention was made of the huge numbers of immigrants going to the U.S. who were illiterate and uneducated. Do you think this could be a further cause of the strong "simplifying" tendency of American English? If yes, how?

4. In light of the chapter, how would you account for the following usages by Huck Finn in Twain's *The Adventures of Huckleberry Finn*?
   sivilization, I dasn't scratch it!, julery, warn't

   Find additional examples of this kind and try to give an explanation for them. What could possibly be Twain's intention with this kind of language?

5. Is rationality present in other, nonlinguistic areas of American life? Think, for example, of the planning of large cities. Or take political decision-making. What kind of rationality can you find here? To get an idea, read the relevant pages in, for instance, D.A. Stone's book *Policy Paradox and Political Reason*.

chapter 14

The "straightforward" American

The general notion that will be used to describe the linguistic and nonlinguistic phenomena under investigation in this chapter is "directness." The
word *direct* is used here in two related senses. First, it is employed in the sense
that a person uses language that is frank and to the point. Second, it is also used
to mean that the language used is easy to understand and follow. It is important
to see that directness is a concept that has mostly to do with language use, and
not necessarily with constructions in grammar or words in the vocabulary in
(American) English, as was the case with other forms of simplicity (e.g., economy and regularity) in the previous two chapters. Nevertheless, we will see that
some grammatical structures and vocabulary items are also involved in the
phenomenon of directness.

For example, a general concern with directness can be seen in English in
the large number of related vocabulary items. These include:

tell it like it is	put one's cards on the table
not mince words	pull no punches
not beat around the bush	get to the point
speak one's mind	wear one's heart on one's sleeve
call a spade a spade	no nonsense
no bullshit	

Another point to keep in mind is that, similarly to economy and regularity, directness can be said to be a property of both British and American English. However,
to the extent that one of these varieties of English makes more extensive use of it,
it can be claimed to be more direct than the other. And here again, it seems that
American English is characterized by more directness, although by a narrow mar-
gin. That directness is very much present in American English can be best seen
in the extent to which it is observed by its professional opponents. For example,
American linguist John Haiman (1995) recently wrote an essay with the title
"The cult of plain speaking," in which he criticizes this property of American
English. This tells us that directness has appeal to a large number of Americans.

As we have seen above, directness here means two things: frankness and
sincerity, on the one hand, and clarity of expression resulting in ease of understanding, on the other. We can put these two ideas in the form of two principles:

(1) "Say the truth and say what you mean," and (2) "say what you want to say explicitly and in a short and clear way." It is obviously the second principle that carries more linguistic implications – at least in the usual sense of "linguistic." However, since the maxims are closely related, it is also important to get an idea of the first.

Sincerity

Sincerity, frankness, honesty, and openness are all manifestations of the principle "say the truth and say what you mean." Americans attach a great deal of value to them. When an American is seen as behaving in accordance with them, he or she is often said to be *outspoken* or *straightforward*. To be outspoken and to be straightforward are normally regarded as desirable properties of people in American society. When people are not sincere, frank, honest, open, and so forth, that is, when they do not do or say what they really mean, they are often called *phony* or *fake*. The derogatory nature of these words, and especially that of *phony*, shows that Americans expect each other to be frank and outspoken all the time. Salinger's novel *The Catcher in the Rye* is to a large degree the story of a conflict between a sincere and outspoken teenager and a "phony" society of adults. Indeed, the notion of sincerity was elevated to the realm of philosophy by, as some say, the "most American" of American philosophers, Ralph Waldo Emerson. This is what he says in one of his best known essays, "Self-Reliance":

> ... let us enter into the state of war and wake, Thor and Woden, courage and constancy, in our Saxon breasts. This is to be done in our smooth times by speaking the truth. Check this lying hospitality and lying affection. Live no longer to the expectation of these deceived and deceiving people with whom we converse. (p. 136)

Unlike some other cultures, Americans despise lying or any kind of fraudulent behavior in most circumstances. For example, while in some cultures cheating in an exam is more or less acceptable, or at least not seriously sanctioned, most American students would rather fail than cheat, or, at least, they would lose face. The American idea of sincerity is not exhausted by the avoidance of lying, cheating, and fraudulent behavior in general. It also covers situations in which other societies suspend the application of sincerity. In many societies, for example, doctors do not tell you or even your close relatives that you are terminally ill. But an American doctor is expected to inform his or her patients of even deeply disturbing truths, like a patient's hopeless condition. To quote Emerson again:

Our sympathy is just as base. We come to them who weep foolishly and sit down and cry for company, instead of imparting to them truth and health in rough electric shocks, putting them once more in communication with their own reason. ("Self-Reliance," p. 139)

Many foreigners, but also some Americans, often perceive this as *bluntness*, a term that designates a certain amount of tactlessness. This arises from an assumed lack of regard for another's feelings on the part of the speaker.

Indeed, American outspokenness and straightforwardness are often seen in a negative light by non-Americans. (But also, when Americans are not being outspoken, this is taken as something not genuine and un-American.) In addition to bluntness, with its potential negative association with lack of tact, American straightforwardness is sometimes interpreted as lack of sophistication or politeness, and even rudeness. Americans have acquired a certain amount of disrepute in this respect – especially in some Western European countries.

Another aspect of the American emphasis on outspokenness is that they are also often perceived as emotional. This is a view that people form especially when Americans are compared with the British, who are typically regarded as calm, cool, reserved, or even aloof.

The principle "say the truth and say what you mean" applies to Americans not only when they speak, but also when they are spoken to. Another reputation that Americans have gained is that they are innocent and even gullible. Not only do they act according to the principle of "say the truth and say what you mean," they also take it for granted that others say the truth and mean what they say. This is why Americans are often regarded as "big babies," that is, adults who are as innocent as "babies" and believe everything they are told. Many American movies portray this kind of character. One example is the movie *Easy Rider*, in which a character (played by Jack Nicholson) fools another with his stories or, as many Americans would put it, engages in *bullshitting* him. And when an American in public office lies, it usually leads to public uproar and major sanctions against him or her, including impeaching a president (as in former president Nixon's case).

The importance of observing the principle of "say the truth and say what you mean" can also be observed in the attitude of the "quintessential American": Benjamin Franklin. Franklin in his *Autobiography* found it important to include sincerity as one of the thirteen virtues that he had followed in his life. In addition to such virtues as temperance, silence, order, resolution, frugality, industry, justice, and others, he said about sincerity: "Use no hurtful deceit; think innocently and justly; and, if you speak, speak accordingly." Thus Franklin, as in some other ways, prefigured some widely held, real or assumed, American traits.

Clear language

The second principle that we will look at has to do not so much with truth as with the clarity of what people say. This principle may be stated in the following form: "Say what you mean explicitly and in a short and clear way." This leads us to a long-debated issue concerning the use of English, both in Britain and America. The key concept, or, we might even say, the catchword here, is "plain English." This is a very popular notion in the English-speaking world in general, but it is not a unitary one. What does it mean? How is it used? According to the authors of *The Oxford Companion to the English Language* (1992), the expression "plain English" can mean four distinct things:

1. English that is straightforward and easy to understand;
2. Blunt, no-nonsense language;
3. Strong or foul language;
4. Movement against overly complex and misleading, especially bureaucratic, language.

Perhaps the most obvious manifestation of the attempt to achieve greater clarity of expression in English is the linguistic movement called "Plain English." This has to do with definition four above. Many Americans believe that ideas, no matter how complex, can be expressed in simple, easy-to-understand language. In their introduction to *The State of the Language*, Ferguson and Heath (1980) write:

> A very widespread notion among Americans is that anything really worth saying can be said in 'plain English.' Almost everyone – including government bureaucrats – decries the use of overwordy, needlessly obfuscatory style of government gobbledygook. (p. xxviii)

But the plain English movement is not an exclusively American phenomenon. It can also be found in Britain (where the movement started), and it is just as strong there as in the United States.

The efforts of the Plain English movement are directed at such "non-plain" uses of English as can be found in *gobbledygook, doublespeak, bafflegab, psychobabble, double Dutch, mumbo jumbo,* and any kind of *bureaucratese.* In the United States, ironic awards, or "anti-awards," are given by the National Council of Teachers of English every year to those whose English is muddled, difficult to understand. The winners are most often government officials or government organizations. Nevertheless, the U.S. Administration is very active against the use of government language that is not plain. Since 1978, five plain English initiatives have been issued by various government offices, including one by President Carter In 1978 (later revoked by President Reagan). Historically speaking, the Puritans favored "puritan plain style" and the Quakers "plain language." Since these two religious groups were, and still are, major determining forces in American society, their preference for plain language can be seen as equally important in the development of American English as well.

Various meanings of "clear language"

The various meanings of "plain English" listed by *The Oxford Companion to the English Language* give us a sense of the complexity of what is involved in "clear language." But there are even more ways to understand our second principle, "Say what you mean explicitly and in a short and clear way."

Transparency of meaning

In some cases, clarity may mean transparency of meaning. Schur (1980), for instance, notes that American English tends to be more transparent than British English. Unfortunately, he provides only one example for the phenomenon. He compares the British word *pram* with the American term for the same thing, which is *baby carriage / buggy*. He finds that it is easier to guess the meaning of *baby carriage / buggy* than that of *pram*. The same applies to some differences observed by Marquis de Chastellux, who was traveling in North America in the 1780s (Baron, 1982:15). The marquis was struck by such American phrases as *blue bird* for *jay*, *red bird* for *cardinal*, and *red duck*, *black duck*, *wood duck* for various *water birds*. These are cases where Americans adopted a simple descriptive name for an opaque term. The marquis took this to be language deprivation, but these examples could also be seen to indicate an American tendency for directness, a tendency observed by commentators on American English two centuries apart.

Explicitness

In other cases, clarity may mean explicitness. An example that Gramley and Pätzold discuss in this connection is the following: "The preposition *through*, as in AmE *Volume one of the dictionary goes from A through G*, is not current in BrE, where the ambiguous *A to G* or the cumbersome *A to G inclusive* might be found" (1992:356). The intended meaning (i.e., that *G* is included) is explicitly expressed in normal, everyday American English. As Gramley and Pätzold observe, British usage is either ambiguous or cumbersome here.

Shortness of expression

A third set of cases of clarity involves the use of short, snappy words. The use of these words is felt to allow a greater degree of directness in denoting things and events than the use of expressions consisting of several words. This sense of directness comes close to linguistic economy, a phenomenon that we discussed in an earlier chapter. Let us take some examples. Besides the Common English expression *to get in touch with somebody*, American English also has *to contact somebody*. The verb *contact* expresses in a compact and direct way what the longer phrase expresses. The verb *cut* was transformed into the noun *cut* in American English. This new noun can replace the common *reduction*. *Reduction* is longer and its meaning is less transparent than that of *cut*. Finally, the American English verb *fix* came to replace the less direct *prepare* and *repair*, corresponding to the two meanings of *fix*.

Directness of reference

This last group of examples has to do with what can be called "directness of reference." A special case of directness of reference involves direct reference to the speaker (writer) or hearer (reader) of a sentence or a piece of discourse. In English in general, this speaker or writer is often not mentioned in the sentence. The linguist Douglas Biber, whose work was already mentioned in the chapter on style, did an extensive study of the difference between British and American English in the use of the pronouns *I/you* (Biber, 1987). (The pronouns *I* and *you* are used to refer to the speaker/writer and listener/reader, respectively.) This was part of a larger study to see whether and to what degree British and American English differ from each other primarily in their syntax used in various types of discourse. Biber concentrated on nine written genres, based on the Lancaster-Oslo-Bergen (LOB) corpus (for British English) and the Brown corpus (for American English). The nine written genres examined in the two corpora consisted of the press, editorials, skills and hobbies, popular lore, government documents, academic prose, belles lettres, general fiction, romantic fiction. The analysis was based on approximately 1,600,000 words. Biber found that in the American genres *I/you* occur more frequently than in the corresponding British genres. This result was consistent for all the genres; that is, all of the nine American genres contained more occurrences of the pronouns *I/you* than the corresponding British ones. Biber's interpretation is that American English reflects a more informal, interactive style than British English. This is correct, and I will make use of this interpretation in a later chapter. However, I make the additional claim that the interactive style reflected in the use of *I/you* is also an issue of directness of reference to writer and reader, and primarily so. The more frequent use of *I/you* in American English shows a greater degree of directness (of reference to writer/reader) that results in a greater degree of interactionality and informality.

Generic one and he/you

We can find the same tendency (i.e., for more direct reference) in a grammatical construction. American English tends to use the pronouns *he* and *you* in places where British English has *one*, namely, where we want to refer back to the generic pronoun *one*. Thus, American usage again shows more directness in referring back to a nonspecific agent. Compare the following examples from Brown and Levinson (1987:198):

> One just goes along as best as one can. (BE)
> One just goes along as best as he can. (mostly AE)
> Wherever one goes in Europe, you hear bullfinches. (only AE)

It should be observed that only American English allows the use of *you* as a generic pronoun. The obvious difference between these examples and the case discussed above is that here the reference is to a generic agent, whereas in the previous case it was to a writer/reader. What is similar is that both cases have to do with directness of reference. And again, American English is more explicit, in that it makes use of the more specific, or less generic, pronouns *he/you* meaning "an individual male" (*he*) and "the listener/reader" (*you*) in referring back to the highly generic (that is, meaning only "one") pronoun *one*. The possibility of using *he* and *you* in this function in American English marks American English as the more direct variety. Brown and Levinson comment:

> The generalization seems to be that in British English the impersonalized point of view is more consistently insisted upon, at least with respect to *one* (an observation which is consistent with other observations about British/American cultural style). (1987:198)

Most likely, the difference that Brown and Levinson have in mind when they talk about "British/American cultural style" is that the British are seen as more reserved than Americans, one manifestation of which being a more "impersonalized point of view" that results in less directness in the use of pronouns.

Tag-questions

American teachers of English often notice that the use of English in *British* textbooks is different from their preferred usage. Some of these differences arise because of the greater directness of American English usage. The case in point is the use of tag-questions in the two varieties. A British English textbook (*International Business English*) has the following examples (Jones and Alexander, 1989:4–5):

> India is very different from Europe, isn't it?
> You haven't been round our works, have you?
> You met Mr Grey yesterday, didn't you?
> You've met Mr Suzuki, haven't you?
> It would be best to send them a reminder, wouldn't it?
> They don't normally pay up immediately, do they?
> You're waiting to see Miss Weber, aren't you?
> Mrs de Souza isn't arriving till tomorrow, is she?
> Your new receptionist doesn't speak English, does she/he?

The American teachers of English I have asked about these sentences seem to agree that there is something "un-American" about them. Their preferred versions would be sentences like these:

> India must be very different from Europe.
> Have you been around our works yet?
> etc.

The sentences used by the Americans seem somehow more direct than their British counterparts. The British sentences suggest more hesitation, uncertainty, or politeness, and they imply less commitment or involvement than their American counterparts. All of this is not to say, however, that Americans do not use tag-questions. They obviously do, but perhaps less frequently and with slightly different purposes and associations than the British tag-questions express. This idea seems to be supported by Gramley and Pätzold (1992:353), who claim that tag-questions of the kind

> He's coming early, isn't he?

are more common in British English than in American English. They note, moreover, that American English prefers tag-questions of the type

> I'll return it tomorrow, okay?

where the tag *okay*, despite being a tag, appears to lend directness rather than indirectness to the speaker. Furthermore, according to Gramley and Pätzold, tag-questions without reversed polarity are rare in American English, as in

They are leaving tomorrow, are they?

Let us now return to the textbook examples of tag-questions offered by Jones and Alexander. Even the less "British English-like" versions of some of the sentences above are likely to be used differently by Americans. Jones and Alexander offer the following as alternatives to the sentences with tags:

I expect India is very different from Europe?
I don't think you've been round our works?
I think you spoke to Mr Grey on the phone. Is that right?

Expressions like *I expect, I don't think, I shouldn't think, I think, I'm afraid, I suppose,* etc. tend to be less frequent in American than in British English. (The common, and often ridiculed, American use of *I guess* is an exception that seems to reinforce, rather than invalidate, this tendency.) Further research would be needed to investigate the details and complexities of the different uses of tag-questions by the British and Americans, together with other linguistic phenoma related to directness, such as hesitation markers, the construction *I'm afraid*, understatement, and others. On a purely intuitive basis, I would suggest that all these are more common in British than in American English.

Directness in discourse

As we saw above, Franklin included sincerity among the thirteen virtues he claimed to have followed in his life. He also had his views about the circumstances under which people should or should not talk. His idea was that people should talk only if it is necessary. He said in his *Autobiography*, "... avoid trifling conversations." If you have nothing informative to say, do not talk.

Contemporary observers of the American linguistic scene note that Americans may have lost their directness in communication – at least on the level of some ordinary types of conversation. Simon Hoggart, a British journalist, remarks: "When Americans meet abroad, or even in America, if they are strangers there is a ritual they must go through, which is a crucial part of their code of behavior" (Hoggart, 1991:73). Hoggart finds the following conversation typical between Americans in this situation:

Party A: Now, where are you folks from?
Party B: We're from Dayton, Ohio.

A: Well, is that so? You know my husband Everett had a cousin – a second cousin, that is – who used to live in Cincinnati, Ohio.

B: Well, hey, I was in Cincinnati only a couple of months back!

A: You were? Now I wish I could remember my cousin's name ... of course, I think he moved to Anchorage, or maybe it was Miami?

This piece of conversation seems to be far removed from the ideal envisioned by Franklin. But I will claim in a later chapter (chapter sixteen) that this kind of conversation has not so much to do with a lack of directness as with the friendly, informal politeness appreciated by many Americans. Since silence in interactions between people is regarded as a sign of impoliteness or unfriendliness, their politeness requires them to talk, often using banalities as in the hypothetical example above. However, we will see in a later section that when a conversation has a specific goal, Americans still very much observe the "rules" of directness in discourse.

The causes of directness

As we saw above, for Franklin, directness was a moral imperative that is most likely to derive from a Puritanical heritage. This may also be present in Webster. One opposite of direct, plain speech is ornamental, "flowery," or, in short, insincere language. As Simpson (1986:69) points out, Webster was suspicious of this:

Not only did he have a natural disaffection for the English ruling class, but he inherited the traditional Puritan suspicion of ornament and affectation, and of everything theatrical (monarchy being but a larger form of theater).

But the moral justification for directness is also complemented by a democratic one. Simpson (1986:59) quotes John Witherspoon:

Absolute monarchies, and the obsequious subjection introduced at the courts of princes, occasions a pompous swelling and compliment to be in request, different from the boldness and sometimes ferocity of republican states. (1802, 3:531)

In other words, the passage tells us that democracy produces boldness, or even ferocity, that is, what we called directness. In this, it is very different from absolute monarchies, which "occasion[s] a pompous swelling."

Directness may also result from pragmatic, or utilitarian, causes. Plainness of speech was a property of Americans that was observed early by travelers. Talking about the Marquis de Chastellux, whose observations we have already come across above and whose book about his trip to North America was published in 1787, Simpson (1986:211) remarks:

> Chastellux, traveling to America in the eighteenth century, had complained of the plain-spoken bluntness of American English, resulting in such trite designations as *blue bird* and *black duck*, and stemming from men's attentions being "employed in objects of utility" with no room or need for a supervening language of poetry. (1787, 1:41-42)

Here the justification for directness is different from either that of Franklin or that of Witherspoon. Chastellux points out a correlation between directness and people's pragmatic, rather than literary, interests. Where people are primarily involved in "objects of utility," there will be "trite designations," rather than "a supervening language of poetry."

Finally, we can also find another pragmatic motive, this time in the realm of the study of language, behind the preference for direct language. Webster suggested that "Nothing facilitates the study of the sciences more effectually than the use of plain intelligible terms" (quoted in Baron, 1982:136). The particular changes that Webster recommended were *name* for *noun* or *substantive*, *substitute* for *pronoun*, *attribute* for *adjective*, *modifier* for *adverb*, *connective* for *conjunction*. But Webster kept the name *verb*, for lack of a better term.

Business talk

Many of the same points made above appear in the way Americans conduct business negotiations – at least some of them, or at least the stereotypical American businessman or woman. The two principles "say the truth and say what you mean" and "say what you say explicitly and in a short and clear manner" often surface in observations of how Americans make business. We will look at two examples.

Hoggart (1991), the British journalist working in the United States as an American correspondent, has this to say about the way businessmen talk in the United States:

> Businessmen's talk, for instance, has a swaggering, no nonsense, 'I'm on top of this' quality. The concept of 'the bottom line' means 'What's in it for me? Don't waste my time with irrelevancies.' (p. 64)

American business negotiations, as perceived by this observer, should be direct; no *bullshitting* is tolerated. American businessmen, not unlike

Americans in general, are rational and goal-oriented, and this is reflected in their language use.

Graham (1983), our second example, describes the main characteristics of American business negotiations. He sees directness and even bluntness as a major property. According to him, American businessmen often resort to what he calls "John Wayne style." Here the principle seems to be: "Shoot first; ask questions later." Graham observes that this might not be the most effective way of doing business; nevertheless the "John Wayne style" prevails in American business. This situation may have given rise to the saying: "America has never lost a war, and never won a conference." We are not concerned with whether or to what degree this is true. For our purposes the important point is that the principles of directness given above are clearly present in American business talk. In addition to directness, informality is another characteristic that Graham mentions. This is captured in the formula: "Just call me John," which indicates that American businessmen try to avoid ceremonial introductions and do not like pulling ranks. Graham's formula for directness is: "Get to the point," an expression we have already mentioned at the beginning of this chapter. This emphasizes efficiency ("Don't waste my time") and a lack of fear of confrontations. Graham illustrates the importance of directness in American business talk by giving two hypothetical examples of business negotiations. The first involves two non-Americans, a manager and an aide:

> *Manager*: I certainly hope this shipment can go out tomorrow.
> *Aide*: I think we may have a few problems, it may be a bit difficult, but we'll try our best.

In the second example, the two businessmen are Americans:

> *Manager*: This shipment must go out tomorrow.
> *Aide*: It's impossible for it to go out tomorrow.

The American version has *must* for *I certainly hope* and *it's impossible* for *I think we may have a few problems, it may be a bit difficult*, etc. The difference in tone and style in the two examples is clearly a matter of directness as defined above. Furthermore, as Graham notes, American businessmen also use the principle of "Lay your cards on the table." This implies that they expect their business partners to say what they want. Both parties should say a clear "yes" or a clear "no" to the suggestions that are made in the course of negotiations.

We can conclude on the basis of the two cases we have examined in this section that directness is a major part of American business talk. This fits in with and reinforces the analysis provided in this chapter for American English in general.

The tension between plain and "unplain" language

However, I do not wish to create the impression that Americans always use and prefer the plain style. This would be simplifying the issue. The plain style may be the ideal, which is often though not always used, but it can also clash with "unplain" language. A clear example of this conflict is reported by Lutz (1990:57-8). Lutz notes that English teachers often say that they prefer clear, simple English. Nevertheless, the same teachers might in reality favor "unplain," heavy style in writing. He describes a study in which two groups of essays were read by teachers of English. Several pairs of the essays differed only in style: One essay was written in simple, clear language, the other in heavy, ponderous style. Concerning the results of the study, it is worth quoting Lutz in full:

> The teachers consistently preferred the essays that had sentences such as, "The absence of priorities and other pertinent data had the result of the preclusions of state office determinations as to the effectiveness of the committtee's actions in targeting funds to the areas in greatest need of program asssistance." The teachers consistently gave lower ratings to the essays that were written with sentences such as this: "Because the state office set no priorities and did not have pertinent data, it could not determine how effectively the committee targeted funds to those areas whose programs most needed assistance." Both of these sentences say the same thing, only the second says it more directly and more clearly. It has all the attributes teachers say good writing should have. Yet teachers overwhelmingly chose the first sentence over the second. Even those of us who should know better can be lured by the siren song of doublespeak. (pp. 57-58)

Thus, ideal and reality do not always coincide. Directness might be an important property of language and can serve as an ideal for many Americans, but in reality the ideal is not always followed.

study questions and activities

1. In his book *Cross-cultural Dialogues,* Craig Storti provides the following conversation that he takes to be illustrative of British and American cultural differences. Bill and Mary are Americans, while Nigel is British.

Bill: How did it go with Nigel?

Mary: Much better than I expected. These English are hard to figure.

Bill: What happened? Did you explain everything to him?

Mary: Yes, completely. I said we were very sorry but we simply weren't going to be able to meet the deadline.

Bill: And?

Mary: He just said, "That's a bit of a nuisance" and changed the subject.

Bill: That's great!

(Storti, 1994: 51)

What does this conversation (including the story behind it) reveal about the different cultural and linguistic styles of the British and Americans?

2. Read the following quotations from articles in the August 9 and 15, 1996, issues of the U.S. newspaper *USA TODAY*. (Remember that this was election year in the U.S. and that the final contestants for the presidency were Senator Bob Dole and President Bill Clinton.)

> Dole's refusal to be an orator on command provides a glimpse into the earthbound person he really is. Up close, he doesn't have the intimidating aura many leaders possess. His embarrassment about introspection is a classic Midwestern trait. Baring emotions is unseemly. Bragging is worse.
>
> He's forthright and blunt, even when he might be better served by swallowing his feelings and using the safer language of politics. His refusal to do that is the real Dole, the one he won't disguise on Thursday, his aides say.
>
> But Dole image-makers have worked long and hard to make the film a portrait of the candidate that they hope reflects his character even in its format: plain-spoken and straightforward.
>
> The theme, Sipple says, is a comparison between President Clinton, "a salesman and a smooth talker," and Dole, "a plain-spoken man of integrity."

How do Dole's image-makers make use of the linguistic and cultural trait of straightforwardness in the campaign? Do they try to put the trait to a political advantage? If yes, whose advantage and why is this possible?

3. Find additional cases and situations where Americans prefer straightforward language. Can you make any generalizations about these? Also, find cases and situations where straightforwardness is clearly not the norm for Americans.

4. Robin Lakoff in her *Talking Power* (1990) observes an interesting difference in public reaction to a statement made by John Lennon in the mid-1960s, when the Beatles were immensely popular both in Britain and the U.S. The statement was this: "The Beatles are more popular than Jesus." Unlike in Britain, the statement generated a great deal of heat and controversy (e.g., some American disc jockeys refused to play music by the Beatles). In light of the discussion in the chapter, how would you explain this? (One clue: think how irony – obviously intended by Lennon – is related to what we called "directness.")

chapter 15

The democratic nature of American English

It is not surprising that in a newly established democracy the use of language will also become more democratic. The democratization of language in America followed a large-scale restructuring of society. In the first half of the nineteenth century, mass democracy arrived in America which demanded a new language. The culture and language of the newly emerging class of citizens is referred to by Cmiel (1990) as "middling culture" or "middling style." Their language was not the "refined speech" of the gentleman anymore, and it contained many elements of the "vulgar." Cmiel describes the situation elegantly: "The men, and to a lesser degree the women, who challenged the gentry for cultural authority were not uneducated rustics. They were men and women of middling culture, people who cultivated refinements but who were not refined" (Cmiel, 1990:58-59).

One clear sign of the linguistic changes in the direction of democratization in American English was the broadening of the meaning of the word *gentleman*, to include not only those who were members of the nobility. In the early part of the nineteenth century, the word *gentleman*, together with *lady*, came to be used for any adult in American society. Although the old social system was gone, many of the old social customs and speech habits survived. It is not the case that everybody enthusiastically welcomed the changes toward democratization in America. One of these people was Cooper, who vehemently opposed the new use of the word *gentleman*. In Cooper's words: "To call a laborer, one who has neither education, manners, accomplishments, tastes, associations, nor any one of the ordinary requisites, a gentleman, is just as absurd as to call one who is thus qualified, a fellow" (quoted in Baron, 1982:23). Cooper also had reservations in connection with words like *boss* and *help*, which began to be used in place of the old words *master* and *servant*. The latter two words are remnants of an undemocratic vocabulary reflecting the old social structure. However, in Cooper's time the old social structure may not have been completely a thing of the past *in reality*. Despite the declaration of equality for all, there were masters and there were servants, but the servants did not want to call their masters *master* and they did not want to be called *servants*. They completed the revolution in language first. This enabled Cooper to conclude that "in all cases in which the people of America have retained the *things* of their ancestors, they should not be ashamed to keep the *names*" (*The American Democrat*, p. 122; quoted in Baron 1982:23).

The person who saw the need for a democratic language in America most clearly was again Webster. Criticizing Johnson's spelling of American *error* as *errour*, he writes:

> The great body of a nation cannot possibly know the powers of letters in a foreign language: and the practice of introducing foreign words in a foreign orthography, generates numerous diversities of pronunciation, and perplexes the mass of a nation. And the practice is, I believe, peculiar to the English. (Preface to the *Compendious Dictionary*, 1806, p. x; quoted in Simpson, 1986:57)

Therefore, Webster realizes the potential danger of even foreign-based spelling to a fledgling democracy: it might be socially divisive. A new democratic country should not allow this to happen.

Standardization

In this section, I will take up the issue of the standardization of American English. It seems reasonable to discuss this issue in relation to a more specific and a more general factor; first, in relation to how Americans responded to attempts at setting up an Academy to regulate language and, second, in relation to what the general American attitude was, and still is, to the standardization of their language.

Academy

One can tell if a language is democratic in its character by whether or not it has an Academy that legislates over linguistic issues. In this respect, English in general is one of the most democratic among Western languages. Although there have been quite a few attempts throughout its history to set up an Academy to make decisions about what is good and bad usage, no Academy was established either in Britain or the United States. In Britain, several famous writers made more or less specific proposals concerning the establishment of such an institution, including Dryden, Defoe, and Swift. In the United States, the most specific proposal was made by a politician – John Adams. Adams was so enthusiastic about the idea that he submitted his plans to Congress in the midst of the American Revolution. But his enthusiasm was not catching on to others. Claiborne (1983:209-10) makes the following comments about the fate of Adams' plans:

> Swift's countrymen, as we know, debated but ultimately rejected his proposal; Adams' fellow citizens, far less respectful of academies and authority generally, hardly even bothered to discuss the matter. (p. 210)

In other words, the idea of establishing an Academy never had a chance in the United States. And if there is no official body to decide what is good and bad usage, speakers have the freedom to make their own decisions. But, as we saw in chapter six, this is not to say that there were no attempts to standardize American English. Clearly, there were some standardizing forces in operation. One of them was the work of the famous American linguist Noah Webster.

Webster again

But the impact of Webster's work was checked significantly by the democratic spirit of the American people. As Claiborne (1983) observes:

> Webster was something of a crank on his chosen specialty, but there
> was a lot of pragmatic method in his crankiness. He sensed that in
> America above all, no single person, no matter how respected, could
> impose standards on the language. (p. 211)

Thus, although Webster would have loved to see American English fully standardized (and at one point even an Academy), his efforts were checked by the powerful spirit of democracy in those whose language he wanted to standardize. However, as Claiborne notes, Webster did not give up his ideas easily. There is a story about how Webster tried to get printers to use his proposed spellings. He went around the printshops of the towns that he visited and gave the printers a list of the spellings that he favored. He then asked the printer to use those spellings in his later work. Claiborne concludes: "Webster knew his countrymen: his incessant persuasion got results as the dictates of an academy could never have done" (p. 211).

The acceptance of standardization in Britain and America

The observations by Claiborne are interesting for an additional reason. They also point to a difference between Britain and the United States in the degree or the acceptance of standardization. Claiborne suggests that Americans are less respectful of authority in general than the British, including linguistic authority. This is an opinion also shared by a well known English linguist Peter Strevens. Strevens (1972), in his comparison of British and American English, writes the following in this connection:

> ... it [the coining of new words and expressions] became established
> as a difference between American and British English that innovation
> was always worth trying in America and might lead to a new word

or expression being taken up by the community, whereas in Britain the forces of standardization and conservatism were and remained stronger and more censorious. (p. 41)

We will have occasion to talk about the innovative character of American English in a later chapter. What is important to point out here is that Strevens mentions "the forces of standardization and conservatism" as being stronger and more characteristic of British English.

Availability of Standard American English

As we have seen, whatever the degree of standardization of American English, there is a dialect-based variety that is usually referred to as "Standard American English" (SAE) and that stands for the language as a whole. It is the Network Standard, a derivative of the earlier General American that comes closest to the regional mid or midwestern-American English. This standard is used by a large percentage of Americans. The large-scale availability of this dialect is the main reason why American English has been seen throughout its history as remarkably uniform. Mencken sees this as one of the major distinctive characteristics of American English. But present-day commentators also make the same point. For example, Baugh and Cable (1983) note:

> The universal spread of education in modern times and the absence of any sharp differentiation of social classes in this country [the US] are not favorable to the development or maintenance of dialect. While a southerner or a man from "down East" can usually be recognized by his speech, there are large sections of the country in which it would be impossible to tell within a thousand miles the district from which an individual came. (p. 380)

This, of course, applies primarily to the midwestern areas of the United States. It is this uniform accent used over a huge area of the country that is closest to the pronunciation of what is viewed as Standard American English, the American English that came to be used by television newscasters. In other words, a large section of the population of the United States speaks the Standard, or at least a variety or accent very close to it. This situation seems to be in sharp contrast to that in Great Britain. The English phonetician W.J. Lewis has this to say about the availability of the standard in England (Lewis, 1971:239):

> Something rather like ninety-five per cent of the population of England exhibit in their speech, fairly frequently, various elements

which are evidence of the locality or region in which they passed their final linguistically formative years, i.e. their teens. The remaining small minority in whose speech no easily observable local character- istics are to be heard speak the variety of English most specifically known as Received Pronunciation (RP).

This is the kind of British English most commonly associated with the largest British radio and television network, the BBC. The people who speak this vari- ety of British English are said to have no accent. The lack of accent is associated with superior social status. As Lewis observes, RP is readily available to a small fraction of the population. This contrasts markedly with the American situation, where a very large percentage of the population (maybe the majority) speak the standard, or a variety closely approximating it. It has to be observed, however, that American newscasters who come from a region different from where a vari- ety closely approximating Standard American is used have to make adjustments to the Network Standard. Dan Rather, one of the best known newscasters, who came from Texas, reportedly had to take speech lessons to correct his Texan speech habits (McCrum, *et al.*, 1986).

Simpson also feels that Americans are less divided by language in social terms. He observes that in England in even basic, everyday exchanges, like a politician talking to the people, the participants are soon made aware of their social differ- ences. He concludes: "This situation is *relatively* less common in the United States today, though it can be perceived in the interactions between northerners and southerners, and between members of different races" (Simpson, 1986:7).

The accent of American presidents

There seems to be a further difference between England and the United States in the social acceptability of the standard accent. Several American presidents have had a local accent. It is the American *attitude* toward their local accent that is noteworthy. McCrum, *et al.* (1986) write in this connection:

> The experience of the network newscasters is in contrast to that of the
> nation's presidents. To America, unlike Britain, the Network Standard
> has virtually no class connotation. A strong regional accent has never
> been a hindrance in reaching the White House. Far from apologizing
> for, or correcting, the speech of their origins, grand or humble, some
> American presidents have worn their accents like a badge. (p. 36)

I have already mentioned some characteristically New England features of for- mer president John F. Kennedy's speech (see chapter five). Jimmy Carter had a

Southern accent, and so does Bill Clinton today. In contrast, it would be quite surprising if the British had a prime minister with a strong regional accent.

Tolerance

Another way in which language use can be said to be democratic or not is the tolerance exhibited by all those concerned in linguistic issues. Obviously, the people most concerned are the speakers of a language, in our case the speakers of American English. I will talk about their attitude to linguistic usage later in this section. At this point, however, I will deal with another group of those concerned: lexicographers, that is, the professionals who make dictionaries.

American dictionaries

The largest, most comprehensive dictionary of American English, commonly called *Webster's Third* or *Webster's Unabridged*, appeared in 1961. This dictionary, which has the full name *Webster's Third New International Dictionary*, contains approximately 450,000 words. What makes it remarkable is not only the size of the enterprise but also the attitude reflected in it toward linguistic usage. Dictionary-making before *Webster's Third* was characterized by linguistic purism in the United States, possibly as a result of prudery (see chapter seventeen). In other words, dictionaries were prescriptive rather than descriptive. *Webster's Third* made it its explicit goal to be descriptive (and this approach was adopted by other American dictionaries as well). It attempted to describe existing usage, rather than legislate over usage problems. The editor, Philip Gove, decided to eliminate usage labels, like *informal* and *colloquial*, that were often interpreted as pejorative by some people and introduced new, more neutral labels (see Bailey in McArthur, ed., 1992). He also passed judgment on fewer items. For example, the words *finalize* and *normalcy*, thought to be unacceptable by many purists, were included without any labels. *Irregardless* received the label *nonstandard*. In general, it can be said that in linguistics to describe is democratic, whereas to prescribe is antidemocratic. A dictionary can also be democratic or antidemocratic in terms of which words it chooses to include or exclude. *Webster's Third* included items like *ain't*. This was in part defined in the following way: "though disapproved by many and more common in less educated speech, used orally in most parts of the U.S. by many cultivated speakers esp. in the phrase *ain't I*." The editor "believed that distinctions of usage were elitist and artificial."

All of these decisions, and some additional ones, provoked a great deal of criticism of *Webster's Third* in the United States. The press and many of the professional reviews found it too permissive. According to Baugh and Cable (1983:386), purism "continues to find expression in the popular press and in lexicographical enterprises." They claim that one example of this in lexicography in the United States is the institution of what is known as the "usage panel."

Usage panels

Usage panels consist of a large number of people (sometimes even more than a hundred) who are acknowledged to be "good writers," that is, people whose English is thought of as exemplary. Members of usage panels give their opinions on contentious points of usage. These opinions are summarized under the item in question in the dictionary. For example, *The American Heritage Dictionary, Second College Edition* (1985), which instituted a usage panel in its 1969 edition, has this to say about *ain't*:

> Usage: *Ain't* has acquired such a stigma over the years that it is beyond rehabilitation, even though it would serve a useful function as a contraction for *am not* and even though its use as an alternate form for *isn't, hasn't, aren't,* and *haven't* has a good historical justification. In questions, the variant *aren't I* is acceptable in speech to a majority of the Usage Panel, but in writing there is no generally acceptable substitute for the stilted *am I not*.

The obvious rationale for the instituting of usage panels is the attempt to legislate over linguistic issues in a democratic way. However, there are several people who do not see the functioning of usage panels in this light. One of them is Baron (1982), who views it as a pseudodemocratic institution:

> The pseudodemocratic arbitration system of the *Harper Dictionary* is an attempt to illustrate the process of decision making in matters of English and thereby to demystify it and give readers a feeling of participation in the process of linguistic self-determination. (p. 232)

It is, however, possible to view the usage panel as an attempt to come to terms with difficult issues of usage in a democratic way. In a sense, the usage panel is like a representative democracy in which people delegate their political power to some elected representatives who will then on make decisions on behalf of the majority. The members of the usage panel can be thought of as experts who are invested with the power of making decisions for those who do not use the language professionally. At the same time, we should remember that the setting up of usage panels also reflects the trust Americans have in experts, a characteristic that was mentioned in chapter six in connection with American conformity.

What should determine linguistic usage?

The discussion of the usage panel and the nature of its role brings up the issue of who should determine questions of linguistic usage. There have been several views about this in the United States. It is well known that Jefferson also participated in the debate, and claimed that priority in linguistic questions should go to common usage and not to grammar. If people use English in a certain way, that should be sufficient for acceptance (Simpson, 1986). Webster seems to have vacillated between three different positions in the course of his career. There were times when he saw common usage as the final arbiter, but also times when reason and analogy played the key role. And also, as Simpson (1986) observes, there were times when he favored the authority of language experts, like linguists and eminent writers. Finally, as we saw in the chapter on rationality, the new grammarians wished to follow reason in the judgment and settling of particular issues. This was a particularly influential trend throughout the nineteenth century. In 1870, Richard Grant White, a successor of the new grammarians of the 1820s, wrote:

> in the development of language ... reason always wins against formal grammar or illogical usage, and that the 'authority' of eminent writers, conforming to, or forming, the usage of their day, ... does not completely justify or establish a use of words inconsistent with reason, or out of direction of the normal growth of language. (quoted in Baron, 1982:201)

Interestingly, Baron observes that White "compares the relationship between those who rely on reason and those who look to authority in language to the relationship between Protestants and Papists (White apparently connects reason with Protestantism) ..." (Baron, 1982:201).

The linguistic tolerance of speakers

So far in this section we have only talked about the tolerance, or intolerance, of the language experts toward linguistic usage. Now we should turn our attention to the attitude of ordinary Americans to problems of usage. The few studies that are available and that bear on this issue seem to indicate that ordinary speakers and users of American English are generally tolerant of linguistic usage. The issue of tolerance in accepting alternative usages in British and American speakers of English has hardly been investigated in an empirical way. Needless to say, this is an important issue in the study of democratic aspects of language use.

Some pilot studies of linguistic tolerance

In an informal, cursory study, my students and I looked at the use of the quantifiers *many* and *much* before plural invariables (nouns ending in *-s*), such as *congratulations, contents, looks, savings,* and *thanks.* We asked six Americans and four Britons to tell us whether these nouns could be preceded by *many* or *much.* A clear tendency that emerged from the answers was that Americans were more divided on this issue. While in many cases (like *congratulations, contents, savings,* and *thanks*) all of the Britons rejected the applicability of *much* as a quantifier, most of the Americans said that *much* can also be used. These findings are supported by those of Varga (1993), whose study had a different focus. The same tendency was observed when we asked informants concerning the use of other examples of contentious linguistic usage, such as whether they use *name after* or *name for; in school* or *at school; hopefully* or *I hope; it don't make any difference* or *it doesn't make any difference; neither are* or *neither is;* and *I wish I was* or *I wish I were.* In all these cases the British informants had a unanimous opinion about the issue and gave one "correct" form as the answer, whereas the Americans were divided.

The results of our admittedly informal studies based on only a small number of Britons and Americans may be interpreted to mean that Americans display their "legendary" linguistic insecurity in these cases, while the British have a confident knowledge of their English. However, if we ask where this confidence comes from, our conclusion may be different. The results may also mean that Americans are somewhat more tolerant concerning linguistic usage and that they are perhaps less governed by prescriptive rules in linguistic usage. This possibility leads us to an account of a study that was conducted to find British and American differences in linguistic usage.

Prescriptivism vs. descriptivism

The only large-scale and systematic study of this issue is that of Biber (1987). We have already mentioned his work in the chapter on directness of American English, where we dealt with the greater use of the pronouns *I/you* in American English. More generally, Biber found that *I/you* co-occurs with other items systematically. It will be recalled that Biber thoroughly investigated nine written genres in both British and American English. He found that *I/you* co-occurs with contractions and the pronoun *it.* That is, contractions, pronoun *it,* and *I/you* tended to be present in these written genres with equally high frequency. These grammatical items reflect, what Biber calls, an "interactional" style in writing. This is a style that reflects a considerable amount of interaction between writer and reader (as opposed to a less interactive style, where these items are less frequent, or are suppressed). The main finding of Biber's study, however, was that American English shows consistently higher frequencies for these items than British English does. Another dimension of British and American writing that Biber studied had to do with such further grammatical items as nominalizations, prepositional phrases, and passives, items that indicate a more abstract, as opposed to a situated, style. Of these, nominalizations and prepositional phrases were found to occur more frequently in American than in British English (while passives occured with roughly the same frequency). Biber's (1987) conclusion is this:

> On Dimension 1, the British genres are characterized by fewer colloquial or interactive features than the American genres. On Dimension 2, the British genres exhibit fewer features associated with a highly nominal and jargon-ridden style (nominalizations and prepositional phrases), a style that students and careful writers are admonished to avoid. In both cases, writing prescriptions appear to play a greater role in the British genres than in the corresponding American genres. (p. 116)

Even more generally, Biber says that "the differences along both dimensions seem to relate to a single underlying functional priority: the greater influence of grammatical and stylistic prescriptions in British writing" (p. 117). If this general conclusion is correct, it may be suggested that British English is slightly less "democratic" than American English, in which "prescriptions" for "good writing" seem to play a less significant role. We should note, however, that this is a conclusion that is not universally accepted. The English linguist Ilson believes, in connection with Biber's views, that they constitute "lingering traces of excolonial linguistic insecurity in the U.S." (1990:39).

Perhaps it is not accidental that this response to such a conclusion comes from an English linguist. It may be that we can witness the long-standing controversy here over the issue of which variety of English is more tolerant and, ultimately, "better."

The acceptance of the "other's" English

Indeed, there seem to be differences between British and American English concerning the tolerance or acceptance of British English by Americans and of American English by the British. Gramley and Pätzold (1992:358) note: "Overall, Americans show a more tolerant attitude towards British loans than vice versa; however, there are far fewer of them in AmE than the other way around." Some Britons resent the great number of Americanisms in British

English. For example, the originally American word *hopefully* has often been unfavourably commented on by British observers of language, or we could say, British purists, together, of course, with their American likes. There is, however, a generational difference in the acceptance of Americanisms in Britain. Young people in Britain seem to be much more favorable to these than the older generation. As we will see, American English uses more new words and expressions than British English. This is a well known difference between the two varieties. It is these innovations or "neologisms," that may produce different responses in speakers of British and American English. Some Britons, possibly belonging to the older generation, may have reservations about the innovative character of American English, and conversely, some Americans may look at British English as conservative. As the English linguist Peter Strevens (1972:60) puts it:

> To the user of a neologizing form of English, another form of English which employs only known, established vocabulary lacks a quality which he recognizes in his own usage. Conversely, to the speaker brought up to regard departure from established usage as something rare and probably undesirable, vivid, new expressions convey a quality which he may not value highly, except in works of literature.

The language of democracy

So far in the chapter, we have examined the American attitude to language. We pointed out as a general conclusion that the American attitude to language is a fairly democratic one. This issue should not be confused with the issue of what the characteristic traits of a democratic language are. In the previous chapter, a connection was pointed out between democracy and directness. To a large degree, directness is only imaginable in a democratic society. This makes directness one feature of American English. In the next chapter, we will discuss the informality of American English. Informality in general language use is another property of a democratic language. In the present chapter, I mentioned the fact that there were early attempts to free American English from a vocabulary that reflected the old and less democratic social structure. These features are all characteristic of American English as a democratic language.

However, there are further observations about the language used in America, some of them less favorable. One of the best known of these is Alexis de Tocqueville's from the 1830s. Tocqueville noted that Americans have a tendency to use a large number of terms that are highly abstract and thus have vague meanings. He said that these are "like a box with a false bottom; you may put into it what ideas you please, and take them out again without being observed" (Tocqueville, 1988:482). Tocqueville regarded this liking for abstractions as a dangerous thing because words that are vague may be given meanings by anyone according to their convenience. This property of a democratic language is in conflict with another property that was mentioned in connection with directness: the transparency and explicitness of meaning.

In his attempt to give an account of why the native Indian languages had such an appeal for Cooper in his novels, Simpson (1986:219) makes the comment that this might have to do with the feature of American English identified by Tocqueville. Simpson writes: "If English in general is a language of general terms, then we may recall Tocqueville's assertion that the English of a democracy in particular is prone to such words, as a means of preserving as much executive ambiguity as is compatible with a minimal degree of honesty." Simpson finds that the highly specific nature of native Indian languages may have contributed to Cooper's favorable attitude to them. He suggests that the specificity of these languages stood in sharp contrast to the highly abstract nature of American English.

Antisexism in America: the linguistic fight

The Oxford Companion to the English Language defines sexism in language in the following way: "... sexism refers to a bias through which patterns and references of male usage are taken to be normative, superordinate, and positive and those of women are taken to be deviant, subordinate, and negative." This bias can manifest itself in a variety of ways.

Examples of sexist usage in English

Before we discuss how American English has changed to give equal status to women in language, let us look at some specific examples of what is commonly referred to as sexist language in English.

Man

The word *man* can be used to refer to "the human race, people in general," as for example in *Man is a talking animal.* This usage is sexist, because it excludes women.

Girl

The use of the word *girl* to refer to adult women may be considered sexist because it places adult women in the category of children, which is the primary application of the term. It is also sexist to use *girl* attributively, as in *girl athlete,* because this usage assumes that athletes are "normally" men. Incidentally, this use of *girl* is not common anymore.

Lady

Expressions such as *lady doctor*, *lady lawyer*, and others also assume that doctors and lawyers are "normally" men, and only deviantly women.

Exclusive naming

In the case of what can be termed "exclusive naming," members of married couples are often addressed in such a way that the husband's social status is explicitly mentioned, while the wife's is not, even though the wife has the same or similar social status. An example of this is when a letter is addressed to Professor John Smith and Mrs. Smith, although Mrs. Smith is also a university professor.

Changes in sexist usage

For the past several decades feminists in the English-speaking world have made a considerable effort to change the English language to free it from sexist usage. In many ways, American feminists have been at the forefront of this struggle and have been leading the way toward what they consider to be a more democratic English. Fundamental to the thinking of many of the advocates of linguistic changes are some ideas from the American linguist Benjamin Lee Whorf (1956), who worked in the first half of this century. One of Whorf's main theses was that language shapes one's thinking. Translated into the feminist argument, this means, in a somewhat simplified form, that if language is sexist, people's thinking will also be sexist. Consequently, if language is freed from its sexist bias, then people will stop being sexist, or at least will be freed from this one (largely unconscious) source of bias. This is a crude form of the argument, but it suffices to show how Whorf's ideas have been significant for and influential in feminist thought about changing American English. Below, I give some examples of the proposed changes.

Ms.

Around 1970, American feminists recommended the use of *Ms.* to address a woman. The reason for this was that women are categorized as married or unmarried by the formulas *Mrs.* and *Miss*, whereas men are not; they are simply addressed as *Mr.*, whether they are married or not. The use of *Ms.* has since caught on and it is quite common in spoken and written address.

"Hurricane language"

In the late 1970s, there were some suggestions made to eliminate certain feminine aspects of weather reports used in the United States. Hurricanes were talked about in terms of some assumed qualities of women. For example, they were called by women's first names such as *Hurricane Hazel*. They were also referred to as being *temperamental* and *flirting with the coast*, reflecting certain stereotypes about women. These usages have since been abandoned, and now hurricanes are named alternately after men and women.

Generic pronouns

The area of sexist usage that came under heavy attack by feminists is the use of masculine pronouns for generic reference in such sentences as *Nobody knew his way home*. In this sentence, *his* is a generic pronoun; it is used in a generalizing sense. Feminists have argued that, instead of *his*, the gender-neutral *his or her* or *their* should be used in these cases. This battle has largely been won by feminists and advocates of more democratic usage in general. Most American publishers honor this suggestion in one way or another.

Person and people

Many words that contained the gender-biased term *man* have been replaced by ones that employ the neutral terms *people* or *person*, or some other gender-neutral word. Thus, *businessmen* has become *business people* and *firemen* is now predominantly *firefighters* in the United States. However, not all suggestions have been enthusiastically received by the population at large. At one point, it was suggested that *chairman* should change into *chairperson*, since it can be both a man and a woman. But somehow *chairperson* has never taken root. Instead, the word *chairman* has been shortened to *chair*, and this has become the dominant usage. The same applies to *anchorman*, which is now widely called *anchor*.

Finally, some recommended nonsexist usages have never been taken seriously. *Fisherman* has not been abandoned for *fisher* and *manhole cover* has not become *personhole cover*.

Lexical one-sidedness

Advocates of democratic usage also point out the lexical one-sidedness of several English words. A *doctor* for most people is a man, and so is a university *professor*, as can be seen from one of the examples above. Most Americans still refer back to these words with the pronoun *he* in sentence sequences like *The doctor came*

... examined the patient. When asked, they tend to fill in the blank with *he*, rather than *she*. The effort to make people realize such cases of lexical one-sidedness may make people more aware of certain social inequalities.

Lexical asymmetries

Similarly, there are many instances of lexical asymmetries in English that people striving for more democracy in language would like to see removed. For example, in English there is the degree *Bachelor of Arts* but not *Spinster of Arts*. In addition, *bachelor* has very positive connotations, whereas *spinster* has clearly negative ones. The same applies to the next higher academic degree, *Master of Arts*. The counterpart of *master* is *mistress*, but, again, there is no *Mistress of Arts*. The connotations of the two words are markedly different in this case as well.

Advocates of democratic usage also object to the relative position of gender-related words in many constructions. Words denoting males are typically placed first, women second in some phrases, thus portraying men as somehow more important than women. Thus, in English it is more common, even more idiomatic, to say *men and women* than *women and men*; *boys and girls* than *girls and boys*; *male or female* than *female and male*; and *host and hostess* than *hostess and host*. The second variants are regarded as special cases reserved for special situations.

In general, then, we can conclude that in American English serious efforts have been made to achieve inclusive usage. This is a very strong movement for the fuller democratization of language. American feminists are leading the world in this general process. It is interesting to note, however, that some feminists object to this movement. Their reason is that the process of changing male-biased usage may hide important social facts – facts that are important to the feminist movement. For example, "to say in the United States that 'The fifteenth amendment ensured the voting rights of former slaves' hides the historical reality that this referred only to *men* who were former slaves" (*The Oxford Companion to the English Language*, p. 923).

study questions and activities

1. Craig Storti (1994) gives a cross-cultural dialogue that is relevant to the chapter. The situation in which the dialogue takes place is a job interview in England. The members of the committee are Arabella (British) and Bob (American). After they have interviewed two applicants, they have the following conversation:

Arabella: I liked the man from Liverpool.
Bob: David Symes? Why is that?
Arabella: I liked his style and his manners. He makes a very good first impression. He's also very well spoken.
Bob: I guess you're right. But I wonder about his technical background. The man from Oxford seemed a bit stronger.
Arabella: The one with the loud tie. Yes, he was stronger.
(Storti, 1994:49)

How can you relate the conversation and the assumptions behind it to the notion of American democracy?

2. "Political correctness" can be interpreted as an attempt to change certain undemocratic linguistic habits. There are many new politically correct terms in use today in the U.S. that have become well established and widely used. They include African American, human resources, chairperson, flight attendant, firefighter, etc. Why were these and other expressions found acceptable by many Americans? Find additional examples of this kind and try to figure out which undemocratic tendencies the expressions are called on to correct.

3. Are you aware of any politically correct terms or expressions that have been suggested but did not become established usages in the U.S.? Why have they not gained currency?

4. How is political correctness viewed in your country? Is it looked at in a positive or negative light, or both? What are the arguments in favor of and against it?

chapter 16

The "casual" American

To a large degree, informality has to do with the amount of attention and effort an activity requires from the participants in a given situation. In the chapter on style, we saw four ways in which Labov collected data: casual speech, reading of a paragraph, reading a list of unrelated words, and reading paired words. It was pointed out that the four ways represent differing degrees of formality, with casual speech being very informal and the reading of paired words being very formal, and that the basis of formality is determined by the amount of attention given to the production of these various kinds of speech. In general, we can say that formality-informality is a matter of how much attention the performance of an activity requires. This applies not only to linguistic behavior (like speech) but to behavior of all kinds. When it applies to linguistic behavior, it can mean at least two things. On the one hand, we can pay more or less attention to the norms and prescriptions of the use of language and, on the other, to the production of speech itself.

We will address these aspects of informality in the use of language in America below. However, we are still left with the question of where that informality comes from. It can be suggested that informality and democracy are connected. In a democratic society one can expect more informality in language use (in both senses above) than in a society that is not, or less, democratic. This obvious relationship is noted by Simpson, writing about Emerson's style (Simpson, 1986:237):

> The striking informalities, localisms, and Americanisms in Emerson's
> diction are famous and obvious to all readers, and they go along with
> a generally avowed commitment to what is democratic, and to the
> linguistic and cultural rights of America as its own place.

We will see that these informalities in the writing of a philosopher also represent a commonly mentioned property of the American way of using English: the mixing of styles. When a philosopher uses informal language, this is considered by some as less than praiseworthy. More generally, "style mixing" is often regarded as unrefined, or even barbarous. This view of Americans ties in with some similar observations we saw in the chapter on American directness. We will discuss style mixing in a later section in this chapter.

The beginnings of American informality

It was pointed out in the previous chapter that mass democracy became a salient characteristic of early nineteenth-century America. Together with the emergence of the new middle class, a new kind of democratic language appeared. This language reflected the speech habits of the "demos," and emphasized informality (Cmiel, 1990). One property of informal speech was the maintenance and use of regional folk dialects. It was not regarded embarrassing to use the speech of the region where one came from. This has been and still is a noteworthy feature of American attitude to regional dialects, as we saw in the discussion of the speech of American presidents (see chapter fifteen). Another aspect of the use of informal language was its reliance on slang. Political speeches were riddled with slang, but its use was not limited to politics. The best public speakers of early nineteenth-century America were not afraid to use slang in their speeches (Cmiel, 1990). One of these was Henry Ward Beecher, a minister, whose sermons "sounded like a familiar conversation" (Cmiel, 1990:59). We find contemporary slang expressions such as *The man who slimes his way, to cuff about the controversies*, and *to make a man cotton to you* in his published sermons. It was observed that Protestant ministers freely talked about *knocking the bottom out of hell* (Cmiel, 1990:63). The new language of mass democracy was also characterized by directness, an aspect of informal language that was discussed in a previous chapter. The directness of mass democracy preferred truth to politeness, and was often rough and blunt. As Cmiel (1990:63) puts it, "it marked the difference between saying, *I think you're mistaken there* and *That's stupid and you're wrong.*" Informality also often took the form of rudeness and was "deliberately insulting" (Cmiel, 1990:63). This was particularly prevalent in politics and the popular press.

These are, according to Cmiel, some of the main aspects of the informal language of early mass democracy in America, but he also observes that informality was just one aspect of this language. Another was the continued respect for "refined speech." It was not the case that refined language was thrown out completely by speakers of the middling style. Democratization in American society brought with it a broadening of public education, which in turn made sure that certain aspects of refined speech continued to be used. This happened particularly thanks to the largely conservative grammars and dictionaries that were popular and widely used in each school. It was the popularity of these traditional grammars and dictionaries that brought about the rejection of the efforts made by the new grammarians, who based their works on principles of rationality (see chapter thirteen). Thus refined language was maintained in early American mass democracy, but it was combined with aspects of informality (Cmiel, 1990).

Nor was it the case that the informal aspects of the new democratic language were used only by the members of the middle class. Successful participation for anyone in politics required the use of a combination of both informal and refined language (Cmiel, 1990). Refined speech alone was no longer sufficient for success in political participation. Public speakers resorted to the new middling style, some not very enthusiastically. For example, one of the most eloquent speakers in America at the time, Daniel Webster, an aristocrat, was asked by his party to give up his classical refined oratory in the campaign of 1840, and rely more on the mixture of refined and informal in his public appearances. The change in style in Webster's oratory was extremely successful (Cmiel, 1990).

In this chapter we will discuss many of the same topics that were touched on above. We will also look at some additional domains of informal language use, as it characterizes American English today. Perhaps the clearest area in which the close connection between democracy and informality manifests itself in everyday language use is the address system. Address systems are linguistic reproductions of power relationships in a society. We now turn to this topic first.

Forms of address

In both British and American English, people generally address other people by making use of a two-term system. This consists of using either First Name (FN) or Title plus Last Name (TLN). A special case of the latter is when Kinship Terms (KT) are used. In some situations, people employ nonreciprocality as a rule. These include the family where the younger generation addresses the older generation by KT and the older generation addresses the younger one by employing FN; in teacher-student situations students use TLN to address the teacher, whereas the teacher uses FN in addressing the students; the boss-employee relationship is also commonly nonreciprocal, in that the boss uses FN and the employee TLN to address each other.

Reciprocality is the rule in most cases where two adults are introduced, both addressing each other with TLN. Young adults use FN reciprocally or FN plus LN reciprocally. In both of these situations there is often a rapid switch to FN plus FN.

As indicated above, this use of the address system is basically common to both British and American English. There are, however, some interesting differences – differences that have to do with differing degrees of formality in the two dialects. Gramley and Pätzold (1992) note that the switch from TLN to FN is slower in British English. Since the FN system is more informal than the TLN system, the quicker change on the part of Americans seems to show again a greater degree of informality in the use of American English. Another observation by Whitcut points to the same conclusion. Whitcut (1980:90) observed that the friendliness associated with the informality of first-naming is viewed as very American in Britain. The practice of first-naming was already discovered in the early nineteenth century. The ladies and gentlemen of the refined class were often referred to as *friend* or *fellow* instead of *Sir* by servants or other employees. Cmiel (1990:69) writes: "Both gentlemen and ladies found their first names used indiscriminately; the respectful distance the formal titles maintained was destroyed."

The use of forms of address in British and American universities provides another interesting case of difference. According to Ervin-Tripp (1974, mentioned in Gramley and Pätzold, 1992), British universities have a three-option system, realized in a sequence from most formal to least formal: (1) There is the use of Title (Dr., Prof.) plus LN. This shows the most deference. (2) As an intermediate stage, M forms (Mr., Mrs.) are used. (3) Finally, FN is used, which is most informal. Other studies indicate that in American universities very often there is no overt address at all. When there is any, it is usually TLN. M forms are also used, especially for female professors. First-naming is also common, especially between male students and male professors. What is remarkable is that first-naming is often initiated by the students and not the professors. (There might be regional and other variation as regards this practice in the U.S. A colleague from the East Coast told me that in his experience students don't use first names unless invited to by the professor. Obviously, the issue requires further study.) Since students are originally in an inferior position in relation to their professors, the fact that initiation is done by the students shows that the social hierarchy is not perceived by American students as something very rigid. This phenomenon does not seem to have its counterpart in Britain. Thus, the use of address in this situation reinforces the conclusion reached above about the greater informality of American English.

Some informal speech acts

Introductions

In both Britain and the United States people use the same formulas when they are introduced to each other. According to Gramley and Pätzold (1992), the formal *How do you do?* is the set expression employed in upper-middle to upper-class circles both in Britain and the U.S. *Hello* is also used in the same circles. However, there are some interesting differences as we go down the social hierarchy. The less formal *Nice/Pleased to meet you* is a formula common to Britain and America in upper working class and lower middle class society. The same seems to hold true, according to Gramley and Pätzold, for the very informal *Hi*. We do not know if this is an accurate description of the social use of these expressions at introductions. What is more relevant for the present discussion is the fact that *Nice/Pleased to meet you* and *Hi* are less formal expressions and that they are regarded as American by speakers of British English. The point is that the informal expressions used by British speakers are still felt to be more American than neutral or British.

Letters to the editor

When people write letters to the editors of newspapers and magazines, they address the editor with *Dear Sir* or simply *Sir*. They seem to do this on both sides of the Atlantic. However, it is also common for Americans to choose *not* to address the editor at all. This is certainly a more informal, and, to some, less polite way of writing a letter to an editor. This situation is similar to the one we observed in connection with the use of forms of address at universities.

Greetings

Most of the greetings that speakers of English use are common to both the British and Americans. They both say *Good morning* and *Good night* to each other. However, Americans use greetings that are either exclusively American or are thought to be characteristically American by speakers of other dialects of English. These include: *How are you?* and *Howdy!*, and even simply the other person's first name (like *John!*). All of these can function as *greetings* in the United States, and are viewed by other speakers of English as very informal.

Thanking

There are even differences in the way the British and the Americans say *Thank you*, an expression which is obviously shared. The British way of informally thanking someone for something is *Ta*. The response to *thank you* can be *you're welcome* in both countries and in Britain it is also very common to repeat *thank you*. Americans often replace these options with the very informal *ah-ha* or *you bet!*

Familiar conversation

In the chapter on directness, we noted that Americans often engage in conversations that apparently lack any kind of directness. Now we can see why that is the case. The simple reason is that some kinds of familiar conversations, like small talk, have a function very different from that of goal-oriented conversations: the maintenance of friendly and democratic relations. Again, we find some illuminating comments on the origin of this characteristically American "genre" in Cmiel's book. Cmiel (1990) argues that the kind of familiar American conversation that foreigners, especially the British, find so annoying, came about as an antidote to traditional refined speech and behavior. In the refined style one showed respect to another person by *not* being familiar to him or her. Politeness and respect equalled distance to the other person. In contrast to this, in the new middling style politeness involved being friendly and familiar, being close. The practice of first-naming and the use of slang were "ways of being *nice*" (p. 70). Distance, in this mode, came to be interpreted as superiority, being an aristocrat, not as showing respect and being polite. A crucial aspect of the middling style became "the idea of familiar conversation" (p. 70).

Informality in pronunciation and spelling

When we talk about the amount of attention given to the actual production of speech, we talk about issues of pronunciation. American English has a number of such features by which it can be said to be very informal or relaxed. This statement might, at first, sound strange. How can pronunciation be informal? If we apply our criterion of the amount of attention to speech for deciding what is formal and informal, we can see why it makes sense to say that the notion of formality can be extended to pronunciation.

American nasality

It has long been recognized that one of the most characteristic features of American English is its nasal sound. Gramley and Pätzold (1992), for example, observe: "Many American speakers, especially from the Middle West, for example, have a 'nasal twang.' This is caused by the articulatory habit of leaving the velum open so that the nasal cavity forms a further resonance chamber" (p. 336). To leave the velum open requires less attention and effort on the part of the speaker than to close it right after the production of a nasal sound (like /m/ and /n/). Strevens (1972) explains what happens in more detail:

> Almost always the switch from *nasal* (through the nose for **m**) to *oral* (through the mouth, for **i:**) is a little slow, so that the vowel has begun before the nose passage has been switched off. When this happens, the beginning of the vowel has a slightly nasal quality. Now, in American pronunciation the duration of the nasalised portion of a vowel following a nasal consonant is slightly longer than in British pronunciations. (p. 78)

The amount of attention and effort used is, of course, no longer conscious, and maybe it never was. The important point is that speakers of American English have developed a form of pronunciation that requires (or, more precisely, would require if it were conscious) less attention and effort.

The American "drawl"

Some Americans are also noted for their "drawl" – a lengthening of vowels. This is especially characteristic of Southern pronunciation: "Southern American speakers, in contrast, are stereotyped by other Americans for their drawl. This drawing out of sounds is due perhaps to an overall lack of tension in articulation" (Gramley and Pätzold, 1992:336). Gramley and Pätzold go on to observe that American and British speakers differ in this respect as well: "British accents are often thought of as 'clipped' by Americans, possibly because of the greater tension and lesser degree of lengthening in stressed vowels...." (p. 336). Bryson (1990:88) also notes the "clipped diction" of the British. Strevens (1972:78) makes the same observation about the perceived "clipped" nature of British pronunciation and the "drawled" nature of the way many Americans speak, but adds: "The difference is characteristic but trivial" (p. 78). This difference is trivial only as long as we see this case as an isolated occurrence in the comparison of the two varieties. However, if we view it as a part of a larger system of differences, it ceases to be trivial. Having a drawl has to do with a less effortful way of producing sounds and is an aspect of the informality of American English. Seen in this light, it can be viewed as consistent with a larger set of British-American differences, most of which we will discuss later in this chapter.

The "flap"

It can also be suggested that the American observance of the so-called "flapping rule" is another instance of the casual, relaxed speaking habits of many Americans. The flapping rule states that, typically, in an intervocalic position the sounds /t/ and /d/ are pronounced /D/. This sound is called the "flap," and it is produced with the tongue quickly touching or flapping against the alveolar ridge. Many Americans produce the flap in word pairs like *writer – rider* and *latter – ladder*, that is, between two vowels. Less typically, it also occurs when it is preceded by an /r/, as in *hurting - herding*; when it is preceded by an /l/, as in *helter – held'er*; when it is followed by an /l/, as in *futile – feudal*; and when it is followed by a syllabic /m/, as in *totem – towed'em*. However, when the /t/ is in a stressed position, it is not pronounced /D/, as in *a'tomic*.

Post-nasal /t/

A well known distinguishing characteristic of American pronunciation is the voicing or complete elimination of /t/ in post-nasal position, that is, after a nasal consonant. Examples of this occurring include *winter* pronounced as *winner*, *enter* as *enner*, and *intercity* as *innercity*, in which the voiceless consonant /t/ is pronounced as voiced /d/. Furthermore, this voiced /d/ may also be eliminated in casual speech after nasals, as in *candidate* becoming *cannidate* and *understand* becoming *unnerstand*. This kind of pronunciation requires less attention to the coordination of the vocal organs and thus reflects a relaxed or casual way of speaking.

Phonetic spelling

We noted in the chapter on rationality that Americans often use phonetic spellings. Phonetic spellings like *thru* for *through* and *tho'* for *though* occur frequently, but are regarded as informal. However, these phonetic spellings may also show up in formal, official use, as in the term *thruway*, for example. Another example that has entered more formal style is the word *hi-fi*.

Style "mixing"

We have already seen that "style mixing" is one of the commonly noted properties of American English (on this, see, for example, A.D. Zwicky, 1981 and T. Williams, 1995). Style mixing occurs when certain linguistic items that are widely regarded as informal are used in registers higher up the stylistic hierarchy, or items that are formal occur in lower registers. It is the former that is more common. Take, for example, the informal phonetic spellings *thru* for *through* and *tho'* for *though*, mentioned earlier. The former generally appear in more informal writing. However, they may also be incorporated into more formal styles.

The phenomenon is not restricted to the American English of today. It was observed as early as 1802 (quoted by Simpson, 1986:107):

> However, I am of the opinion, that even local vulgarisms find admission into the discourse of people of better ranks more easily here [America] than in Europe.

Simpson quotes Witherspoon here. He maintains that people of a certain rank are not supposed to use certain linguistic items in their speech, but obviously, they did. A few decades after Witherspoon's observation, Tocqueville (1988) noticed the same thing: "Americans often mix styles together in an odd way, sometimes putting words together which, in the mother tongue, are carefully kept apart." The mother tongue is of course British English, and it seems that, as we will see in this section, Americans have developed and kept this habit more so than the British. The British linguist Ilson (1990:39) notes that Americans are more prone to mixing levels of style than the British. He feels that what is sometimes termed "the vigor of American English" comes from the inappropriate mixing of different levels of formality. Ilson's example is the coexistence in the same informal letter of the informal address *Hi Chuck* with the formal pronominalization construction *reservation finalizing*. We will consider some further examples of such style mixing in American English.

The use of slang

One interesting aspect of slang in America is that Americans appear to be quite liberal about their use of slang. They are not particularly concerned about what others may say or think of them if they use slang. This may have to do with what we said about the language of mass democracy in America, namely, that slang was a part and parcel of public oratory of all kinds, and also of everyday conversations. Given this situation, it is not surprising that a significant portion of the vocabulary of the average speaker of American English is made up of slang words and expressions (see the chapter on slang). British commentators on the American linguistic scene, both past and present, often note that Americans are fond of using slang. Strevens (1972:63) makes this comment on the issue: "There is little doubt that American usage is less formal than British and that the average American speaker or writer is less concerned than his British opposite number about whether or not other people will regard his English as containing slang."

Another British observer, Hoggart, gives us a specific example of the use of slang in relatively formal domains. Writing about his experiences with "mild office workers" in Washington, Hoggart finds it noteworthy that these office workers employ, for Hoggart's taste, a large number of slang expressions, which include:

> I've been kicking some ass around here today. ("I have worked very intensely today.")
> Lissen, pal, I wrestled him to the mat. ("I have defeated him in an argument.")
> We'll clean his clock. ("We will defeat him.")
> He hit it out of the park. ("It was a successful speech.")
> He's home safe. ("He's won a close decision.")
> Getting to first base. ("first success")
> Throw a curveball. ("pose a difficult problem")
> (Hoggart, 1991:64-65)

The use, and, just as important, the wide acceptance of slang in domains outside what other nationalities might consider formal may be a reflection and remnant of the cultural traditions mentioned at the beginning of this chapter.

Use of formal words

There is also some evidence of the converse situation, that is, that Americans tend to use less formal words in general. (American snobs are of course not considered here.) Some English words are generally viewed by speakers of English as formal. One of these is the verb *alight*. This verb is used in England in the sign *Alighting only* (Gramley and Pätzold, 1992). When the British use a more formal word, Americans tend to use a less formal one. Some examples include *Toilet engaged*, which is *Lavatory occupied* in America and *At risk*, which is *In danger* or *Endangered* in American English. Instead of *supporter*, Americans are more likely to say *fan* or *booster*, both of which are more informal than the first word. Some further well known cases in this category include *whilst* and *while*, *amongst* and *among*, and *amidst* and *amid*. The first words of these pairs are more formal and more likely to be found in British English usage (Crystal, 1991).

Adverbs

There are interesting differences between British and American English in the use of adverbs as well. I will mention two of these here, because they both bear on the issue of informality. In Standard English, verbs expressing actions require adverbs of manner, not adjectives. Thus, a sentence like *She swims well* is standard English. This contrasts with *She swims good*, which occurs in colloquial speech and is considered by many as substandard or, more appropriately, nonstandard. Crystal (1991) also notes that it is especially American usage. Thus Americans appear to make more extensive use of this colloquial or informal usage (involving such adjectives as *bad*, *nice*, etc.) than do the British.

Another point of divergence is in the use of adjectives as intensifiers of other adjectives. This happens in sentences like *You did that real good*. According to the rules of Standard English, adjectives must be preceded by adverbs in an intensifying function. Thus, *real* would have to be *really* in the example. Gramley and Pätzold (1992:357) observe in connection with this sentence that "adjectives as intensifiers (*real* in the example) are used much further up the stylistic scale [in American English]."

Use of nonstandard forms

Crystal's observation about the use of *good* above is relevant for an additional reason. It suggests that speakers of American English are fairly tolerant when it comes to nonstandard usage. The ready acceptance of nonstandard forms in language use is another sign of informality, which may go back to the period when the middling style mentioned by Cmiel emerged. The same seems to hold for the ready acceptance of slang on the part of Americans. Another example of the phenomenon is the word *ain't*. As we saw in the previous chapter, *ain't* is one of the prime examples of nonstandard usage in the English language – no matter which variety. Nonetheless, it seems to be employed by many educated Americans, as Crystal (1991:8) observes: "forms with *ain't* are widespread in informal educated American English." This is not the case with other varieties of English. (Interestingly, and as an exception to this generalization, the form also occurs as an affectation among upper-class British speakers of English.) However, Crystal's view is vehemently opposed by many Americans. Clearly, there is a need for further research concerning the use of *ain't* in the U.S. As a final example of the use of nonstandard forms higher up the stylistic scale, consider nonstandard past tense forms. This happens especially in the case of verbs like *spring*. The standard past tense form of this verb is *sprang*. However, the form *sprung* also occurs in American English in linguistic usage above the nonstandard level. The same applies to past tense forms like *rung* for *rang*, *shrunk* for *shrank*, *sung* for *sang*, *stunk* for *stank*, and *swung* for *swang* (Gramley and Pätzold, 1992:350).

Informality in writing

Biber's (1987) study referred to in the preceding chapters shows that Americans employ a more informal style of writing than the British. Here's what Biber (1987:111-113) has to say about this:

> ... there are systematic differences in the frequencies of contractions, pronoun *it*, and pronouns *I/you*; each American genre consistently shows a substantially higher frequency for these features than the corresponding British genre. The systematic difference between British and American writing ... thus seems to reflect a substantially greater use (or tolerance) of informal, colloquial, and interactional features in American writing.

It is not necessary to add anything to this conclusion, except to say that apparently American English has preserved many of its informal characteristics that it had acquired in its early formative years. This informality has become one of the hallmarks of American English and was capitalized on by many American writers. One of the greatest of these was Walt Whitman, of whom Simpson (1986:238) offers the following comment: "That Walt Whitman's identity as a true man of the people is so often taken for granted has much to do with the studied informality of his style." Obviously, one of Whitman's talents was to be able to capture the "true" spirit of being an American.

study questions and activities

1. Try to check the validity of the claim that Americans use informal language in situations (or genres) that otherwise require more formal language. Read some nonfiction (such as Steve Pinker's *The Language Instinct* or an article from *Newsweek* magazine) and see if you can find informal words, sentence structures, or spellings in what you read. If you can, explain why these informal usages are present. What function(s) could they possibly serve?

2. In what ways does American informality show up in nonlinguistic behavior? Analyze, for example, how many Americans dress or eat. If you compare these ways of behavior with those of other European nations (e.g., the British), what conclusions can you draw?

3. What aspect(s) of informality does the following American dialogue (or "mini-drama") indicate? (The mini-drama is taken from Andrew F. Murphy's *Cultural Encounters* in the *USA*, 1991.)

> **Bo:** Hey, you guys! I want you to meet Lamchul Adiprachan. He's here from Bangkok for a few months to study how we drill oil wells.
> **Red:** (Shaking Adiprachan's hand)
> Pull up a chair, Lam, and let me get you a beer. It's nice to meet you. Sis, say hello to Lam.
> **Sis:** (Several people stand up to shake Adiprachan's hand.) Hi, Lam.
> **Lam:** Bo, Red, Sis – I've never heard these names before. My English books are full of names like Robert, Patricia, Jennifer, and Michael.
> **Red:** Well, around here we mostly use nicknames. I came by mine naturally. I don't know if you can tell through all this gray hair, my hair used to be red.
> **Sis:** My brother named me when I was little. And his full name is Beauregard.
> **Lam:** So you're his sister. I get it.

chapter 17

American prudery in language

A t least from a historical perspective, it can be claimed that American English contains more of what can be called verbal prudery or propriety than British English does. Verbal prudery simply means that the use of certain words and phrases falls under social sanction, that is, their use is forbidden. This tendency in American English in the nineteenth century was observed, for example, by Mencken, who made the following comment (1963:356): "The nasty revival of prudery associated with the name of Victoria went to extreme lengths in the United States, and proceeded so far that it was frequently remarked and deplored by visiting Englishmen." An example of this is the surprise of a British visitor who noticed that Americans use the term *rooster* for the English term *cock* ("male chicken"). This was probably the result of the sexual meaning that had been acquired by the latter (the new American meaning for *cock* being "penis," a metaphorical identification commonly used in many languages). This example reflects a process that was going on in the language habits of many Americans. They censored themselves, and when a word could be understood to have "unfavorable connotations," they resorted to the use of words that were "safe" in this respect. Sexuality was repressed on a large scale. This account of Victorian prudery based on the idea of repression is rather traditional. The interested reader should turn to Foucault (1978) for a much more complex view of Victorian prudery, a view in which Foucault criticizes what he calls the "repressive hypothesis."

I will extend the interpretation of verbal prudery to some domains that are not usually included under that term. Verbal prudery is primarily applied to domains that have to do with sexuality or human biological functions. I will also include under the term such areas as swearing, death, and other related domains. This is because the linguistic processes that are at work in these cases are more or less the same as in the case of sexuality or bodily functions.

The social and historical context

Sketch of the historical background

The social and linguistic process of "prudery," according to Mencken, peaked in the United States in the 1830s and 40s, but remained strong throughout the nineteenth century. This period coincides with the rule of Queen Victoria in

Britain, who reigned from 1837 to 1901. This was a period of remarkable growth and vigor for the British Empire as large portions of the world came under its political, economic, cultural, and linguistic influence. The English language truly became a "world language" during this period, and what came to be known as "Victorian values" spread all over the world. These values involved certain attitudes toward certain aspects of life. One of the major values of the Victorian era was a taboo against swearing or any strong language and direct reference to sexual activities. Victorian values spread beyond the English-speaking world and were adopted in many European countries, and remnants of the attitudes they carry survive to the present day. As Mencken observed, the influence of Victorian attitudes was especially strong in the United States, stronger than in Britain. The reason for this is probably that Victorian values were coupled with and reinforced by the strong Puritan heritage in the United States. Indeed, Foucault, in his work mentioned above, uses the term "Victorian puritanism" in his account. For American Victorian prudery in linguistic usage to peak in the 1830s and 40s, as Mencken (1963) and Cmiel (1990) claim, it must have started long before the Victorian period proper.

Who promotes verbal prudery?

But who are the people that engage in verbal prudery in the United States? Simpson (1986) suggests that it is primarily the middle class:

> Euphemisms have usually been more fashionable among the aspiring, middle order of society, those most anxious about the proprieties they themselves created, but which they tend to regard as imposed from above. The lower and upper orders are both, then as now, less self-conscious about such matters. (p. 190)

This makes sense in light of Labov's similar observations concerning the phenomenon of hypercorrection among Americans. In chapter six, we saw that middle-class Americans in general engage in more hypercorrection than people belonging to the lower or upper classes. This is the most "fluid" and mobile social layer, whose members apparently assume that there is more at stake for them in terms of social advancement. This creates a great deal of linguistic insecurity in many Americans (see also Baron, 1982).

Webster as "purifier" of the Bible

There were also some individuals in America who thought it their duty to help Americans and American English get rid of words and phrases that could

possibly hurt people's sensitivity. It is of some significance that one such individual in the United States was Noah Webster. First, he went to great lengths to
make his dictionaries free from any improprieties. Second, as a prominent (if not
the leading) American linguist for a long time after the American Revolution,
Webster found time not only to lead his church choir but also to contribute to
the "purification" of one of the main resources of American English. He was so
unhappy with the language of the Bible that in 1833 he undertook to bowdler-
ize it. In the sanitized version of the Bible produced by Webster, Onan does not
spill his seed but *frustrates his purpose* and men do not have *testicles* (stones) but
peculiar members. In addition to these changes, he suggested a number of others.
He got rid of the verb *stink* and substituted *smell* for it; instead of *to give suck* he
used *to nurse* or *to nourish*; *whore* was substituted by *lewd woman* and *prostitute*;
and the phrase *to go a-whoring* became *to go astray* (examples taken from
Mencken, 1963). Webster's argument for the "purification" of the Bible was that
the Bible was made at a "half-civilized" stage of human society, but society
reached a refined stage at his time. Webster's conclusion was: "Purity of mind is
a Christian virtue that ought to be carefully cherished; and purity of language is
one of the guards which protect this virtue" (quoted in Cmiel, 1990:102).

As the examples above indicate, verbal prudery works especially in such
domains as body functions (*to give suck*), sexuality (*to go a-whoring*), and anything
that can be regarded as "offensive" (*stink*). In what follows in this chapter, we will
look at these and other semantic areas where taboos were especially visible in that
they produced a number of expressions in American English as a response to
the taboos.

Swearing

Profanity (contempt for God or holy things in general) is the clearest example of
things that fall under taboo in the Christian world. Swearing often (though not
exclusively) makes use of religious terms. Swearing of this kind was especially forbidden by the Puritans both in England and America. However, the ban on these
did not really help decrease their number. On the contrary, as Marckwardt (rev.
Dillard, 1980) note, "American English developed a whole lexicon of near-
swearing, ..." (p. 134). These include *darn*, *drat*, *doggone*, *blasted*, *Sam Hill*, *gee
whiz*, and dozens of others. What is common to them is that they are words
whose phonetic shape is similar to the pronunciation of the religious term
involved in the swearing. Thus, the pronunciation of *darn* resembles that of
damn, the pronunciation of *doggone it* that of *God damn it*, the pronunciation
of *gee whiz* that of *Jesus*, and so forth. The resemblance in sound shape is
enough to evoke the religious term. Speakers of American English can in this
way achieve two goals: swear (by using a religious term) and not swear (by using

a non-religious term) at the same time. That is, they can engage in profanity and avoid it in one act. Nevertheless, it is obvious to everyone that the words above amount to thinly disguised swearing.

We might wonder about the possible causes that may have led to disguised swearing. Baron (1982:125) offers an explanation:

> Speech was as important as literacy, and there was a tendency in Puritan New England to equate speech with morality. Physical punishments were meted out to those considered guilty of various linguistic infractions, including swearing, anger, scolding, and gossiping. Verbal behavior was subject to correction by the rod – appropriateness of speech is still of great concern to American teachers – but there was also a very positive emphasis on the stereotype that America was a nation of public speakers.

This explanation links the tabooed activity of swearing with the strict moral values of the Puritans. With disguised swearing one can get the best of both worlds: one can remain moral and give vent to anger simultaneously.

Death and some related areas

It is likely that death is regarded as less than a pleasant experience in any culture, and thus it is possibly a universal taboo topic. But Americans are nevertheless notorious for their desire to prolong life and for their varied "avoidance mechanisms" (see, for example, Walmsley, 1987). This attitude has certain linguistic manifestations. The time-honored word in English for the container in which people are buried is *coffin*. In American English this was replaced by the more delicate sounding *casket*, a word that possibly comes from *burial casket*. The person who arranges funerals has been called *undertaker* for a long time. However, this was found too explicit and suggestive of death by Americans, who produced *mortician* as an alternative. Another American term for the same person is *funeral director*, which not only avoids the explicitness of *undertaker* but dignifies the job itself. The word *undertaker* is considered by most speakers of American English as old-fashioned. The place where dead bodies are kept before the funeral is called *mortuary* in common (general) English. In America this has become a *funeral parlor* or a *funeral home*, truly reflecting the American love for euphemisms in talking about topics that are unpleasant for people.

But the euphemizing process did not stop at this stage. We find that today *perpetual rest consultants* can sell us an *underground condominium* or an *eternal condominium*. When translated to simple language, this amounts to saying that undertakers can sell us a cemetery lot (Lutz, 1990). Furthermore, instead of gravediggers digging the graves, people specializing in *internment excavation prepare* them. Any detailed study of this semantic domain in, for instance, advertisements would reveal hundreds of expressions of this kind.

Old age

Old age is regarded, possibly because of its relation to death, unfavorably by many Americans. To stay *forever young* (as in the popular song) is a major American desire. People who are old tend not to be called *old people*, since, presumably, this would hurt their sensibilities. They are called *senior citizens* instead. The traditional expression for the institution where old people are cared for is not *old folks' home* anymore; it has been replaced by *nursing home* or *retirement residence*. The general tendency is not to refer to old age at all. Today's medical science is no exception. Aging is referred to as *cell drop out*, or *decreased propensity for cell replication* (Lutz, 1990:64).

War and death

But the conceptual domain of death extends beyond death as such. One major reason for death is war. As Fussell (1992) remarks, war is often referred to as a *campaign* in the U.S., a term that is much less explicit and transparent than *war*. Also, the U.S. has a Department of Defense and a Secretary of Defense, in which the word *defense* is a euphemism for war, and may hide aspects of war that are regarded as unfair by many people, for instance, the possibility that the U.S. is the initiator of or the "attacker" in a war. Similarly, expressions like *to suppress* (or *neutralize*) *a target* may be used to "beautify" some ugly facts about people killing other people.

The military commonly conceals embarrassing facts by relying on what Lutz (1990) calls "doublespeak." Thus when American soldiers are killed by American bombs or artillary shells, this is called *friendly casualties* caused by the *accidental delivery of ordnance equipment*. And when civilians are bombed by American forces, this might be referred to as *eroding the will of the population* (Lutz, 1990:176). The Grenada invasion in 1984 started out as an *invasion* proper, but then it turned into a *pre-dawn vertical insertion* in the words of the Pentagon (p. 183). As these examples suggest, the military is one major supplier of euphemistic doublespeak in the U.S.

The human body

Certain parts of the human body fall under linguistic taboo in many cultures. One of the main reasons is that these body parts participate in or are used to perform activities that are tabooed themselves. Such activities include sexual activities and the emptying of the body of waste materials (which is a euphemism itself). One wonders which of these is at work in the case of words like *leg*. There is a popular anecdote concerning the use of this word in America in the first half of the nineteenth century. A woman injured her leg and a man asked her politely: *Did you hurt your leg much?*. The woman's response was that the word *leg* should not be mentioned in the company of ladies, and that the proper word to use is *limb*. Probably Baron (1982:24) makes reference to the same story when he writes about an incident that involved a certain Captain Frederick Marryat, an Englishman traveling in America in the 1820s:

> ... he [Captain Marryat] finds that Americans are too dependent on euphemisms. He relates an incident in which a woman became offended at his use of the word *leg*, informing him that *limb* was the preferred term, and adding, "I am not so particular as some people are, for I know those who always say limb of a table, or limb of a piano-forte." Marryat then tells of his visit to a seminary for young ladies where, to ensure good taste, a four-limbed pianoforte had had its limbs dressed "in modest little trousers, with frills at the bottom of them!" (Diary, pp. 246-47)

What's more, as Mencken (1963) tells us, *feet* was also banned at the beginning of the nineteenth century in America. The taboo on the use of *leg* extended to the legs of fowls as well. In the Victorian period, chicken legs were called *joints*, a completely neutral term. That the British also participated in all this is shown by the word *drumstick* for chicken leg, which is of British origin.

The use of the word *breast* was also forbidden. The now literary term *bosom* was used in its place. Even chicken breast disappeared, giving way to *white meat*. This phrase was originally used of such light-colored meat as veal and pork.

Body wastes

One of the semantic areas that is capable of producing a large number of euphemisms is that of *body wastes* (the compound being a euphemism itself). It is especially instructive to look at the socially institutionalized place where the two main activities related to body wastes, urination and defecation, are performed. Americans are, in the words of Fussell (1992), extremely "shamefaced" about this place. The British English term for this is *water closet* (or *W.C.*), whereas Americans originally chose the word *toilet*, a fairly opaque term that does not say anything about what is happening in the place (i.e., that water is used). Despite its nontransparent, and thus slightly euphemistic, character, this word is avoided by Americans today. However, American English abounds in other euphemistic expressions to describe this location. In the home, *bathroom* is the main American word to refer to it. *Restroom* and *washroom* are commonly used today for public toilets. *Comfort station* has the same meaning, but it is rarely used. *Powder room* denotes a public toilet for women. The most common slang or colloquial term is *john* in America, and the corresponding British word is *loo*. *Toilet* has later found its way into British English and it remains, together with *lavatory* and *W.C.*, the main term in Britain. *Facilities* is yet another euphemism favored by many Americans. Humor is also employed by Americans to dull the potential offensiveness of expressions that refer to taboo topics such as toilets. For example, some Southern Californians resort to humorous expressions like *tinkling factory* in certain situations. Looking for the public toilet in the streets of a European city, one adult Southern Californian asked: *Where's the tinkling factory here?*

We observed in chapter fourteen that directness is one major property of the way Americans speak. One would expect that this is especially so among "macho" working class Americans. But Fussell (1992) noted that this is not so, at least in relation to the use of toilets. The portable toilets in construction sites are called *Porto-Potty, Potty Queen, Por-to-let, Port-o-John,* and *Sani-John,* words not exactly matching the stereotype of construction workers as "tough and outspoken." However, to settle this "issue" of inconsistency in a conclusive way, we would have to know whether these words have been created by the construction workers themselves or the manufacturers of portable toilets.

Mencken (1963) notes that women's rooms (a euphemism itself) were not called anything in the heyday of using euphemism for toilets. What was indicated, however, was *whose* facilities they were: men's or women's. The rest had to be figured out. Usual signs (on the doors of toilets) included *For Ladies Only, Ladies Only, Ladies,* and *Women.* Similarly for men: *Gents Only, Gents, Gentlemen,* and *Men's.* Today the most common signs are *Women* and *Men.*

The activities of urination and defecation performed in this place are commonly expressed through euphemisms in English. Thus, we find a huge number of euphemistic expressions in all styles and registers of English, including medical, slang, juvenile, informal, and formal usage. Below is a small selection of these, gleaned from Richard A. Spears' (1982) *Slang and Euphemism* and Jonathon Green's (1998) *The Cassell Dictionary of Slang.* The expressions come from a variety of registers and styles and they may have slightly different meanings. If an item is given in either source as originating in the U.S., the expression is marked with the abbreviation US.

Urination:
do number one, evacuate the bladder, go (US), go to the bathroom

(US), make water, micturate, pass urine, pass water, potty (US), take a leak (US), urinate, void, water the dragon, water the horses, water the mule (US), wet (one's pants)

Defecation:
do number two, ease oneself, evacuate the bowels, go (US), go to the bathroom (US), have the runs ("diarrhea"), have the trots ("diarrhea"), Montezuma's revenge (US, "diarrhea"), movies (US, "diarrhea"), perform the work of nature, poop, poo-poo (US), potty (US), quickstep (US, "diarrhea"), relieve oneself, squat, stool, unfeed (US), void

As can be seen, the expression *go to the bathroom* is used for both urination and defecation by Americans. (The British equivalent of this is the less euphemistic *go to the toilet*.) The American tendency for prudery in this domain is further demonstrated by the phenomenon that Americans use the same expression to talk about the "needs" of domestic animals, such as cats and dogs. Thus, in the U.S. even a cat or dog can be said to want to go to the bathroom.

Sexuality

Areas that gave rise to a prevalant use of verbal prudery in American English have to do with sexuality in some form. Since certain pieces of clothing cover the sexual organs they fell under heavy taboo. These garments were variously called *undergarments, sub-trousers, nether garments,* and *panties.* More interestingly, they were also *unmentionables* and *inexpressibles.* Mention of the word *corset* was regarded as insulting. Going to bed had, as it still does, sexual connotations because the assumed prototypical place for sexual activity is the bed. Now since it was impossible for the nineteenth-century American to say that he or she *is going to bed* (that is, to sleep), they used *retire* instead. Servant girls in this century were not *seduced,* they were *betrayed. Confined* meant *pregnant* (Cmiel, 1990). Female stockings were called *hoses* or *long socks,* possibly for the same reason. This taboo based on sexual connotations extended to the animal domain as well. A case that was already mentioned serves as a good example. After the word *cock* acquired the meaning of the male sexual organ, Americans did not use that term to refer to the male of chickens. The word that replaced it was *rooster.* Moreover, the word *haycock* that was present in English for centuries was replaced by *haystack* in American English. It was perhaps the assumed sexuality of bulls that led to the disappearance of the word *bull* to refer to the males of cows. Bulls at this time became, in a development that would probably please many feminists today, *male cows, cow creatures,* and *seed oxen.* Following this development, bulls were not castrated anymore; they were *changed, arranged, altered,* and, according to Mencken, in Georgia they even *made a Baptist minister of them.*

On the other hand, there is also an unprecedented surge of sexual explicitness today in the United States. We noted in the chapter on slang that the word *fuck* and its derivatives occupy twelve pages in the *Historical Dictionary of American Slang.* Fussell (1992) observed that sexual explicitness in T-shirts is greater than ever. A restaurant in Indiana issued a T-shirt with the following inscription: LICK ME, SUCK ME, EAT ME ALL NIGHT LONG. True, the T-shirt invites people to eat, but the sexual reference of the sign is obvious.

Despite occasional surges in sexual explicitness, the main tendency in (American) English still is to use euphemistic language about sexuality, including the sexual act itself. The following list is just a small sample taken from Spears' and Green's work and Stephen Glazier's (1997) *Random House Word Menu.* Here again, expressions given as originating in the U.S. are marked US.

> ease nature (US), be familiar with, be intimate, coit, consummate, do, do it, do the naughty, fornicate, get laid (US), get some, get some action, give oneself, go all the way, go to bed with, go to town (US), have a roll in the hay (US, "to engage in an act of spontaneous copulation"), have sex, have sexual intercourse with (US), know, let nature take its course (US, "to permit sexual attraction to accomplish some appropriate task such as breeding animals or restoring harmony in a marriage"), lie with, love, make it, make love, mount, perform (US), play hide the salami (US), possess, score (US), sleep around (US), sleep with (US), womanize, yield one's favors

There are literally hundreds of such euphemistic expressions in (American) English. As can be seen in the list above, they can be found in all styles and registers, but the style that is especially productive of them is slang.

Prostitution

A domain that resulted in a wide variety of terms especially in the nineteenth century is that of prostitution. What was originally called simply and directly a *whorehouse* came to be called by a variety of names in this period. This is understandable since the institution, the place, and the associated activities were, and still are, under taboo in middle-class America. Marckwardt (1980; rev. Dillard) mentions *assignation house, sporting house,* and *crib* as alternatives that are American in origin. Maybe the best known of the terms he cites are *cat house* and *call house,* which are still current as slang expressions today. It might be the popularity of the expression *call girl* that also keeps *call house* alive. *Fancy house* and *cow bag* were also coined in this general period. Two additional terms, *disorderly house* and *house of ill fame* (or *ill repute*), are further examples of the process at this time to "camouflage" the real referent, or meaning, behind them.

Amazingly enough, prostitutes can also be called *available casual indigenous female companions.* Lutz (1990) tells us that these were the words that the State Department used in 1988 to warn embassy employees in Budapest that some of the local prostitutes are probably spies for the Hungarian government: "it must be assumed that available casual indigenous female companions work for or cooperate with the Hungarian government" (Lutz, 1990:207-208). Together with Lutz, we must acknowledge the linguistic creativity and talent of the author of this sentence in using euphemistic language.

Euphemistic language is a kind of refined language. As Cmiel (1990) points out, euphemisms in nineteenth-century America were not necessarily welcomed by the refined class, which often thought it was a false and pretentious language. The users of euphemisms were regarded as trying to be refined but in fact being unrefined. Euphemistic language "reflected the rise of the half-educated" (Cmiel, 1990:66). Many educated Americans still consider lower-class users of euphemisms "half-educated," or not educated at all.

study questions and activities

1. The terms below indicate another area (or semantic domain) – not dealt with in the chapter – where Americans use highly euphemistic language. Can you guess from the examples which area they are about and what they mean? *Negotiated departure, redundancy elimination, be excessed, involuntary separation, right-sizing.* If you know what area they have to do with and what they mean, try to find more examples from your own sources. Why do you think this area is so heavily euphemistic?

2. One characteristic feature of politically correct language is that it abounds in euphemisms. What are some of the major linguistic means of creating politically correct language, as exemplified by the following expressions? *Metabolically challenged, alternative dentation, animal companion, chemically inconvenienced, sobriety-deprived, copper woman, differently abled, hair-disadvantaged, melanin impoverished, lookism, mentally challenged, metabolically different, motivationally deficient, native Alaskan, sun people.*

3. Most of the items listed in the previous question have not become accepted by many Americans. Who have and who have not accepted them? What do you think the reasons are?

4. Do a linguistic study of sexual explicitness in American English. If you are American, study in detail the way your teachers, your parents, and your friends talk about sexuality. If you are not American, study in detail the ways sexuality is talked about in various literary sources (e.g., Salinger's *The Catcher in the Rye* and Hemingway's *For Whom the Bell Tolls*). Make a detailed inventory of what is used, and by whom in each case, and compare your findings. What general conclusions can you come to in light of what was said in the chapter? You can also do a comparison with what you find in corresponding British sources.

chapter 18

Tall talk and grandiloquence

The focus of this chapter will be on two related aspects of American speech: tall talk and grandiloquence. We begin with tall talk because it provides a historical perspective on grandiloquence, which is the phenomenon of dignifying or elevating things that are not viewed as being dignified or elevated.

Tall talk

What is tall talk?

It is a common stereotype about Americans that they are excellent rhetoricians. Several authors who have studied American English also noted that Americans are a nation of good public speakers. In the last chapter we saw how, according to Baron (1982), this idea goes back to at least the New England Puritans. Mencken (1963) makes a similar observation when he writes: "The American, from the beginning, has been the most ardent of recorded rhetoricians" (p. 99). Mencken appears to believe that this American skill has in part to do with tall talk. He continues: "His politics bristles with pungent epithets; his whole history has been bedizened with tall talk ..." (p. 99). But what are some of the defining properties of this form of talk?

One property of tall talk is undoubtedly humor. This does not have to be intentional. The user of the sentence *She slings the nastiest ankle in old Kentuck* (Mencken, 1963) may not have intended any humor when he expressed the meaning "She was the best dancer in Kentucky," but it would be difficult to take the sentence with a straight face. Mencken provides further examples in which humor is combined with some other features of tall talk, when he says:

> Such a term as *rubberneck* is almost a complete treatise on American psychology; it has precisely the boldness and contempt for ordered forms that is so characteristically American. The same qualities are in *roughhouse, has-been, lame-duck*, and a thousand other such racy substantives.... (p. 99)

This humor and boldness in language are often expressed in the form of "ingeniously contrived epithets," "wild hyperbole," and "fantastic simile and metaphor." This kind of oratory has a "bombastic" effect, and its main purpose is "to impress the listener with the physical prowess or general superiority of the speaker or of his friends" (Mencken, 1963:149), as we will see in some of the examples below.

But the words used in tall talk are not always based on metaphor or simile. Many are, such as *ringtailed roarer* ("a big hearty fellow") and *screamer* ("strong man"), but many are not, such as *to absquatulate* ("to depart stealthily"), *bodaciously* ("completely"), *conbobberation* ("disturbance"), and *rambunctious* ("uncontrollable"). They are often what are called high-sounding or mouth-filling words, including such additional examples as *kankarriferous, angeliferous, splendiferous*, based on such suffixes as *-acious, -ticate, -iferous, -icute*. Most of these words were created or invented in the 1830s or 1840s. Interestingly, the verb *teetotal* is also a product of this general process and was created in 1837. Baron mentions slightly different but related examples from the same time period, quoting Harrison, a British clergyman, from the 1840s (Baron, 1982:189): "Harrison seems to feel that the following examples are characteristic of American usage, stereotyped as full of tall talk and fancified phrasing: *the advent of fun and fashiondom; a foot like a jolly fat clam; pocketually speaking; unletupable nature, plumptitude, wide-awakeity, betweenity*, and *go-awayness*."

Where does all this come from?

Marckwardt (1980; rev. Dillard) sees the possible source of tall talk in Elizabethan literature (p. 111). Dillard (1985) also connects this hyperbolic form of American talk with Black trappers and cowboys, groups that have elaborate oral traditions. The Black version of tall talk is called "fancy talk." The spirit behind the process is also attributed to the hard life on the frontier and the effort to somehow compensate for the hardships of life. Carmer (quoted in Marckwardt, 1980:109; rev. Dillard) explains:

> At the end of a hard day's work the American cowboys or miners or lumberjacks or applepickers have had their fun out of making up stories about men who do jobs that could just not be done, and in an impossibly short time with one hand tied behind them. The dreams of American workers, naturally enough, have never been delicate, exquisite, or polite – like most fairy stories. They have been big and powerful, and a strong wind is always blowing through them.

And we can add that perhaps the diversity of immigrants has also contributed to this.

The historical context for tall talk

If what was mentioned above are some of the causes or sources of tall talk, then the context for it was the unbound belief that anything and everything is possible in the new country. The belief was also fueled by national feelings. 1828 was the year when Andrew Jackson was elected, and it was also the year when the linguistically and culturally important event of the publication of Webster's *American Dictionary of the English Language* took place. The general belief and expectation was that everything American is to be grand, including the territory of the country, its population, products, science, and political institutions. There was also unbound confidence in the material development of the country. The resulting general outlook of most Americans was that America has a grand future (Mencken, 1963:145).

Tall talk in politics

Given these sources and the context of tall talk, it is only natural that tall talk permeated such rhetorically-charged activities as political speeches. Mencken (1963) gives the following example of a speech in Congress from this period:

> The proudest bird upon the mountain is upon the American ensign,
> and not one feather shall fall from her plumage there. She's American
> in design, and an emblem of wilderness and freedom. (p. 146)

This speech was given in Congress, but tall talk is even more characteristic of what is called *stump speaking*, a prevalent practice throughout the nineteenth century in American political speeches. The excerpt above is surely "bombastic" and contains "wild hyperbole" and "fantastic simile and metaphor." Indeed, for Mencken the very basis of American political life is rhetoric based in part on tall talk: "His [the American's] politics bristles with pungent epithets; his whole history has been bedizened with tall talk; his fundamental institutions rest far more upon brilliant phrases than upon logical ideas" (p. 99). The same view seems to have been held by Washington Irving, more than half a century before Mencken. Simpson, quoting some ideas from Irving, writes: "The United States is parodied as a society ruled by a 'pure unadulterated LOGOCRACY or *governmnent of words*,' ... in which anyone with a 'plentiful stock of verbosity' may succeed, ..." (Simpson, 1986:112). For a politician to be a good rhetorician is just as important today in the United States as it was in the first half of the nineteenth century. Many Americans believe that it is *the* most important quality in politicians. The example that is most frequently mentioned in making this point is former President Ronald Reagan, who was considered to be the "great communicator."

Tall talk in literature

Regarded as the "first truly American writer" by Faulkner, the American author who continued the tradition of tall talk in his literary fiction was Mark Twain. Twain is of course best known for the simplicity of his style and thus as the writer who continued the plain style in American literature. Nevertheless, he was greatly affected by tall talk, and he used it effectively as a literary device, as in the following passage from his *Life on the Mississippi*:

> Whoo-oop! I'm the the old original iron-jawed, brass-mounted, copper-bellied corpse-maker from the wilds of Arkansaw! Look at me! I'm the man they call Sudden Death and General Desolation! Sired by a hurricane, dam'd by an earthquake, half-brother to the cholera, nearly related to the smallpox on the mother's side!

Mencken, who quotes this passage (1963:146), says that it contains "grotesque metaphors and farfetched exaggerations," some of the characteristic features of tall talk.

Twain used tall talk extensively in his books, including perhaps his least successful book, *A Tramp Abroad*, which he wrote about his trip to Europe in 1878. Here is a passage from that work:

> The captain of the raft, who was as full of history as he could stick, said that in the Middle Ages a most prodigious fire-breathing dragon used to live in that region, and made more trouble than a tax collector. He was as long as a railway train, and had the customary impenetrable green scales all over him. His breath bred pestilence and conflagration, and his appetite bred famine. He ate men and cattle impartially, and was exceedingly unpopular. The German emperor of that day made the usual offer; he would grant to the destroyer of the dragon, any one solitary thing he might ask for; for he had a surplusage of daughters, and it was customary for dragon-killers to take a daughter for pay.

This legend is the product of Twain's imagination, and, as a commentator on Twain's trip to Germany, Harry B. Davis (1985:67), tells us, it prefigures Twain's later and much more successful book, *A Connecticut Yankee in King Arthur's Court*. And one of Twain's most popular short stories, "The Celebrated Jumping Frog of Calaveras County," can be said to be based on tall talk as well. These and many other examples seem to indicate that Twain had been greatly influenced by this "American genre" and had a life-long affection for it, parallel to his deep devotion to plain style. He was a master of both.

Some popular figures in early American tall talk

There are several well-known characters in American folklore who come from the speech form of tall talk. Paul Bunyan could cut down two trees with a double-bladed ax. Mike Fink could jump across rivers. John Henry could carry a bale of cotton under each arm and two on his head. Strap Buckner used to knock down bulls with a single blow of an iron pestle. As Marckwardt (1980; rev. Dillard) remarks, frontier exaggeration found outlet in tall talk.

But tall talk was characteristic not only of folk heroes but also of some real individuals like Davy Crockett, who said making a political comment: "... fresh from the back-woods, half horse, half alligator, a little touched with snapping turtle, can wade the Mississippi, leap the Ohio, ride a streak of lightning, ... and eat any man opposed to Jackson" (Marckwardt, 1980:110; rev. Dillard).

Tall talk today

However, tall talk was not an exclusive property of the nineteenth century. It exists in many forms in the twentieth century as well. According to Marckwardt (1980; rev. Dillard), the mouth-filling word *gobbledygook* was first used by Senator Maverick in its modern sense of "talk that is pompous and wordy, full of long, especially Latinized words" in the late 1940s. What is known as *psychobabble* today is also a form of tall talk, the exaggerated jargon of psychotherapists. But tall talk also pervades the everyday. What is called *bullshitting*, a common linguistic phenomenon, often takes the form of tall talk. Marckwardt (1980; rev. Dillard) notes that many Americans have a rather positive attitude to "the verbally esoteric." Indeed, there is a popular colloquial American saying that reflects this lay attitude to forms of tall talk in a clear way: "If you can't impress them with brilliance, dazzle them with bullshit."

Place names

Tall talk also shows up in areas where we would not expect it. Bryson (1990:208) mentions that Americans have "a legacy of colorful names." If we look at some of the examples Bryson provides, we must agree with him. Here are some of them:

Chocolate Bayou, Ding Dong, Lick Skillet – in Texas
Sweet Gum Head – in Louisiana
Why – in Arizona
Whynot – in Mississippi
Zzyzx Springs – in California

Stiffknee Knob, Rabbit Shuffle – in North Carolina
Scratch Ankle – in Alabama
Fertile – in Minnesota
Climax – in Michigan
Intercourse – in Pennsylvania
Ninety-six – in South Carolina
Eighty-eight, Bug – in Kentucky
Dull, Only, Peeled Chestnut – in Tennessee
Hog Heaven – in Idaho
Dead Bastard Peak, Crazy Woman Creek, Maggie's Nipples
– in Wyoming

Bryson notes that some of these have been changed. Nonetheless, the point remains that these place names are likely to be reflections of the American love for tall talk, and, as such, to be typically American names.

As another example of the contemporary use of tall talk, let us take the nicknames of some states:

Iowa – Hawkeye State
California – Golden State
New Mexico – Land of Enchantment

These names reveal the same American attraction to playful exaggeration.

Sports teams

The names of sports teams are also revealing. It is only in the United States that we find sports teams and clubs with such names as the *Pirates*, the *Devils*, the *Red Sox* (i.e., Socks), the *Tigers*, the *Cowboys*, the *Bulls*, the *Angels*, the *Mighty Ducks,* and many others. In European countries, for example, these names are unthinkable, or would only be used as a result of American influence in some professional sports. "Wild hyperbole" is widely regarded as a characteristically American phenomenon.

Cars

Hyperbole and exaggeration can also be found in the names American car manufacturers give to their products. Some examples in this category include *Mustang*, *Impala, Cougar, Bronco*. These are obviously also names that try to make a point about the cars, highlighting some of their desirable features, such as speed and power. On the other hand, they also fit in with the tendency for tall talk.

Another interesting American phenomenon connected with cars is what is called *vanity plates* on cars. In the United States car owners are entitled to have a license plate of their own choice (after paying some extra money to the Department of Motor Vehicles). Thus car owners get a chance to express themselves not only through the kind of car that they drive, but also through the license plate they use. These "creative" license plates are often reminiscent of tall talk. We find plates such as *L84AD8*, meaning "late for a date," which was Nicole Brown Simpson's license plate.

Grandiloquence, or dignifying the not-so-dignified

By dignifying I mean a process through which a domain or aspect of life is elevated by making reference to it by a word or phrase that lends the domain more importance and respect than it would otherwise have. For this purpose, euphemism – a linguistic device we have already come across in the previous chapter – is commonly employed. In this, the process is similar to what we find in verbal prudery. However, the basic difference between prudery and grandiloquence lies in the fact that whereas prudery involves a domain that is taboo, grandiloquence involves one that is lowly or down-to-earth but not necessarily taboo. Grandiloquence is the opposite of plain or direct English, and it also makes simple things more complicated than they really are, thus giving them more importance. Dignifying the not-so-dignified is a process that is related to tall talk, in that more importance and respect is given to someone or something that does not quite deserve so much of it. Let us now turn to some examples of this process in American English.

Some frontier "institutions"

As was noted above, the place where tall talk and grandiloquence were most popular was the frontier and the West. We will briefly discuss only two "institutions" of the West: the saloon and the opera. Much of the discussion below is based on Marckwardt (1980; rev. Dillard).

The saloon

The word *saloon* is an early eighteenth-century adaptation of the French *salon*. The French word designated a large, elegant room where guests are often received. In America, this word was applied to an establishment where alcoholic drinks are drunk. The British equivalent is *public house*, or *pub* for short. Today *saloon* is an old-fashioned word in American English. At the time it came to be used in the sense of the British English *pub*, it often referred to a cheap and dirty place where alcohol was sold in the frontier region. The establishment is typified in the *saloon* of many Western movies. In other words, there was a big gap between the connotations of the original French word and those of the word as used in American English. *Saloon* served the function of giving dignity to an establishment that was less than dignified. The word acquired clearly negative connotations before and during the Prohibition era. As a result, the owners of saloons began not to call themselves *saloonkeepers*, which was the original word for that purpose. The words that are in common use today in American English are *bar* and *bartender*. It is interesting to note that the positive connotations of elegance and fashion that we find in the French word *salon* are still present in some words in the United States. For example, the place where people, especially women, go for hair styling, facial massages, manicures, etc. is called a *beauty salon* (or *shop* or *parlor*).

The opera house

But frontier towns did not only consist of saloons. The communities on or behind the frontier usually also had their local theaters. These were called *opera houses*. However, these institutions in the nineteenth and early twentieth century were very different from the opera houses of today – both in architecture and the performances presented. As Marckwardt (1980; rev. Dillard) notes, in Muncie, Indiana, some of the "operas" performed in the local "opera house" included such titles as *The Telephone Girl, Over the Garden Wall, The Black Crook*, and *Uncle Tom's Cabin*. As the titles suggest, the performances did not bear too much resemblance to what was or is usually understood by operas. The term *opera house* was used to elevate the status of the institution.

Education

The domain of education provides a large number of examples for the same process. The attempt to elevate the standing of certain institutions and roles within those institutions often resulted in differences between British and American English usage. The American educational system is a good example. It is an interesting question why the process of dignifying was so prevalent in this particular domain. The answer may have to do with American feelings of insecurity that derive from the assumed superior educational system of the mother country.

College and university

To begin, the term *college* seems to have developed a more extensive range of reference in the U.S. than in Great Britain. While in Britain a *college* is a part of a university (as in the *colleges of Oxford University*), in American English it can designate not just institutions that are a part of higher education. In the United States, the word *college* primarily refers to an institution where undergradutate or graduate studies are conducted. A college is a place where you go to obtain your first academic degree or your doctoral degree. In addition to this usage, Americans have used it to refer to institutions that are not a part of what is considered higher education. Thus, *college* may designate a place where secretarial training is given or a place where people learned to become, say, barbers. In the U.S., there have been *business or secretarial colleges* and *barber colleges*. In these cases, a more dignified term is used to describe less dignified institutions. This has broadened the range of reference for the term in American English in ways in which this has not happened in British English.

Fussell (1992) notes that in many cases, especially during the Kennedy and Johnson administrations, many second-rate colleges and other lower-level educational institutions were given university status. Fussell writes: "The goal was to widen access to 'educational opportunity,' and in pursuit of this end verbal inflation ... was called on to promote to university status numerous normal schools and teachers colleges, business academies, secretarial institutes, provincial theological seminaries, and trade schools" (pp. 65-66). What is especially important for our purposes is Fussell's use of the phrase "verbal inflation." This phrase covers exactly the kind of process that is being characterized here. Fussell continues: "The technique was not to turn them into universities ... but simply to call them universities" (p. 66). This illustrates how verbal aggrandizement can serve social purposes.

In the nineteenth century, the term *university* was also used more extensively in American English. A nice illustration of this is a statement by an American "patriot" quoted by Marckwardt (1980; rev. Dillard): "There are two universities in England, four in France, ten in Prussia, and thirty-seven in Ohio" (p. 121). Today, however, Americans employ the term differently. For most Americans, a *university* is an institution of higher education that has both undergraduate and graduate programs. Thus, a university is different from college in that it must have a graduate program, whereas a college may have just an undergraduate program.

High school

The American use of the term *high school* represents the same tendency we have seen for the words above. A *high school* is a secondary school, especially for grades 9, 10, 11, and 12. According to Marckwardt (1980; rev. Dillard), it began to be used in this sense in 1824, when it also included grades 7 and 8. This use of *high school* does not exist in England or in Europe, where the institution of high school is on the third and highest level in the educational system, namely, where universities and colleges are. The fact that the term *high school* was accepted for a secondary-level institution in America indicates that it was felt to be an adequate and satisfactory way of designating this kind of school. The perceived adequacy of the "upgraded" term shows that the attitude is not alien to the American character.

Professor

Perhaps one of the best examples of the American tendency to elevate status can be found in the use of the word *professor* in the sense of a teacher at a school of higher education. Although some dictionaries make a careful distinction between the various senses of the term and its range of application, most speakers of American English use it indiscriminately and ignore the distinctions drawn by dictionaries. For example, *Webster's New World Dictionary* provides the following definition of the relevant sense:

> 2. a) a college or university teacher of the highest academic rank, usually in a specific field; full professor b) *short for* assistant professor & associate professor c) loosely, any college, university, or, occas., secondary-school teacher

For everyday purposes, *professor* is practically not used in sense 2. a); it is used mostly in senses 2. b) and especially 2. c). This means that, in the course of natural speech in everyday contexts, Americans tend to elevate the status of all teachers below the rank of full professor at a university. They can use it to include not only all university and college teachers but also secondary-school teachers. In contrast, *professor* in England means a "university teacher of the highest grade who holds a chair in a subject" (*Oxford Advanced Learner's Dictionary*), that is, the equivalent of the American *full professor*. This difference in range of application tells us not only that the word has a broader range of reference in American English, but also that the difference has a certain "direction" that fits the general pattern: the tendency to elevate lower status to a higher one. In the twentieth century *professor* has even been used of dancing teachers and magicians.

School as an exception

But this is just a tendency and not a watertight rule. Exceptions to it can easily be found. One such exception comes from the same domain. British and Americans use the word *school* in interestingly different ways. In Britain, *school* is applied to primary and secondary schools. In the U.S., it covers both, but it is also used of colleges and universities. Thus, someone might say *Berkeley is the best school in the country*, meaning the University of California at Berkeley, or a 40-year-old woman might say *I'm going to go back to school next year*, meaning that she wants to continue her university studies. This use of *school* is not available in Great Britain. In a way, the American use of the word goes against the tendency we pointed out in this section. It can be suggested that by calling the university *school*, Americans actually lower or, in this sense, "downgrade" the highest level of their educational system to the elementary and secondary levels, where the word's primary application lies.

Fraternity

A widely known student institution at American universities or colleges is called *fraternity*. The current definition of *fraternity* is a men's student organization at a college or university chiefly for social or scholastic purposes (like a *debating fraternity*). These organizations usually have secret rites. The name of fraternities commonly consists of Greek letters. The original meaning of the word has to do with brotherhood. According to Marckwardt (1980; rev. Dillard), shortly after the Declaration of Independence a group of students at William and Mary College formed a literary society which was called Phi Beta Kappa. Members of the society pledged eternal brotherhood to each other and called their organization a *fraternity*. Later, other student organizations that were based on the idea of brotherhood also called themselves *fraternities*. Today, any collegiate society can have this name. Given this history of the term, we can see the by now familiar pattern in its development. The meaning of a term which designates a group of men at a university or college formed on the noble principle of brotherhood comes to be extended to any, especially male, student organization. In the course of the extension, the meaning first covers a group of men organized for an elevated cause and then it comes to refer to student organizations that have nothing to do with this cause. In the process, the term comes to designate an ordinary student organization. Indeed, fraternities today have acquired a negative connotation. The related term *frat rat* designates a male student who is a member of a fraternity, but the connotations are rather negative. *Frat rats* are commonly assumed to be rowdy and mostly interested in beer, women, and parties. This development of meaning illustrates how an organization that is no longer noble or elevated is dignified with the name that had a very positive meaning.

Occupational terminology

Occupational terminology abounds in examples of the same process. Many of the differences between the use of British and American occupational terms result from the fact that Americans tend to apply a term that designates an occupation that is highly regarded to something that is less dignified or highly respected, a process whereby the latter domain or concept becomes dignified.

Doctor

The word *doctor* has different ranges of application in British and American English. The British use involves physicians, but excludes surgeons and veterinarians. The American use of the term is broader, and its breadth is due to the American liking for dignifying. This is not obvious in the case of surgeons. Surgeons in British English are not called *doctors*; they are simply *Mr. Surgeons*. In other words, British English usage appears to draw a line between surgical and nonsurgical aspects of medicine, and uses the term *doctor* for the latter domain. This may or may not have to do with the issue of dignifying. More clearcut examples involve veterinarians, who are doctors in the U.S. but not in Great Britain. Moreover, Americans seem to be at more liberty than the British to apply the term to such professions as osteopaths, chiropractors, optometrists, chiropodists, and so forth. There is also a more general tendency in the U.S. to call anyone with remarkable skills a *doctor*, even in the domain of sports, as the example of *Dr. J.* (Julius Erving), the former basketball star, indicates. This usage might be jocular, but the point is that it seems to be more widespread in the U.S.

Mortician and its synonyms

Sometimes it is difficult to say whether a given term in American English is the product of verbal prudery, the tendency to elevate the lowly, or the result of both processes that are jointly at work. As was observed, death is a topic that is not commonly talked about in an explicit way; it falls under taboo. Thus the use of the word *funeral director* and especially that of *mortician* (first documented in 1895) is less direct than the use of *undertaker*, a word going back to the beginning of the seventeenth century. However, it is also conceivable that the American terms *funeral director* and *mortician* come from the American urge to dignify a profession that is not highly regarded. And there is also the possibility that these processes are both at work behind the creation of these two American words.

Beautician

A clearer case is represented by the American word *beautician* (a word coined around 1924). The work that a cosmetologist, a near-equivalent of beautician, does is not a taboo activity that needs to be expressed in acceptable ways. Therefore, it is unlikely that it is verbal prudery that is at work here. More likely is the possibility that it is a job that is not as highly esteemed as other jobs whose names bear the suffix *-ician*, such as *phonetician* (deriving from around 1848). It should be noticed that *mortician* has the same suffix. This is indication that it is the suffix *-ician* that is involved in the process of dignifying.

Engineer

According to some estimates, the term *engineer* has over 2000 uses in American English. The attempt to dignify an occupation has led to some interesting differences between British and American English. In British English the driver of a locomotive is an *engine-driver*. The American counterpart has obviously been influenced by the process of grandiloquence: it is *(train) engineer*. The British word for a person who takes care of an apartment house is a *caretaker*, while Americans use *janitor*. However, it was proposed in America that a janitor should be called an *engineer-custodian,* or *custodial engineer*, a word that dignifies the job of janitors and which sounds like an exaggeration for European ears.

Grandiloquence and occupational jargon

Many Americans are greatly impressed by complicated occupational jargon. In a way, they expect professionals to use jargon even if it is not completely intelligible to them. A doctor is regarded as somehow less competent if he or she does not use the "sophisticated" vocabulary of medicine (see, for example, the video presentation *Social dialects of American English*). Long and especially Latinate words can be particularly impressive. This kind of impressibility by jargon also goes back to the rise of middling culture. But in the nineteenth century if a politician used jargon-filled language in his public speeches, this "was associated with lack of breeding" – at least by refined audiences (Cmiel, 1990:65).

Long words can also make a good impression on some people. Words that consist of more syllables are taken to carry more "weight" than words that consist of less. Fussell (1992) provides some examples, when he writes:

> Thus the popularity of *wellness* as a replacement for *health,* the use of *assist* instead of *help, a great dining experience* for *a great dinner, a great reading experience* for *a great read,* etc.... a *watch* becomes a *timepiece,* just as a *choice* ascends a bit and becomes an *option* – twice as desirable because requiring twice the syllables. (p. 103)

The home

Another recent example of, and an on-going tendency for, dignifying the not-so-dignified is provided by the domain of the home. As will be shown, in this case some critiques of contemporary American society see outright fraudulence behind the semantic process of dignifying.

Home and house

Several authors comment on the American abuse of the word *home*. It is commonly used in the U.S. instead of the more direct word *house*. Thus Marckwardt (1980; rev. Dillard) notes that instead of *housebuilder*, *houseowner*, and *house appliances* Americans talk about *homebuilder*, *homeowner*, and *home appliances*. In these and many other instances the word *home* lends "a warm, snuggly association" to a compound that it would not have if the simple word *house* was used. Fussell (1983, 1991) calls these and similar usages "fraudulent" (1991:107). He makes the point that the terms *house* and *home* originally meant two different things, but that the difference is disappearing from recent American usage. A main reason for the disappearance, according to Fussell, is money-greed. The real-estate industry can sell more houses if they try to sell them with the positive connotations of the word *home*, rather than with the neutral word *house*. Thus when Americans want to buy a new house, in the process they are used to encountering such compound words as *model homes*, *homesites*, and *townhomes*, in place of the more honest but less impressive *model house*, *building site*, and *townhouse*.

　　As the examples above show, many Americans use, and many fall victim of, verbal pomposity. Grandiloquence or verbal aggrandizement seems to be a characteristic feature of American English. This is a property that may find its roots in tall talk, the exaggerated and high-sounding form of speech used especially in the frontier. The verbal pomposity we have seen in this chapter is deeply engrained, and it is thus often hardly perceptible. It pervades not only American talk, but also much of thought and behavior.

study questions and activities

1. Can you find more examples of bombastic language in American English?

2. In your judgment, what are the areas, or domains, that are especially likely to produce exaggerated linguistic expressions in American English? Give examples.

3. Do research on the names of soccer teams in Great Britain and those of football, basketball or ice-hockey teams in the United States. What do you find in terms of bombastic language?

4. Find passages in American literature where bombastic language prevails. What artistic functions do you think these passages serve?

5. Can you find examples of bombastic language in American politics? And in your country? Why is this kind of language used?

chapter 19

The inventiveness of American English

This chapter will explore the inventive or innovative character of American English. Inventiveness is conceived here as a property of language that produces new words. We will examine exactly which word-formation processes have been most productive in American English. Another aspect of inventiveness, what I will call "imaginativeness," will be the topic of the next chapter.

Inventiveness as a major property of American English

That American English is perhaps the most innovative variety of English is a commonplace. Both native and foreign observers of the English language in the United States note, almost without exception, that American English is highly innovative or inventive. For example, in their survey of American English, Ferguson and Heath (1980) remark that there are frequent comments "on the greater amount of innovation in the USA than in England" (p. xxxvii). Max Lerner (1987) in his *America as a Civilization* called American speech "the richest product of the American experience." Some early politicians were also impressed by and commented on the innovative character of American English. Jefferson (quoted in Baugh and Cable, 1983), for example, made this remark: "Here where all is new, no innovation is feared which offers good" (p. 381). Indeed, innovation is regarded as a hallmark of American English by several linguists and other commentators, including H.L. Mencken. Mencken devoted a long chapter to the topic in his *The American Language* and emphasized its importance in determining the character of American English throughout his book. Marckwardt (1980; rev. Dillard) also paid a great deal of attention to American inventiveness in language, and considered it as the single most important feature of American English.

Is inventiveness good or bad?

However, opinions differ as to whether inventiveness or innovation should be regarded as necessarily a good thing. Summarizing opinions about inventiveness, Ferguson and Heath write: "These characteristics and others like them may be either admired or deplored. For example, the innovations may be regarded as corruptions or as an example of creativity, ..." (p. xxxvii). The issue is not new.

Ferguson and Heath wrote about it in 1980, but it goes back a long way in the history of American English. For example, Jefferson and Franklin held contradictory opinions about it. Jefferson was very much in favor of innovation "which offers good," and saw it as something very positive for the political and cultural development of the country. Franklin, on the other hand, was not enthusiastic about it at all, as the following (given in Baugh and Cable, 1983:381) makes it clear: "The introducing new words, where we are already possessed of old ones sufficiently expressive, I confess must be generally wrong, as it tends to change the language." This view reflects fairly conservative ideas on Franklin's part not only of language but also of the relationship between language and society. Franklin apparently believed that for language to change is bad and for it to be "stationary" is good, and that there is an ideal form of language that should not change. Jefferson, in contrast, had just the opposite view concerning this issue:

> And should the language of England continue stationary, we shall probably enlarge our employment of it, until its new character may separate it in name, as well as in power, from the mother tongue. (quoted in Baugh and Cable, 1983:381)

Jefferson, more than anyone else, saw a clear *need* for changing the language. Language is only appropriate if it reflects the needs of its users. He offered some weighty reasons:

> There are so many differences between us and England, of soil, climate, culture, productions, laws, religion, and government, that we must be left far behind the march of circumstances, were we to hold ourselves rigorously, to their standard.... Judicious neology can alone give strength and copiousness to language, and enable it to be the vehicle of new ideas. (quoted in Baron, 1982:109)

The linguistic issue was obviously a political one as well. For many, or perhaps most, American linguists and politicians around the turn of the nineteenth century, innovations were clearly favorable, in the same way as the political changes were favorable. Among linguists, it is again Webster who, in his *Dissertations on the English Language*, states the relationship between political and linguistic reform most clearly: "Here men are prepared to receive improvements, which would be rejected by nations, whose habits have not been shaken by similar events" (quoted in Simpson, 1986:61).

The locus of inventiveness

Another question we will deal with briefly is this: Where is the inventiveness of American English most visible? We have seen throughout this book that language consists of several areas, including sounds, words, syntax, rules of language use, and more. In which of these areas can we put our finger on American inventiveness; or where is it easiest to identify? The answer is that the area most noted for innovations is the vocabulary of American English. As was pointed out in earlier chapters (especially in chapter three), a large number of new words were produced in the nineteenth century in the course of the westward movement of the nation. These were times when, as Claiborne (1983:212) puts it, nobody could have "contained the American vocabulary which was expanding vigorously, if not quite as rapidly, as the country itself." But this process is still going on. As Ferguson and Heath (1980) note: "The innovative tendency of American English is also continuing, most obviously in words," and they add "but also in syntactic constructions" (p. xxxvii). In the previous chapters we have seen a number of typically American syntactic constructions. Furthermore, Strevens (1972) also observes that, in addition to the vocabulary, "in spelling ... the tendency to innovation and playfulness is noticeably stronger in American than in British English." The bulk of innovations, however, can be found in the vocabulary. The new words that come into American English are often called "neologisms" by linguists.

Americanisms

At this point the question arises as to which words and phrases can be regarded as *American*. More generally, the question is: What counts as an Americanism? Mencken, among others, dealt extensively and in great detail with the issue. Simply put, an expression is an Americanism either if it was coined in the United States, or if it has a uniquely American meaning, or if its use is more typical or more frequent in the United States than it is in Britain. I have pointed out different sources for Americanisms, and I repeat only some of the most important ones here, based on a classification by Trudgill and Hannah (1982). (1) Americanisms often come from archaic words, as in the case of *fall* ("autumn"). (2) They also arise as a result of responses to new objects and circumstances not found in Britain. An expression may be borrowed from Indian languages (such as *squash*) or other colonial or immigrant languages (such as the French *prairie*). They may also be created by English word-formation processes such as compounding (as in *cottonwood*). (3) Many Americanisms represent independent development of technologies (as the railroad, giving rise to terms such as *switch* in American English). (4) Some Americanisms refer to institutions and practices that developed in the United States. Examples here include *Congressional, gubernatorial,* and *gerrymander.*

In this chapter, we will primarily be concerned with a part of the second category, that is, with cases where an Americanism is the result of some common and productive word-formation processes in English. In many of these cases, British and American differences will be seen as a result of the greater productivity of these processes in American than in British English.

Making new words in American English

Algeo (1991) suggests that there are six basic ways in which new words are made in English in general: creating, borrowing, combining, shortening, blending, and shifting. Briefly, creating is a process in which a new word is made from elements that did not previously exist in the language. In borrowing, words are taken from another language. Combining yields new words by putting together two already existing words or other meaning-bearing elements. In the case of shortening, already existing words are made shorter to yield new ones. Blending is a combination of combining and shortening. Finally, shifting produces new words by changing the grammatical category and/or meaning of a word to another category and/or meaning. Below, we will see examples for each of these processes.

Not all of these processes are equally productive. The processes produce differing percentages of new words in English. According to some studies reported by Algeo (1991), the productivity of making new words is highest in combining and lowest in creating, yielding the following order from highest to lowest: combining, shifting, shortening, blending, borrowing, and creating. This finding meshes with and gives some support to informal studies of Americanisms listed in *Webster's New World Dictionary* (see chapter ten).

As we saw in chapter one, the invention of new words by Americans is Prince Charles' pet hate concerning American English. He deplored the fact that they "invent all sorts of new nouns and verbs." He contended that Americans "make words that shouldn't be." He would probably be very upset if he found out that Americans make use of the entire range of word-formation processes that are available in English in order to express themselves as fully as possible.

Combining

Combining subsumes two distinct word-formational mechanisms: compounding and derivation. We begin with compounding.

Compounding

In compounding, two existing words are put together to form a new word. The resulting new word is called a "compound." Some typically American nominal compounds (i.e., whose word class is noun) include *walkie talkie*, *hitchhike*, *milk shake*, and *uptown*. In all of these cases, two words that can be used independently are put together: *walk* and *talk*, *hitch* and *hike*, *milk* and *shake*, and so forth. This is an extremely common way of making new words in English. This process has been very productive in American English in giving names to new things and expressing new experiences. This is especially obvious in many of the new words created to name plants and animals. I have already mentioned *cottonwood*, and other examples include *mockingbird*, *eggplant*, *grasshopper*, *catfish*, and *rattlesnake*. As Marckwardt (1980; rev. Dillard) notes, farming was another domain that produced a large number of new compounds in American English. Words like *log cabin*, *hired hand*, and *corn belt* are examples of the process in this domain. Politics is a third area that is rich in compounds, as words like *lame duck*, *dark horse*, and *top secret* demonstrate. Yet another domain is *show business*, a word which itself is the result of the American liking for compounds. Other examples include such almost universally known terms as *soap opera*, *disc jockey*, and *strip tease*. The American world of business produces a large number of compounds. The words *bank account*, *sandwich man*, and *sales clerk* derive from this kind of linguistic creativity. Finally, American sports have also been very creative. Such major American sports as baseball, football, and basketball have all contributed to the process of compounding: for example, *bush league* for baseball, *quarterback* for football, and *slam dunk* for basketball.

So far all the examples we have seen for compounds are nominal, that is, the two words when put together produced a noun. However, adverbials and verbs are also often used for the purpose of making a new word: adjectives, adverbs, nouns, or verbs. In the expressions *up and up*, *down and out*, and many others, two adverbials are joined with *and* to yield a compound. Verbs are also often combined with adverbials, as can be seen in examples like *dropout*, *hold up*, *set up*, *drive-in*, *meet with*, *comedown*, etc. These originally American English examples reflect the American talent and liking for linguistic innovations. A comment by the *Oxford Companion to the English Language* is pertinent here: "Phrasal verbs have always been common, but have increased in number since the mid-19c and even more so since the mid-20c, especially in AmE" (p. 775).

An almost exclusively American case of compounding is the one in which a verb and a noun are combined and the noun has the semantic function of an adverbial. Quirk, *et al.* (1985) provide examples like the following: *swimsuit*, *frypan*, *restroom*. In these instances and many others, the first part of the compound is a verb (*swim*, *fry*, and *rest*). The verb is combined with a noun (*suit*, *pan*, and *room*) in such a way that the noun can be thought of as the instrument or location with or in which the activity is performed. Thus, we *swim in a suit*, *fry in a pan*, and *rest in a room*. According to Quirk, *et al.* (1985), this way of producing compounds is characteristically American.

Derivation

In another mechanism producing compounds, we do not have two full-blown words, as was the case above. There are many compounds in which one element is a full-blown word and the other is an affix. Affixes are meaning-bearing elements (morphemes) that do not stand alone. They have to be attached to fully independent words. Affixes can be attached either to the front of a word (these are called "prefixes") or to the end (these are called "suffixes"). This way of combining two linguistic elements is called "derivation." English has a large number of affixes. Many of these are more productive in American than in British English.

Prefixes
Take the prefix *semi-* as an example. In addition to many of its shared combinations with British English, it has a number of originally American uses in examples like *semimonthly*, *semiweekly*, *semi-nude*, *semi-indirect*, and *semipro*.

Another case is the prefix *de-*. This prefix also seems to be much more productive in American English. Perhaps the most famous example is *demoralize*, a word coined by Webster. But other instances abound, such as *deregulate*, *derealization*, *dewimp*, *delist*, *defoliant*, *defeminize*. The "Americanness" of the prefix *de-* is nicely illustrated in the following quotation from Simpson (1986), in which he talks about the early American poet Barlow: "There are a host of poetic licences (e.g., *buffle* for "buffalo") and some strangely prophetic coinages, such as *derouted* and *condependent*, words that might seem incipiently plausible to the modern reader used to words of the *deplaning* class" (pp. 99-100).

The prefix *anti-* produces a large number of words that do not exist, or are much less accepted in British English, such as *antifreeze* and *antiknock*. However, many of the "*anti-* words" originated in American English, but now are in widespread use in England and, indeed, all over the world. These include scientific terms such as *antibiotic* and *antibody*. Others have to do with special American political institutions, such as *antislavery*, *antifederalist*, and *antitrust*.

Suffixes
Now let us take a look at some suffixes. Some suffixes are more productive in American English since the suffix has acquired a new meaning. Perhaps the

suffix that best illustrates the process is *-wise*. This suffix has two meanings that are shared by British and American English and one that is exclusively, or at least predominantly, American. The sense "in the direction of" is common. This is what we find in words like *clockwise* and *anticlockwise* and the specifically American word *counterclockwise*. Another sense is "in the manner of," exemplified by such words as *crabwise*. A third sense of the suffix is "as far as something is concerned." This is the sense that is made use of in the sentences below:

How are we doing timewise?
The cafeteria is just terrible foodwise.
Healthwise I'm OK, but moneywise I'm broke.
Profitwise we're facing a bleak future.

In these sentences the suffix *-wise* occurs with a specifically (or predominantly) American sense. This sense is extremely productive in American English.

Two additional suffixes are commonly viewed as being more productive in American English: *-ee* and *-ery*. Many words that are combinations of a verb plus *-ee* are perceived by Brits as typically American. These include *divorcee*, *advisee*, *draftee*, *retiree*. The suffix *-ery* also has a uniquely American sense. Marckwardt (1980:102; rev. Dillard) points out that while *bakery* and *grocery* in England mean primarily the trade of the baker and the grocer, respectively, in America they also mean the place where baked products and the merchandise of grocers are sold.

"Prefix words" and "suffix words"
There is a word-formation mechanism that falls between compounding (two independent words) and derivation (one independent and one dependent word). These are cases where it is not entirely clear whether we have to do with an independent word or a dependent word. Consider a word like *-happy* in such combinations as *slap-happy*, *trigger-happy*, and *dollar-happy*. On the one hand, *happy* is an independent, full-blown word that can stand alone, as in *She's happy*. On the other hand, it can function as a word that has a particular meaning only in combination with other words, like the ones above (*slap*, *trigger*, *dollar*). When it is attached to these words, it has special meanings. One is "to act in an irresponsibly quick way," as in *trigger-happy*. The other is "to behave as if one was intoxicated," as in *slap-happy*. In these senses, *-happy* can only occur in combination with other words. This is why *happy* has uncertain status. Another word that is similar to this is *artist*. In addition to its regular use, it can be found in such combinations as *bullshit-artist* and *ripoff-artist*, both of which are slang expressions. *-Artist* in these compounds has the sense "a person who is particularly good or talented at an activity." Both *-happy* and *-artist* are American inventions. When full-blown words are used in this way,

sometimes they are called "prefix-" or "suffix-words" (e.g., Wentworth and Flexner, 1975). The two cases we have seen above are both suffix-words.

There are many other suffix-words that are characteristically American. Like the ones above, they tend to produce informal or slang expressions. The suffix-word *-burger* is used in such combinations as *cheeseburger, fishburger, -bug* occurs in *firebug, TV-bug*. The prefix-word *for* produces such combinations as *for real, for kicks, for good, for free, for sure*. *Down* is also commonly used as a suffix-word. It forms such combinations as *comedown, bringdown, countdown, showdown, dress down, jew down* (an offensive word), *lowdown*. It is a suffix word that is more common in American than in British English. Some of these innovative American compounds employing suffix-words (such as *countdown*) have been taken over by speakers of British English.

A productive American prefix-word is *no*. It occurs in such combinations as *no-show* (a noun meaning "person who fails to show up"), *no nonsense, no go, no-account* ("worthless," "good-for-nothing"), *no-fault* (an adjective meaning a "form of insurance which covers certain losses of all persons injured"), *no-hitter* (a noun), and *no name* (an adjective).

Shifting

Shifting as a word-formation device is sometimes called conversion or functional shift. Shifting can occur in basically two ways: the shift goes either from one grammatical category to another, or from one meaning to another. We begin with cases where new words are created as a result of shifting the grammatical category of a word.

Noun to verb

The most frequent grammatical shift in American English is from noun to verb. This is also the case that is most commonly recognized as typically American. Some of the best known examples of words that originated in this way include: *to host, to guest* ("to be a guest on a program"), *to contact, to progress, to pressure, to network, to author, to gift, to premiere, to rev, to ground, to figure, to advocate, to notice, to radio, to input, to chair, to ghost*. Nominal compounds may also emerge as a result of this process: *to car pool, to island hop, to quarterback, to mastermind, to microwave, to spot check, to wolf whistle, to speed-zone, to redshirt, to skyrocket, to spearhead*. And even proper names may participate in the process, as in *to Miranda* ("to inform an arrested person of his/her legal rights"). As Simpson notes, this characteristically American process of making new words did not always meet with the approval of the English-speaking world. Even some Americans complained: "... American writers were frequently taken to task for their habit of making verbs out of nouns and adjectives. Benjamin Franklin himself had complained of *to progress* and *to advocate* in exactly these terms ... and many other commentators followed him in so doing" (Simpson, 1986:96). One of the verbs produced this way that has been criticized frequently is *to critique* (see Baron, 1982).

Verb to noun

The process of making verbs out of nouns is less productive but clearly present in American English. Examples in this category include *dump, strike, cut,* and *scrub.* These are all established nouns in English in general. The process has also affected compounds made up of verbs plus particles: *build-up, brush-off, a run-down, a checkup, a run-around,* provided by Strevens (1972) and many others, such as *run-down, countdown, showdown, hairdo, cutback, hold-up, hangup, knowhow, overkill, sit-in, meltdown, retread, spin-off, splashdown, wannabe, have-not, never-was-has-been.*

Proper nouns to common nouns

Proper nouns can also be converted into common nouns. American English makes use of the possibility in examples like *Miranda* ("the legal rights of an arrested person"), *Oscar* ("an Academy Award"), *Mae West* ("an inflatable life jacket vest").

Nouns to adjectives

American English also fondly converts nouns to adjectives: *acid, cafeteria, girlie/girly, key.* Perhaps the best known example of this kind is the word *lengthy,* the use of which was supported by Jefferson. The process also extends to compounds. Examples of nominal compounds include *back burner, ball park (figure), blue collar (worker), bottom line,* and *dime store. Pushbutton* and *off-peak (hours)* represent verbal and adverbial compounds.

Adjective to verb

Adjectives are turned into verbs. The single most celebrated example is the verb *to belittle,* an invention of Jefferson himself.

Changes of meaning

New words may also be created by the process of changing not the grammatical category but the meaning of a word. This can be based on a number of semantic processes: specialization, generalization, adding new meaning, metaphor, and metonymy.

Specialization

Specialization occurs when the original meaning of a word is narrowed down. Two examples will suffice. One is the word *to jiggle*, which originally meant a form of dance, and later its meaning was specialized to "move in a sexually suggestive way," obviously a part of the dance itself. A second example is *to streak*, a verb which meant "to move or run at a fast speed." One of its more present American meanings is "to run naked in public." This is a prank that was popular on many American college campuses in the 1970s.

Generalization

Generalization is the opposite of specialization. A more specific meaning becomes more general, as in the example *full-dress* changing its meaning from "requiring full dress" to "complete in all details," as in *a full-dress inquiry*.

Old word-new meaning

An old word may receive a new meaning based on some similarity. Some of the specifically American English words that have been formed in this manner include *robin, oriole (crow), walnut, beech, partridge, hemlock*. In addition, many of the words that Lewis and Clark used (see chapter three) also belong to this category, words such as *creek, bottom, bluff* and *slay* (in the sense of *sleigh*). These words all have a specifically American meaning. Simpson comments: "In this respect they are indeed demonstrating the principle that Webster and others had argued as central to the practice of neologisms in America; extending the senses of old words to new objects, rather than inventing new words out of nowhere" (Simpson, 1986:119).

Words like *hopefully* represent a special case within this category. The word has the meaning of "in a hopeful way." So it can be used in sentences like *She went there hopefully, but was disappointed*. However, Americans extended the meaning of *hopefully* to "it is hoped." Thus in American English it is perfectly acceptable to say *Hopefully, she'll come*, which does not mean that she will come in a hopeful way, but that it is hoped or the speaker hopes that she will come. This use of *hopefully* attracted a great deal of criticism both from British and American purists (see Baron, 1982).

Metaphor and metonymy

A new word with a new meaning is often made by "metaphoric or metonymic transfer." An example of metaphoric transfer can be seen in an example like *virus*, which has acquired the figuratively similar sense of "a surreptitiously introduced and self-replicating computer program." Metonymy is at work when a part of a situation stands for another part of the same situation. The word *scuttlebutt* refers to a water fountain on a ship. This is also the place where much of the gossiping on a ship goes on. Consequently, *scuttlebutt* also means "gossip or rumor." I will say more about these imaginative processes in American English in the next chapter.

Shortening

I will mention two common ways of shortening: backformation and clipping. Neither of them is extremely productive, but both produced some well-known American words.

Backformation

In backformation, a new word is made by removing a part of another word, typically the end. This is often done for the sake of creating an effect. Some American examples include *location – locate, donation – donate, bulldozer – bulldoze, enthusiasm – enthuse, emotion – emote, burglar – burgle, housekeeper – housekeep*. These words have been the object of criticism on both sides of the Atlantic.

Clipping

Perhaps the two best known clippings in American English are *gym* from *gymnasium* and *movie* from *moving picture*. Clipping is a shortening in which either a syllable (or syllables), or, in the case of compounds, a whole word is left out. Place names may also be clipped, as in *Vegas* from *Las Vegas*, *Frisco* from *San Francisco*. A special kind of clipping is *LA* from *Los Angeles*.

Blending

Blending is a combination of compounding and shortening. Some American examples include *motel* from *motorist* and *hotel* and *Reaganomics* from *Reagan* and *economics*.

Borrowing

In chapter two we saw a large number of examples for cases in which American English acquired new words from other languages. Americans were not picky about their sources. As Claiborne (1983:212) put it, they were "borrowing from any source that happened to be handy."

Creating

Americans have also been coining new words out of no previously existing words or affixes. These words are called "coinages." *Rambunctious, hornswoggle, fun,* and *pun* are examples of words that are not made from the known materials of English. Speculating on the motivation for this, Claiborne (1983) suggests that Americans were "inventing brand-new words out of sheer high spirits and delight in 'tall talk.'" To a large degree, this is still going on today in the fashion industry and advertising. Many of the new words of this kind are created on New York's Madison Avenue, the center of advertising.

Archaic words

Finally, several words in the vocabulary of American English derive from archaic words once used in the English language. We saw several examples of this in chapter two.

We can conclude this discussion with the German linguist Manfred Görlach, who suggested that

> Americans have remained more open to colloquial innovation, and more inclined towards linguistic experiments in word-formation, than have the British, who have apparently inherited more restrictive attitudes towards neologisms from the 18th century. However, all the patterns used in AmE are also used in BrE; the two varieties – in so far as differences still exist – differ mainly in the frequencies and stylistic values of such coinages. (Görlach, 1995:73)

Where were neologisms created?

There is some agreement that the most exuberant growth of the vocabulary of American English took place in the course of the nineteenth century, the century of the "westward movement" (see chapter three). It makes sense to suggest, together with others, that most of the innovations or neologisms were born on the frontier or during the westward movement of the nation. This is the place and the time where and when new words were most needed. This was also the place that had enough of the democratic spirit to maintain the new inventions, where the scholars, the schoolbooks, and the schoolteachers could not intervene. In Claiborne's (1983:212) words: "Nowhere were these processes so active as along the westward-moving frontier, whose trappers, explorers and pioneering settlers were remote from scholars and schoolbooks, and in contact with new peoples whose vocabularies could be raided for new words." However, some contemporary observers in the nineteenth century were less enthusiastic about the process than Claiborne today. For them, this liberty of the frontier was not necessarily a good thing. Baron (1982:163) quotes William Chauncey Fowler, who wrote the following in 1868:

> As our countrymen are spreading westward across the continent, and are brought into contact with other races, and adopt new modes of thought, there is some danger that, in the use of their liberty, they may break loose from the laws of the English language, and become marked not only by one, but a thousand Shibboleths.

In this context the word *shibboleth* means any phrase that is distinctive of, or unique to, a group of people. Fowler was concerned that Americans would develop ways of speaking that would make them deviate "from the laws of the English language."

The causes of American inventiveness

The most important cause of the innovative character of American English is the fact that Americans had to adapt their language to the new circumstances. In this regard, innovation was, for them, simply a necessity, as again Jefferson put it so succinctly: "Necessity obliges us to neologize" (quoted in Baron, 1982:102).

Second, the nineteenth century was also a period of "an outburst of national pride, national consciousness and national self-assertiveness" (Claiborne, 1983). American national identity was formed, and, as a result, all "symbols" of that identity had to reflect separateness and independence from England. This included language: American English which, according to Webster, was to become a completely different language from British English.

Given these perspectives on the formation of American English, Franklin's view that "there are words enough already" and, later, Cooper's ideas to this effect (Simpson, 1986) do not make too much sense. They were simply beside the point. The important thing was that Americans *had to* and *wanted* to innovate (in spite of the resistance to this by some people like Fowler). Innovation, for them, was a matter of survival and a matter of desire. What enabled them to innovate and what allowed them to revel in the exuberant production of new words was the spirit of freedom – a spirit that was most clearly present on the frontier and which was institutionalized by the political principles of American democracy.

study questions and activities

1. Find as many further examples of American compounds as you can. What properties of compounds do the ones that you found reveal?

2. As Prince Charles said, "Americans invent words that shouldn't be." One large category of this is when Americans produce verbs from already existing nouns. Why are many of these criticized, such as the verb *to critique*? On the other hand, do they offer any advantages in communication?

3. In the *Oxford Companion to the English Language* this is what we find in connection with phrasal verbs (McArthur, 1992:775): "Phrasal verbs have always been common, but have increased in number since the mid-19c and even more so since the mid-20c, especially in AmE" (American English). Collect examples of phrasal verbs that originated in America. Why do you think they are so popular with speakers of American English?

4. Speakers of English often create what are called "sentence words," expressions such as *I-don't-understand-you-look*, as in *He gave me this I-don't-understand-you-look*. Take a look at some popular British and American magazines and do a study of sentence words. In which variety of English is it more common? What is the function or use of sentence words in general?

5. Does American inventiveness show up in areas other than language?

chapter 20

The imaginativeness of American English

In the previous chapter we have looked at the many ways in which American English displays inventiveness. In discussing the innovative character of this variety of English we have come across several examples of imaginativeness as well. Indeed, imaginativeness can be regarded as another form of inventiveness – inventiveness where new words and phrases are created not simply with the help of a word-formation process but also with the help of such imaginative processes of linguistic creativity as metaphor and metonymy. By imaginativeness, then, we mean the process in which metaphor or metonymy also participate in the invention or creation of new words or phrases.

The nature of imaginativeness

This imaginativeness is just as frequently commented on as the inventiveness of American English. Mencken (1963), among others, often talks about the "pungent," "bold," "muscular," "vigorous," "racy," "picturesque" character of American English. Others frequently mention "colorfulness" and "expressiveness" (e.g., Svejcer, 1978). These features usually manifest themselves in metaphorical and metonymical language. Baugh and Cable (1983) also note the American talent for being inventive in an imaginative way:

> He [the American] is perhaps at his best when inventing simple homely words like *apple butter, sidewalk,* and *lightning rod, spelling bee* and *crazy quilt, low-down,* and *know-nothing,* or when striking off a terse metaphor like *log rolling, wire pulling, to have an ax to grind, to be on the fence.* (p. 365)

They also tell us that this property of American English began to show as early as colonial times:

> The American early manifested the gift, which he continues to show, of the imaginative, slightly humorous phrase. To it we owe *to bark up the wrong tree, to face the music, fly off the handle, go on the warpath, bury the hatchet, come out at the little end of the horn, saw wood,* and many more, with the breath of the country and sometimes of the

frontier about them. In this way, the American began her contributions to the English language.... (p. 365)

We will see in this chapter that, in addition to the colonists, others have also
played a part in turning American English into a highly imaginative variety of
English. At this point, I simply wish to note that the feature of imaginativeness
goes back a long way in the history of American English. Furthermore, we
should also keep in mind, as Baugh and Cable observe, that the process is still
going on at the present time. It is not the case that American English was imaginative for some time at its beginnings and then its imaginativeness went away.
A further point worth emphasizing on the basis of the passage above is that the
imaginative aspect of American English is frequently linked with humor.
Many of the expressions quoted in the passages above (like *saw wood, bark up
the wrong tree*), as well as many of the others we will look at below, reflect the
humorous nature of American metaphors. Finally, as the passage above
reminds us, imaginativeness often derives from the experiences of Americans
in the country and the frontier. We will also deal with this issue in more detail
in this chapter.

But imaginativeness is not related to inventiveness alone. I have touched on
the imaginative aspects of American English in several earlier chapters.
Wherever it was necessary to mention or call on such figures of speech as
metaphor or metonymy as part of the explanation of a particular phenomenon,
the notion of imaginativeness was raised. In the sections to follow I will take up
the most important phenomena with which imaginativeness is connected. I will
look at these in some detail from the perspective of the imaginative character of
American English.

Why items are borrowed from American English

In the chapter on vocabulary differences, we looked at several reasons why items
are borrowed from American English by British English. Among these reasons
is metaphor. Gramley and Pätzold (1992), for example, talk about how "the
vivid and expressive nature of a number of [American] words and phrases is
held to have helped them expand" (p. 359). Svejcer (1978) maintains that
"words and set phrases which have a distinct expressive-stylistic coloring" are
used for stylistically neutral ones (p. 158). Among the examples he provides we
find the American word to *steamroller* or *steamroll* for Common English *suppress,
crush, defeat, override*, or *overpower*; *boost* for *publicize*; *foolproof* for *simple*; *up-
and-coming* for *promising*; *brainwashing* for *indoctrination*. These American
English words show a more imaginative character than their Common English
counterparts. *To steamroller, boost, foolproof, up-and-coming*, and *brainwashing*

are vivid, picturesque words that evoke a forceful image. In this respect, they resemble Mencken's famous example of *rubberneck*. It is informative to look at the list of examples provided by Svejcer (pp. 158-159):

AE:	Common E:
brush-off	rejection
fill-in	summary
rundown	account
run-in	quarrel
try-out	test
tie-up	strike
toss-up	even chance
hangover	relic
cookout	picnic
firebug	arsonist
sparkplug	inspire
skyrocket	rise
rabble-rouser	demagogue
grill	cross-examine
race	election campaign

In his discussion of the same issue, Strevens (1972:61-62) provides a similar list: *to blow one's top* ("to fly into a rage"), *to case a joint* ("to spy out the land before a robbery"), *to give the once-over* ("to inspect something"), *to hijack* ("to take over a plane, ship or train or motor vehicle by force"), *to moonlight* ("to work clandestinely at a second job"), *blue movie* ("pornographic or erotic film"), *cliffhanger* ("suspenseful happening"), *handout* ("free gift"), *hard-boiled* ("experienced, unemotional"), *in the doghouse* ("temporarily unpopular"), and so on. Commenting on the list, Strevens (1972) notes:

> There are two reasons for having given a number of examples of these expressions. The first is to illustrate the kind of vivid, affective use of language which American English has produced for around two centuries, and which has provided a constant flow of linguistic exports to Britain. (p. 62)

But, we can ask, why do the more imaginative – the metaphorical – American words appeal to the British? This is a more general issue and is not limited to Americans and British alone. There seem to be a number of things involved. First, the American words are easier to form images of. We can have an image of *grill*, *steamroller*, *race*, and so forth, in a way in which we cannot in the case of *cross-examine*, *defeat*, and *election campaign*. They evoke an image that the Common English words do not, and, as a result, are easier to understand. Second, they also appear to be simpler. They are simpler in the sense that they come from concrete, physical domains of experience – domains of experience that most people can relate to. Most of us have experienced what fire is and how it can affect things (in the case of *grill*); most of us have experienced what it is like when a heavy object moves over a softer surface (in the case of *steamroller*); and most of us have experienced the activity of running a race in some form (in the case of *race*). Third, the meaning may also become richer. This happens, for example, in the case of such words as *foolproof* or *sparkplug*. The word *foolproof* implies that something is so simple that even a fool cannot mishandle or misunderstand it; that is, the meaning of *simple* is enriched by the aspect of intensity. In the case of *sparkplug*, as in John *sparkplugged* the operations or John is the *sparkplug* of the team, the word additionally implies that John activates others in such a way that when they seem to lose enthusiasm or want to give up, he can reactivate them just as a sparkplug could, and that if John loses heart, the operations or the whole team are in trouble, just as a car would be whose sparkplug has broken down. These, and several others, are implications that the word *inspire* does not have at all. Given these reasons, the American words may be felt to be more effective by the British. Or, in the words of Baugh and Cable (1983) again:

> Generally speaking, it may be said that when an American word expresses an idea in a way that appeals to the English as fitting or effective, the word is ultimately adopted in England. Mr. Ernest Weekley, in his *Adjectives – and Other Words*, says: "It is difficult now to imagine how we got on so long without the word stunt, how we expressed the characteristics so conveniently summed up in *dope-fiend* or *high-brow*, or any other possible way of describing that mixture of the cheap pathetic and the ludicrous which is now universally labelled *sob-stuff*." (pp. 388-89)

It has also been observed that it is the clarity or explicitness of some expressions that may help them get into British English (Svejcer, 1978). We have discussed the notions of clarity and explicitness in the chapter on directness. Metaphor may also make a word or expression's meaning more transparent. The meaning of *fill-in* is more transparent than that of *summary* because it is based on the concrete physical experience of filling up a container. The same applies to *strike oil* because striking oil is a subcase of being successful, and to *baby-buggy* because of the similarity of shape and function between a *horse-drawn buggy* and the one in which babies travel (as opposed to British English *pram*, which does not evoke any kind of similarity).

Informality

Imaginativeness also has to do with informality. I have suggested that speakers of American English often use highly informal and metaphorical language in domains where it would not be felt to be quite appropriate by speakers of British English. This idea was based, among other things, on the reported experiences of a British journalist working in the U.S. He observed that American government officials (and we may reasonably suspect that not only them) use fierce, aggressive, masculine, or "macho" language in connection with their generally rather timid work. Some of the examples mentioned are *We'll clean his clock* (from boxing) and *He hit it out of the park* (from baseball). In general, it can be suggested that in the U.S. talk about politics is largely couched in an informal and metaphorical language that is taken from American sports. (Some American presidents are famous or even notorious for their heavy use of sports language for politics. One example is former president Nixon.) I will substantiate this claim further in a later section in the chapter.

Verbal prudery

It was noted above that in some cases metaphor can help people express their meanings more directly and explicitly. In other cases, however, the opposite effect can be achieved with the help of imaginative language; namely, a taboo topic may be talked about through the use of metaphor and metonymy. In the discussion of verbal prudery in a previous chapter, I mentioned such examples as *restroom* and *washroom* for toilet, which is a taboo topic. Both of these examples employ metonymy. Metonymy in these two examples involves a process in which a part of a larger situation is used to stand for another part of the situation. When we use a public toilet, we often interrupt whatever we do. For example, we take a break from work and this means that we do not have to work for the few minutes we are in the room that contains the toilet. This is a kind of rest from work. Resting plus the room where resting occurs can then be used to refer to the public facility where the activities of urinating and defecating take place. A similar explanation holds for *washroom*, except that, in this case, another activity, washing the hands or the body, is used to mark the place where the taboo activities occur.

But why was the expression *going to bed*, in the sense of "go to sleep," abandoned by Americans? When we go to sleep, we actually go into our bed. So going into our bed is a part of the larger situation, and, given the explanation above, speakers should legitimately be able to use it to talk about going to sleep. Yet, as was noted in chapter fifteen, the expression was avoided and replaced by the now archaic word *retire*. Why? The reason is that going to bed is a part of two situations: going to sleep and having sex with someone. Going to bed is a part of having sex in the sense that we think of sexual activity as primarily occurring in bed. Thus, going to bed also evokes the situation of having sex. Because of this, Americans avoided the expression *to go to bed* for "to go to sleep." They did so, because it evoked, for them, a situation that was itself a taboo domain.

Tall talk

As was noted in chapter eighteen, tall talk often employs metaphor, or in Mencken's words (1963:149), "fantastic simile and metaphor." Tall talk, for Mencken, also included "ingeniously contrived epithets," "wild hyperbole," "a bombastic display of oratory," linguistic devices that all have something or other to do with metaphor.

A special kind of tall talk, in which the less dignified is made to appear more dignified, can also be based on a special kind of metaphor. We noted how longer words are frequently used to impress people. In the case of expressions of the type *a great dining experience* for *a great dinner* and *timepiece* for *watch*, we have a longer expression that is used to enhance the status or importance of what we are talking about. A special kind of metaphor is at work here. A more favorable impression of the thing in question can be made because the presence of more word form is understood as carrying more importance by the hearer. There seems to be a correlation between word form and the content of words to the effect that "more form creates more content" (for a detailed discussion of this phenomenon, see Lakoff and Johnson, 1980). This is how bombast and pomposity often work.

Inventiveness

In the discussion of inventiveness, it was mentioned that metaphor and metonymy play an important role in the creation of new words, in that the new meanings of words are often based on metaphoric or metonymic transfer of meaning. We have called this phenomenon the "shifting of meaning." We have also pointed out that many American compounds employ metaphorical transfers. In addition, there can be shifting based on the grammatical category of words; nouns may become verbs and verbs nouns. We will see in a later section that these grammatical shifts are often based on metonymy.

Some major metaphorical domains in American English

So far, we have seen a large number of individual examples of metaphor that were all created by Americans. Some that were mentioned or briefly discussed include *brush-off, fill-in, rundown, run-in, try-out, tie-up, toss-up, hangover, cook-out, firebug, sparkplug, skyrocket, rabble-rouser, grill, race*. However, individual metaphors can be commonly found to co-occur, that is, to cluster around a certain concept. When a number of metaphors reflect a single concept or domain as regards both their origin (such as sports) and their target (such as politics), we will say that we are dealing with a "conceptual metaphor." Thus, the notion of conceptual metaphor is opposed to "linguistic metaphor" (Lakoff and Johnson, 1980). Linguistic metaphors may occur in isolation or in systems. When they cluster around a given source concept, we have a conceptual metaphor.

So far in this chapter we have primarily dealt with metaphors that were isolated or individual linguistic metaphors. There was only one exception: the conceptual metaphor that had politics or life as its target of application and sports as its origin. In this case, for example, politics is understood and talked about by making use of the conceptual domain of sports. Following the terminology of cognitive linguistics (see, for example, Lakoff and Johnson, 1980), I will call the target of the application of linguistic expressions (e.g., politics) the "target domain" and the origin of the linguistic expressions (e.g., sports) the "source domain."

Given the notion of conceptual metaphor, we can now ask if there are any characteristically American conceptual metaphors. In other words, the question is whether there are any source domains in terms of which Americans typically understand their experiences. One such domain, I would suggest, is sports.

"Sport" as metaphor

The language of American sports may be viewed as a special variety of American English, in addition to that of the railroad, automobile, drug culture, and many others. When this language is used to understand other domains, like politics, the way Americans comprehend sports is imposed on these other domains as well. Of all the special varieties of American English that have played any role in the development of a special American English vocabulary, the domain of sports contributed a great deal, maybe the most.

Politics as sport

Sports, as has been pointed out above, is a major source domain for politics in the United States. In addition to the examples already discussed, we find many more. Politicians can sometimes employ *hardball tactics*; they may have a *game plan*; they may *play it safe* or *play for time*; a politician can be a *good team player*; a presidential candidate has a *running mate*; the election campaign may be a *close race*; senators and congressmen can *quarterback an operation*; they can have a secret consultation called a *huddle;* a politician may be a *frontrunner* and a *heavyweight* or a *lightweight*, as the case may be; and some of them often *play hardball* in their political activities.

Business as sport/game

But the American experience of sports is not limited to the comprehension of politics. It also extends to the world of business. That is, business may be the target domain with sports being the source domain, as the following examples illustrate: some businessmen may play *for high stakes;* they are also often advised to *quit while they are ahead;* they sometimes *plunge right into an investment;* if they are successful, they can *make a killing* or at least *break even.*

Love and sex as sport

Love and sex are also the target of sports metaphors. An American given to seducing women can be said to *play the field;* a successful attempt at seduction is *scoring;* when he starts his "operations," he *makes a pass at* or *makes a play for* somebody; initial success in a relationship is expressed as *getting to first base;* and, after a rejection by an unwilling partner, Americans may marry somebody *on the rebound.*

Life as sport

Given that Americans understand all these different aspects of life in terms of sports, it is not surprising that their understanding of life in general also derives in part from the domain of sports. Some of them do, while others don't like to participate in what they call the *rat race;* especially young people may *drop out* of mainstream society; it is an American slogan that *life is not a spectator game* and that *life is hard, play it tough;* they can also encourage each other with the words *when the going gets tough, the tough get going.*

Many of the following expressions Gramley and Pätzold (1992:363-64) mention in their discussion of the language of the favorite American and British pastimes, baseball and cricket, respectively, can apply to various aspects of life. They point out that some of the expressions are shared by baseball and cricket, due to the common origin of the two sports. Most of them, however, are specific to either baseball or cricket.

Many of the expressions used in cricket and baseball have extended meanings, which are based on metaphor. I begin by giving a list of expressions shared by baseball and cricket (first the baseball or cricket expression, then its extended metaphor-based meaning is given in double quotation marks):

batting order	"order to do things"
to field	"to enter a competition"
to take the field	"to begin campaign"

The expressions that are used for cricket only include:

sticky wicket	"difficult situation"
something is not cricket	"unfair"
to hit something for six	"to score a big success"
to queer someone's pitch	"to spoil somebody's plans"
to be caught out	"to be trapped/found out"
a hat trick (also soccer)	"something very well done"
to have had a good innings	"to have had a long life"

The expressions that are used for baseball only include:

to play hard ball	"to be serious about something"
to touch base	"to keep in contact"
not to get to first base	"not to be successful"
to pinch hit for somebody	"to stand in for somebody"
to strike out	"to fail"
to have a strike/ two strikes against somebody	"to have a disadvantage"
to play in the big leagues	"to work/be with powerful people"
a double play	"two successes in one move"
a rain check	"postponement"
a grand slam	"smashing success/victory"
a blooper	"a mistake or a failure"
a doubleheader	"a combined event with lots to offer"
batting average	"a person's performance"
out of the ball park	"phenomenal feat"
out in left field	"remote, out of touch, unrealistic"
off base	"wrong"

Clearly, sports and sport terminologies are commonly used metaphorically in an effort to comprehend various abstract ideas. What is especially interesting about the expressions above is that many of them have to do with the notions of success and failure. This applies to both the cricket and the baseball expressions. This suggests that the concepts of success and failure in life in general are understood in terms of the more specific successes and failures associated with various sports activities. In other words, sport is a general metaphor for life.

The following expressions have to do with aspects of success:

> **BE:** hit something for six, a hat trick
> **AE:** a double play, a grand slam, batting average, out of the ball park

The ones below are related to failure:

> **BE:** to queer someone's pitch, to be caught out
> **AE:** not get to first base, a blooper, off base

In all these cases, the notions of success and failure in general are comprehended through the more specific success and failure experienced in sports. We will come back to this issue in the next chapter.

In addition to sports, there are other special varieties of American English that serve as source domains for the metaphorical understanding of some aspects of American culture and society.

The frontier

The frontier provides a major source of metaphors for American life. Life on the frontier was hard and different. As we saw in chapter three, the plants, animals, physical objects, landscape, activities, people were all different, and hence they had to be named. But the spirit on the frontier was also different; it was new, dangerous, and exciting. This new spirit found expression in many metaphorical expressions created on the frontier. Bryson (1990:164) describes this in these words: "Settlers moving west not only had to find new expressions to describe features of their new outsized continent – *mesa, butte, bluff,* and so on – but also outsized words that reflected their zestful, virile, wildcat-wrassling, hell-for-leather approach to life." Many colorful expressions were created; some of them were not metaphorical, like *hornswoggle* and *rambunctious,* but many of them were. These include *to move like greased lightning, to kick the bucket, to be in cahoots with somebody,* and *to root hog or die.*

We noted in chapter two that it was mainly the Scots-Irish (like the famous Davy Crockett) who moved inland and became the pioneers. These people were well suited to the task before them. They were tough, and also rough, and they were linguistically inventive and imaginative. Their inventiveness came from the rich oral culture that they inherited:

> The Scots-Irish brought with them a rich oral culture: aphorisms, proverbs, superstitions, and an ability to turn a striking phrase – *mad as a meat axe, dead as a hammer, so drunk he couldn't hit the wall*

with a handful of beans. It was the frontiersmen who first spoke of someone with *an axe to grind,* or someone who *sat on the fence* when he should perhaps *go the whole hog.* (McCrum, *et al.,* 1986:157)

Many aspects of frontier life have contributed metaphorical expressions to American English, expressions that are commonly used to the present day. I present some examples below.

Cowboys

The cowboys' activities gave rise to a number of metaphorical expressions. When an American today says that someone can't even *hold down a job,* he or she is using an idiom that goes back to how cowboys tried to hold down a cow for branding. A *tenderfoot* was originally a calf and later became a "beginner, novice, an inexperienced person."

Indians

Several American metaphors derive from aspects of Indian culture with which the settlers came into contact. Some of the best known ones include *go on a scalp hunt, smoke a peace pipe, put on the warpaint, play possum, bury the hatchet, go on the warpath.* These and other idioms, now viewed as inappropriate, have found their way into many languages outside American English.

Gambling

Many aspects of American life are comprehended through the frontier activity of gambling. Some of the metaphorical idioms that gambling produced in American English include *I'll call your bluff, pass the buck, square deal, poker face, big deal, the cards weren't stacked against you, play a wild card,* and *the chips are down.*

Backwoodsmen

Other colorful metaphors derive from the activities of the backwoodsmen. When an American loses control over his anger, he can be said to *fly off the handle.* The frontier bully put a chip on his shoulder, where the expression *chip on one's shoulder* today means "an inclination to fight or quarrel." Backwoodsmen hunted for racoons or opossums, and when a 'coon or 'possum hound was on a false scent, it was barking up the wrong tree. Hence the metaphor *bark up the wrong tree,* meaning "to be mistaken."

Mining

Mining expressions were also adopted as metaphors for aspects of American life. The following is a selection of these metaphors:

> strike oil ("get rich"), pan out ("turn out well, succeed"), hit pay dirt ("discover a source of wealth"), peter out, strike it rich, stake a claim to, diggings (or digs), big strike, lucky strike.

Many of these examples have to do with the concept of success; that is, they indicate that someone is successful in some activity.

Farming

The backwoodsmen, the cowboys, and the miners were soon followed by farmers on the frontier. Interestingly, the imagery and vocabulary of farming did not have an important impact on other domains; that is, it was not used to the same degree as the others as a metaphorical source domain by Americans. Dillard (1976:xix) observes in this connection:

> To assert that phrases originating with miners ... were important to the development of American English is not to say that farmer's terms (slop bucket/swill pail, whiffletree, hay doodle/stack/cock, roasting ears, leadhorse) were not. A test of the ability to express metaphorical concepts in other contexts might, however, tend to favor the other group.

In other words, Dillard suggests that the vocabulary of farming was a less important source domain of American metaphors than that of (gold) mining and oil drilling.

Railroad

In chapter three we talked about the significance of the railroad in the disappearance of the frontier and the West. It also functioned as a source domain for the understanding of several American concepts. Some examples include *to railroad* ("to coerce"), *to sidetrack* ("to divert from the main issue"), *streamlining*, *jerk water town*, and *whistle stop tour*.

Additional source domains

There are many domains or concepts that developed after the frontier was closed. These more recent domains provide additional source domains for comprehending aspects of American culture. We mention two of these.

Automobile

As was noted in chapter three, American culture is frequently referred to as a "car, or wheel, culture" due to the importance of the automobile in American life. For example, the metaphorical expression *spin one's wheels* indicates a lack of progress in an endeavor and *mileage* means "the benefit one gets from something," as in *I got a lot of mileage out of this*. Interestingly, several current slang idioms that have to do with sexuality also take the automobile as their source domain. The idiom to *check one's oil* means "to have sexual intercourse" and when someone has *his motor running*, he is "sexually aroused."

Drug culture

Drug culture provides another contemporary source domain for Americans. The expressions of drug culture that are made use of in other domains have primarily to do with either "loss of control" or "very pleasant experience." Thus, we find metaphors such as *spaced out, mind-blowing, out of this world, freak out, zonk out* from drug culture being used in an extended or more general sense.

Some target domains

So far in this section we have looked at particular source domains that are uniquely or at least characteristically American domains for the understanding of various areas of American culture and society (the target domains). The expressions generated by these source domains (like the frontier) may have been borrowed by other cultures, but they seem to originate from the United States. Below we will consider some characteristically American target domains and see how they are metaphorically comprehended. The first of these is immigration.

Immigration

The role of immigration was discussed in chapter two. This is a crucial aspect of American society. This is also an aspect that has generated a great deal of controversy. The main issue has been for a long time: Should America allow more or fewer immigrants into the United States? A corollary of this issue is the American attitude to immigration. We can get a sense of this if we look at the major conceptual metaphor for immigration. The metaphor is "immigration is a flood." In other words, much of the understanding of this aspect of American history derives from how the concept of flood is comprehended. Some of the terms used include *flow*, *influx*, *tide*, *wave*, *deluge*, and, of course, *flood*. All these disasters can then *drown* or *swamp* the people who are already in the United States. Given this negative consequence of the metaphorical image, it becomes natural to apply *sieves* for immigrants. These are just some of the examples that are used to talk about the process of immigration in terms of the "flood" metaphor (examples taken from Frick, 1990). They seem to reveal an unfriendly attitude toward immigrants – especially if they come in large numbers and from certain ethnic groups (see Frick, 1990).

Democracy

The United States has always been regarded as the best example, or even *the* example, of a democratic society. In conceptualizing American democracy and the liberty that Americans enjoy, authors use a variety of conceptual metaphors. For example, Stevenson (1987:10) uses a "house" metaphor for American democracy, with a family, Americans, living in the house. Debates about problems in American society are viewed as *family fights* inside the house. However, as is fitting for a democratic society, the fights are going on in the house *with all the windows open*. Stevenson states that "Specific laws require that the *windows be kept open*" (p. 10). Moreover, the application of the metaphor continues, "The press, too, does not deal kindly with the *family fight*, and is known for its aggressiveness" (p. 10). This metaphor gives us a positive evaluation of democracy in America. However, not all evaluations of American democracy are necessarily positive. Perhaps the best known foreign commentator, Alexis de Tocqueville (1835/1987), makes us see American democracy in a less favorable light. Tocqueville uses the common metaphor "society as a person," and given that metaphor he portrays American democracy as a "highly defective person" that cannot control its passions, that is often irrational, whose activities are unrestrained, and so on (Kövecses, 1994).

America

The concept of America itself has undergone a number of interpretations. Maybe the best known of these is the notion that "America is a melting pot." The idea of melting the various nationalities and races together goes back to the beginning of the history of the United States. The term *melting pot* was applied to America by Israel Zangwill as the title of a play produced in 1908. It is an interesting question how precisely this metaphor has been employed through the centuries: Who were included in the melting pot?; who were excluded?; how much melting or assimilation took place?; was there a dominant element in the pot to which the others assimilated?; which parts of the United States came closest to the ideal of complete "melting"?; and so forth.

The opposite of the notion of the melting pot is the view that America is a "mosaic." This view emphasizes the idea that America is a collection of separate ethnic groups. The idea of America as a nation of various ethnic groups fitting together in a mosaic, rather than "melted together," arose in the wake of renewed interest in ethnicity in the 1960s. A currently more popular metaphor is America as "tossed salad."

Some conceptual metonymies

American imaginativeness manifests itself in the creation of new words with the help of metonymic processes as well. Metonymies can be given as "stand for" relationships between two entities. Thus, in a metonymy, one entity or thing is said to stand for another entity or thing. We have seen some individual linguistic examples of metonymy, for instance, in the chapter on verbal prudery. However, just like metaphors, metonymies can also be systematic, that is, they can occur in systems (see Lakoff and Johnson, 1980; Kövecses and Radden, 1998). One of the favorite American metonymic processes is the one in which a part of a longer expression is used to stand for the whole expression. Here are some examples for the "part of an expression for the whole expression" metonymy in American English:

Danish	for	Danish pastry
shocks	for	shock absorbers
wallets	for	wallet-sized photos
Ridgemont High	for	Ridgemont High School
the States	for	the United States

Some productive metonymic systems

In a study of nouns that become verbs in English, Clark and Clark (1979) distinguished among eight types. The three most productive types account for the majority of their more than one thousand examples. Most of their examples were drawn from American English. The three types are what Clark and Clark call "locatum verbs," "location verbs," and "agent verbs." We can reinterpret their findings in such a way that the groups of verbs that they identify as locatum verbs, location verbs, and agent verbs are in fact productive conceptual metonymies. Many of the verbs below are not conventionalized in the lexicon of English, but most of them would be understood by native speakers.

Locatum verbs: N→V

In the case of locatum verbs, a noun indicating an object that moves toward another object becomes a verb. Here are some examples:

> blanket the bed, sheet the furniture, newspaper the shelves, wallpaper the wall, litter the highway, parquet the floor, butter the bread, tenant the building, sweater the child, initial the memo, straitjacket the patient, beard the actor, lemon the tea, gas the car, cream the coffee, Christmas-gift each other, rotten-egg the speaker, billboard the highway, tunnel the mountain

In all of these examples, the noun-object moves toward another object. This can be reinterpreted as the metonymy "the object of motion stands for the motion itself." Thus the blanket, the sheet, the newspaper, the wallpaper, and so on stands for the motion of the blanket, the sheet, the newspaper, the wallpaper, and so on.

Location verbs: N→V

In the case of location verbs, a noun indicating the destination of motion becomes a verb. Examples of this process include:

> ground the planes, bench the players, doormat the boots, shelve the books, blacklist the director, sick-list the patient, front-page the scandal, headline the story, floor the opponent, sidewalk the merchandise, the boat landed, field the candidates, jail the prisoner, house the people, kennel the dog, closet the clothes, silo the corn, garage the car, film the action, photograph the children, bed the child, porch the newspaper, mothball the sweaters, footnote her colleagues, sun oneself, floor the accelerator

Here again, the noun indicating destination is used to stand for the motion itself. The appropriate conceptual metonymy seems to be "the destination of a moving object stands for the motion directed to that destination."

Agent verbs: N→V

With agent verbs, a noun indicating a typical agent (or doer) becomes a verb. Here are some examples:

> butcher the cow, jockey the horse, referee the game, author the book, to housewife, mother someone, father someone, uncle someone, bully the children, chairman the department, don't Bogart that joint, houseguest with the Joneses, quarterback for the Giants, tourist through the East Coast, watchdog the house, out-fox his followers, chicken out of a fight, hare down the road, cat it up the waterpipe

In this case, the noun indicating an agent becomes a verb indicating a characteristic activity or property of that agent. We can account for examples of this kind with the following conceptual metonymy: "the agent stands for a characteristic activity or property of that agent."

The general point that I wish to make here is that one important aspect of imaginativeness in American English is metonymy. There are distinct types of metonymic processes, and some of these contribute significantly to the imaginative character of American English.

British and American attitudes to imaginativeness

There might be an interesting difference between the British and American attitude to imaginative aspects of language. While it seems that many Americans are attracted to colorful, vivid figurative speech and writing, some Britons are less enthusiastic about it. The British linguist Strevens (1972:60) writes:

> Americans often express pride in the vividness and vitality of their speech and writing, and contrast it with what they regard as the staid and conservative usages of British English. The British, for their part, tend to regard much American writing and speech as brash, highly-coloured, even vulgar.

In this and previous chapters, we have seen that vivid, picturesque idioms pervade many areas of language use in America. Imaginativeness has always been a hallmark of American English. This imaginative inventiveness may be looked upon as being a good or a bad thing. There is controversy about the issue both inside and outside the United States. The issue may also have to do with prescriptivism in the use of language. Strevens (1972) tells us that the British follow established usage more so than Americans, and that this creates differing opinions about imaginativeness in the two countries:

> ... to the speaker brought up to regard departure from established usage as something rare and probably undesirable, vivid new expressions convey a quality which he may not value highly, except in works of literature.

On the other hand, the situation must be more complicated. At the beginning of this chapter, we saw that there must be a sufficiently large number of Britons who do like and hence adopt the imaginative language use of Americans. One of the major reasons the British take over Americanisms is the highly imaginative – primarily metaphorical – character of American English (which is, of course, not to say that British English is not metaphorical; all languages and dialects are).

If this view expressed above by Strevens is by and large correct, it also means that the British see a wider gap between the ordinary, everyday and the literary use of language and that the realm of the imaginative, for them, is in "high" literature. In contrast, Americans have long been characterized by tall talk and grandiloquence – ways of speaking that give imaginativeness a central place in the realm of ordinary language use. But this comparison between the British and Americans is of course extremely tentative, since we lack empirical sociolinguistic studies that would enable us to draw more serious conclusions.

study questions and activities

1. You have seen that many American slang expressions are metaphorical. (You probably believed so far that only high literature is pervaded by metaphor.) What could possibly be the explanation for this?

2. Read a few longer articles in American newpapers and magazines about American politics. Find the examples that come from the domain of sports. What do these sports metaphors tell you about American politics? Can you imagine political life without them?

3. Try to check how pervasive the "frontier metaphor" is in American English. Collect as many examples as you can and try to determine which aspects of American culture and life they are used to understand.

4. America has been conceptualized by a set of successive metaphorical source domains, one of them being the "melting pot" metaphor. Find other, older and newer, metaphors for America and analyze them. What changes in attitude do they reflect?

5. The following conversation demonstrates how misunderstanding can occur from the American love of imaginative language. (The conversation is taken from Andrew F. Murphy, *Cultural Encounters in the USA*.)

> **Mahmoud:** (To a passing conductor) Excuse me. Is this Amtrak schedule correct? Will we arrive in Chicago at three-thirty?
> **Conductor:** You got it. (The conductor walks away.)
> **Mahmoud:** (To a woman sitting beside him) I got what?
> **Passenger:** You've got the correct information. It's a short way of saying "you're correct."
> **Mahmoud:** I see. I studied English in Iran, but some of the idioms and pronunciation are still difficult for me.
> **Passenger:** Is this your first trip to the Windy City?
> **Mahmoud:** I beg your pardon?
> **Passenger:** Chicago. I think they call it that because there's so much wind.
> **Mahmoud:** Yes, it's my first trip. I'm touring the country by train. The U.S. countryside is beautiful.
> **Passenger:** It certainly is, especially in my neck of the woods. I'm from Alabama. Do you all plan to travel down that way?
> **Mahmoud:** I'm traveling alone.
> (Murphy, 1991:22)

Find the cases where misunderstanding occurs. Discuss what these cases have to do with the use of imaginative language.

chapter 21

Action and success in American English

In this chapter, we look at the concepts of success and action-orientedness as expressed in American English. It will be pointed out that the two are intimately connected and that success is the dominant category. Success and action-orientedness are concepts that, in addition to others, are frequently mentioned as typical American traits (see, for example, Bellah, *et al.*, 1985). I will show that these traits also manifest themselves in American English, beginning with a brief characterization of the concept of success in the American mind.

The components of American success

There are obviously many different conceptions of success in the United States, but it is possible to give a characterization that can be regarded as prototypical, that is, an idea of success that somehow functions as an ideal and with respect to which other differing conceptions can be defined. If we read Studs Terkel's (1980) interviews with successful Americans, a structurally remarkably uniform, though in the details diverse, picture of success emerges. It is this structurally uniform notion that can be called the American prototype of success. Many of the things that are uniform about American success can be found in Robertson (1980). Significantly, the title of Robertson's book is *American Myth, American Reality*. Thus, I do not claim to describe a sociologically real notion of success, but only one that is used as a "blueprint" of success by many Americans. This notion can be described as follows:

> Success for most Americans means financial success. The idea is that if you have a lot of money, you are successful. It follows that in this conception of success the starting point is that you are not wealthy; many American success stories build on the situation in which someone born poor becomes rich. Also, American history is, to a large degree, the poor going to America to get rich. As Emma Lazarus's poem states: "Give me your tired, your poor, your huddled masses yearning to breathe free...." The poor in America or the poor people who come to America are characterized by a desire to be successful. If you do not desire success, you are "unmotivated" in or for life and there is something wrong with you. Furthermore, to become

successful is a matter of how much you want to be successful. In America if you want it very much, you can achieve it. The American idea of success is specific in terms of its goal; as mentioned above, the typical goal is to become wealthy.

In addition, many Americans believe that America as a natural, political, and cultural entity has the resources for someone to become wealthy. America is still imagined by many as the "land of possibilities," and, for some, even as that of "infinite possibilities." Another prevalent belief is that if you have the "inner resources," you can achieve success; in other words, you must have the talent, the intelligence, the right attitude. The idea is that if you have the inner resources (and if you work hard), these will lead to eventual success. The converse also holds. If you are not successful, it is because you do not have the inner resources. The appropriate American slogan here is this: *If you are so smart, how come you are not rich?* Success comes through competition with others, and not everyone can become successful. If you are smarter, stronger, more industrious, and so forth, than others, then you will be successful. You must also set the appropriate goal, and you have to do everything in your power to achieve that goal. You must have the right attitude, which primarily means that you have to be goal-oriented. In addition, you have to be confident that you as a person have everything that's needed (*I know I can do it*). Only things outside yourself can stop you.

Together with confidence, we can find a fear of failure in many Americans. This anxiety is a natural consequence of something uncertain. You must also take risks; without risk-taking, you cannot achieve success. This requires courage: people who are not courageous and do not take risks deserve to remain poor. But most importantly, you have to be dynamic; you have to be an "actor," an "agent." Without at least trying, nothing can be achieved. Passivity does not take you anywhere. The main kind of action is work, hard work. If you work hard, you can become anything and everything. Action-orientedness goes together with some beliefs. One is the belief that human beings control, or at least can control, their environment. Second, you have to change things, if you want progress. Without effecting change, the "old order" remains. Third, you have to believe in the changeability of the future. The future can be shaped. If you have these beliefs, if you work hard, and if you have the right attitude, you will achieve your goal; you can be successful (*You can make it*).

As can be seen, the idealized conception of success in America is largely based on some major American notions: the Protestant work ethic, the "American Dream," and the spirit of competition.

Linguistic reflections of success in American English

Given this description of the American idea of success, let us now see how it is revealed through language.

Competition

It was noted in the previous chapter that several areas of American culture are comprehended through metaphors of sport. What is the reason for the prevalence of sports metaphors in American culture? At least part of the reason, I believe, is that in American society success and failure are major measures and forces, not only in politics or business but also in human relationships, like love or sex. Since, as suggested, sports is the primary domain in which success and failure are explicitly accepted and measured, it serves as an ideal source domain for the comprehension of a number of other domains.

Goal-orientedness

An interesting example of the goal-oriented nature of American English in comparison with other varieties of English is what can be called the "*take*-construction." There are many expressions in American English that make use of the verb *take*: *take a look at, take a walk, take a bath, take a lick, take a sip, take a pee*, and others. In other varieties of English, including British English, the same idea is expressed with the help of the verb *have*, rather than *take*, yielding *have a look at, have a walk, have a bath*, and so on. In discussing this construction, Wierzbicka (1988) suggests that the American version with *take* reflects a conceptualization of these actions as quick and pre-planned. This is in line with the image of Americans as being decisive and determined. The property of goal-orientedness is opposed to the hedonistic connotations of the construction with *have*. Further examples of the same difference may be American English *take exams* and *write tests*, as opposed to British *sit (for) an exam*. The verb *take* again suggests more determination and even more confidence in getting good results.

Risk-taking

It was mentioned above that risk-taking is an important part of the American idea of success. On the way to success, one has to take risks. This shows up in a variety of metaphors that Americans use and that come from the frontier activity of gambling. Here are some examples from Lakoff and Johnson (1980):

> I'll take my chances. The odds are against me. I've got an ace up my sleeve. He's holding all the aces. It's a toss-up. If you play your cards right, you can do it. He won big. He's a real loser. Where's he when the chips are down? That's my ace in the hole. He's bluffing. The president is playing it close to his vest. Let's up the ante. Maybe we need to sweeten the pot. I think we should stand pat. That's the luck of the draw. Those are high stakes.

The major theme of this "life is a gambling game" metaphor is the risk involved in major decisions. However, the metaphor as a whole is also clearly concerned with the notion of success.

Action-orientedness

The prototypical American is active and impatient. To change the world, he or she has to act, and act quickly without delay. This property resonates with and might explain why Nike chose the slogan *Just do it* to sell its products in America. It might also have to do with one of the characteristically American word-formation processes, shifting, especially the shifting of nouns into the category of verbs that we saw in the previous chapter. In the chapter on slang I pointed out the action-orientedness of many American slang idioms, employing such verbs as *hit*, *grab*, and *kick*. These and others occur in idioms that do not really call for such "active" or even "violent" imagery. Furthermore, according to Marckwardt (1980; rev. Dillard), the *-er* ending is one of the most productive ones in American English. Our informal studies also show that it is more productive in American than British English. American innovations with *-er* include such words as *rock and roller*, *bra-burner*, *tripper*, *women's libber*, and *babysitter*. In all these examples it is the "doer" that is emphasized. In addition, such "action suffixes" as *-ize* and *-ify* appear to be more productive in American than in British English. Thus, American English has created *finalize*, *burglarize*, *winterize*, *editorialize* with *-ize* and *beautify*, *glorify*, *falsify*, *mistify*, *pacify* (in one of its senses) with *-ify*. Indeed, the prototype of a successful person is a *go-getter*, a *doer*, a person who can get things done.

Here again, we find a typically American philosopher who made action and work an integral part of a typically American philosophy: transcendentalism. The philosopher is Ralph Waldo Emerson. In his "Self-Reliance" Emerson (1841) writes: "I ask primary evidence that you are a man, and refuse this appeal from the man to his actions" (p. 124). And in the same essay, he goes further:

The objection to conforming to usages that have become dead to you is that it scatters your force. It loses your time and blurs the impression of your character ... under all these screens I have difficulty to detect the precise man you are; and, of course, so much force is withdrawn from your proper life. But do your work, and I shall know you. Do your work, and you shall reinforce yourself. (p. 125)

Progress

Americans see their goals as destinations of a journey. The American preoccupation with the amount of progress made in their endeavors can be seen from the large number of metaphorical linguistic expressions that are used to gage how close they are to their destination on the way to success. This can be found in how Americans think about life in general and their career and personal relationships in particular. Here is a selection of examples that have to do with these domains (taken from Lakoff, 1993):

Life:
He got a head start in life. I'm where I want to be in life. He'll go places in life. He's never let anyone get in his way. He's gone through a lot in life.

Career:
He clawed his way to the top. He's over the hill. She's on the fast track. He's climbing the corporate ladder. She's moving up in the ranks quickly.

Love:
Look how far we've come. We're at a crossroads. We can't turn back now. I don't think this relationship is going anywhere. Where are we? We're stuck. It's been a long bumpy road. This relationship is a dead-end street. We're just spinning our wheels. Our marriage is on the rocks. We've gotten off the track. This relationship is foundering.

All of these expressions are based on the metaphor of "journey." Given this metaphor for life, career, and love, progress can be measured in terms of the distance to one's destination. Reaching one's destination is achieving success.

Achieving success

This final aspect of success is highly eleborated in American English. Many of the "sports" metaphors we saw in the previous chapter are concerned with the notion of achieving success, one example being *to get to first base with someone*. The "journey" metaphors for progress also often highlight the ultimate goal – reaching one's destination. One expression like this from the metaphors above is *to go places*. But the richest source of metaphors for achieving success is the frontier. Some of the "gambling" metaphors for life have to do with success and the fear of failure. The expression *to win big* indicates achieving success, while the sentence *Those are high stakes* reflects concern about the final outcome. Most of the success metaphors, however, come from mining: *strike oil* ("get rich"), *pan out* ("turn out well, succeed"), *hit pay dirt* ("discover a source of wealth"), *strike it rich, big strike, lucky strike*. In a way, of course, this is not surprising. The act of finding gold or oil was indeed an act of finding wealth for many Americans. This has made the expressions describing these acts natural metaphors for achieving success in general.

British and American differences

In the previous section I have been concerned with describing some of the ways in which Americans talk about success. I have also indicated that there are some linguistic differences between British and American English in how the notions of success and especially action-orientedness reveal themselves in language. But do we have any independent, nonlinguistic evidence to show national differences in this regard? The answer is yes, and it comes from Gordon Allport's classic study of prejudice. Allport (1979:103) writes:

> A number of American and English insurance clerks were asked to write a completion of the following sentence, "The qualities I admire most in a person are...." The replies were diverse, and many of them showed no national difference whatsoever; for example, a sense of humor was mentioned with equal frequency in both countries. But qualities having to do with ability to control and exploit the environment ("go-getting") were mentioned by 31 percent of the Americans, and by only 7 percent of the English. On the other hand, the ability to control one's own impulses was mentioned by 30 percent of the English, and only 8 percent of the Americans. Here we seem to have a bit of evidence for the *assertiveness* of the American and the *reticence* of the English.

This kind of nonlinguistic evidence is extremely important for our purposes. It shows that the subtle linguistic differences I have pointed out between British and American English are correlated with real (nonlinguistic) differences in national character. The sociological study done by Allport provides us with some evidence for the claim that British and American linguistic differences arise from independently existing differences in cultural style or national character.

study questions and activities

1. Try to find some accounts of life stories by successful Americans. What language do they use to talk about their success in life? To what extent does their idea of success fit the "prototype" given in the chapter?

2. Can you find examples of American action-orientedness outside language? If yes, discuss them.

3. Craig Storti (1994) offers the following dialogue that takes place between a British and an American businessperson who both work for the same company in England. Which one is British and which American?

    > **Ms. Foster:** I had hoped we could develop some new accounts with this new software program.
    > **Colin Davies:** Oh, yes. I think this product will definitely help us penetrate some new markets.
    > **Ms. Foster:** We'll be kicking off the promotion campaign by the end of next month.
    > **Colin Davies:** We've already made some preliminary contacts. There's a lot of interest. We plan to make some initial visits starting week after next.
    > **Ms. Foster:** Great! That should boost our fourth-quarter numbers a bit.
    > **Colin Davies:** How do you mean?
    > **Ms. Foster:** You know, increased sales.
    > **Colin Davies:** A bit early to say, I'm afraid.
    > (Storti, 1994:97)

    What kind of attitude and behavior characterizes Ms. Foster and Colin Davies, respectively? How are these attitudes and behaviors related to the characterization of American English and Americans in general as presented in this chapter and some of the previous ones?

4. Read the following conversation between an American woman, Marge, and an Englishman, Jeremy. (The dialogue is taken from Storti, 1994, again.)

Marge: Why don't you try more freelancing? Selling to some publications in the United States, for example.
Jeremy: I'd like that, actually. Any help you could give me would be most appreciated.
Marge: Oh, you don't need me. Just put together a selection of your pieces and send them out.
Jeremy: But I don't know any editors.
Marge: Doesn't matter. Just send a cover letter explaining you'd like to be their man in London. Or something like that.
Jeremy: Oh, I couldn't do that.
(Storti, 1994:17)

How do the assumptions behind what is said in the conversation relate to Emerson's ideas as quoted in the chapter?

chapter 22

A new mind

More then two hundred years ago a French traveller to America, Hector St. Jean de Crévecoeur, asked: "What then is the American, this new man?... Here [in America] individuals of all nations are melted into a new race of man, whose labours and posterity will one day cause great changes in the world" (quoted in Mitchell and Maidment, 1994:19). We can now ask with him: What, then, is the mind of "this new man" like? We can only give a partial answer to this question, as based on our study of American English and what this reveals about the "mind" of its users. What I attempt to do in this chapter is to describe, at least partially, what the new mind is like on the basis of the main features of American English and the major forces that have shaped it. To do this, we must review the major forces that have shaped American English first, as presented in this work.

The effects of social history on American English

There are two major historical events that have left their lasting mark on American English: the settling of North America from Europe and later from around the world, and the westward march of the nation, creating what became known as "the frontier." I briefly summarize their impact on the development of American English.

Settlement and immigration

It is a commonplace that in America, with the exception of the Native Americans, everybody is a newcomer. It is customary to talk about the people who came to America after the American Revolution as *immigrants*, while to refer to those who arrived in America before the Revolution as *settlers* (or *colonists*). Since most of the settlers in the first two hundred years spoke English, the dominant language of the new country was, and remained, English. This language preserved many archaic features from the English of England in the sixteenth and seventeenth centuries. The first settlers found speakers of other languages in North America. Of these, the Native Americans had lived in America long before the settlers arrived. The Spanish, the Dutch, and the French came shortly before the English settlers, and the Germans began to arrive shortly after them, while the blacks from Africa came simultaneously with the white settlers. The English of these first settlers was greatly influenced by the languages spoken by all of these races and nationalities. Spanish, Dutch, French, and German are typically referred to as colonial languages. Black English has been a major factor shaping several aspects of American English. The language of the later immigrants has been less influential, partly because they were striving toward uniformity in their speech habits and the model that they most commonly followed was the English of the native-born white Americans.

Westward movement

We may begin with some minor but interesting ways in which American English and, consequently, the American mind has been influenced by the westward march, looking at two spatial particles, *back* and *out*, first. To see what is uniquely American about them, we may compare their American usage with how these words are used in British English.

Back

In both British and American English, the dominant sense of the particle or adverb *back* can be given as "to the rear; to the origin of movement." This is exemplified in sentences such as

> She went back to the office,

which is used if she was in the office before. Now take a sentence such as

> She went back East.

There is an important difference in the use of this sentence between British and American English. In British English it can only be used if she actually worked or lived east of the place where she is now. In American English, in contrast, the sentence can be appropriately used even if the person in question has never been in the eastern part of the United States. The difference is even more transparent in cases such as

> My brother lives back East.

This can be said by a Californian whose family has never been outside California. For an American, East is "back," hence *back East*. This is because the history of the United States, the westward movement in particular, defined a certain point of view for Americans as regards the conceptualization of "East and West." As Robertson (1980) observes, this is the major division of space in the American mind. The westward expansion of the nation gave Americans a special point of view for viewing space that is missing from other nations. This shows up in American English, and raises the question: How, then, is the west conceptualized by Americans?

Out

To see this, consider again another particle or adverb, *out*, as used in British and American English. *Out* is used in the same way in the two dialects in examples such as

> She ran out of the house.
> Get up and go out.

The meaning of *out* in cases like these can be given as "not inside a place." However, sentences such as the following are typically American:

> Out West you'll find your fortune.

If the east is viewed as "back" in the American mind, the west is conceived as "out." This is based on the notion that the east is metaphorically a "closed container." This explains the use of *out West* in American English. Interestingly, it may be noted that British English uses *out* in a similar way to indicate "out" of the U.K., except to Europe (where "over" or "across" is used) – "out to America," "out to Canada," "out to Australia," especially in the sense of "emigrating (out) to somewhere." However, there is also a conceptualization of the west in which it is a closed container as well. By getting out of the closed container of the east and going west, the limited resources of a closed container become the unlimited resources of the much larger space outside that container. But this much larger space is a closed container, too. We can find this conception of the West in examples like:

> The West gradually opened up before the settlers.

By *opening up* before the settlers, the west offered its new resources and possibilities to them.

Up – down

In the two cases above, we saw how a major event, the westward march of the nation, shaped the conceptualization of space in America. Now we will look at a case in which the political organization of the United States affects the understanding of another set of spatial concepts, that of *up – down*. Here again, the best way to point out what is uniquely American about the understanding of these spatial particles is to compare their American usage with British usage. The usage that is obviously shared is when *up* means "from south to north" and *down* means "from north to south." Thus, both dialects would have sentences such as:

> I'm going up to London. (from south of London)
> I'm going up to New York. (from south of New York)
> I'm going down to London. (from north of London)
> I'm going down to New York. (from north of New York)

However, *up* and *down* have an additional meaning in British English but not in American English (or at least much less clearly so). For *up*, this meaning is "from periphery to the center or place of importance." *Down* means the reverse. In characterizing this sense of *up* and *down*, Crystal (1991:47) writes:

> (iv) especially in British English, *down* meaning 'from a place of importance to a place of lesser importance' (London and the leading university towns being traditionally seen as more important in this respect), *up* being the reverse.

Crystal continues: "Speakers from all parts of the country might say *I'm going up to London*, ..." This includes people from north of London. American usage clearly contrasts with British usage in examples like the following:

> I'm going up to London. (from north of London)
> *I'm going up to Washington. (from, say, New York)

The star indicates that the sentence is not acceptable in American English. The reason is that socio-political importance does not seem to play a role in the choice of *up* and *down* in American English, whereas it does in British English. The more centralized socio-political position of London and some other cities in England contrasts with the less centralized geopolitical organization of the United States.

The frontier

The influence of the frontier on American English has been enormous (see, for example, Dillard, 1985 and 1992). We have seen throughout this book how the frontier contributed in many ways to the development of a unique variety of English. First, as was pointed out in chapter three, it provided a large bulk of the vocabulary of American English. Second, it was also the place where directness became a characteristically American property of language use. Third, it was on the frontier that the American genre of "tall talk" was born. This was made ample use of by several American authors, including Mark Twain. Fourth, to a large degree, the spirit of democracy and one of its attendant properties, informality, also developed most fully on the frontier. They have left their indelible mark on American English. Fifth, two such important characteristics as inventiveness and imaginativeness were produced by the frontier as well. Sixth, the dynamism and success and action-orientedness of Americans and American English were shaped here. Moreover, not only did the frontier provide metaphors for many aspects of American life and culture, it also became a metaphor for America. For many people, both inside and outside the United States, America is seen through a stereotype of the frontier (Limerick, 1994). Given all these contributions of the frontier to American English and to a view of America itself, it is appropriate here to quote a "pioneer" historian of the frontier, Frederick Jackson Turner, at this point. In a famous passage, Turner summarized the major traits of the frontier in 1893 with the following words:

> That coarseness and strength combined with acuteness and inquisitiveness; that practical, inventive turn of mind, quick to find expedients; that masterful grasp of material things, lacking in the artistic but powerful to effect great ends; that restless, nervous energy; that dominant individualism, working for good and for evil, and withal that bouyancy and exuberance which comes with freedom – these are the traits of the frontier, or traits called out elsewhere because of the existence of the frontier.

As can be seen, many of the traits mentioned by Turner coincide with the ones that we have found important in the characterization of American English. Moreover, such "can-do" language as this may also have endorsed the belief in Manifest Destiny.

Properties of American English

We have noted several properties of American English in this book. These may not be the only ones, but these are the ones that stand out in the light of a comparison with British English. Here's the list of these properties, given in the order in which they were discussed:

economical
regular/uniform
direct

democratic
tolerant/nonstandardized
informal
prudish
inflated/self-aggrandizing
inventive
imaginative
success and action-oriented

The economical nature of American English was seen in several principles that were formulated on the basis of linguistic data. The principles included: "use as little form as possible," "use forms you already have," "avoid redundancy," and "one meaning, one form."

Regularity was found in how American English makes use of paradigms that have a tendency to eliminate members of the paradigm that are irregular.

Directness was observed in linguistic phenomena that appear to adhere to two principles: "say what you mean and say the truth" and "say what you want to say in clear language."

Even more so than the other features, the democratic nature of American English is a relative feature. It was pointed out that English in general can be claimed to be a democratic language. The democratic character of American English was found in such areas as the relative uniformity of American English and the availability of the prestigious standard dialect for a large number of people in the United States.

Tolerance was seen in the apparently low degree to which Americans observe prescriptive linguistic rules. Furthermore, tolerance exhibits itself in how Americans create new forms and constructions that deviate from the canons of standard usage, as well as in the widespread use and acceptance of these forms and constructions by Americans.

The notion that American English is highly informal was based, among other things, on the use of the pronoun system, relationship-markers in discourse, and the mixing of styles within a single discourse or text.

The prudishness of American English is displayed by the tendency for Americans to use highly euphemistic language to talk about aspects of life that they regard as in any way offensive, unpleasant, or sensitive.

The high-sounding, inflated phrases of American English historically derive from the tall talk of the frontier. In today's speech it can be noticed in the language of several institutions that try to portray themselves as more prestigious, important, and dignified than they really are.

Inventiveness in American English manifests itself in the high degree to which American English is contributing to the English vocabulary. All the processes of word formation in English are put to maximum use to create new words. Additional devices of word formation are also employed.

Imaginativeness seems to pervade several aspects of the use of American English (e.g., the "exporting" of American words, informality, inventiveness, etc.). Imaginativeness is one form of inventiveness, in which linguistic devices like metaphor and metonymy are put to use in the creation of novel words and expressions. There are some uniquely American experiences that serve as metaphorical "source domains" (such as the frontier) for the understanding of many aspects of American life.

American English can be said to be dynamic or active, rather than passive. This property shows itself most clearly in the American preference for goal-oriented and action words where there is a choice, in the selection of action-related metaphorical "source domains" (sports, frontier), and the general emphasis on success as a concept.

American English and the American character

However, the properties listed above do not properly belong to American English as such. They characterize the people who speak American English, or, alternatively, the stereotype of the people (either stereotypes that outsiders have of Americans, or stereotypes that they have of themselves, or both). Strictly speaking, American English (or any language) cannot be economical, direct, democratic, tolerant, informal, prudish, inventive, imaginative, and so forth – only the people speaking American English can. In other words, the list of features for American English should instead be regarded as a list of properties for the characterization of the (stereotype of the) people who speak American English.

Indeed, in some chapters of the book I have employed terms that are more appropriate for the characterization of the people than for that of the language spoken by them. Thus, I used the adjective "straightforward," rather than "direct," in the title of chapter fourteen; the title of chapter sixteen was "The casual American," and not "The informal American"; and we talked about "linguistic economy in American English," rather than about American English being economical. The properties identified in this book belong more appropriately to Americans than to their language. Is this borne out by other than linguistic evidence?

Many of these properties have been offered by several nonlinguists as essential aspects of the American character. In the preceding chapters I have tried to adduce other than linguistic evidence for these American traits. For example, I quoted from Allport's classic study on prejudice to substantiate the claim based on linguistic evidence that Americans are characterized by a high

degree of success and action-orientedness. I also mentioned Levinson's observation about differences in cultural patterns in England and the U.S. in connection with "directness." There is a great deal of evidence of this kind around
in sociological, anthropological, literary, and cultural studies, but for the purposes of this book, there is no need to survey all this literature. Also, several of
the properties listed above reflect generally known and widespread notions
about Americans. Americans are commonly viewed and characterized (also by
themselves) as casual, straightforward, democratic, inventive, and so on. In
these cases the stereotype of Americans and the properties of American English
match each other strikingly.

American intellectual traditions

It would be difficult not to notice some connections between the properties
of American English and/or the American character traits, on the one hand,
and some American intellectual traditions, on the other. It seems legitimate
to suggest that the properties listed above can be connected to certain intellectual traditions. As a matter of fact, I already made these connections explicit
in previous chapters. Nevertheless, it is useful to provide a summary at this
point to facilitate the discussion to follow.

It was argued that "linguistic economy" derives in part from the puritan
value of thriftiness – the notion that we should be economical with resources
in general. It was also shown that linguistic economy may have to do with
rationality – in its emphasis on the avoidance of redundancy and on "one-to-
one" meaning-form relationships. What was called "verbal prudery" may also
be in part the product of Puritan ideas about morality, and especially ideas
concerning religion and sexuality. American verbal prudery, however, is also
linked with Victorianism, the set of values that evolved during Queen
Victoria's reign from the 1830s to the first decade of the twentieth century. It
was suggested, furthermore, that Victorianism may have been more influential
in America than in Britain because of the particularly strong Puritan heritage
in American thought.

The feature of "regularity" or "uniformity" in American English goes back
to some ideas about logic and rationality. In the formative years of American
English, reason was (as it is now) regarded as being universal, and it was claimed
to be more "logical" to have a linguistic system that is regular than one that is
not. Rationality ultimately comes from the Age of the Enlightenment, and the
new nation made conscious efforts to implement many of its ideas. As, for
example, philosopher Francis Fukuyama (1992) puts it: "Liberal democracy in
its Anglo-Saxon variant represents the emergence of a kind of cold calculation
at the expense of earlier moral and cultural horizons" (p. 214). The ideals of

rationality were reinforced by some ideas of utilitarianism that emerged mainly from the work of Bentham and Adam Smith.

Utilitarianism may have been one driving force behind the property of "directness." Sincerity and clarity are based in part on the principle of least effort. However, this also requires a special social context. The principle can only be implemented in a democratic society, where in the process of communication speakers do not have to observe elaborate codes for verbal behavior. Finally, directness may also be based on Puritan morality, as it manifests itself in various forms of plain style, either Puritan or Quaker.

The feature of "democracy" is obviously connected with certain republican ideals, especially equality and justice for all. "Informality" in language can be considered as a manifestation of democracy, in the sense that in a democratic society there are no, or fewer, forms of deference than in a less democratic one. It is also not surprising that in such a society there is a higher degree of "tolerance" of deviation from linguistic norms and that, consequently, prescriptivism is less at work. In other words, the features of American English as democratic, tolerant, and informal may be seen as all stemming from the republican heritage of American intellectual traditions.

The "inflated" character of much of American English is apparently connected with the spirit of freedom in the frontier, which was in part responsible for people being able to express themselves – through work and speech – without the rigid restraints of more traditional societies. The frontier also produced the "action-orientedness" of American English – especially through the notion of success. What was happening in the frontier in much of the nineteenth century coincided with the period of American Romanticism, which was embodied in the works of authors like Emerson, Poe, Whitman, Dickinson, and others (see Bickman, 1988). This factor further contributed to the tendency for people to express themselves freely and to be inventive. The "inventiveness" and "imaginativeness" of American English are products of the same mechanisms.

In summary, we find the following intellectual traditions that have historically shaped American English on a large scale:

Puritanism
Victorianism
Rationality
Utilitarianism
Republicanism
Romanticism

These intellectual traditions largely coincide with what Bellah, *et al.* (1985) have found as characterizing the everyday thought of middle-class Americans on the basis of hundreds of interviews. Bellah, *et al.,* in their book *Habits of the Heart*, distinguish four kinds or traditions of individualism: the Biblical tradition, the republican tradition, the utilitarian tradition, and expressive individualism. The correspondences between the set of traditions we have found as shaping American English and those found by Bellah, *et al.* as shaping American thought are obvious:

> *Biblical tradition*: Puritanism manifested in economy, directness, ("Victorian puritanism" in) prudery.
> *Republican tradition*: Republicanism manifested in democracy, tolerance, informality.
> *Utilitarian tradition*: Rational utilitarianism manifested in directness, regularity, economy.
> *Expressive individualism*: Romanticism manifested in inventiveness, imaginativeness, inflated speech, and action-orientedness

As can be seen, intellectual traditions may blend with each other. For example, it was pointed out in the chapter on directness that utilitarianism combines forces with rationality to produce directness and in the chapter on verbal prudery it was suggested that Puritanism may be jointly at work with Victorianism. Furthermore, some of the properties of American English may be motivated by more than one intellectual tradition, as is the case for economy and directness.

Tensions

But all this is not to say that we have a neat set of linguistic properties existing side by side and a neat set of intellectual traditions also existing side by side. Instead, the proper conclusion that we can draw is that both the properties of American English and the intellectual traditions shaping them may, and do, conflict with each other. In an obvious way, linguistic economy can be said to conflict, say, with inventiveness and directness with imaginativeness.

Moreover, in the previous chapters we have discussed properties of American English that clash with the properties that were found to be important and highlighted in this work. For example, in the chapter on directness it was noted that an overwordy, "unplain" style is preferred to plain, direct English by some speakers of American English. In addition, we can see a different interpretation of what might be taken to be "linguistic insecurity" on the part of many speakers of American English. The alternative account I have offered is that cases of "linguistic insecurity" may be reinterpreted as a lack of prescriptive norms imposed on speakers.

To return to our initial question: What is the "new mind" of "this new man" like, then? On the basis of our linguistic evidence, we can offer the following short answer: It contains all of the properties listed above in this chapter, as well as all the tensions that exist among these properties. It would require another, and a very different, book to show how these features of American English and those of Americans interact with each other. Just like any other nation's, the American "mind" is complex and has been shaped by a variety of geographical, social, historical, and intellectual factors. Some of these are unique to America (like the frontier experience) and some are not (like rationality). But the uniqueness of American English does not involve only what is unique, that is, exclusively American to its development. Instead, its uniqueness, in addition, derives from the particular blend of influences and the degree to which each of these applied to the American situation. It is the combination of all of these factors that make American English a special, and at the end of the twentieth century a highly successful, variety of the English language.

American English and modernity

We have seen that the intellectual traditions of puritanism, rationality, utilitarianism, republicanism, and expresssive individualism (as this last one is manifest in inventiveness, imaginativeness, and inflated language) have been major forces that have shaped American English. We have robust evidence for the presence of these forces in American English.

The chief reason why I felt it was necessary in this book to go through this list of features and the major forces that have presumably shaped them is to be able to show that it is these same forces that have contributed most to our idealized conception of liberal democracy (see Fukuyama, 1989, 1992). In liberal democracy, production and economy are predominantly governed by ideas of rationality and utilitarianism (see, for example, Weber, 1965). Political organization is also based on rationality (see, for instance, D.A. Stone, 1988) and, in an obvious way, on principles of Enlightenment republicanism. American liberalism draws on and goes back to at least the "expressive" tradition of American individualism. As regards the role of the "Biblical" tradition, it provides an ethic – both for work and the home (see Weber, 1965) – that is clearly present in the current notion of liberal democracy as we know it today. It can even be claimed that the Biblical tradition is the basis of the division of American political life into "liberal" and "conservative" views (see Lakoff, 1996).

It is in this sense that I suggest that English, and especially American English, can be taken to be the language of (an idealized view of) liberal democracy; it is also in this sense that it can be viewed as the language of modernity. The cornerstone of liberal democracy is rationality – the notion that underlies both its view of democracy and its theory of production. The importance of this notion in liberal democracy is shown by the fact that it is the idea of rationality that has been criticized most vehemently by the French poststructuralists and postmodernists (for an interesting summary, see Appignanesi and Garratt, 1995), who see liberal democracy and its means of production – capitalism – as the fullest embodiment of modernity.

Based on this conclusion, my prediction is that as long as these intellectual trends, taken individually or together, have a market in the world, the language that seems to express them most fully – (American) English – will also have a market for hundreds of millions of non-native speakers of English around the world.

study questions and activities

1. Analyze the most popular European sport, soccer, and its highly popular American counterpart, football. Why do Europeans love soccer and why do Americans love football? What differences does your analysis reveal about cultural norms, values, preferences, expectations, attitudes, etc. between Europeans and Americans?

2. It's been predicted recently by Bernard Vincent (1997) that American English is dying. He argues that once a language acquires universal status, it inevitably begins to die. He draws an analogy between Classical Latin and (American) English and suggests that the latter will die for the same reasons that the former did. Do you agree or disagree with this prediction? Why?

References

Algeo, J. (1986). The two streams: British and American English. *Journal of English Linguistics*, 19.2, 269-284.

Algeo, J. (1989). British-American lexical differences: A typology of inter-dialectal variation. In: O. Garcia and R. Otheguy (eds.), *English across Cultures, Cultures across English. A Reader in Cross-Cultural Communication.* Berlin and New York: de Gruyter, 219-241.

Algeo, J. (1991). *Fifty Years among the New Words. A Dictionary of Neologisms, 1941-1991.* New York: Cambridge University Press.

Algeo, J. (1992a). American English. In: T. McArthur (ed.), *The Oxford Companion to the English Language.* Oxford: Oxford University Press, 37-41.

Algeo, J. (1992b). American place-names. In: T. McArthur (ed.), *The Oxford Companion to the English Language.* Oxford: Oxford University Press, 53-56.

Allen, I.L. (1993). *The City in Slang. New York Life and Popular Speech.* New York: Oxford.

Allport, G.W. (1979). *The Nature of Prejudice.* Reading, MA: Addison-Wesley.

Amastae, J. (1992). Chicano English. In: T. McArthur (ed.), *The Oxford Companion to the English Language.* Oxford: Oxford University Press, 210.

The American Heritage Dictionary. (1985). 2nd ed. Boston: Houghton Mifflin.

András, L., and Z. Kövecses (1989). *Magyar-Angol Szlengszótár (Hungarian-English Slang Dictionary).* Budapest: Maecenas.

Appignanesi, R., and C. Garratt (1995). *Postmodernism for Beginners.* Cambridge: Icon Books.

Ayto, J., and J. Simpson (1993). *The Oxford Dictionary of Modern Slang.* Oxford: Oxford University Press.

Bailey, G., N. Maynor, and P. Cukor-Avila, eds. (1991). *The Emergence of Black English: Text and Commentary.* Amsterdam: John Benjamins.

Bailey, R.W. (1992). Dialect in America. In: T. McArthur (ed.), *The Oxford Companion to the English Language.* Oxford: Oxford University Press, 291-296.

Baron, D.E. (1982). *Grammar and Good Taste.* New Haven: Yale University Press.

Baugh, A.C., and T. Cable (1983). *A History of the English Language*. 3rd ed. London: Routledge and Kegan Paul.

Baugh, J. (1992). Black English Vernacular. In: T. McArthur (ed.), *The Oxford Companion to the English Language*. Oxford: Oxford University Press, 133-135.

Bellah, R.N., R. Madsen, W.M. Sullivan, A. Swidler, and S.M. Tipton (1985). *Habits of the Heart: Individualism and Commitment in American Life*. Berkeley: University of California Press.

Benson, M., E. Benson, and R. Ilson (1986). *Lexicographic Description of English*. Amsterdam: John Benjamins.

Berrey, L.V., and M. Van der Bark (1947). *The American Thesaurus of Slang*. 2nd ed.

Biber, D. (1987). A textual comparison of British and American writing. *American Speech*, 62.2, 99-119.

Biber, D. (1988). *Variation Across Speech and Writing*. Cambridge: Cambridge University Press.

Bickman, M. (1988). *American Romantic Psychology*. 2nd ed. Dallas: Spring Publications.

Bigsby, C.W.E. (1975). Europe, America and the cultural debate. In: C.W.E. Bigsby (ed.), *Superculture*. London: Paul Elek, 1-27.

Bigsby, C.W.E., ed. (1975). *Superculture*. London: Paul Elek.

Brogger, F.C. (1992). *Culture, Language, Text: Culture Studies within the Study of English as a Foreign Language*. Oslo: Scandinavian University Press.

Brown, P., and S. Levinson (1987). *Politeness: Some Universals in Linguistic Usage*. Cambridge: Cambridge University Press.

Bryson, B. (1990). *The Mother Tongue: English and How It Got That Way*. New York: Avon Books.

Bryson, B. (1994). *Made in America: An Informal History of the English Language in the United States*. New York: William Morrow.

Cameron, D. (1992). Naming of parts: gender, culture, and terms for the penis among American college students. *American Speech*, 67.4, 367-382.

Carver, C.M. (1987). *American Regional Dialects: A Word Geography*. Ann Arbor: University of Michigan Press.

Cassidy, F.G., ed. (1985). *Dictionary of American Regional English*. Vol. 1: A-C. Cambridge, MA: Belknap Press.

Cassidy, F.G., and J.H. Hall, eds. (1991). *Dictionary of American Regional English*. Vol. 2: D-H. Cambridge, MA: Belknap Press.

Cassidy, F.G., and J.H. Hall, eds. (1996). *Dictionary of American Regional English*. Vol. 3. Cambridge, MA: Belknap Press.

Chapman, R.L. (1986). *New Dictionary of American Slang*. New York: Harper and Row.

Chapman, R.L. (1989). *Thesaurus of American Slang*. New York: Harper and Row.

Claiborne, R. (1983). *Our Marvelous Native Tongue: The Life and Times of the English Language*. New York: Times Books.

Clarence, M. (1994). *Juba to Jive: A Dictionary of African-American Slang*. New York: Penguin Books.

Clark, H., and E. Clark (1979). When nouns surface as verbs. *Language*, 55:4, 767-811.

Cmiel, K. (1990). *Democratic Eloquence: The Fight over Popular Speech in Nineteenth-Century America*. Berkeley: University of California Press.

Cmiel, K. (1992). "A broad fluid language of democracy": Discovering the American idiom. *The Journal of American History*, 79:3, 913-936.

Cowley, M. (1973). *A Second Flowering*. New York: The Viking Press.

Crystal, D. (1975). American English in Europe. In: C.W.E. Bigsby (ed.), *Superculture*. London: Paul Elek, 57-68.

Crystal, D. (1991). *Making Sense of English Usage*. Edinburgh: Chambers.

Crystal, D. (1997). *English as a Global Language*. Cambridge: Cambridge University Press.

Davis, H.B. (1985). *Mark Twain in Heidelberg and the Neckar Valley*. Heidelberg: Verlag Brausdruck.

Dillard, J.L. (1972). *Black English, its History and Usage in the United States*. New York: Random House.

Dillard, J.L. (1975). *American Talk*. New York: Random House.

Dillard, J.L. (1985). *Toward a Social History of American English*. Berlin: Mouton.

Dillard, J.L. (1992). *A History of American English*. Harlow, Essex: Longman.

Eble, C. (1996). *Slang and Sociability*. Chapel Hill: University of North Carolina Press.

Eble, C. (1998). American college slang. In E.W. Schneider, ed. *Focus on the USA*. Amsterdam: John Benjamins.

Emerson, R.W. (1941/1841). Self-Reliance. In: *The Best of R.W. Emerson*. N.P.: Walter J. Black, Inc.

Ferguson, C.A., and S.B. Heath, eds. (1980). *Language in the USA*. Cambridge: Cambridge University Press.

Finegan, E. (1980). *Attitudes toward English Usage: The History of a War of Words*. New York: Teachers College Press.

Finegan, E., and N. Besnier. (1989). *Language: Its Structure and Use*. San Diego: Harcourt Brace Jovanovich.

Flexner, S.B. (1960). Preface to H. Wentworth and S.B. Flexner (eds.), *Dictionary of American Slang*. New York: Crowell, vi-xv.

Foucault, M. (1978). *The History of Sexuality. Volume 1: An Introduction.* New York: Vintage Books.

Frazer, T.C. (1998). The dialects of the Middle West. In: E.D. Schneider, (ed.), *Focus on the USA.* Amsterdam: John Benjamins, 81-102.

Frick, E. (1990). Metaphors and motives of language-restriction movements. In: H.A. Daniels (ed.), *Not Only English: Affirming America's Multilingual Heritage.* Urbana, IL: National Council of Teachers of English, 27-36.

Fromkin, V., and R. Rodman (1993). *An Introduction to Language.* 5th ed. Orlando: Harcourt, Brace, Jovanovich.

Fukuyama, F. (1989). The End of History? *The National Interest,* 16 (Summer), 3-18.

Fukuyama, F. (1992). *The End of History and the Last Man.* New York: Avon Books.

Fussel, P. (1983). *Class: A Guide through the American Status System.* New York: Random House.

Fussel, P. (1992). *Bad, or the Dumbing of America.* New York: Touchstone.

Gilligan, C. (1982). *In a Different Voice.* Cambridge, MA: Harvard University Press.

Glazier, S. (1997). *Random House Word Menu.* New York: Random House.

Glowka, A.W., and D.M. Lance, eds. (1993). *Language Variation in North American English.* New York: The Modern Language Association of America.

Görlach, M. (1991). *Englishes.* Amsterdam: John Benjamins.

Görlach, M. (1995). *More Englishes.* Amsterdam: John Benjamins.

Gozzi, R. (1990). *New Words and a Changing American Culture.* Columbia: University of South Carolina Press.

Graham, J.L. (1983). Negotiators abroad - Don't shoot from the hip. *Harvard Business Review,* 61(4): 160-168.

Gramley, S. and K. -M. Pätzold (1992). *A Survey of Modern English.* London: Routledge.

Green, J. (1999). *The Cassell Dictionary of Slang.* London: Cassell.

Haiman, J. (1995). The cult of plain speaking. In Z. Kövecses (ed.), *New Approaches to American English.*

Haiman, J., ed. (1985). *Iconicity in Syntax.* Amsterdam: John Benjamins.

Hendrickson, R. (1986). *American Talk. The Ways and Words of American Dialects.* New York: Penguin.

Hoggart, S. (1991). *America: A User's Guide.* London: Fontana.

Holloway, J.E., and W. Vass. (1997). *The African Heritage of American English.* Bloomington: Indiana University Press.

Ilson, R. (1990). British and American English: ex uno plura? In: C. Ricks and L. Michaels (eds.), *The State of the Language.* 2nd ed. Berkeley: University of California Press, 33-41.

Janicki, K. (1977). *Elements of British and American English*. Warsaw: Panstwowe Wydawnictwo Naukowe.

Jones, L., and R. Alexander (1989). *International Business English*. Cambridge: Cambridge University Press

Joos, M. (1967). *The Five Clocks*. New York: Harcourt, Brace, & World.

Kochman, T. (1981). *Black and White Styles in Conflict*. Chicago: University of Chicago Press.

Kövecses, Z. (1994). Tocqueville's passionate "beast": A linguistic analysis of the concept of American democracy. *Metaphor and Symbolic Activity*, 9(2), 113-133.

Kövecses, Z., ed. (1995). *New Approaches to American English*. Budapest: Department of American Studies, ELTE.

Kövecses, Z., and G. Radden (1998). Metonymy: a cognitive linguistic view. *Cognitive Linguistics*, 9(1), 37-77.

Krapp, G.P. (1924-56). *The English Language in America*. 2 vols. New York: Century.

Kretzschmar, W.A., Jr. (1998). Foundations of American English. In: E.W. Schneider (ed.), *Focus on the USA*. Amsterdam: John Benjamins, 25-50.

Kurath, H. (1949). *A Word Geography of the Eastern United States*. Ann Arbor: University of Michigan Press.

Kurath, H. (1971). What do you call it? In: J.V. Williamson and V. M. Burke (eds.), *A Various Language: Perspectives on American Dialects*. New York: Holt, 246-254.

Labov, W. (1966). *The Social Stratification of English in New York City*. Washington, DC: Center for Applied Linguistics.

Labov, W. (1972). *Sociolinguistic Patterns*. Philadelphia: University of Pennsylvania Press.

Lakoff, G. (1993). The contemporary theory of metaphor. In: A. Ortony (ed.), *Metaphor and Thought*. 2nd ed. Cambridge: Cambridge University Press.

Lakoff, G. (1996). *Moral Politics: What Conservatives Know that Liberals Don't*. Chicago: The University of Chicago Press.

Lakoff, G., and M. Johnson (1980). *Metaphors We Live By*. Chicago: University of Chicago Press.

Lakoff, R. (1975). *Language and Woman's Place*. New York: Harper.

Leisi, E. (1985). *Das Heutige Englisch*. Heidelberg: Carl Winter.

Lerner, M. 1987. *America as a Civilization*. New York: Holt.

Lewis, W.J. (1971). The American and British Accents of English. *English Language Teaching*, 25, 239-248.

Lighter, J.E. (1994). *Historical Dictionary of American Slang*. Vol. 1. New York: Random House.

Lighter, J.E. (1997). *Historical Dictionary of American Slang*. Vol. 2. New York: Random House.

Limerick, P.N. (1994). *The Frontier in American Culture*. Berkeley: University of California Press.

Lutz, W. (1990). *Doublespeak*. New York: HarperPerennial.

Malmstrom, J., and A. Ashley (1958). *Dialects—USA*. Champaign, IL: National Council of Teachers of English.

Marckwardt, A.H. (1980). *American English*. Revised by J.L. Dillard. New York: Oxford University Press.

Marckwardt, A.H., and R. Quirk (1964). *A Common Language: British and American English*. London and Washington: British Broadcasting Corporation and Voice of America.

McArthur, T. (1992). *The Oxford Companion to the English Language*. Oxford: Oxford University Press.

McCrum, R., W. Cran, and R. MacNeil (1986). *The Story of English*. New York: Penguin Books.

Medgyes, P. (1982). Which to teach: British or American? *English Teaching Forum*, Vol. XX/1, 9-16.

Mencken, H.L. (1919). *The American Language*. 1st ed. New York: Knopf.

Mencken, H.L. (1963). *The American Language: The Fourth Edition and the Two Supplements, Abridged with Annotations and New Material*. Ed. by R.I. McDavid, Jr., with the assistance of D.W. Maurer. New York: Knopf.

Mitchell, J., and R. Maidment, eds. (1994). *The United States in the Twentieth Century. Culture*. Milton Keynes: The Open University.

Moore, M.E. (1991). *Understanding British English*. New York: Citadel Press.

Moss, N. (1973). *What's the Difference?* London: Hutchinson.

Munro, P. (1990). *Slang U*. New York: Harmony Books.

Murphy, A.F. (1991). *Cultural Encounters in the U.S.A.: Cross-cultural Dialogues and Mini-Dramas*. Lincolnwood, IL: National Textbook Company.

Murray, S.O. (1998). *American Sociolinguistics. Theories and Theory Groups*. Amsterdam: John Benjamins.

The Oxford Advanced Learner's Dictionary. (1989). New edition. Oxford: Oxford University Press.

Parshall, G. (1994). Words with attitude. *U.S. News and World Report*, June 27, 61-67.

Partridge, E. (1984). *Dictionary of Slang and Unconventional English*. 8th ed. London.

Penfield, J., and J.L. Ornstein-Galicia (1985). *Chicano English: An Ethnic Contact Dialect*. Amsterdam: John Benjamins.

Plumb, J.H. (1978). Britain and America. The cultural heritage. In: J.H. Plumb, F.A. Youngs, H.L. Snyder, E.A. Reitan, and D.M. Fahey, *The English Heritage*. St. Louis: Forum Press, 1-14.

Preston, D.R. (1998). Where the worst English is spoken. In: E.W. Schneider (ed.), *Focus on the USA*. Amsterdam: John Benjamins, 297-390.

Quirk, R., S. Greenbaum, G. Leech, and J. Svartvik (1985). *A Comprehensive Grammar of the English Language*. London: Longman.

Reed, C.E. (1977). *Dialects of American English*. Rev. ed. N.P.: The University of Massachusetts Press.

Robertson, J.O. (1980). *American Myth, American Reality*. New York: Hill and Wang.

Ryabov, G., and O. Petrova (1992). Why learn American English? *English Teaching Forum*, 46-47.

Schneider, E.W., ed. (1998). *Focus on the USA*. Amsterdam: John Benjamins.

Schur, N.W. (1980). *English English*. Essex, CT: Verbatim.

Simpson, D. (1986). *The Politics of American English, 1776-1850*. Oxford: Oxford University Press.

Spears, R.A. (1982). *Slang and Euphemisms*. New York: Jonathan David Publishers.

Stevenson, D.K. (1987). *American Life and Institutions*. Stuttgart: Ernst Klett Verlag.

Stewart, G.R. (1970). *American Place-Names*. New York: Oxford University Press.

Stone, D.A. (1988). *Policy Paradox and Political Reason*. N.P.: HarperCollins.

Strevens, P. (1972). *British and American English*. London: Collier-Macmillan.

Svejcer, A.D. (1978). *Standard English in the United States and England*. The Hague: Mouton.

Tannen, D. (1990). *You Just Don't Understand: Women and Men in Conversation*. New York: Ballantine.

Terkel, S. (1980). *American Dreams: Lost and Found*. New York: Random House.

Thorne, T. (1990). *The Contemporary Dictionary of Slang*. New York: Pantheon.

Tierney, J. (1995). Can we talk? *The New York Times Magazine*, January, 16.

Tocqueville, A. de (1835/1987). *Democracy in America*. New York: Knopf. Also (1988). New York: Harper and Row.

Trudgill, P., and J. Hannah (1982). *International English*. London: Edward Arnold.

Varga, L. (1993). On common nouns that are neither count nor mass. In: Z. Kövecses (ed.), *Voices of Friendship. Linguistic Essays in Honor of László T. András*. Budapest: Eötvös Loránd University, 91-101.

Vincent, B. (1997). From dead Latin to dead English: On the lethal effects of linguistic universalism. In: C. Giorcelli and R. Kroes (eds.), *Living*

With America, 1946-1996. Amsterdam: VU University Press.

Walmsley, J. (1987). *Brit-Think, Ameri-Think*. New York: Penguin.

Weber, M. (1965). Die Protestantische Ethik und der Geist des Kapitalismus. In: J. Winckermann (ed.), *Die Protestantische Ethik*. Tübingen: J.C.B. Mohr.

Webster's New World Dictionary. (1991). Third college edition. New York: Prentice Hall.

Wentworth, H., and S.B. Flexner (1960). *Dictionary of American Slang*. New York: Crowell.

Wentworth, H., and S.B. Flexner (1975). *Dictionary of American Slang*. 2nd supplemented edition. New York: Crowell.

Whitcut, J. (1980). The language of address. In: L. Michaels and C. Ricks (eds.), *The State of the Language*. Berkeley: University of California Press, 89-97.

Wierzbicka, A. (1986). Does language reflect culture? Evidence from Australian English. *Language and Society*, 15, 349-374.

Wierzbicka, A. (1988). *The Semantics of Grammar*. Amsterdam / Philadelphia: John Benjamins.

Wilkinson, R. (1988). *The Pursuit of American Character*. New York: Harper and Row.

Williams, T. (1995). Register mixing in American written discourse. In: Z. Kövecses (ed.), *New Approaches to American English*. Budapest: Department of American Studies, ELTE.

Wills, G. (1992). *Lincoln at Gettysburg: The Words that Remade America*. New York: Simon and Schuster.

Whorf, B.L. (1956). *Language, Thought, and Reality*. Ed. J.B. Carroll. Cambridge, MA: MIT Press.

Wolfram, W. (1974). *The Study of Social Dialects in American English*. Englewood Cliffs, NJ: Prentice.

Wolfram, W. and D. Christian (1989). *Dialects and Education: Issues and Answers*. Englewood Cliffs, NJ: Prentice Hall.

Wolfram, W., and N. Schilling-Estes (1998a). *American English: Dialects and Variation*. Oxford: Blackwell.

Wolfram, W., and N. Schilling-Estes (1998b). Dialect change and maintenance in a post-insular island community. In: E.W. Schneider (ed.), *Focus on the USA*. Amsterdam: John Benjamins, 103-148.

Wolfson, N. (1989). *Perspectives: Sociolinguistics and TESOL*. New York: Harper and Row.

Zwicky, A.D. (1981). Styles. In: T. Schopen and J.M. Williams (eds.), *Style and Variables in English*. Cambridge, MA: Winthrop Publishers, 61-83.

Index

immigrants/immigration
    as target metaphor domain 301-02
    effects of on American mind 317-18
    influence of 19-22, 34-35
incident names 45
informality in AE 235-46, 293
    in pronunciation and spelling 240-42
    in writing 245-46
    of speech acts 238-40
    origins of 236-37
insecurity, linguistic 326
institutions, establishing 44-48
intellectual traditions approach 9-10, 162-64, 324-26
interactional vs. informational dimension 110
interdialectal diversity 160
interdialectal polysemy 160
interdialectal synonymy 159
interlocking terms 161
International English 11
introductions 238-39
inventiveness of AE 275-88, 294
inversion 198
Irish
    immigrants 20
    influence of 298-99
isogloss 56
Italian
    immigrants 21
    influence of 35

jargon 108-09
Jefferson, Thomas 8, 165-66, 226, 276
Joos, Martin 110-11

Kennedy, John F. 67, 223
Kurath, Hans 51-52, 56-57, 58, 59, 63

Labov, William 75-78, 79, 87, 112
Lakoff, Robin 79
landscape, naming of 39
letters to the editor 239

standardization of 86
    Western dialect 71
prostitution, as source of prudery 255-56
prudery, verbal 247-57, 293-94
    social and historical background of 247-49
Puritanism 20, 168, 171-72, 248, 249-50, 259
purpose, expression of 182-83

Quakers 20
questions 184
    tag 209-11

race 80
railroad 42-43, 300
rationality in AE 177-202
Received Pronunciation (RP) 223
redundancy, elimination of 179-85, *see also* economy
referential gap 159
region, urban vs. rural 80
regional dialects of AE 63-74, *see also* linguistic geography
    American attitudes toward 87
regular and irregular verbs 190
regularity of AE 189-99
religious names 47
republican tradition 325-26
rhoticity 64, 66, 67, 74, 75-78, 112
risk-taking 311-12

saloon, *see* drinking
Schilling-Estes, Natalie 64
Scottish
    immigrants 20, 298-99
sectional atlas studies 57
setting 105-08
sexism 230-33
sexuality 127-28
    as source of prudery 254-55
Shakespeare, William 24, 27
shift names 46
shifting 282-85
shortening 285